Orphan Trains

Orphan Trains

*The Story of
Charles Loring Brace
and the Children
He Saved and Failed*

Stephen O'Connor

HOUGHTON MIFFLIN COMPANY
BOSTON · NEW YORK   2001

Copyright © 2001 by Stephen O'Connor
All rights reserved

For information about permission to reproduce selections from
this book, write to Permissions, Houghton Mifflin Company,
215 Park Avenue South, New York, New York 10003.

Visit our Web site: www.houghtonmifflinbooks.com.

Library of Congress Cataloging-in-Publication Data
O'Connor, Stephen.
Orphan trains : the story of Charles Loring Brace
and the children he saved and failed / Stephen O'Connor.
    p.   cm.
    Includes index.
    ISBN 0-395-84173-9
1. Orphan trains — History. 2. Brace, Charles Loring, 1826–1890.
3. Children's Aid Society (New York, N.Y.) — History. I. Title.
HV985 .O36 2001
362.73 4 0973—dc21   00-053881

Printed in the United States of America

Book design by Robert Overholtzer

QUM 10 9 8 7 6 5 4 3 2 1

All illustrations courtesy of the Children's Aid Society

To Simon and Emma

Contents

Acknowledgments

This book could never have been written without the help of many people. First and foremost is Janet Graham, codirector of the PBS documentary *The Orphan Trains,* who so generously passed on her topic to me, shared her insights and copious research materials, and arranged for me to be granted access to the archives of the Children's Aid Society. Her moving and intelligent film was an inspiration and touchstone throughout my research and writing.

I also want to thank Robert Dykstra for his advice and encouragement and for the hours of work he put into saving me from my own ignorance; and Nesta King for her generosity and intelligence. What mistakes remain in this book are entirely my own.

This book also could not have come into existence without the wisdom, trust, and kindness of many people at the Children's Aid Society: Phil Coltoff, T. Jewett, Anne McCabe, Michael Wagner, Lydia King, and Lisa Glazer. I particularly want to thank Victor Remmer, a former CAS director and its present archivist, for helping me find my way around the dusty filing cabinets and weighty tomes that he watches over on East Forty-fifth Street, and for sharing his hard-earned insights, both as a longtime worker in the trenches of child welfare and as a historian of the CAS.

I owe an immense debt of gratitude to all the former orphan train riders who spoke so candidly and movingly with me about their experiences: Alice Bullis Ayler, Marguerite Thomson, Arthur Smith, Howard Hurd, Anne Harrison, and Harold Williams. Thanks also to Mary Ellen Johnson, the founder of the Orphan Train Heritage Society of America, for her hospitality and advice, and for having had the compassion and courage to help so many people.

For doing so much to help me understand the true nature of foster care now and in the past, I want to thank Keith Hefner and Al Desetta at Foster Care Youth United, and Baudilio Lozado, Donald Stroman, Matthew Dedewo, Yamina McDonald, and Diana Moreno, who endured my interrogations so patiently.

Many other people gave me invaluable aid in understanding the complexities of child welfare now and in the past. They include: Marcia Robinson Lowry of Children's Rights; Bruce Henry, Maxine Shoulders, and Ximena Rua-Merkin of Covenant House; Verna Eggleston and Joyce Hunter of the Hetrick Martin Institute; Philip Genty of Columbia University Law School; Liz Squires of the Administration for Children's Services; and Ellen Schutz, Mary Jane Sclafani, Jill Hayes, Fred Magovern, Hank Orenstein, John Courtney, Edith Holtzer, LynNell Hancock, Janis Ruden, Steve Shapiro, and Christina Lem.

I also want to thank the American Antiquarian Society, the Virginia Center for the Creative Arts, and the MacDowell Colony for doing so much to make me a wiser, saner, and better writer.

My thanks also to Kathy Newman, Paul Attewell, Rob Cohen, and Claudia Cooper for their good food and conversation, and comfortable beds, during my Worcester sojourns; Wendy Holt and Janet Silver for all their patience and invaluable help with the manuscript; Steve Fraser for getting me off to such a good start; Kim Witherspoon for her years of faith and friendship; and Lyda Schuster for all of her help on two books.

And finally, I want to thank Simon and Emma for putting up with so many bouts of half-orphanhood during the years I worked on this book; and Helen, for everything, always.

There's a great work wants doing in this our generation, Charley—let's off jacket and go about it.

Frederick Law Olmsted

Prologue:
Working for Human Happiness

ON THE MORNING of October 1, 1854, forty-five children sat on the front benches of a meetinghouse in Dowagiac, Michigan. Most were between ten and twelve years old, though at least one was six and a few were young teenagers. During the week the meetinghouse served as a school, but on that day, a Sunday, it was a Presbyterian church, and more than usually crowded, not only because the children had taken so many seats, but because the regular parishioners had been augmented by less devout neighbors curious to see the "orphans."

For the last couple of weeks notices had been running in the newspapers, and bills had been posted at the general store, the tavern, and the railroad station asking families to take in homeless boys and girls from New York City. The children had arrived on the train from Detroit at three that morning and had huddled together on the station platform until sunup. They had spent the previous night on a steamer crossing Lake Erie from Buffalo, New York, and not a one of them had avoided being soiled by seasickness — their own or their fellow passengers' — or by the excreta of the animals traveling on the deck above. The night before, they had slept on the floor of an absolutely dark freight car, amid a crowd of German and Irish immigrants heading west from Albany. During their first night out from New York City, on a riverboat traveling up the Hudson, they had slept in proper berths, with blankets and mattresses — but only because the boat's captain, after hearing the tales they told of their lives, had taken pity on them.

The children's days of hard travel were clearly evident in their pallor and the subtle deflation of their features. Their clothes — which had been new when they left New York—were stained and ripped and emitted a distinct animal rankness. Their expressions were wary, as if they had been caught doing something wrong and were wondering whether they were going to be punished. In some of the younger children this wariness verged on fear, but most of the older boys and girls had known too much disappointment and loneliness to be afraid of what was about to happen to them, or at least to reveal that fear, even to themselves. Some of them cast glances—challenging, or ingratiating—back at the men and women seated behind them; some looked down at their shoes, while others stared straight ahead at the young man beside the altar, whose enthusiasm, accent, and fluid gestures marked him as a city preacher. His name was E. P. Smith, and he was telling the audience about the organization he represented: the Children's Aid Society, which had been founded only one and a half years earlier by a young minister named Charles Loring Brace.

Brace, a native of Hartford, Connecticut, had come to New York in 1848 to study theology and had been horrified both by the hordes of vagrant children—beggars, bootblacks, flower sellers, and prostitutes—who crowded the city's streets and by the way civil authorities treated them. Mass poverty was a new problem during that era. Up through the early nineteenth century there had been no slums in American cities. There had been poor people, of course, and run-down houses on the back streets and disreputable taverns on the waterfronts, but none of the large, decaying neighborhoods of fear and despair that are so ubiquitous in urban America today. Beginning shortly after the War of 1812, torrential immigration and the nation's uneasy transition to industrial capitalism had divided American cities into hostile camps of the affluent and the desperately poor. In no city was this division more pronounced than New York, which started the nineteenth century with a population of less than 40,000 and ended it with close to a million and a half. In 1849 New York's first police chief reported that 3,000 children[1]—or close to 1 percent of the city's total population—lived on the streets and had no place to sleep but in alleys and abandoned buildings or under stairways. At first the authorities had dealt with these vagrant children mainly by incarcerating them in adult prisons and almshouses, and then, beginning in the 1820s, by building juvenile prisons and asylums, which were barely less harsh or punitive.

Brace believed that most of these children were not criminals but victims of miserable economic and social conditions. Incarceration did nothing but "harden" them in the ways of crime. What they really needed, he maintained, was education, jobs, and good homes—and in March 1853 he established an organization to provide them with just such benefits.

During its first year the Children's Aid Society primarily offered its young beneficiaries religious guidance at Sunday meetings and vocational and academic instruction at its industrial schools. It also established the nation's first runaway shelter, the Newsboys' Lodging House, where vagrant boys received inexpensive room and board and basic education. From the beginning Brace and his colleagues attempted to find jobs and homes for individual children, but they soon became overwhelmed by the numbers needing placement. Unable to raise enough money to increase his staff, Brace hit on the idea of sending groups of children to the country and letting local residents simply pick out the child they wanted for themselves. The forty-five young people sitting in the Dowagiac meetinghouse were the first of these groups—and the first riders of what would come to be called the "orphan trains."

As Smith explained the program to his audience, he appealed equally to their consciences and pocketbooks. These were the "little ones of Christ," he said, who had the same capacities, the same need of good influences, and the same immortal soul as "our own" children. Kind men and women who opened their homes to one of this "ragged regiment" would be expected to raise them as they would their natural-born children, providing them with decent food and clothing, a "common" education, and $100 when they turned twenty-one. There would be no loss in the charity, Smith assured his audience. The boys were handy and active and would soon learn any common trade or labor. The girls could be used for all types of housework.

When he had finished speaking, bench-legs squawked on the floorboards and the congregation came forward to get a better look at the children. Some of these men and women were shopkeepers, carpenters, or blacksmiths, and one was a physician; most, however, were farmers. Their faces were gaunt (only the wealthy were fat in the nineteenth century) and reddened by sun, wind, and, in not a few cases, whiskey. As they mingled with Smith's party, some blinked back tears that such innocents should already have known so much hardship, others looked them up and down and asked questions, trying to assess their strength and honesty, while one or two went so far as to squeeze the children's muscles or plunge a finger into their mouths to check their teeth.

The actual distribution of the children commenced the following morning at the tavern where they were staying. In an account of the trip published by the Children's Aid Society, Smith said that in order to get a child, applicants had to have recommendations from their pastor and a justice of the peace, but it is unlikely that this require-ment was strictly enforced. In the early days the society's agents tended to be very casual in both the acquisition and dispersal of their charges. Smith himself had let a passenger on the riverboat from Manhattan take one of the boys and had replaced him with another he met in the Albany railroad yard—a boy whose claim to orphan-hood Smith never bothered to verify. When applicants did not have the required documents, Smith probably did what was done routinely by later CAS agents: he looked at the quality and cleanness of the applicants' clothes, asked them about their property, professions, and church attendance, and, if he saw no evidence that they were liars or degenerates, gave them a child.

By the end of that first day (a Monday), fifteen boys and girls had gone to live with local farmers or craftsmen, and by Thursday evening, twenty-two more had been taken. On Friday, Smith and the eight unclaimed children—the youngest and therefore the least able work-ers—continued west from Dowagiac by train. In Chicago, Smith put them by themselves on a train to Iowa City (one and a half days' jour-ney), where a Reverend C. C. Townsend, who ran a local orphanage, took them in and attempted to find them foster families. As for Smith, he caught the first train back to New York.

Despite the fact that the Children's Aid Society heard practically nothing of most of these children ever again, this first expedition was considered such a success that in January the society sent out two more parties of homeless children, both to Pennsylvania. Over the next seventy-five years the CAS orphan trains carried an estimated 105,000 children to all of the contiguous forty-eight states except Ari-zona. For most of those years the children were distributed to their new "parents" or "employers" (both terms were used) much as they had been by E. P. Smith, through a sort of auction held in a church, opera house, or large store. Applicants for children were supposed to be screened by committees of local businessmen, ministers, or physicians, but the screening was rarely very thorough. The monitoring of placements was equally lax. Because of the great difficulty and expense of travel in nineteenth-century rural America, CAS agents rarely checked up in person on the boys and girls they had placed. The society tried to keep tabs on placements by sending both the children and their foster parents regular letters of inquiry, but these mostly went unanswered.

Sustained by a monitoring system that seriously underreported failure and by a prodigious quantity of blind faith, Charles Loring Brace tirelessly promoted what he called the "Emigration Plan" during his thirty-seven years at the head of the Children's Aid Society. In moving and persuasive books, articles, speeches, and annual reports, he portrayed his system of placing needy and orphaned children in families as more humane and effective than even the best institutional care, and also as vastly cheaper. As a result, Brace's system was imitated by many organizations, initially only in the East but eventually all across the country. The New York Foundling Hospital alone sent some 30,000 children west.

All told, by 1929, when the CAS sent its last true orphan train to Texas, roughly 250,000 city children had found foster homes through these programs. Some of these children were abused by their new families in all the ways that we are familiar with from present-day news reports about the tragedies of foster care, and some were just as happy as the literature of their placement agencies said they were. Two boys placed by the CAS became governors, one became a Supreme Court justice, and several others became mayors, congressmen, or local representatives. Many children grew up to become drifters and thieves, and at least one became a murderer. The vast majority led lives of absolutely ordinary accomplishment and satisfaction. And many, perhaps also a majority (because there is nothing extraordinary about unhappiness), saw no end to the misery into which they had been born.

This book concentrates on the CAS orphan trains, not only because the society placed considerably more children over a much longer period than any other agency, but because Charles Loring Brace almost single-handedly forged the philosophical foundations of the movement, and of many other efforts on behalf of poor children, and remains to this day perhaps the preeminent figure in American child welfare history. Until well into the twentieth century, virtually every program seeking to help homeless and needy children was either inspired by or a response to Brace's work and ideas. His notion that children are better cared for by families than in institutions is the most basic tenet of present-day foster care. And his abiding belief in the capability and fundamental goodness of poor city children, while occasionally echoed in the speeches of politicians and child welfare experts, is one that our nation dearly needs to reclaim.

Brace was an exceedingly hardworking, intelligent, and complex man whose life can hardly be defined by his work with the Children's Aid Society. He was jailed in Hungary for supposed revolutionary activities, and he was a prominent abolitionist, author, and journalist. As a *New York Times* correspondent during the Civil War, he was present at some of the Union Army's most stunning early defeats. Brace's best friend for much of his young manhood was Frederick Law Olmsted, the celebrated designer of Central Park, and his social contacts included Charles Darwin, John Stuart Mill, Ralph Waldo Emerson, Washington Irving, and George Eliot.

With all of his drive and accomplishment, Brace was a man of many contradictions. He was ferociously ambitious, yet believed that ambition was a sin. He constantly excoriated himself for not living up to his own ideals—for not working hard enough, loving well enough, or having motives that were pure enough—but he never seems to have doubted the exemplariness of his character. He could speak quite openly about his "abounding courage and hope." He proclaimed without the slightest shred of irony, "I am striving after perfect truth," and admitted, as if it were only self-evident, that "few human beings have ever had a more real sense of things unseen than I habitually have." And yet he believed that virtue existed only in humility and self-denial. He wanted always to live more simply and to endure greater hardship. What he called his "brightest of all visions" was "a humble, self-controlled life, all devoted, given up, to working for human happiness."[2]

As much as Brace's work with the Children's Aid Society may have satisfied his desire for prestige and power, it was nevertheless the single greatest moral effort of his life. In simplest terms, this book is an attempt to measure the virtue of that effort by examining its motives and by tracing its consequences, both during Brace's lifetime and after. The earliest chapters explore what in Brace's experiences and era made the idea of sending even small children hundreds of miles from home to live with total strangers seem natural and good. Later chapters discuss the successes and failures of Brace's efforts, and those of his imitators, and show how changing ideas of childhood, work, bondage, and the nature of society caused what had once seemed an act of nearly unassailable wisdom and compassion to appear cruelly indifferent to the very children it had been designed to help.

The true measure of the virtue of Brace's effort lies in its effect on the lives of these children. This book illustrates that effect by looking at the fates of orphan train riders in aggregate, and by telling the stories of particular children: John Jackson, who at five years old walked off after a marching band and never found his way home again; a lame street peddler named Johnny Morrow, who won over the Children's Aid Society staff by fulfilling their most sentimental fantasies; Lotte Stern, a ragpicker's fourteen-year-old daughter who, like so many girls of her time, was forced into prostitution and then damned for it by society; John Brady and Andrew Burke, who rode the same orphan train in 1859 and became, respectively, the governors of Alaska and North Dakota; and Charley Miller, who shot two young men dead on a boxcar in Wyoming because, as he put it at his trial, he was lonely and cold and so far from home.

A cautionary note: although the term "orphan trains" has a poetic resonance and a degree of recognition that made it the all-but-inevitable title for this book, in some ways it misrepresents the placement efforts of the CAS and other agencies. During the orphan train era itself, none of these agencies ever actually used the term in their official publications. The CAS referred to its relevant division first as the Emigration Department, then as the Home-Finding Department, and finally, as the Department of Foster Care. The Foundling Hospital sent out what it called "baby" or "mercy" trains. And almost everybody else referred to the practice as "family placement" or "out-placement" ("out" to distinguish it from the placement of children "in" orphanages or asylums). The term "orphan trains" may have been coined by a journalist sometime in the early twentieth century, but it did not come into its present wide currency until long after the close of the era, perhaps as recently as 1978, when CBS aired a fictional miniseries entitled *The Orphan Trains.*

One reason the term was not used by placement agencies was that less than half of the children who rode the trains were in fact orphans, and as many as 25 percent had two living parents. Children with both parents living ended up on the trains—or in orphanages—because their families did not have the money or desire to raise them or because they had been abused or abandoned or had run away. And many teenage boys and girls went to orphan train sponsoring organizations simply in search of work or a free ticket out of the city.

The term "orphan trains" is also misleading because a substantial number of the placed-out children never took the railroad to their new homes, or even traveled very far. Although the majority of children placed by the CAS went to the Midwest and West, the state that received the greatest number by far (nearly one-third of the total) was New York; Connecticut, New Jersey, and Pennsylvania also received substantial numbers of children. The main goal of the Emigration Plan was to remove children from slums, where opportunities were scant and "immoral influences" plentiful, and to place them in "good Christian homes." In part because Brace considered the country fundamentally more beneficent, and in part because the demand for children (as laborers and for adoption) was always highest in the least-settled areas, the typical good Christian home was a farm. But the CAS did place many children not only near New York but right in the city itself.

What is more, for most of the orphan train era, the CAS bureaucracy made no distinction between local placements and even its most distant ones. They were all written up in the same record books and, on the whole, managed by the same people. Also, the same child might be placed one time in the West and the next time—if the first home did not work out—in New York City. The decision about where to place a child was made almost entirely on the basis of which alternative was most readily available at the moment the child needed help.

Because distant and local placements were so functionally interchangeable, discussing only what might be called "classic" orphan train placement—groups of children distributed far from New York City—would distort the nature and goals of orphan train programs and misrepresent the experiences of many of the placed children. Such a focus would also obscure the fact that, in an important sense, the orphan train era never ended. What really happened is that during the first decades of the twentieth century, as a result of demographic, political, and social changes, fewer and fewer children were sent to homes in other states and more and more were placed locally. Decades before the last orphan train left for Texas, all of the main placement organizations—including the CAS—had become primarily what we would call foster care and adoption agencies. But for the people operating these agencies, the transformation was only in how they did their work (more screening and monitoring of placements), not in the work's fundamental nature and goals.

It is important—even consummately important—not to obscure the connection between the orphan trains and our own child welfare programs, because the consequences of Brace's moral effort end—if they may be said to have ended at all—only now, in this moment, and in each succeeding moment, as we ourselves decide what we can and should do to help the "poor and friendless" children of our own time. It is my hope that, as we discover how well or ill Brace and his followers promoted the happiness of children during the nineteenth and early twentieth centuries, we will better understand how we might serve those children who most need our help at the start of this new millennium.

PART I

Want

TESTIMONY

JOHN BRADY

ℐℛ I cannot speak of my parents with any certainty at all. I recollect having an aunt by the name of Julia B———. She had me in charge for some time, and made known some things to me of which I have a faint remembrance. She married a gentleman in Boston, and left me to shift for myself in the streets of [New York City]. I could not have been more than seven or eight years of age at the time. She is greatly to be excused for this act, since I was a very bad boy, having an abundance of self-will.

At this period I became a vagrant, roaming over all parts of the city. I would often pick up a meal at the markets or at the docks, where they were unloading fruit. At a later hour in the night I would find a resting-place in some box or hogshead, or in some dark hole under a staircase.

The boys that I fell in company with would steal and swear, and of course I contracted those habits too. I have a distinct recollection of stealing up upon houses to tear lead from the chimneys, and then take it privily away to some junk-shop, as they call it; with the proceeds I would buy a ticket for the pit in the Chatham-street Theatre, and something to eat with the remainder. This is the manner in which I was drifting out in the stream of life, when some kind person from your Society persuaded me to go to Randall's Island. I remained at this place two years. Sometime in July, 1859, one of your agents came there and asked how many boys who had no parents would love to have nice homes in the West, where they could drive horses and oxen, and have as many apples and melons as they could wish. I happened to be one of the many who responded in the affirmative.

On the fourth of August twenty-one of us had homes procured for us at N———, Ind. A lawyer from T———, who chanced to be engaged in court matters, was at N——— at the time. He desired to take a boy home with him, and I was the one assigned him. He owns a farm of two hundred acres lying close to town. Care was taken that I should be occupied there and not in town. I was always treated as one of the family. In sickness I was ever cared for by prompt attention. In winter I was sent to the Public School. The family room was a good school to me, for there I found the daily papers and a fair library.

After a period of several years . . . I had accumulated some property on the farm in the shape of a horse, a yoke of oxen, etc., amounting in all to some $300. These I turned into cash, and left for a preparatory school. . . . I remained there three years, relying greatly on my own efforts for support. . . . I have now resumed my duties as a Sophomore [at Yale], in faith in Him who has ever been my best friend. If I can prepare myself for acting well my part in life by going through the college curriculum, I shall be satisfied.

I shall ever acknowledge with gratitude that the Children's Aid Society has been the instrument of my elevation.

To be taken from the gutters of New York City and placed in a college is almost a miracle.[1]

HARRY MORRIS

◊ When I arrived at N.Y., I never seen so many relations as I had and all was tickled to see me. The Pennsylvania Station has several entrances to get through so as not to miss me, they were coupled at every one. My sister-in-law was the lucky one to see me first.

My, but what a home-coming that was, I will never forget it as long as I live. Would of the Aid Society done justice I would of found my parents long, long before I did. After the reunion I told mother that I was going to the Aid Society and I wanted her to go along. . . . The moment I stepped in the door, the elderly man sitting at the desk recognized my mother and said to her, "This isn't the son that we had, is it? The one we sent out west." My mother said to him, yes, he wants to speak to you in person. Well, what a fine lad this is, he had no more than got lad out of his tongue, then I told him what I thought of the Childrens Aid Society of N.Y.C. and I told him I was going to let the whole world know what kind of people you were and also how you made misrepresentations and I had the pleasure of telling him that the Aid Society never placed me in any home to make me what I was. He sure did back water and he was just like a whipped dog when I got through telling him facts about the life I went through. He begged me to keep mum and offered me reward for not mention of the statements but his money was just like his representatives, — FALSE.[2]

The Good Father

CHARLES LORING BRACE was born on June 19, 1826, in Litchfield, Connecticut, a small but prosperous village, wholly lacking in urban luxury or vice, but providing its residents with something approaching urban levels of learning and culture. It was the home of the nation's first law school, founded by Tapping Reeve in 1784, which numbered among its graduates Vice Presidents Aaron Burr and John C. Calhoun and the educator Horace Mann. It was also the home of one of the first secondary schools for girls in the United States, the Litchfield Female Academy, graduates of which included Harriet Beecher Stowe and her sister Catharine Beecher. Litchfield's best-known native son was Ethan Allen, leader of a Revolutionary War militia group, the Green Mountain Boys, but during the Brace family's tenure the village's most illustrious resident was the Congregational preacher Lyman Beecher — the father not only of Catharine and Harriet but also of the celebrated (and at times infamous) liberal minister Henry Ward Beecher. The Braces and the Beechers would become deeply intertwined over the years, and each family would exert a profound influence on the development of the other's social activism.

One of the most important of these influences was in some ways the most indirect. Among his many other accomplishments, Lyman Beecher was a founder of the social movement in which Charles Loring Brace would make his career. In 1812, distressed by increasing drunkenness, crime, and irreligious behavior, especially in America's rapidly growing cities, Beecher told some thirty Congregational clergymen whom he had invited to a meeting in New Haven: "The mass is changing. We are becoming another people. Our habits have held us long after those moral causes that formed them have ceased to operate. These habits, at length, are giving way." If swift action were not taken, Beecher warned, the nation would soon be overrun by a tide of "Sabbath-breakers, rum-selling, tippling folk, infidels" and "ruff-scruff." Beecher proposed combating this tide through the foundation of a "Society for the Suppression of Vice and the Promotion of Good Morals." This organization would be a "moral militia" composed of "wise and good" citizens who would oppose vice and "infidelity" by preaching to likely perpetrators, holding prayer meetings, and passing out religious literature.[1]

Partly through Beecher's example and vocal advocacy, similar moral reform societies were soon founded all along the Eastern Seaboard and as far west as Saint Louis. The "wise and good" who staffed these societies were generally evangelical clerics whose primary goal was to attract converts. Over time, however, these domestic missionaries learned that the best way to draw people to their sermons was by offering benefits such as food, clothing, and schooling. This was the aspect of the movement that ultimately would most impress Charles Loring Brace. He would carry it a step further, however, and thereby help pave the way for the emergence of modern social work, all but abandoning conversion and making service (or "aid") the top priority of his own moral reform society.

Lyman Beecher never played any direct role in Brace's choice of career. He moved to Boston the year Brace was born and was living in Cincinnati when Brace began working with the poor in New York City. The elder Beecher and the Brace family also stood on opposite sides of their era's culture wars. Whereas the Braces, though devout Congregationalists, were dedicated rationalists with a strong interest in natural science, Lyman Beecher was a conservative Calvinist who saw science and rationalism as the enemies of faith. It was Lyman's children, especially his two famous daughters, who would forge the strongest ties with the Brace family. But, at the very least, Lyman Beecher presided over Charles's childhood and youth as an exemplar — a man who made the career of activist-minister a compelling possibility.

John Pierce Brace, Charles's father, first knew Lyman Beecher as a landlord. John Brace came to Litchfield to be chief instructor at the Litchfield Female Academy and rented a room in the Beechers' plain, often added-to clapboard parsonage — described by Stowe as "a wide, roomy, windy edifice that seemed to have been built by a series of afterthoughts."[2] Despite their philosophical differences, John Brace soon won at least the cordial respect of the famous minister, if for no other reason than that Brace was the favorite teacher of Beecher's younger daughter, Harriet. In her autobiography, Stowe called John Brace "one of the most stimulating and inspiring instructors I ever knew"[3] and made him the model for Mr. Rossiter, the brilliant teacher in her novel *Oldtown Folks:*

> Mr. Jonathan Rossiter held us all by the sheer force of his personal character and will, just as the ancient mariner held the wedding guest with his glittering eye. . . . He scorned all conventional rules in teaching, and he would not tolerate a mechanical lesson, and took delight in puzzling his pupils and breaking up all routine business by startling and unexpected questions and assertions. He compelled everyone to think and to think for himself. "Your heads may not be the best in the world," was one of his sharp off-hand sayings, "but they are the best God has given you, and you must use them for yourselves."[4]

John Brace had come to the Litchfield Female Academy through sheer nepotism. His aunt, Sarah Pierce, founded the school in her dining room in 1792, and she seemed to have pegged her nephew as a potential teacher from his earliest childhood. She and her sister Mary oversaw his education in Hartford, where he had been born, and paid his tuition at Williams College. For a while John seems to have considered entering the ministry, but in 1814 he acceded to Sarah's wishes and moved to Litchfield to become the head teacher at her school.

By the time John Brace arrived, the academy had long since moved from the Pierce sisters' dining room to a large, white, Greek Revival building, on the village's fashionable North Street, just one hundred yards closer to the center of town than the Beechers' roomy residence. Each year up to 140 students came to the school from as far away as Ohio and the West Indies, as well as from New York and all parts of New England. Although Sarah Pierce had intended the school to "vindicate the equality of the female intellect," she had not herself received the level of education she desired to provide her students and had been heavily influenced by condescending British advice books on teaching young women. Catharine Beecher, who attended the academy before John Brace's arrival, recalled in her autobiography: "At that time, the higher branches had not entered the female schools. Map drawing, painting, embroidery and the piano were the accom-

plishments sought, and history was the only study added to geography, grammar, and arithmetic."[5] In their assigned essays the girls were
expected to meditate only on such "female" virtues as contentment,
cheerfulness, charity, and forgiveness.

All this changed once John Brace became the head teacher. His first
assignment to Catharine's younger sister Harriet, for example, was to
write about "The Difference Between the Natural and the Moral Sub-
lime." And Harriet's earliest literary triumph was an essay responding
to Brace's question: "Can the immortality of the soul be proved by the
light of nature?"[6]

Under John Brace's direction, Litchfield girls undertook a curriculum — including science, higher mathematics, logic, and Latin —
that at the very least equaled that of most boys' academies. In one subject area Litchfield girls clearly exceeded their counterparts at the male
schools, and that was moral philosophy, which boys were not expected
to study until college.

Although John Brace was far from being above the sexist double
standards that prevailed in his day, his educational agenda had a decidedly feminist slant. He specifically worked against the stereotype of
women as charming but superficial creatures who lacked the intellectual fortitude to master their emotional impulses. In an address to the
graduating class of 1816, he explained that he wanted students "to feel
but to feel in subordination to reason." Education, he told the new
graduates, would improve woman's "rank in society, placing her as the
rational companion of man, not the slave of his pleasures or the victim of tyranny."[7]

As significant a figure as John Brace would be in Harriet Beecher
Stowe's life, and later also in Catharine Beecher's, it was in fact
through his marriage that he became most intimately connected with
the Beecher family. Lucy Porter, Lyman Beecher's sister-in-law, came
to Litchfield for an extended visit in 1819. By early 1820 she and John
Brace had married, and later that same year their first child, Mary,
was born. The Braces continued to live with the Beechers until 1822,
when they moved to a home of their own nearby. It was in this house,
some four years afterward, that John and Lucy's second child, Charles,
was born.

જ

During the early nineteenth century the United States was undergoing
a dramatic shift in social organization. An economy composed pri-

marily of small-scale independent entrepreneurs — farmers, crafts-people, and shopkeepers — was giving way to one of large-scale capitalists and industrialists, and decidedly economically dependent wage earners. Many people became wonderfully rich as a result of this transformation, and many became desperately poor. All of these changes — especially the fact that people increasingly worked outside the home — profoundly altered the roles of men and women, and the ways in which they understood and raised their children. Charles Loring Brace's upbringing, like that of most of his generation, was the product of a clash between the old and the new ways — a clash that affected both the sort of "aid" he came to feel poor children most needed and the way that aid was understood by the larger society.

The Puritans of the seventeenth and eighteenth centuries believed that children were born damned. This was not mere theology, but a fact parents witnessed every day in their children's behavior. To Anne Bradstreet, sinning commenced with a child's first breath:

> Stained from birth with Adams sinfull fact,
> Thence I began to sin as soon as act:
> A perverse will, a love to what's forbid,
> A serpents sting in pleasing face lay hid:
> A lying tongue as soon as it could speak,
> And the fifth Commandment do daily break.[8]

In essence, the Puritans had what most people today would think of as an inverted image of the soul's progress: starting in corruption and, through God's grace, ending in innocence. The mechanism by which the soul was cleansed of original sin ("Adams sinfull fact") was "conversion," or being "born again" — a spontaneous and often ecstatic union of the individual with God. The problem was that there was no way to *achieve* conversion. God was almighty, absolutely free, and could not be constrained even by the obligation to reward goodness and punish sin. He had chosen that small portion of humanity he was going to save — the "elect" — for his own inscrutable reasons back before the beginning of time, and there was no way for men or women to change his mind. There was also no way to know for certain who was among the elect. Even one's own apparent conversion might be an illusion spun by the Devil to lure one into the sin of pride. Some theologians maintained that the elect would not know they were saved until they found themselves in Paradise. Although God was technically free to grant second birth even to the most loathsome of sinners, most people assumed that he did not have much use for this freedom, and that the elect could be identified by their superior virtue — especially by their capacity for self-denial.

Adam and Eve fell because they were ambitious and put their own desires ahead of God's. They wanted knowledge and to move up in the world ("Your eyes shall be opened," said the serpent, "and ye shall be as gods, knowing both good and evil"). The child in Anne Bradstreet's poem was not merely stained by the consequences of their ambition, but still possessed, from birth, by their "perverse will, a love to what's forbid." Puritans believed that virtue lay only in the suppression of what they called "self-will" and its replacement by a desire to serve, obey, and glorify God. For many Puritans the mere existence of a child's will was nigh unto a perversity all by itself. John Robinson, the original minister at the Pilgrims' Plymouth Colony, advised his parishioners:

> Surely there is in all children . . . a stubbornness, and stoutness of mind arising from natural pride, which must, in the first place, be broken and beaten down; . . . Children should not know, if it could be kept from them, that they have a will in their own, but in the parents' keeping; neither should these words be heard from them, save by way of consent, "I will" or "I will not."[9]

Puritan parents loved their children as much as parents ever have, but they did not see love as the unalloyed blessing we generally understand it to be today. Love was, after all, yet another carnal impulse, and as such it might lead parents to shirk their responsibility both to God and to their children. Letting a "pleasing face" divert one from subjecting a child to necessary discipline was not only sinful but possibly a sign that both parent and child were headed for eternal damnation. According to one Puritan adviser, parents were to keep "due distance" from their offspring because "fondness and familiarity breeds and causeth contempt and irreverence in children."[10]

In certain instances, parental love could even be equated with sin. When an impoverished couple in Northampton, Massachusetts, went to court in 1680 to stop their children from being forcibly indentured by the civil authorities, the judge rejected their arguments, declaring that "what the Parents Spoke [was] more out of fond affection and sinful Indulgence than any Reason or Rule."[11]

Slowly during the eighteenth century, and more rapidly during the nineteenth, the foundations for many of these beliefs began to crumble, partly under the assault of rationalism and Romanticism, but mostly through the successes of capitalism. Between 1820 and 1860 per capita income rose 50 percent[12] — although not among industrial workers — and thanks to the advent of mass production and inexpensive transportation, many goods became much cheaper. Women no longer had to spend days weaving cloth and stitching it into clothing but could outfit their families through a single shopping trip. Infection rates declined because of the piping of fresh water into cities and the easy accessibility of factory-produced soap and cotton underwear. And both heating and cooking became more efficient through the development of cast-iron stoves. For many people, especially in the expanding middle and upper classes, life was much easier, and the idea of a strict and vengeful God no longer seemed as natural as it had during earlier, harder eras. More to the point, growing numbers of people began to believe that the true elect were not those who most loved God, but those who most loved money.

Puritan culture was also undermined by capitalism's disconcerting effect on sex roles. Many affluent women found that they had become what some scholars call "economically superfluous." Whereas their mothers had added to the family coffers by tending livestock and gardens and making clothing, these women only spent their husband's money at stores and on the servants who performed almost every household labor. Understanding, at least intuitively, that in most ways life would have gone on unchanged in their homes without them, affluent women increasingly tied their sense of self-worth to the non-economically productive aspects of their lives — to their roles as wives, hostesses, and, especially, mothers.

The Victorian enshrinement of motherhood came to pass, in part, because of the equally disconcerting effect that capitalism had on the male sex role. During the colonial era farmers, artisans, and merchants alike had tended to work at home and were hardly ever out of earshot of their wives and children. But by the early 1800s ever greater numbers of men — manufacturers, merchants, and bankers as well as their employees — were spending their days away from home. As a result, they could no longer perform one of the most essential duties allotted them under Puritan tradition: the religious and moral instruction of their children. When "economically superfluous" upper-class women quite naturally stepped into the breach, prevailing notions of child-rearing, and of the nature of children themselves, were radically transformed.

John Locke may have dealt the concept of infant damnation a mortal blow with his assertion that the child is, at birth, a *tabula rasa,* or blank slate, on which character is written by experience, but we owe our notion that children are innocent at birth primarily to Romanticism.

To Romantic philosophers and writers, civilization was a corruptive process that despoiled the soul's natural purity just as the products of civilization (smoke-belching, filth-oozing cities and factories) despoiled nature itself. Not only was the child's soul still nearly as it had been created by God ("Heaven lies about us in our infancy!" proclaimed Wordsworth), but the child's natural character was seen as more Christian, at least when childish ignorance was construed as innocence, weakness as gentleness, and dependence as love. Under the influence of such notions, children gained an utterly unprecedented stature in literature during the eighteenth and nineteenth centuries: portrayed as holy innocents by such writers as William Blake and William Wordsworth, and as victims, again by Blake, and victim-heroes in the novels of Charles Dickens.

This beatification of children came to pass for many reasons, one of which was Victorian culture's attempt to make women's new non-economically productive role more palatable. But it was also encouraged by the Romantic critique of masculinity. Romanticism began as a reaction against that consummately "masculine" virtue — reason — and asserted the superiority of "feminine" virtues such as compassion, intuition, gentleness, introspection, and spontaneity.

Many Victorians were quite disturbed by the way the new economy redefined men, and not merely because it forced them to abandon their traditional child-rearing responsibilities. As the work of men, especially in the upper classes, became less physical — less a matter of plowing, shearing, hammering, and hauling and more a matter of contracts and balance sheets, stocks and bonds, profit and loss — it was harder to see such work as dignified, God-sanctioned labor and to separate it from simple greed. Disturbed by what they saw as an ever more avaricious, ugly, and unnatural world wrought by men, Victorians found refuge in the image of the home as a feminine preserve, and of mothers as the protectors of innocent, lamblike children. As one early-nineteenth-century minister put it:

> I believe that if Christianity should be compelled to flee from the mansions of the great, the academies of the philosophers, the halls of the legislators, or the throng of busy men, we should find her last and purest retreat with woman at the fireside; her last altar would be the female heart; her last audience would be the children gathered around the knees of the mother.[13]

The early Victorian middle- and upper-middle-class mother was helped to take on her new responsibilities by a new genre of literature: the mother's guide. These books portrayed raising children as the consummate fulfillment of femininity and as critical to the survival of a new nation. *The Mother's Book* by Lydia Maria Child (who is now best known as the author of "Over the River and Through the Woods") was dedicated to "American mothers on whose intelligence and discretion the safety and prosperity of our Republic so much depend." And Lydia H. Sigourney, in her *Letters to Mothers,* maintained that "the mother, kneeling by the cradle-bed, hath her hand upon the ark of a nation."[14]

The authors of these guides had abandoned the harsh rhetoric of earlier generations. In none of them are mothers told that their children are "better whipped than damned," as Cotton Mather had warned. None of these authors echo John Robinson's declaration that children's "stoutness of mind, arising from natural pride . . . must . . . be broken and beaten down." Rather, mothers were repeatedly instructed to be gentle and affectionate with their children, and not to expect too much of them. In *Hints for the Improvement of Early Education and Nursery Discipline,* Mrs. Louisa Gurney Hoare presents nature as a guide rather than as something needing correction:

> The minds of children, as their bodies, are not to be forced, we are to follow the leading of nature — "to go her pace" — . . . it is to be remembered that nature may be cramped or forced, rather than corrected and improved; and that, in every doubtful case, it is wise to in-

cline to the lenient, rather than to the severe side of the question; because an excess of freedom is safer than too much restraint.[15]

These authors also cast aside the Puritan emphasis on sermons and precepts as the most effective means of moral instruction. Rather, as a Mrs. Barbauld says in an epigraph to Child's book: "Do you ask what will educate your son? Your example will educate him; your conversation; the business he sees you transact; the likings and dislikings you express, — these will educate him — the society you live in will educate him."[16]

Also, far from counseling mothers to restrain their love for their children or to guard themselves against the seduction of a "pleasing face," these authors generally shared Lydia Sigourney's view: "To love children, is the dictate of our nature. Apart from the promptings of kindred blood, it is a spontaneous tribute to their helplessness, their innocence, or their beauty. The total absence of this love induces a suspicion that the heart is not right."[17]

For the most part, however, these authors still did not see love in the modern sense, as beneficial in and of itself. Love's virtue was primarily instrumental: a mother's love for her child was what enabled her to give so much of herself, and a child's love of his or her mother was what made the child want to follow the mother's example and advice. Only from Lydia Maria Child do we hear anything that approaches our present era's conviction of the supreme importance of love, but interestingly, not until a decade after the publication of her *Mother's Book:*

> "What shall be our reward," says Swedenborg, "for loving our neighbor *as* ourselves in this life? That when we become angels, we shall be enabled to love him *better* than ourselves." . . . A mother's love has the same angelic character; more completely unselfish, but lacking in the charm of perfect reciprocity. The cure for all the ills and wrongs, the cares, the sorrows, and the crimes of humanity, all lie in that one word, LOVE.[18]

However modern much of the advice of these mother's guides was, their philosophy retained the strong influence of the Puritan forefathers in one significant aspect. A glance at the table of contents of modern child-rearing guides by Dr. Spock or Penelope Leach shows that they are primarily compendiums of technical advice about diapering, feeding, and recognizing and managing chicken pox, whooping cough, and other childhood diseases. Although the mother's guides of the early nineteenth century also contained such advice, their authors primarily intended them as handbooks for moral instruction. Catharine Beecher's popular mother's guide was even called *The Moral Instructor*. A simple list of the chapter headings of Mrs. Hoare's *Hints for the Improvement* . . . gives the clearest indication of how important the inculcation of morality was to early Victorians:

General Principles of Education
Truth and Sincerity
Authority and Obedience
Rewards and Punishments, Praise and Blame
Temper
Justice
Harmony, Generosity &c.
Fearfulness and Fortitude
Independence
Industry, Perseverance, and Attention
Vanity and Affectation
Delicacy
Manners and Order
Religious Instruction and Religious Habits
Religious Habits

None of these titles would have seemed out of place in a Puritan father's guide of a century before, nor much of the advice in the text that followed. Industry and frugality were as strongly recommended as ever. Lydia Maria Child told her readers: "As far as possible keep a child always employed — either sewing or knitting, or reading, or playing, or studying, or walking."[19] Catharine Beecher said: "It is sinful to waste money or any kind of property." And: "Any amusement is a sinful waste of time that does not prepare us for a better discharge of duty."[20]

Clichés of the "idle poor" aside, idleness has always been a sin more likely to be indulged by the rich, and it must have been of particular concern to these newly leisured mothers of children whom wealth had also freed from the need to work. Likewise, these women —

who, along with their children, were more dependent on their husbands than any of their ancestors were likely to have been — must
have been particularly sensitive about the "sin" of dependence.
Child's pronouncements on this evil could hardly be more grave:
"Children should be brought up with a dread of being dependent on
others."[21]

✤

John and Lucy Brace raised their children in a manner that combined
equal parts of the Romantic veneration of childhood and nature with
the old-fashioned Calvinist insistence on duty, diligence, and self-
sacrifice. In part because Lucy was occupied in caring for the two
youngest Brace children, Emma and the baby James, who was sickly,
Charles was educated, in accordance with Puritan tradition, by his father. In the early years that education, apart from basic instruction in
reading and writing, seems to have been largely informal. Charles
would sometimes sit in on his father's classes or tag along when John
took Litchfield girls on woodland "tramps," during which all members
of the party would eagerly gather samples for their herbariums and
mineralogical cabinets. But most of Charles's education came in the
form of his father's extemporaneous lectures and inquisitions in the
midst of daily routines. One of Charles's favorite activities as a child
was to go on solitary expeditions with his father to mountain streams,
where, sitting on a broad rock or grassy bank, under the shifting shade
of beeches, oaks, and larches, they would bait hooks, watch the glint of
sunlight on the rushing water, and wait until they saw the line go stiff
and felt the tug of a silvery life's determination to endure.

Although Charles was to spend most of his life working in cities, the
deep pleasure in nature that was first nourished in Litchfield was to
stay with him until the day he died. All of his writings, but especially
his letters, are filled with evocations of natural beauty, even when that
beauty is only a certain quality of sunlight on a brick wall. In his early
twenties he would frequently speak of nature as an "expression of God
to us," or as containing some of "God's qualities," but these were only
the rationalizations of a divinity student who felt the need to justify
his every pleasure and interest by seeing it as some kind of communication with God.[22] Brace's love of nature was so much more basic, so
much more a matter of simple sensuality and of the body's joy at its
own workings. He never felt so alive as when he was at what he once
described as "my trouting, my ramblings over mountains and by wil-

low-fringed brooks, all my ecstasies over the fresh green meadows and waving woods and bright flowers and trout streams."[23]

In 1833, when Charles was seven, his family moved to Hartford so that John could become the principal of Catharine Beecher's Hartford Female Seminary. It was during this period — according to Charles's biographer, his daughter Emma — that his education began in earnest.

John Brace could hardly have been a more devoted teacher. For two hours every day, until Charles was fourteen, John read to him from the classic works of Greek, Roman, European, and American history, interspersing them with selections from Shakespeare and Sir Walter Scott. By the time Charles attended Yale at sixteen, he could speak at least some French, German, Spanish, and Latin, and he also had received instruction in mathematics, biology, botany, entomology, and geology, but not much in chemistry or physics.

John Brace was so devoted to his son that he would often neglect his seminary students. Emma Brace told a favorite family story about her father:

His curiosity on subjects of history was insatiable, until his questions and his father's elaborate replies became a torment to the young ladies of the school. When, finally, the child selected the dinner hour to propound his queries, and their teacher laid down his carving knife and fork, and the roast grew cold, the pupils, after suffering thus, silent and hungry on several occasions, rebelled. Charles was threatened. If he did not stay away with his questions, he should be kissed. Dreading this terror, after the manner of small boys, he desisted.[24]

With all of his indulgence of Charles's intellectual curiosity, John Brace was very capable of being hard on his son, even cruel, in the interest of developing fortitude and self-control. In a letter John wrote shortly after Charles moved to New York, he explained:

Very early I exposed you to danger, urged you to climb, to swim, to do many things that many parents thought wrong and dangerous, for the very purpose of so familiarizing you to danger that you should be superior to fear. Do you remember in Litchfield my keeping you near the cannon when firing on review day, until you nearly fainted, and I had to take you into Mr. Deming's house?[25]

This was the side of John Brace's character that caused even adoring students like Harriet Beecher Stowe to be afraid of him. He was a charming man, a published (though decidedly minor) novelist, and an author of humorous poetry who had little difficulty setting "the table in a roar" with his jokes and was, to his own mind, excessively fond of "female society."[26] But he was nevertheless driven and deeply serious — very much in the tradition of his Puritan ancestors.

The fact that John Brace chose to introduce his Litchfield Female Academy girls to moral philosophy well ahead of their counterparts at the boys' academies is an indication of just how important he believed the subject to be. Moral philosophy was never a mere exercise in mental agility for him, but simply the most basic and definitively human of all activities. Nothing mattered more to the elder Brace, or to his son, than the attempt to determine the nature of one's obligation to one's fellow man — and to God — and the attempt to discipline one's character so as to fulfill that obligation to perfection. For the Braces, as indeed for most thinking people of their era, it was impossible to separate moral philosophy from theology. Although investigation of the good surely occupied a portion of every one of their weekdays, it always came into a particularly sharp focus on Sundays when they attended church.

Apart from his father, the single most important figure in Charles Loring Brace's early education was Horace Bushnell, minister of the North Congregational Church, which the Brace family attended during their Hartford years.

Bushnell is regarded by many as the most important American religious thinker of the nineteenth century. He devoted his life to mediating between the vengeful God of the Puritan founders of his church and the Unitarian God of love who seemed to better express the spirit of his prosperous and increasingly easy era. More than any single theologian, Bushnell helped diminish American Calvinism's emphasis on infant damnation and depravity, largely by showing how one's religious identity — including one's readiness for salvation — could be shaped during the earliest years of life. In this regard he was not only reflecting some of the child-rearing notions promulgated by his Hartford neighbors Lydia Sigourney and Catharine Beecher but also incorporating the Unitarian emphasis on lifelong religious development. His most influential work on this topic, and one that nearly earned him official condemnation for heresy, was *Christian Nurture,* which was published in 1847. Some of the core ideas for this book were first presented in a sermon entitled "Unconscious Influence," which he delivered at the North Congregational Church on February 20, 1842, to an audience that included the young Charles Loring Brace.

Brace was fifteen years old at the time, about six months away from beginning his studies at Yale College. He was gaunt and broad-shouldered, with a jutting forehead, deep-set, pale eyes, and a long, heavy-nostriled nose — all features that were held during the nineteenth century to betoken strong character but whose effect was diminished in Brace by an exceedingly long and narrow jaw. In one photograph from around this time he seems to lurch toward the camera, his eyes weighty and his broad mouth dangling open, as if he were drunk. But in other photographs his gaze is tranquil, intelligent, searching, and just slightly impatient — the gaze of a young man who expects a tremendous amount both of himself and of everyone with whom he comes into contact.

The account of Bushnell's sermon that Brace inscribed into his diary that afternoon was brief, punctuated by self-consciously smart remarks, and consisted primarily of a recapitulation of Bushnell's grandiose presentation of "unconscious influence" as something akin to a force of nature, on the order of earthquakes and the rising of the sun. But many years later Brace would write to a young friend that that morning's sermon had "affected my whole life."[27]

cJ/p

Hear how [an earthquake] comes thundering through the solid foundation of nature. It rocks a whole continent. The noblest works of man, cities, monuments, and temples, are in a moment leveled to the ground, or swallowed down the opening gulfs of fire. Little do [people] think that the light of every morning, the soft, and genial, and silent light, is an agent many times more powerful. But let the light of the morning cease and return no more, let the hour of the morning come, and bring with it no dawn: the out-cries of a horror-stricken world fill the air, and make, as it were, the darkness audible. The beasts go wild and frantic at the loss of the sun. The vegetable growths turn pale and die. A chill creeps on, and frosty winds begin to howl across the freezing earth. Colder, and yet colder, is the night. The vital blood, at length, of all creatures, stops congealed. Down goes the frost towards the earth's centre. The heart of the sea is frozen, nay the earthquakes are themselves frozen in, under their fiery caverns. The very

globe itself too, and all the fellow planets that have lost their sun, are become balls of ice, swinging silent in the darkness. Such is the light which
revisits us in the silence of the morning.[28]

— Horace Bushnell

All of his life Charles Loring Brace was attracted to grand hypothe-
ses that aspired to be as comprehensive as God's own thoughts. Preeminent among these was Darwin's theory of natural selection, which
was to have a profound effect on Brace's understanding of his work
among the urban poor. Brace himself would write two massive tomes
that each strove to take as comprehensive a view of existence as Darwin's. One purported to show how God used all the oldest religions
of the world to prepare humanity for the revelation of the "highest truth," Christianity; the other was a proto-anthropological attempt at a definitive survey of the "races" of the "old world." Bushnell
was Brace's kind of thinker — never one to shy away from the cosmic
implications of his ideas. And this, perhaps, is why it was Bushnell's
theological expression of ideas prefigured by Sigourney, Beecher,
and Child — and to some extent already truisms among Hartford's
elite — that was to have the most powerful effect on fifteen-year-old
Charles.

Bushnell began his sermon with a quotation so brief most of his audience probably missed it: "There went in also that other disciple."
The line comes from the twentieth chapter of the Gospel of John, in
which the apostle, who always referred to himself as "that other disciple," said that when he and Peter heard from Mary Magdalene that Jesus had risen, they hurried together to see the evidence of this miracle
with their own eyes. John arrived first at the cave where Jesus had been
entombed, but stopped and — out of confusion, doubt, fear? (the
motive is not named) — did not go in. Only after Peter arrived and
entered the cave without hesitation did John follow him and both "*see
and believe.*"

Bushnell reminded his audience of this story and went on to introduce his main point:

And just so, unawares to himself, is every man the whole race through,
laying hold of his fellow-man, to lead him where otherwise he would
not go. We overrun the boundaries of our personality — we flow together. A Peter leads a John, a John goes after a Peter, both of them un-

conscious of any influence exerted or received. And thus our life and conduct are ever propagating themselves, by a law of social contagion, throughout the circles and times in which we live.[29]

Bushnell held that "unconscious influences," such as lured John to follow Peter, are so powerful because, unaware of them as we are, they often feel like our own, natural impulses and so we put up no resistance to them. They are also powerful because, far more than our conscious attempts to influence others, they flow out of our true natures. Even just acts or statements (or laws, or institutions) can have a profoundly negative effect if we perceive that they are hypocritical, just as false or inadequate acts or statements can have positive effects if we see that they are well intentioned. And finally, unconscious influences are so powerful because they affect us in earliest infancy — even before we can speak or understand the way people represent their actions to us:

> The child looks and listens, and whatsoever tone of feeling or manner of conduct is displayed around him, sinks into his plastic, passive soul, and becomes a mould of his being ever after. . . . [Children] watch us every moment, in the family, before the hearth, and at the table; and when we are meaning them no good or evil, when we are conscious of exerting no influence over them, they are drawing from us impressions and moulds of habit, which, if wrong, no patience or discipline can wholly remove; or if right, no future exposure utterly dissipate.[30]

It is with this point that Bushnell made his clearest break from the Puritan doctrine that God's grace works almost exclusively through adult "conversion" (being "born again") and that he commenced the argument that would ultimately help inspire Charles Loring Brace to spend his life working with children and families. Bushnell's belief that these early unconscious influences have a direct effect on the child's preparation for salvation caused him to speak of the responsibilities of parents — and of all people — in dire terms:

> [F]irst make it sure that you are not every hour infusing moral death insensibly into your children, wives, husbands, friends, and acquaintances. By a mere look or glance, not unlikely, you are conveying the influence that shall turn the scale of someone's immortality. Dismiss,

therefore, the thought that you are living without responsibility; that is impossible. Better is it frankly to admit the truth; and if you will risk the influence of a character unsanctified by duty and religion, prepare to meet your reckoning manfully, and "receive the just recompense of reward."[31]

When Bushnell told his parishioners that they must be responsible for — and therefore attempt to control — even those influences they were not aware of having on others and did not intend to have, he was placing a tremendous burden on them. Almost any act or statement, including those his parishioners believed most virtuous, could infuse "moral death" into their children, family, and friends. What is striking is that, rather than acknowledging the onerousness of this burden, Bushnell seemed to grow excited by it. His recommendation for how one might "sanctify" one's character in order to avoid destroying the characters of others was uninflected by the slightest recognition of its difficulty; indeed, it was decidedly celebratory: "It is, first of all and principally, to be good — to have a character, that will of itself communicate good. . . . In order to act with effect on others, [the Christian] must walk in the spirit, and thus become the image of goodness: he must be so akin to God, and so filled with his dispositions, that he shall seem to surround himself with a hallowed atmosphere."[32]

During the early nineteenth century, when, for better and for worse, one's moral character occupied a place in the public imagination akin to "fitness" and "success" today, certain expansive natures like that of Bushnell — and of his young parishioner Charles Loring Brace — responded to moral challenges the way contemporary joggers respond to marathons, or venture capitalists to promising start-ups. They understood the risks of accepting those challenges. They also knew their own limitations. They may even have known that they were likely to fail. But they felt that submitting to the most demanding moral discipline was worthwhile in and of itself, not only because it might bring some good into the world, or win them praise, or afford them moments of self-satisfaction, but because it represented something essential about what it was to be a human being, and to be alive.

Charles would have enrolled at Yale in 1840, when he was only fourteen, had his mother not become seriously ill. Never very healthy, she died after only a short period of illness, and Charles and his family were so distraught that he put off attending college for two years. Lucy Porter Brace is hardly referred to in the Brace family's correspondence, and Charles seems almost never to have spoken about her to his friends or children. In Emma Brace's biography of her father, she says only that Lucy was "a self-devoted, anxious mother with hardly strength enough for the many cares of her little home."[33] The explanation for her absence from family correspondence was simply that she and John were never apart long enough for either to write.

Charles finally entered Yale in the fall of 1842 and, despite his youth, seems to have had little academic difficulty. He did so well in fact that if he was not ranked at the top of his class, he was very close to it — a situation that soon inspired an odd anxiety in him.

Enough orthodox Puritanism survived in the Brace household — or at least in the mind of young Charles — for him to believe that virtue must be entirely selfless. One could not be truly good if one performed even the most apparently moral acts for any reason other than to serve God or humanity. Charles's anxiety at Yale (or at least the anxiety he publicly acknowledged) was not over how his grades compared to those of other scholars, but over the fact that he wanted so desperately to be at the top of his class. He wrote about this moral failing to his sister Emma, who, apart from his father, was his closest soulmate within the family. She responded: "I do not see why you cannot be ambitious and at the same time have this feeling in subservience to God's will; why can you not perform your duties to God at the same time, and ask his blessing upon your efforts." Despite her sympathy for her brother's problem, Emma had no hesitation about being ambitious on his behalf: "Though you have noble antagonists, I should think you may attain, if not the first (which I hardly dare to hope), at least one of the first."[34]

Charles also brought up his misgivings about his ambition in a letter to his father: "It is Sunday, and from some thoughts I have had, I thought I would ask your advice. All to-day, at the most solemn times, I have thoughts come over me which completely carry me away. These thoughts are principally on ambition, my studies, and things connected with them, and I want to know whether a person can be ambitious and still attend to his Christian duties." Charles went on to explain that when he had been at church that morning, he had not been able to prevent himself from being utterly distracted from the sermon by thoughts of "some dire struggle going on between this and that fellow." Borrowing from Bushnell, Charles speculated in this letter that he might try to study out of the desire to be a good influence on his fellow students rather than out of personal ambition. But immediately recognizing the hypocrisy of this stratagem, he concluded, almost in despair: "I should like to know whether you, when a young man, had such feelings come over you, and exclude everything else."[35]

What is most intriguing about this question is that Charles seems to have believed that, if not in the past, then certainly in the present, his father had so supremely mastered his own being that he was never distracted during sermons or, perhaps, on any other occasion. It is hard to imagine even the most devout sixteen-year-old today — especially one as well educated as Charles — asking his father whether he had ever been distracted. But during the early nineteenth century complete control of the mind and body was still seen as both a real possibility and an ideal. And nurturing that control, perhaps especially among the Braces and their social circle, was a passionately conducted group effort and lifelong project.

Many of the letters exchanged between Charles, his family, and his friends contain confessions of one or another weakness and requests for advice about how that weakness might be corrected. Charles constantly worried about being too comfortable and not self-sacrificing enough. To his father he wrote: "[I]f I am going to do any good in life, I must begin by denying myself now."[36] And to a friend: "I should like a less easy life, where there is more of responsibility and strong influence. For I think the firm Christian character is made best in hard duties."[37]

With all of his faith that virtue lay in subordinating himself to others, Charles seems nevertheless to have been equally convinced that he could not be truly admirable unless he stood apart from and, indeed, somewhat above his fellow human beings. He wanted to be "independent" — as in being an "independent" thinker, but also as in being "self-reliant," especially financially. Lydia Maria Child's recommendation that children be brought up with a "dread of being dependent on others" had been perfectly realized in Charles, who had a mortal aversion even to the *appearance* of being "dependent" for money, luxury, or even simple pleasures on anyone outside his family. The intensity of his aversion is revealed in yet another letter asking for advice from his father, this time about his relations with his great friend and college roommate, John Olmsted.

Olmsted's father was a prosperous Hartford dry goods merchant who made considerably more money than John Brace. At Yale, John Olmsted was constantly receiving shipments of pies and other confections from home and buying dumbbells, fencing foils, and boxing gloves, all of which he was more than willing to share with Charles. Owning little more than his books and clothing, and receiving comparatively meager shipments from home, Charles was anxious about accepting such favors when he was unable to return them. "I want to know," he told his father, "whether it will seem at all dependent in me to use these things. If the slightest expression that way should ever drop from [John], I should separate from him immediately, but as it is, I don't hardly think he considers it so at all." What is surprising about this inquiry is that Charles's concern — again, perhaps, reflecting the ideas of Horace Bushnell — was not for his own morality or reputation, but for John's. "I have to be much more careful of myself than I would be at home, or than persons generally would, for John notices very particularly, and is influenced in his own conduct by what he sees in mine."[38]

With all of his anxiety about his moral character, and all of his emphasis on Christian humility and denial, Charles seems never to have had much doubt about his moral and intellectual superiority. Not only an excellent student at Yale and a good boxer, he was the animating force of his small social circle — including, among others, John Olmsted and John's older brother, the future author and landscape architect Frederick Law Olmsted. One member of that group, Fred Kingsbury, first set eyes on Brace while the latter — having decided to risk his independence — was engaged in a boxing match with John Olmsted. In his own autobiography, Kingsbury explained that in Brace he saw "something . . . in the intense earnestness with which he went into the boxing that impressed me at once, and it was a true index of his character."[39]

That "intense earnestness," and the magnetism it exerted on his closest friends, is visible in an 1846 photograph of Brace, the Olmsted brothers, Fred Kingsbury, and Charles Trask. The broad-shouldered Brace, with long, greasy hair, a tight dark jacket, rumpled waistcoat, and flamboyant silk tie, sits at a table surrounded by his friends. He is looking straight into the camera with a brooding impatience, as if he could not bear sitting still even so long as it took the photographer's phosphorus to flash, while the hardy and handsome Frederick

Law Olmsted gazes over at him with an expression of contemplative appreciation.

Far from resenting Brace's attempts to "influence" them, the Olmsted brothers responded with eagerness to his ideas and example. Once, when they were separated for a few months, John Olmsted wrote Brace to say how much he missed his "influence."[40] And in 1848, just as Brace was about to move from New Haven to New York City, where the Olmsted brothers had already gone to live, Frederick wrote, "Let us help each other . . . to give our thoughts a practical turn. . . . Throw your light on the paths in Politics and Social Improvement and encourage me to put my foot down and forwards. There's a great work wants doing in this our generation, Charley — let's off jacket and go about it."[41]

Brace would indeed have a profound effect on Frederick Law Olmsted's career. He introduced his old friend to the *New York Daily Times* editor who assigned him to write the series of articles on southern slavery — collected in *The Cotton Kingdom,* Olmsted's first great public success. Brace also introduced Olmsted to Charles W. Elliot, a member of the commission to develop Central Park. When Olmsted was campaigning to be appointed superintendent of the park, Brace got him the recommendation letter from Washington Irving that ultimately convinced the Democratic city authorities that Olmsted deserved the position despite his Republican sympathies. And finally, a letter from Brace's uncle, Asa Gray, the world-famous botanist, would help Olmsted and his partner, Calvert Vaux, win the job of actually designing the park.

But the influence definitely went two ways. Without Frederick Olmsted's practical-mindedness and passion for argument, Charles might never have undertaken social service work but pursued instead a career as a minister-philosopher that, in all likelihood, would have been decidedly less auspicious. Brace had enormous intellectual ambition and breadth of learning and — despite his early self-image — an astute *practical* imagination, but he lacked the capacity for rigorous and original thought that would have allowed him to emulate his first mentor, Horace Bushnell.

જ઼ર

Frederick Law Olmsted was in love with Emma Brace. "Yes, certainly, I really love her, love her dearly," he confessed to his brother (who also claimed to love Charley's little sister — to have loved her in fact since he was five years old), "but," Fred continued, "I've no intention of marrying her, and she knows it, and moreover I know that she's no intention of marrying me, whatever I wish."[42] Proclamations of love were a common motif in Frederick Olmsted's correspondence. In a single letter he might declare himself smitten by one woman in the first sentence, by a second in the next, by a third in the following, and so on — never wholly serious, never only joking. And as it was with love, so had it been with almost every other aspect of his life.

In 1837, when fifteen-year-old Fred Olmsted entered Yale, he had already been to thirteen schools — the result of his own restlessness and his father's indecision about what sort of education might best suit him — and his commitment to college was to prove no more durable. He dropped out during his first year, ostensibly because of temporary blindness from a bad case of sumac poisoning, and he would never officially re-enroll or get a degree from any university. Over the next few years he studied engineering, taught at the Phillips Academy in Andover, Massachusetts, and worked for an importer in New York City. In the fall of 1842, when he was twenty years old and his younger brother John and their good friend Charley Brace had just enrolled at Yale, Frederick returned to New Haven and sat in on some classes, but he was off again before the spring term was over, sailing out of New York as a seaman on a ship bound for Hong Kong. A year later he was back at Yale, full of stories about his adventures on the far side of the world and nursing the lingering effects of a shipboard case of typhus. But after a couple of months in New Haven, he was off again, this time to study farming in upstate New York, and then to run a farm, with considerable ineptitude, that his father bought for him in Sachem's Head, Connecticut. The farm went bust after only one season.

As unsteady as his early career may have been, Frederick Olmsted had decidedly firm opinions and a passion for expressing them. In a letter to Fred Kingsbury, Brace described the "torrent of fierce argument, mixed with diverse oaths on Fred's part," that he and Olmsted, much to their mutual enjoyment and illumination, were having almost every time they saw each other. "I must say," Brace continued, "Fred is getting to argue with the utmost keenness, — a regular Dr. Taylor mind in its analytic power! But what is queerest, never able to exercise that power except in discussion! . . . I shouldn't be surprised if he turned out something rather remarkable among men yet."[43]

Brace and Olmsted had two main bones of contention: abolition and religion. Charles was a passionate opponent of slavery, as well as a

friend of the prominent abolitionists William Lloyd Garrison and
Theodore Parker. Olmsted also abhorred slavery but, unlike Brace, did
not want it abolished by law or by force. Describing himself as a
"peace man," he maintained that slavery should be brought to an end
through rational persuasion — and indeed, his book *The Cotton Kingdom* attempted to do just that, by demonstrating that, morality aside,
slavery did not make economic sense.

Brace and Olmsted had always argued about religion, but their
theological disputes came to a head in 1847, when, after a stint teaching at Connecticut country schools, Brace enrolled at Yale's Divinity
School with the intention of becoming a minister. Olmsted was a
deeply religious man, but also passionately honest and determinedly
pragmatic, to say nothing of being "independent" to the point of re-
belliousness. He had little time for theology, especially when it presented unverifiable assertions as truth. He objected in particular to
any doctrine that elevated blind faith over sincere exploration of religious ideas, and he believed that good conscience and good works
mattered more to one's ultimate salvation than doctrinal purity or
even faith itself.

In many ways Frederick Law Olmsted was precisely the sort of
young man who had helped spawn a fashion among American Protestants for youthful conversion. The advance of capitalism had created
the now-familiar social problem of the "generation gap." Prior to the
eighteenth century the lives of most children were essentially identical
to those of their parents. But as the pace of social change accelerated,
the world into which children matured was ever more different from
that of the previous generation. The new demands and possibilities
that young people encountered, especially the growing need to travel
far from home to find work, were a source of anxiety to parents and
children alike. The countless young Americans who, like Frederick
Olmsted, were overwhelmed by choice and took long years to settle on
a career were seen as particularly susceptible to vice and dangerous
ideas. Since the moral certainty that followed "rebirth" was held to be
the most effective inoculation against temptation, a fashion for early
conversion swept the nation. Prior to the American Revolution, people were typically "born again" in their thirties, forties, or even fifties,
but by the start of the Victorian era conversions in the late teens or
early twenties were all but the norm.

Several of the Olmsted children were "saved" at this age, shortly after the death of their sister. John's conversion came at a revival at Yale

in February 1846, when he was nineteen, and Charles Brace heard his call to the ministry when he too was "reborn," at twenty, later that same year. But the elder of the Olmsted brothers was never to be similarly united with God, a fact that caused him some dismay but also seemed a result of dearly held principles. He often trumpeted the virtues of his "unsettled" state in his arguments with Charley.

In a letter written in March 1848, when Brace had nearly finished his year at Yale's Divinity School and was preparing to move to the more liberal Union Theological Seminary in New York City, Olmsted declared, with typical sensitivity to his friend's feelings:

> I never knew the man that had graduated at a Theological Seminary that showed ordinary *charity* at his heart. I do believe it is harder for an editor and a clergyman to enter the Kingdom than for a rich man. . . . I thank God, Charley, you are not *settled* yet, not absolutely pinned down to any or but comparatively few Theological dogmas (I hope *political* too). For if you reach this state it will be perfectly impossible for you practically to have charity for those that differ from you — and I believe that one spark of charity is of more value than all the *results, settlings* of all the study, the light, or Grace of Belief of Drs. Taylor, Edwards, Luther, Calvin (whose opinions have been a terrible curse).[44]

Brace seems to have been unperturbed by his friend's attacks, perhaps because, while clearly disagreeing with Olmsted on the virtues of ministers and theology, he was as staunch a supporter of unfettered inquiry as Olmsted. Several months *before* receiving this letter he had written to a friend:

> [T]hat there can be anything wrong in searching for truth freely, or in uprooting the dearest opinion to see what lies under it, or in applying our individual judgment to any truth (be it even of God's existence), I do not see. . . . I am determined never for a moment to refuse hearing a truth because it is new, and never to be afraid to dig under a belief because it is old and dearly loved. God help me in it. I have no more fear of Freethinking than I have of charity.[45]

ৡৢ

In the conservative atmosphere of Yale's Divinity School, there were many who found Brace's religious speculations "dangerous." To one of these critics he wrote that the times when his faith was all "unsettled"

were long past, and that, in any event, God was merciful regarding er-
rors that resulted from a sincere quest for the truth. The main topic of
the letter, however, was Brace's notion of God's mercy, a notion that
would play a key role in both his rejection of orthodox religion and
his embrace of social activism.

He began the letter by objecting to Calvinism's emphasis on God as
"The Lawgiver" and to its constant references to the "Throne of Law"
and the "Dignity of the Law." "It seems to me," he said, that "the government of a State does not present the best type of God's government
(if we may call his influence a government)." On the contrary, Brace
maintained, "[i]t isn't a Lawgiver which we find presented in the New
Testament, but a Father seeking our happiness. The only abstract justice I can see, which He must uphold, is whatever will tend to the most
happiness." The main reason human government (as embodied in
law) is not a good model for God's government is that law can apply
only to the "overt" acts of man. No human law can pardon an offender
merely because he repents, because human beings cannot look into
the heart of a man to determine whether his repentance is sincere.
And this is precisely what makes human law both inferior to God's
and an inferior metaphor for God's governance. Instead, Brace believed, "family government" was a more appropriate metaphor for
God's relationship to humanity:

> A father governs by love. His will may be all, for a time, the children
> know of right. He does, to a degree, know the hearts of his subjects,
> and can almost determine when repentance is sincere. He tries to gov-
> ern the motives and dispositions, as well as overt action. Now I do not
> believe there is a kind, judicious father anywhere but would forgive a
> child who had done wrong if he were only sure of his repentance.[46]

In this letter Brace revealed four of the fundamental beliefs on
which his work with poor families and children would rest. First, during an era when the majority of upper-class Americans thought of
poverty and criminality as more or less synonyms, Brace denigrated
the mechanisms (the law and its executive institutions) that supposedly determined who was "criminal." He asserted that the highest justice understood that lawbreakers might have motives or other qualities that redeemed them, and that God cared less about the law than
about promoting human happiness.

Second, Brace elevated the family beyond being the prime instrument by which God shaped human beings, as it had been for Bushnell, to the very image of God's relationship to humanity: God was a father who loved all of His children and wanted only their happiness.

Third, Brace's notion that the good father — like God — "tries to govern motives and dispositions, as well as overt action" implied that those doing God's work through charity were at least sanctioned to engineer the souls of those they helped. And indeed, all of Brace's charitable work would aim to "improve" the character of its beneficiaries — a goal he had in common with most Protestant charities.

And finally, Brace chose to illustrate God's beneficence by His forgiving of sins in cases of sincere repentance. The encouragement of such repentance would be Brace's primary goal when he first began to work with the miserable and the poor of New York City, but it would also be one that he would shortly disregard as tragically insufficient.

ᵔ 2

Flood of Humanity

THE UNITED STATES changed more rapidly during the early nineteenth century than at any other time before or since. To the average citizen the most noticeable change was the rocketing population expansion, particularly in cities. Between 1790 and 1830 the rate of urban population growth was nearly double that of the nation as a whole. Philadelphia more than tripled in size during this period, only to be surpassed as the nation's most populous city by New York.

At the time of the first U.S. census in 1790, only 33,131 people lived in Manhattan. Population increased steadily throughout the first quarter of the nineteenth century, but only began to explode when the Erie Canal was opened in 1826 — the year of Brace's birth — making New York the prime gateway for trade and immigration to the East Coast and the whole of the Midwest. Throughout the remainder of the 1800s nearly 1,000 people a day poured into Manhattan from abroad and all parts of the American continent. By 1848, when Brace went to New York to attend Union Theological Seminary, the city had half a million inhabitants. By 1860 New York's population would be more than 800,000, and by 1890 it was close to one and a half million.[1]

People came to New York to escape famine, oppression, or the law. They were running away from their families or rejoining them. They came to find work, to build reputations, to get rich. Many people who came to the city were only on their way someplace else, to a homestead on the prairie, to California's gold country, or, conversely, back to Europe. But one way or another, New York's flagstone and granite sidewalks were filled with people driven by a vision of a better life. It was a city of hope and of hope destroyed, of furious energy and of simple fury.

Most people who wrote about New York in the nineteenth century found the city's soul on its grandest and longest street: Broadway, a corridor of three- and four-story brick and limestone buildings, running, in 1848, from Battery Park to Union Square. Here were many of New York's finest shops, hotels, and theaters; here were City Hall, Trinity Church, Saint Paul's Chapel, some of the city's grandest mansions and the enormously popular P. T. Barnum Museum. Here too were the crush and cacophony that even then seemed to typify New York City.

Carts, cabs, lumbering omnibuses, and grand carriages decked out with uniformed footmen clanked and clattered over Broadway's rounded cobbles. The air was dense with the curses of draymen, with whiffs of manure and gutter water, with the hoarse cries of newsboys and the singspiel of the corn girls ("Hot corn! Hot corn! Here's your lily-white corn. All you that's got money — Poor me that's got none"). By all accounts the sidewalks of Broadway were as crowded throughout the Victorian era as they are today, with the difference that pedestrians then had to watch out not only for traffic — unregulated, in those pre-stoplight days, by anything other than audacity and dumb luck — but also for stray pigs, which were famous for barreling unexpectedly out of side streets and bowling over anyone in their path.

According to George Templeton Strong, a conservative lawyer and diarist of mid-nineteenth-century New York, two-thirds of the throng that always crowded Broadway were "whores and blackguards,"[2] but the imagination of nineteenth-century commentators was most often captivated by the more elevated segment of the street's pedestrian traffic, the belles and beaus of high society, as well as the "Byrons of the desk," who would come to Broadway to show off their finery and look one another over.[3] Almost every portrait of New York life during that era contains extended rhapsodies about the gaudy splendor of Broadway's afternoon and evening promenades. That so young a nation could produce so many silk dresses, white collars, and brightly colored parasols, to say nothing of so much vanity and presumption, seemed almost miraculous to early observers. Broadway was a wholly new phenomenon. There was no street to match it — not anywhere in America, and by some accounts, not anywhere in the world.

Two blocks east of Broadway and a three-minute walk from City Hall was another wholly new phenomenon, at least for North America, one not nearly so miraculous but no less astounding. This was Five Points, a district named for the pie-slice buildings at the intersection of its four major streets. Five Points was Manhattan's poorest, most crowded, and most dangerous neighborhood. It had been built on unstable landfill near the start of the century, and by the 1840s most of its two-story buildings were cockeyed with cracked walls and swaybacked roofs. Its streets were bogs in the driest of weathers, buzzing with mosquitoes and flies and stinking of the horse and pig dung that had been worked into the mud by decades of traffic. According to Charles Dickens, who visited Five Points under police protection in 1842, pedestrians who strayed into the district's maze of back alleys could sink in this fetid stew up to their knees.[4]

Five Points was the place where ambition went sour, where people who had endured much found they could endure no more. The only businesses that thrived there were taverns, some of which, run by free blacks and featuring entertainers such as the renowned dancer Juba, were the nineteenth-century equivalent of 1920s Harlem nightclubs. The neighborhood was reputed to be overrun with thugs and thieves and to be home to most of the prostitutes who plied their trade along Broadway and in City Hall Park, as well as in Five Points' numerous bordellos. The area's most infamous building, a rambling, ramshackle brick structure called the Old Brewery, was said to have been the site of more murders than any other structure in the city.

It is hard to imagine today how deeply shocking, even baffling, Five Points was to most Americans, especially during the first half of the nineteenth century. It was not that there had never been violence, drunkenness, or prostitution in the United States, only that such ills had never existed on so vast a scale — a scale that represented not merely an escalation in frequency but a transformation of their very nature. A few country thugs and burglars are a far cry from the powerful gangs that tyrannized Five Points. And a small-town tavern with an entrepreneurial waitress is nothing like block after city block of women, girls, and, presumably, boys offering their bodies to anyone with coins to spare.

Five Points was also an affront to democracy. Not only had there been no slums in eighteenth-century American cities, but there had been little social segregation. Ben Franklin's closest neighbors in Philadelphia, for example, had been a plumber, a barrel-maker, and a shopkeeper. Many Americans had thought that the marked stratification of urban society represented by neighborhoods such as Five Points, as well the "vice" and class resentment that flourished within them, were wholly European artifacts, impossible within a democratic republic. And almost everyone believed that these were only temporary aberrations that would clear up as soon as the largely foreign-born poor got over their habits of "idleness" and "dependence."

The real causes of the poverty in Five Points, and in the growing slums of other American cities, had a lot less to do with individual moral weakness and a lot more to do with the nation's coming of age. New York in the nineteenth century was very much like a Third World city today — like Rio de Janeiro or Bombay. Many of New York's afflictions during that era were those that accompany the transition from a traditional to an industrial economy. They were what happens when the economic foundation of a society changes more rapidly than its cultural habits.

During the eighteenth century most Americans were farmers, artisans, or shopkeepers who primarily lived in their places of business and "employed" only their own families and maybe an apprentice or two. Work was done when people got around to it. Punctuality was a minor virtue. Profits were shared by the family, and apprentices were given basic necessities, training, and some schooling. In 1750 only 6 percent of New York City's workforce labored for wages, a proportion that expanded more than fourfold, to 27 percent, over the next one hundred years.[5] The expansion of wage labor was encouraged by the development of new industries within the city. There had been no more than a handful of printers and book publishers in New York in 1810, for example, but by 1860 there were 154 such businesses — and they were fairly big operations, employing, on average, 26 people each. But the rise in wage labor was also the result of individual artisans being driven under by competition from businesses that practiced consolidated production. In 1810 almost all clothing was still made by individual seamstresses and tailors or in the home, or it was imported from England; the U.S. census listed no garment manufacturing companies in New York. But by 1860 there were 398 such companies in the city, employing an average of 67 workers each.[6]

Mass production brought down the price of goods and helped make life easier, more comfortable, and even healthier, at least for the upper classes, but these benefits came at a price. The wage laborers who produced these cheaper goods had to contend with the new perils of the mechanized workplace, and with the unsanitary conditions of the crowded neighborhoods where they lived. They also suffered a great deal more financial insecurity than their more economically independent counterparts of an earlier era.

Artisans and farmers were comparatively self-sufficient. They grew

or made much of what they needed to survive, and when times
got hard they could compensate to some extent by working a little
harder or by lowering prices. Industrial workers, by contrast, were entirely dependent on wages. They had to buy virtually everything they
needed, and virtually everything they produced went to their employers. When times got hard, wage laborers could not compensate by
working harder, because they would often be out of a job and thus
could not work at all. And in cities like New York, where immigration ensured that there were always many more willing workers than
jobs, employers had no compunctions about laying people off when
business took a bad turn, or even just during seasonal lulls. Working-
class Americans were constantly losing their jobs through no fault of
their own. Moreover, with no strong unions, pay remained low. At
midcentury, when rents for the humblest two-room apartment averaged two to three dollars weekly, wage workers in New York rarely
earned more than five dollars a week.[7] And during the first half of the
century industrial wages tended to fall rather than to rise. In a Philadelphia cotton mill, for example, the pay of hand-loom weavers de-
creased from one dollar per cut in 1820 to seventy cents in 1833, to only
sixty cents in 1840.[8] Many workers throughout the 1800s were paid so
meagerly that they could not afford to miss a single day on the job.
They also had little protection against accident or illness. If one member of a farmer's or cobbler's family could not work for some reason,
other members could compensate by taking over his or her duties. But
there was no way a woman who helped support her family through
the needle trades could suddenly take her husband's place in the iron-
works when he was injured or fell ill. The result was that working-class
families lived constantly on the edge of destitution. When they fell
over that edge, as they often did, they had no choices but begging, the
workhouse, or crime.

Even when both parents were employed, earnings were so meager
that many families depended heavily on the income of their children.
As late as 1880, working-class children contributed between 28 and 46
percent of household income in two-parent families.[9] The littlest children scavenged coal, wood, or rags wherever they could find them.
Those six or older might sell newspapers, matches, or flowers on the
streets or perform menial tasks in shops or factories. They would also
help their mothers by watching younger siblings, keeping house, and
doing some of the sewing, hat-making, or other piecework by which
women commonly helped support their families. At the start of the

1800s many children, especially in poor families, were indentured or "bound out" until age twenty-one. But by midcentury, when the indenture system had been substantially eroded by wage labor, overwhelmed parents would still often send their children to live with relatives or friends during financial or domestic crises. These informal foster parents commonly expected the children to work in order to "earn their keep."

Domestic violence and substance abuse were problems at least as serious during the nineteenth century as they are now — although the "substance" abused was almost exclusively alcohol. The streets of American cities were filled with children who had been forced from their homes or who had simply left when a father became violent or a mother took to drink. And in an era when women frequently died in childbirth and epidemics of cholera and typhoid fever regularly swept American cities — especially in poor, overcrowded, and unsanitary neighborhoods like Five Points — children were much more likely than now to lose one or both parents and often wound up destitute and on the streets.

Immigration helped swell the number of New York's street children mainly by adding to the oversupply of willing workers in the city and thus placing a downward pressure on already meager wages. It was also not uncommon, however, during an immigrant family's short stopover in New York before heading west for a child to wander off on the street and become permanently lost. And in the days before radio transmission made it possible to know in advance exactly when a boat was to dock, parents whose children had followed them from the old country only after they themselves were securely settled sometimes did not hear for hours or even days that the ship bearing their children had arrived — more than long enough for a child to become lost, or worse, in a tumultuous and utterly unfamiliar port city. And finally, parents emigrating west in search of greater opportunity quite often left behind even very young children who had good jobs. Such parents were not necessarily heartless or mercenary; generally they saw themselves as sparing the child from the serious risks and hardship of frontier life. Unfortunately, those young workers often ended up losing their jobs and then, with no income, no home, and no way of rejoining their families, they had to make their way alone out on the streets.

It is not surprising in an era overwhelmingly inclined to see poverty as a sign of moral failure or of God's disfavor that the first response of civic authorities to the swelling numbers of vagrant children in American cities should be to treat them as criminals. For the first quarter of the nineteenth century the police routinely rounded up unaccompanied children and threw them into adult prisons and almshouses.

Not everyone shared this dim view of street children, of course. In 1825 a group of New Yorkers who believed that the incarceration of children was cruel, unfair, and only likely to make them more disposed to criminality founded an institution specifically for juvenile criminals and vagrants: the House of Refuge. As its name implies, this institution, which was soon duplicated in Philadelphia and Boston, was intended to provide children with shelter, food, education, job training, and moral guidance — a worthy program, certainly, but not one that the public was willing to fund. From the beginning, these "refuges" were understaffed by underqualified and underpaid men and women and very soon became as brutal and punitive as the institutions they were intended to replace. Nor did their existence mean that children were no longer being thrown in with adult criminals. As late as 1851 there were still 4,000 inmates under twenty-one years old in New York's adult prison, 800 of whom were fourteen or younger, and 175 of whom were younger than ten.[10] And civic authorities continued to see poor and vagrant children not merely as criminal but sometimes as less than human.

In 1849 New York's first police chief, George Matsell, issued a report estimating that 3,000 children lived on the streets of Manhattan. (The other boroughs were not incorporated into the city until 1898, but Brooklyn at least had substantial child vagrancy as well.) Matsell hoped his report would boost support for the newly unified police department, but even such a motive hardly explains the extremity of his language. He portrayed the city as in the midst of a dangerous infestation by "degrading and disgusting . . . almost infants," who were "addicted to immoralities of the most loathsome description" and whom, he claimed, it was humiliating to recognize as "part and portion of the human family."[11]

Even couched in such absurd rhetoric, Matsell's estimate of child vagrancy was widely accepted during his day and was far more conservative than the estimates of social reformers, who commonly put the number of vagrant children at 10,000, and sometimes even 30,000 or 40,000.[12]

ℐℛ

> I think I should enjoy studying in New York for a year, but not much more.
> The novelty must wear away then. But now it is the greatest possible relief
> after study, to take a walk down Broadway and look at the perfect flood of
> humanity as it sweeps along. Faces and coats of all patterns, bright eyes,
> whiskers, spectacles, hats, bonnets, caps, all hurrying along in the most ap-
> parently inextricable confusion. One would think it a grand gala-day. And
> it's rather over powering to think of that rush and whirl being their regular
> everyday life.
>
> — Charles Loring Brace[13]

Brace came to New York in the fall of 1848 ostensibly to study at Union
Theological Seminary but perhaps equally to be with his friends John
and Fred Olmsted. John had moved to the city to study medicine
with Dr. Willard Parker, and Fred was working a new farm on Staten
Island.

In 1848 the city occupied only the lower quarter of Manhattan Island and petered out into open countryside beyond the Croton Reser-
voir at Forty-second Street (the present site of the main public library
and Bryant Park). "Downtown" was the area around Wall Street, while
Greenwich Village was a nearly suburban "uptown." In those days Union Theological Seminary was located in the Village, a block west of
Broadway, on University Place, just above Washington Square.

John and Charley shared a basement room in a boardinghouse
nearby where they were bothered by mosquitoes and the noise of
constant pedestrian traffic. Their fellow boarders, who seem to have
annoyed Charles almost as much as the mosquitoes, consisted of
self-important theological students with bad table manners, music
teachers who complained incessantly about the musical tastes of the
average American, and snooty schoolteachers who demonstrated
their overall superiority through excessively distinct enunciation, as in
ri-t-ee-uss-ness-ss.

Brace was himself a schoolteacher at that time. He taught Latin at
the Rutgers Institute four and a half hours a day for six dollars a week
— very good money he thought.[14] He also wrote regular articles for
several publications, including the *New York Daily Times* and the *Independent* — the Congregationalist newspaper associated with Henry
Ward Beecher's Plymouth Church in Brooklyn. In the evenings Brace
went to clubs and hotels with other young writers and journalists and
smoked cigars, drank ale, and engaged in rampant speculation in
which, according to Fred Kingsbury, "nothing was regarded as settled,

and if so regarded, there was all the more reason why it should be un-settled at once."[15]

With all of this activity on top of his regular studies, Brace had be-come thoroughly involved in the "rush and whirl" of Manhattan that had so impressed and slightly daunted him on his first arrival. As in-toxicated as he was by his life as a New Yorker, it wearied him, and he worried, as he wrote to Fred Kingsbury, that it was numbing his moral sensibilities:

> [D]o you not feel afraid . . . of this crowding of life's business, in wear-ing off some of our best *human* feelings too, as well as our love for God? Just look around and see how few men keep any of the warm or noble sentiments which they had once. I am inclined to think it is par-ticularly so in this country. Perhaps money-making is more entirely absorbing. . . . I don't believe we have any idea how long devotion to some inferior object or how the wear and rubbing of poverty may rub away the best and noblest impulses we have. Can a man be an earnest, enthusiastic worshiper of principle when he finds it doesn't bring him in eighteen pence a day? Shall we *love* and clasp men to us when we don't get five minutes out of the twenty-four to kiss our wives?[16]

Frederick Law Olmsted's Staten Island farm, "South Side" — paid for by a $12,000 loan from his father — encompassed 130 acres near Seguine Point, looking out over the Atlantic Ocean just south of the entrance to New York Harbor. The house was Dutch, with a broad wooden porch — or piazza — running around its seaward sides. Olmsted believed that farming was the healthiest, happiest, and most virtuous life a man could have, and he often declared that he loved no work so much as plowing. The fact that he was, at best, a middling ag-riculturalist who never managed to turn a profit at either of his two farms did nothing to diminish his appreciation for the calling.

Every weekend that they could manage, especially during the sum-mers, Charley and John would escape the heat and noise of Man-hattan for the tranquillity of South Side, where they would take walks along the pebbly shore or through a thick wood of oak, maple, sweet gum, and sassafras and sit on the broad piazza eating peaches, writing letters, and watching ships pass by under tan sails or plumes of black smoke. Fred Olmsted, occupied with farmwork from dawn until six in the evening on Saturday, would return to launch into debates with Charley that, fueled by good food and wine, lasted until the early hours of the morning and then continued all day Sunday. Not infrequently, however, these passionate disputations were relieved by visits from young women — in particular from nineteen-year-old Mary Perkins, who was the granddaughter of one of Fred's neighbors. She and John became engaged in February 1850 and were wed the following fall. After John's death of consumption in 1857, Fred married his sister-in-law and adopted John's son, who had been christened John Charles but was called Charles.

As stimulating as Brace may have found the company at South Side, what he most loved about his visits to the farm was the opportunity to reimmerse himself in nature. Almost every one of the letters he wrote from the island contained an extended meditation on the landscape that surrounded him and on its relationship to the divine. In the early spring of 1849 he wrote to his sister, who was then living in Georgia:

> *My dear Emma:* Sunday again on the Island, about nine o'clock in the evening, and such a beautiful day! Since I have learned to look more on beauty as the expression of God to us, I have explained many of the peculiar feelings I have always had about it. That strange sadness — dreaminess — the pure effect it always had on me, — for I believe in the strongest sense of the Infinite, or of some of God's qualities, in the lines and colors of nature. I took a long walk alone on the beach this afternoon, — the old golden light on everything, with the blue, dreamy highlands, and the gray sky in the east, against which everything stood out so beautifully, the sea sparkling and deep blue, with the same unceasing whisper on the beach — hush! hush! I did enjoy that walk. And could not help but think of Him who was over it all, and who looked through all upon me. You, too, came in, and my own foolish, imperfect life, and all I might be and the little I was.[17]

The spring of 1849 was one of the most catastrophic in New York City's history. On May 10, fans of the celebrated American actor Edwin Forrest gathered in front of the Italian Opera House on Astor Place to protest a performance by Forrest's British rival, William Charles Macready. Police surrounded the crowd and, when the protesters refused to disperse, fired into it, killing thirty-one people and wounding forty-eight — and, not incidentally, setting off what is still the bloodiest civil disturbance ever to occur in New York apart from the draft riots of 1863. Over the next two days, in what became known as the Astor Place Riot, seventy police officers were wounded and at least three more people were killed. Most of the protesters in front of the opera house were Irish immigrants. Despite the aesthetic and nationalistic dispute that had ostensibly brought them there, the ensuing riot was widely interpreted as an expression of the class and ethnic antagonisms that had already spawned nine serious riots in New York City since the start of the century.[18] The violence particularly disturbed many city residents because it followed so hard on the heels of the European revolutions of 1848, which were also fueled by ethnic and class antagonism. But the riot also came in the midst of New York's most virulent cholera epidemic ever. By New Year's Eve of 1849, 1 percent of the city's population — or 5,071 people — would die of the disease, and many residents began to feel that the foundations of civilization were crumbling beneath their feet.[19]

Brace was involved in both catastrophes. Although he apparently only witnessed the riot, he came close enough for his father to call him "foolhardy." And he ministered to at least one dying cholera victim, an experience he described to his father as "the first of those poor efforts I should be glad to lay at the feet of Christ."[20]

The spring of 1849 did indeed mark the beginning of Brace's career of social activism. But despite his long-term aspirations, the actual commencement of his career was a response less to the need of the community than to a calamity within his own family.

As inspiring a teacher as John Brace may have been, he had never been able to earn enough money to raise his family above the lower edge of middle-class respectability — a fact that seems not to have diminished his children's admiration for him in the least. When it came time to start earning a living, Charles and Emma both chose to follow in their father's footsteps by becoming teachers, and they did so simultaneously, in the autumn of 1846. Charles had just finished his undergraduate studies at Yale and had taken a job at a Connecticut country academy in part so as to save up enough money to attend Yale's Divinity School. Emma, however, never went to college. Her formal education ended when she graduated from the Hartford Female Seminary. Although she thought teaching a noble profession, and one that would inspire her to improve her own character (as she put it, the need of her students "to hear of God and his mercies" would provide her with strong "inducements to do good"[21]), the primary reason she took a job at a rural school in Garrettsburg, Kentucky, was that she wanted to relieve her father of the financial burden of supporting her.

Emma stayed in Garrettsburg for two years. In the autumn of 1848 (around the time Charles moved to New York), she took a new job at a school in Georgia. Toward the end of her first term there John Brace decided to give up his own teaching career and to take a job as the editor of the *Hartford Courant,* a move that caused Charles perhaps his first major disappointment in his father. Writing in response to the news, Charles accused John Brace of becoming a "mere party-instrument" and declared: "We had better, all of us, for our own self-respect and God's respect, too, be digging potatoes for a living than hanging on the skirts of a party for an office."[22]

It is not clear why John Brace decided to give up the tranquil purity of the female seminary for the brutality and corruption of city politics, but it is at least sadly ironic that in the very season when he at last acquired the financial wherewithal to enable Emma to give up her job and return home she contracted tuberculosis.

Her illness began with what appeared to be a severe cold in the spring of 1849. After a month or two of bed rest, during which Charles came to visit her, she was at last well enough to return north and recuperate in Litchfield, at the home of her aunts, Sarah and Mary Pierce. Charles was there to greet her on July 18 and wrote a letter to their father that first evening:

> Emma came today. She is much better than she was at the South. . . . I think this air will benefit her, and Aunt Mary's kind care. If she will only be prudent, and I think she will. She is cheerful, yet looking at things as they are. We may have hope, and yet must be ready for the worst. Let us leave her in God's hands. My heart is almost crushed sometimes as I think of her, and yet I see that God is never more truly kind than in such trials.

Brace chose to find kindness in the illness that was destroying his beloved sister by seizing on it as the force that would motivate him, finally, to act on his beliefs. In this same letter, he told his father that he was able to bear his sister's situation "cheerfully" only by concentrating on the labors he might perform "for human happiness, for *God*. My future as I draw it, has not for some time been one of happiness. I do intensely long to give every effort and thought to the good of men, to truth."[23] Again and again in the letters that he wrote over the next seven months he portrayed Emma's illness as the "kindness" that would inspire him to labor for others — a labor that he habitually portrayed as self-sacrifice: "I believe I can serve God by suffering."[24]

In late October, as Emma's condition grew steadily worse, he began to minister to the terminally ill young women at the New York Charity Hospital on Blackwell's Island.

For more than two centuries Blackwell's Island (now Roosevelt Island) had been one of the more isolated and picturesque spots in the archipelago that made up greater New York City. Nearly two miles long, and lying in the East River between Manhattan and Queens, the island had been the refuge to which Captain John Manning fled in disgrace after losing New York to the Dutch in 1673. And for some five generations, starting in the early eighteenth century, it had been farmed by members of the Blackwell family, from whom the island derived its name. During the 1840s it was still possible to stroll through the island's many arbors and past its willow-shaded wells, to look out across the roiling East River at the white houses scattered on the green hills of Manhattan, and feel that one was in the midst of a rustic paradise. That impression, however, would be sadly dissipated as soon as one turned one's gaze to the island's four major structures, each of which served as a receptacle for a different variety of New York City's human refuse.

The Department of Charities and Corrections had purchased the island from the Blackwells in 1828, primarily because the fierce tidal currents surrounding it would make it difficult for anyone confined there to escape. At the island's extreme northern end was the city's madhouse, a large building with an octagonal tower that, according to the day's theories, would help orient the disoriented by harnessing the earth's magnetic forces. For those poor souls whom magnetism failed to improve, however, a standard nineteenth-century fare of cold baths, shackles, and locked cells was also available.

At the island's southern end lay the Charity Hospital, where the city's poor and destitute came to be treated for any number of ailments, primarily alcoholism and venereal disease. The largest portion of the patients were prostitutes suffering the final and most grotesque stages of syphilis. The hospital had separate sections for men and women as well as a children's ward, which Lydia Maria Child, the abolitionist and mother's guide author, visited in 1842: "This establishment," she wrote of the children's ward, though clean and well supplied with outward comforts, was the most painful sight I ever witnessed. About one hundred and fifty children were there, mostly orphans, inheriting every variety of disease from vicious and sickly parents. In beds all of a row, or rolling by dozens over clean matting on the floor, the poor, little, pale, shriveled, and blinded creatures were waiting for death to come and release them. Here the absence of a mother's love was most agonizing; not even the patience and gentleness of a saint could supply its place; and saints are rarely hired by the public.[25]

Near the center of the island was the city's newest almshouse, an institution where those who had committed no other crime than being destitute were incarcerated. Almshouses had existed in the United States from the earliest colonial days. New York's first was built by the Dutch in 1653. Although they were considered charitable institutions, they had been designed to grant their charity — chiefly shelter and food — in such a way that no one would think of accepting it except in the direst of circumstances. On Blackwell's Island the men and women were housed in separate buildings, even if they were married, and their children were taken away from them and placed in nurseries on nearby Randall's Island. Lest the "able-bodied" — men in particular, but also women — should be tempted to live off public expense rather than take whatever job (at whatever pay) they could find, all residents of the almshouse who were physically capable were required to work. The men broke stones in a quarry on the island, cared for the almshouse grounds, and worked in vegetable gardens. The women were set to sewing and knitting and housework, especially brushing mattresses and floors to keep down the population of vermin.

The largest and oldest structure on the island was the New York Penitentiary, a massive edifice of hewn stone and rubble masonry that stood four stories high and was close to 500 feet across. The building housed both men and women, with the vast majority of the women being prostitutes. This institution was called a "penitentiary" rather than a "prison" because it was intended to redeem prisoners rather than merely punish them. As in the almshouse, and orphanages and houses of refuge, reform was to be accomplished through hard work, strict discipline, rigid schedules, and compulsory religion. Some penal institutions took additional steps to encourage penitence. At Sing Sing, for example, prisoners were not allowed to speak to one another so that they might better contemplate their sins and repent. At the Eastern Penitentiary outside of Philadelphia such contemplation and repentance were encouraged — at least ostensibly — by keeping prisoners in solitary confinement for the whole term of their incarceration. But neither of these moral reform techniques was practiced on Blackwell's Island. Inmates there were allowed to talk freely, and although the penitentiary's 756 stone cells had been designed for single occupancy, they often contained two and even three prisoners. For the most part, the men and women in the penitentiary did exactly the same work as those in the almshouse, with the difference that they wore black and buff striped woolen clothing, were kept in shackles, and were watched by armed guards.

Lydia Maria Child also visited the prison on her tour, with a decidedly radical agenda that she took no pains to conceal from the people accompanying her. When one of these companions was prompted to ask, regarding the prisoners, "Would you have them prey on society?" she replied:

> I am troubled that society has preyed upon them. I will not enter into an argument about the right of society to punish these sinners; but I say she *made* them sinners. . . . The world would be in a happier condition if legislators spent half as much time and labour to *prevent* crime, as they do to *punish* it. The poor need houses of *encouragement*; and society gives them houses of *correction*. Benevolent institutions and reformatory societies perform but a limited and temporary use. They do not reach the ground-work of evil; and it is reproduced too rapidly for them to keep even the surface healed. The natural, spontaneous influence of society should be such as to supply men with healthy motives and give full, free play to the affections, and the faculties. It is horrible to see our young men goaded on by the fierce speculating spirit of the age, from the contagion of which it is almost impossible to escape, and then see them tortured into madness, or driven to crime, by fluctuating changes of the money-market. The young soul is, as it were, entangled in the great merciless machine of a falsely-constructed society; the steam he had no hand in raising, whirls him hither and thither, and it is altogether a lottery-chance whether it crushes or propels him.[26]

While Charles Loring Brace would never have condemned the "speculating spirit" of his age quite so ferociously, he would absolutely have concurred with Child's basic premises — published when Brace was sixteen and still a devoted member of Horace Bushnell's congregation — that society ought to prevent crime by giving men "healthy motives" and "full, free play to the affections, and the faculties." In particular, he would agree with the opinions of the superintendent of the penitentiary, who — "unmasked," as Child put it — told her

> that ten years' experience had convinced him that the whole system tended to *increase* crime. He said of the lads who came there, a large proportion had already been in the house of refuge; and a large proportion of those who left, afterward went to Sing Sing. "It is as regular a succession as the classes in a college," said he, "from the house of refuge to the penitentiary, and from the penitentiary to the State prison."[27]

One Sunday near the end of October 1849, Brace was rowed by two convicts from the rocky shore of Manhattan across the churning East River to Blackwell's Island. Most of the leaves were already off the trees, and the bare branches were the color of the walls of the enormous prison that dominated the island. The armed ferryman had checked Brace's papers before departure to make sure that his passage had been approved by the Department of Charities and Corrections, and during the voyage the small ferry passed another boat in which two convicts rowed a gun-toting guard against the current to keep an eye out for escaping prisoners. Other guards with guns were mounted in turrets at the prison's corners and atop its central building.

Whatever Brace may have thought of the penitentiary or the almshouse, his purposes that day exactly corresponded with theirs. He had come to help the lost souls on the island earn God's forgiveness through sincere repentance. He went first to the almshouse chapel, where he preached without notes to an assemblage of paupers about a God who loved them no matter what they had done. In the afternoon he had more informal talks with inmates of the madhouse and the penitentiary, but he was most affected, as he wrote to his father, by the patients in the charity hospital:

> I have never had my whole nature so stirred up within me, as at what met my eyes in those hospital wards. Standing in a long room, with beds on each side, and speaking to the poor creatures as they lay

there. They are nearly all, you know, diseased prostitutes, brought there mostly to die. Though some do recover. If a man could ever speak of the realities he believed, or of the love of Jesus to the guilty, 'twould be there. Ghastly faces peering from bandages around you, and others all festering with disease, or worn and seamed with passion, and some where pure, kind expressions must have dwelt once. You felt that you were standing among the wrecks of the Soul; creatures cast out from everything but God's mercy. Oh! 'twas the saddest most hopeless sight. Some were young and delicate looking, seduced and deserted. God help them! I had a long day's work.[28]

He described this same visit in a letter to Fred Kingsbury, dwelling on details that perhaps he felt he could not mention to his father:

There was a beautiful face amongst them, voluptuous, but really with very fine expression. She had seen better days, I suspect, than most of them, and seemed to look on almost proudly as we spoke. But as we — no, I — alluded to old friends, and home and the love which they had once, and the kind hearts which had been around them in old days, and then told them in the simplest, most untechnical words I could use, of the Friendship they might have in Jesus, and His love to them, she could not refrain her tears, as I hardly could mine. Oh, what a gleam they gave for a moment on that life of pain and sin and remorse she had had! God help her! It's as near hopeless as can be for the prostitute to reform.[29]

After Brace began his Sunday visits to Blackwell's Island, he all but ceased talking of a career in the pulpit. His letters were full of meditations on the "inefficiency of religion" and particularly on that "Calvin piety" that sees Christian duty as being fulfilled merely by regular attendance at church, revival meetings, and the like, rather than by following the example of Christ and sacrificing oneself to help others. Brace was determined to "serve God by suffering," but he was not sure exactly what he should do. For a while he continued to assert in his letters that he should help others by applying the craft that he had just spent two years acquiring — that is, by preaching — but his enthusiasm for this goal seemed to steadily diminish.

During the bleak fall and winter of 1849 and 1850 Brace was in the midst of the most severe challenge to his faith of his entire life. He had flirted with atheism while in divinity school, but really only so that he could maintain afterward that his belief in God had remained unshaken by the most thorough and rational examination. The doubt he endured during Emma's long, awful decline was of a wholly different order. Despite all of his assertions to the contrary, Brace was having grave difficulty believing in the kindness of the God who was killing his sister. In the letter to John Olmsted in which he confessed his doubts, he also said that, for the first time in his life, he wished for his own death, so that he might be "some place where these pains and heartaches would be all over forevermore."[30]

But for all his suffering and confusion, Brace remained true to his resolution that his sister's death should have the best possible effect on him. It was during her last terrible months that he finally and irrevocably shifted his ambitions from the "theological" to the "practical." And perhaps most significantly of all, it was in a letter to Emma, written on February 15, 1850, just two days before she died, that he first mentioned the social problem that would occupy him for the rest of his life:

> *My dear Emma:* Isn't this a wonderful winter? We have hardly had any here, it is so mild and clear. And then when it is cold you would hardly know it, the sun is so bright. I think, after all, there is a great deal of beauty in winter, especially when there's snow over everything. The sky is uncommonly beautiful this season with us, and we have towards night a peculiar cold gray tint which I have not often seen described. Have you ever noticed the effect produced this season of the year by the afternoon sunlight tingeing a cloud of steam, the most delicate, fading away, not-to-be-looked-at purple color, you ever could see. Try it. New York is whirling on as usual. You can have no idea, Emma, what an immense vat of misery and crime and filth much of this great city is! I realize it more and more. Think of *ten thousand children* growing up almost sure to be prostitutes and rogues![31]

જ઼ૈ

When Emma died, on a Sunday, Charles locked himself in his basement room for three days and three nights and emerged, by his own account, "not gloomy" but determined to be purified by his sorrow. Although the most important part of that purification was to come through work, Charles decided that it should begin with some play: a walking tour of England and Ireland in the company of the Olmsted brothers.

Initially, only Charles and John were to make the tour — Charles, so that he might get over his grief, and John, only just engaged to Mary Perkins (the granddaughter of Fred's Staten Island neighbor), to have a last adventure as a single man. John also hoped that the trip would improve his health. He had been sickly ever since contracting a lung ailment during his first year at Yale and had suffered a particularly severe bout of illness that winter — a bout made all the more frightening by what was happening to his childhood sweetheart. Fred had not been invited because the two friends had assumed that he would not be able to leave his farm during the peak growing season, and in any event, they knew he did not have the money. Fred, however, could not bear the idea of his brother and best friend going off on such an adventure without him. So he begged cash off his father and left South Side in the care of his Irish farmhands.

Their ship sailed out of New York Harbor on May 2, after an aborted mutiny by its drunken crew, and arrived at Liverpool nearly a month later. Brace and the Olmsted brothers spent a few days exploring Liverpool before crossing the Mersey and, knapsacks over their shoulders, officially commencing their walking tour. Over a period of four weeks they meandered south through Gloucester and Salisbury to the Isle of Wight, and then headed north to London. Although they occasionally traveled by train, they spent most of their time on small country roads, stopping when the fancy took them to look in on farms, markets, and orchards and making more purposeful visits to well-known parks and gardens, and to jails, debtors' prisons, and schools for the poor, as well as to more common tourist spots, such as Tintern Abbey and Stonehenge. Brace was particularly interested in visiting the "ragged schools," which offered education to children whose poverty and tattered, stinking clothes made them unwelcome in standard schools.

From London they traveled by sailing ship to Belfast, where they spent several days as the guests of Robert Neill, a passionate opponent of American slavery who had played host to many abolitionists on European speaking tours, including William Lloyd Garrison and Frederick Douglass. The person who most interested Brace during the visit, however, was Neill's daughter, Letitia, who shared his interest in spiritual matters. The two of them would often take long walks about the city and its environs.

In a letter to John Olmsted written in Germany several months later, Brace described his relationship with Letitia as a "delightful sisterly friendship."[32] In another letter, written to Letitia at about the same time, he seemed to be bidding her a final farewell: "[Y]ou, dear, trustful friend, how much I hope for a happy and useful future to you. Not, either, happy, but one which shall best fit you for the progress in the life beyond. God aid you, and may we both become more spiritual and nearer Him in our lives. You *can* have a noble future. It is to be seen whether you will."[33]

Despite the implications of this letter, Brace returned to Belfast at the end of his European tour — more than a year after his first visit. By the time he left to return to America, he and Letitia had begun to talk, at the very least, about the possibility of marrying.

In early October 1850, Fred and John Olmsted set sail on the *City of Glasgow*, returning to farm and fiancé, respectively, and Brace went on to Hamburg to study politics and theology. His original plan was to return to the United States just before Christmas, but much to the consternation of his family, who worried that a prolonged stay in Europe would unsuit him for the "practical" life of his native country, Brace decided to remain in Germany until spring, and then move on to tour Austria, Hungary, Switzerland, and Italy.

Brace had a wonderful time in Germany. His studies were stimulating, he made very good friends, drank gallons of potent German coffee, and was a popular guest at dinner parties. He loved the spirited, affectionate, and straightforward — if occasionally risqué — social interaction of the Germans, whose gatherings made American parties, especially in New England, seem so dreary, stiff, and superficial by comparison. But it was the life of the ordinary German family that he most admired and envied: "There are not in all my memories," he wrote,

> pictures so warm and glowing, as of some of these families in North Germany; families where the look and language of Affection were not blurred by that everlasting formalism and coldness and selfishness which hangs over our households; where love was without dissimulation, neither worn for duty, nor worn for effect; where mutual kindness

and self-sacrifice and affection had so long been, that the very air and
aspect seemed to welcome and sun the stranger.[34]

Brace believed that the simple and honest affection of the Germans
"manifested the great principle of Christ's self-sacrificing love" far
more authentically than the superficial "formalism" of the United
States, where one's virtue — or Christianity — was thought to be determined by how rigidly one conformed to certain prescribed behaviors, like going to church and saying grace. Brace earned vilification as
an infidel and a drunk when, in an article he wrote from Germany for
the Congregationalist weekly *The Independent,* he declared that America needed a "revival in home life" more than a "revival of religion."

But Brace did not think that excessive formality of religion and social manner were the only factors contributing to America's anemic
family life. Rather, the prime culprits he cited in his book *Home-Life in
Germany,* published after his return to the United States, were a "universal greed for money, [the] clangor and whirl of American life,
[and] the wasteful habits everywhere growing up."[35]

Brace had always been a critic of American materialism, especially
that of New York City, which he called "the *materialist* place in our
country."[36] In part, he objected to American commercial culture as a
matter of moral principle: his highest virtue was self-sacrifice, and he
saw materialism as consummately selfish. But during his year and a
half in New York he had also become acutely aware of the more con-
crete consequences of commercialism: the impoverishment and abject
misery of an unprecedentedly large segment of the population.

One of the reasons Brace had found it difficult, in the wake of his
sister's illness, to figure out exactly how he might labor "for human
happiness" was that in the United States there were really only two
methods for dealing with the poor: preaching at them and incarcerating them. In Germany, however, he discovered a third alternative, one
guided by Christian ideals but fundamentally practical in its execution.

The German institution that most interested Brace was the *Rauhe
Haus* (Rough House), a residential school for vagrant children outside
of Hamburg. The *Rauhe Haus* had been founded by Johann Hinrich
Wichern, the leader of the Inner Mission, a Christian socialist movement that had started in the 1830s but underwent a substantial rise in
prominence in 1848 — the year of the revolutions and the publication

of *The Communist Manifesto* — as the middle classes grew increasingly anxious about the rage of the poor.

In the United States, orphaned and vagrant children were confined to institutions founded on the superficial conformity to ritual and rules that Brace so objected to in American society generally. Orphanages and houses of refuge often vowed, in the words of a New York Orphan Asylum report, to treat the children in a "strictly parental" manner and to clothe "the Institution as far as possible with those hallowed associations which usually cluster about home."[37] In practice, however, the children got nothing like parental or homelike treatment. They were dressed in identical uniforms. They ate, slept, and marched in long anonymous rows. And they were subjected to strict, unvarying routines. As for religion, which the institutions ostensibly considered essential to the reform of vice-prone children, it could hardly have been more superficial. When, for example, Lydia Maria Child toured an orphan asylum in rural Queens, New York, her guide informed her with evident pride that it was "beautiful to see [the children] pray; for at the first tip of a whistle, they all dropped on their knees."[38]

In his book *Home-Life in Germany,* Brace amply illustrated his vision of the superiority of the *Rauhe Haus* to American institutional care for vagrant children:

An omnibus ride of three miles carried me to its neighborhood, and after a walk through a pleasant wooded lane, I reached the place. The whole looked as little like the usual home for vagrants, as is possible. I saw no squads of boys walking demurely about, but looking as though the very devil was in them, if they could only let it out. There were no heavy-looking overseers, discoursing piously of the number whom Providence had committed to their charge — and thinking of their pockets. And there was not even the invariable home for forsaken children — the huge stone building, with one bare sunny court-yard. The idea seems to have been here, that those who have no home of their own, as much as possible should be given of the home which God has prepared for all.

It was a large, open garden, full of trees and walks and flowers and beds for vegetables, while on each side stretched away green cornfields. Among the trees there were some dozen plain, comfortable little wood houses, like old fashioned farm-houses, scattered about, and one quiet shaded chapel. The boys visible outside were busy cleaning the flower-beds, or working in the harvest field; some also, repairing fences and buildings.[39]

These children were not merely doing busy work or practicing two or three isolated skills, such as cleaning lanterns or stitching on buttons, as they would have at an American institution. The residents of the *Rauhe Haus* participated in all the varied labors that ordinary farm children normally performed, and did so not as an exercise in discipline but for the benefit of the whole community — or so it seemed to Brace. In addition to working in the garden and on the surrounding farm, the children took turns in a variety of workshops for tailoring, joining, spinning, and baking and had several hours of school each day, as well as time off for play.

As much as Brace appreciated the harmonious integration of the *Rauhe Haus* with its natural environment, it was the institution's attempt to approximate natural home life that most impressed him. In each of the little wood houses a "family" of some twelve boys or girls lived with an adult theological student, who was assisted by a devout farmer or mechanic. The intimacy of this arrangement may not have reproduced the bonds of a loving family, but it certainly made it possible for supervisors and children to get to know and perhaps trust one another much more thoroughly than they would have under the standard American model.

Most of the children stayed at the *Rauhe Haus* for five or six years and then, like their counterparts in the United States, were bound out to farmers, mechanics, or craftsmen. Some of them, however, did their apprenticeship at the *Rauhe Haus* printing press, which, to Brace's amazement, managed to turn a profit and help support the institution.

Brace completed *Home-Life in Germany* in March 1853, the very month when he and a group of concerned New York businessmen and Protestant clergy announced the foundation of the Children's Aid Society, and one can detect in the conclusion of his almost rapturous account of the *Rauhe Haus* an idealized vision of what his own organization might accomplish:

"A Home among the Flowers" [Brace's preferred name for the *Rauhe Haus*], where the vagrant — the child nourished amid filth and squalor — in the dark cellars of a great city, should at length see something of God's beautiful world; where among friends, in the midst of or-chards and corn-fields, he could grow up, invigorated by healthful la-bor, to manhood — all this would seem alone more like the dream of a philanthropic French novelist, than the reality.[40]

A month or so after touring the *Rauhe Haus*, Brace visited a coun-try pastor whose philanthropy would also inspire some of his projects in New York. Brace was most impressed by two lodging houses where vagrants were given clean, comfortable, and dry places to stay for a nominal rent. He also was intrigued by a savings bank in which the poor deposited money once a week. At the end of each season their in-vestments were returned to them, not as cash but as food or fuel fur-nished at wholesale rather than retail prices. What most appealed to Brace about both of these projects was that they required the poor to make some contribution toward the benefits they received, so that their character was not destroyed by becoming dependent on mere charity.

After Hamburg, Brace moved to Berlin, where he lived for the first four months of 1851, supporting himself by writing for American newspapers such as the *Independent* and the *Christian Union*. He wrote to Fred Kingsbury that he thought all of his traveling was mak-ing him a "much better man. . . . It makes one love humanity better to meet so many kind-hearted people, and to receive so many entirely unselfish favors and kindness." He thought that he was becoming more disposed now to "look all around a question, and less and less apt to feel either very strong admiration or contempt at things." He re-gretted a certain "loss of earnestness" but felt that he was wiser for be-ing less likely to launch into "unmitigated tirades," the like of which he believed had "delayed the progress of truth so, especially among the clerical gentry."[41]

Despite the supposed mellowing of his character, Brace expressed many of his most radical and uncompromising opinions during his solitary travels in Europe, his controversial critique of American reli-gion being only one example. In letters home he excoriated his father for publishing an antisocialist article in the *Courant,* condemned John and Fred Olmsted for not actively opposing the recently passed Fugi-tive Slave Act, and claimed that he would rather "be sent to Sing Sing for life" than abide by a law that could require him to participate in the apprehension of escaped slaves and their return to their masters in the South.[42]

The cause that most engaged his passions, however, was the Hungarian struggle for independence. In March 1848, inspired by the revolution that had just commenced in Paris, the Hungarians had briefly — and vainly — risen up in arms against the Austrians, who had dominated their country since the sixteenth century. The most charismatic of the revolution's leaders had been Lajos Kossuth. A man very much after Brace's heart, Kossuth was a dynamic political figure and a brilliant writer and speaker who gained an almost mythic stature not only in his own country but all over Europe and even in the United States. During the summer of 1849, however, the Austrians, with the help of Russian troops, crushed the Hungarian revolution, and Kossuth fled to Turkey, never to return to his native land.

In the spring of 1851 Brace decided — against the advice of almost everyone who heard of his plans — to crown his European travels by touring Hungary and witnessing firsthand the nation's enduring underground struggle, which he called "[t]he best effort for freedom this century."[43]

The idea of visiting Hungary had actually been suggested by John Olmsted one grim, wet afternoon when they were tramping a muddy road in England. And it was John who made the visit financially feasible by getting Brace named foreign correspondent for both the *Philadelphia Bulletin* and the most widely respected of all American newspapers, the *New York Tribune,* which was edited by Horace Greeley.

Brace left Germany for Vienna on April 15, 1851, and in early May he started down the Danube with an official Austrian government pass allowing him to visit Hungary. Although he saw signs of oppression everywhere, even in the "long line of monotonous willow bushes" he observed on the shore and in "the melancholy pine forest on the hills," Brace was tremendously excited by his trip — the earliest part of it at least.[44]

As in Germany, Brace had no shortage of social invitations. He had taken great care before arriving in the country to acquire plenty of letters of introduction from Hungarians living abroad. And whatever his personal charms, he also had great social cachet merely by virtue of his nationality. Less than seventy-five years after Americans had fought and won their own struggle for independence from a foreign power, they still retained some revolutionary glamour, especially in nations like Hungary that could only aspire to democracy. For many of Brace's hosts, merely having an American sitting at the dinner table was an act of insurrection, even if not a word was exchanged about politics.

Brace would not become acutely aware of how thoroughly tyranny could invest even the simplest words and gestures with dire implications until he entered the city of Gros Wardein (now Oradea in Rumania), where a substantial contingent of Austrian troops was stationed. In Budapest, still a well-traveled and cosmopolitan city despite the Austrian crackdown, and in the backroad towns that he had already visited, people had been more or less normal in their conversations with him — even feeling free to talk about the revolution, at least in private. But almost as soon as Brace arrived at Gros Wardein he noticed people cutting off their own jokes midsentence, or interrupting one another with sudden intakes of breath and sharp glances. The city was bustling, even prosperous — but joyless, and he resolved to leave as soon as he could do so without offending his hosts.

During his first afternoon in the city his host, a Professor C., took him to lunch at a hotel. Partly to impress two men at the next table with the fact that his guest was American, C. asked Brace what he thought of Laszlo Ujhazy, a wealthy Hungarian landowner and republican who had given his fortune to the revolution and then fled to the United States, where he founded a celebrated utopian colony. Finding something unsettling in the manner of the men at the next table, Brace confined himself to making noncontroversial remarks ("Ujhazy was much respected in America &c") of the sort that he had heard from almost everyone he had spoken to that day. He was happy when the meal was over and he could leave.[45]

The following morning Brace and C. went to visit Gros Wardein's Austrian governor, who cut off Brace's greeting by telling C., "This gentleman is under suspicion for not having handed in his pass to the police."

Brace tried to explain that he had assumed he had the customary twenty-four hours before turning in his pass. When the governor would not listen, Brace bid him a hasty good-bye and went straight to the police station. There the functionary he dealt with was all smiles and solicitation, explaining that, while he had to hold on to Brace's pass so that a general could inspect it, there would be no further difficulties and Brace should simply send for the pass that afternoon.

Some hours later, as Brace was finishing a meal at the home of some Hungarian friends, the door flew open and in walked the chief of police with two gendarmes and a warrant for Brace's arrest.

Brace invited the chief to sit down and join him in a plate of strudel, and then, to prove his utter indifference to Austrian authority, he consumed not one but two helpings of the dessert, followed by a cup of coffee and a cigar.

The police drove Brace back to C.'s estate, informing him along the way that he was being charged with possession of "proclamations." Not knowing that he was staying at a private home, the police had spent the whole of the previous night searching for him at every hotel and boardinghouse in the city. It was only thanks to his visit to the police station that they had been able to find him.

When the carriage arrived at C.'s estate, Brace noticed a police officer standing guard beside a bundle of books and writings that had been confiscated from his room. Brace laughed at the thought that anyone might expect to find dangerous political sentiments in his religious "effusions" or affectionate letters to friends — all written in his appallingly illegible hand — but the police were unimpressed. They loaded him and his belongings back into the carriage and took him first to the police barracks, and then to an old castle outside of the city.

This castle, which dated from the Middle Ages, was a massive turreted structure built around the four sides of a central square. Outside its walls was a deep fosse (or ditch) crossed by a drawbridge. On the far side of the fosse was a second wall that had crumbled into vine-covered ruins at several places and in others supported the walls of wine and beer shops. During the revolution the castle had been a gun factory for the republican forces, but it had since been transformed into an Austrian state prison for political offenders.

Two soldiers with rifles and fixed bayonets took Brace through the iron gates of the castle and into a hall where he was processed for imprisonment. "Every possible hole and corner was searched in my pockets," Brace wrote in *Hungary in 1851,* his account of his travels and imprisonment, "and everything to the last *Kreutser,* and smallest bit of paper, taken out, and carefully noted down; my watch and tooth-pick being the only things left me. I said not a word during the whole search, though I must say, if there is anything calculated to make a man feel like a felon, it is such a procedure."

From this hall he was taken through one dirty cell, in which there were half a dozen prisoners, into another cell, even dirtier, occupied by only two. When Brace asked whether he might not have a better cell, the guard only answered, "It will be part of your experience as a traveler. *Gute Nacht!*"[46] The heavy door slammed, and Brace turned to face his cellmates.

One was a revolutionary foot soldier who had been convicted for traveling with a false pass, and the other a tailor sentenced to five months for carrying a concealed weapon. The cell they shared was fairly large, built entirely of stone, with weighty arches that met at the center of the ceiling. The only window had been boarded up outside its bars to within a few inches of its lintel. The air in the cell was rank with mildew and the smell of unwashed men — not just Brace's cellmates but all the state prisoners who had preceded them. When he lay down on his bed, he found it roiling with fleas. By morning his eyes were black from lack of sleep, and he was covered with so many red, itching bites that he seemed to have a ferocious skin disease — which is to say that he looked very like the inhabitants of Blackwell's Island to whom he had once preached repentance.

During the weeks of his imprisonment Brace was interrogated daily by four jurists, the leader of whom was a keen-eyed, intellectual-looking man whose official title was "auditor." Outraged and, as he would discover, sorrowfully naive during his first interrogation, Brace responded to the auditor's hostile question "What are your objects in Hungary?" by declaring contemptuously,

> I am traveling in Hungary, gentlemen, as I have traveled in other lands, with the purpose of studying the character and manners of the people, and with the particular object of investigating the old political institutions of the Hungarians. There has always been a want of good reports in America, with respect to the old Constitution of this Nation. I wished to see its workings on the spot. My object has been no other than that of a candid investigator.

As soon as Brace finished this speech he realized not only that his affectation of superior indifference had been entirely laughable given the absolute power these four men had over him, but that by speaking so boldly he had only given them evidence that they could use against him. His reference to the constitution — an early proto-democratic document — had been his biggest error, since it had been by this constitution that Kossuth and his allies had justified all of their claims to independence, great and small, including the revolution.

"We do not believe your account, sir," the auditor stated with a weary finality. "We know the sympathy of Americans with these revolutionists here. We know that no American traveler would leave the great routes of travel for such a vague purpose as this. . . . We know your object!" Brace asked for proof, but the auditor only continued:

> Sir, we understand you. We can prove that every one of your acquaintances has some connection or relative among the emigrants in America. We can prove that you are in a wide conspiracy. We understand this route of travel, and these many acquaintances. There is a wide complot here. I have been accustomed to trace plots for many years. I see your object. Speak out openly and confess.

The evidence that the court had against Brace consisted of two pamphlets about the Hungarian cause: one had a picture of Kossuth as a frontispiece, and on the other someone — not Brace — had inscribed in pencil a quote from Virgil: "Oh! ye who have too sorely suffered, God shall at length bring an end to this too!" The court also claimed to have evidence, which it never divulged, but which could only have consisted of testimony from the two men at the hotel restaurant, that Brace was an agent of Ujhazy. And they considered this evidence confirmed when Brace confessed that he had once seen Ujhazy on the sidewalk in New York. The most damning evidence, at least from the auditor's point of view, was Brace's carefully accumulated letters of introduction. When he attempted to assert their utter innocence, the auditor begged to differ:

> We understand the countersigns and secret devices of your Democratic Society. You hide a conspiracy under a few words. You will enter a room and only say "*Good Morning!*" and you can convey at once under those words, some political sign. There is some plot hidden under this introduction. Explain to the court. Your only hope is confession.

On hearing these absurd assertions, Brace became frightened — so frightened that for a moment he had "that *dreamy* sense, as if it were not I, but some one else, here in that strange peril" — for he now understood full well that common rationality or standards of evidence would offer him no protection, that even if he made no further mistakes and gave the court nothing to confirm its ridiculous charges, the auditor could still suborn enough witnesses to convict him of anything he wanted.

Back in his cell, having been informed that his extended imprisonment was all but certain, Brace threw himself down on his stinking and flea-infested bed and, in mounting despair, thought first — characteristically — of his ambition: "Perhaps *my* LIFE, — all that I had wished and hoped for — all that I had been preparing for, was to end here, to close in this mean, miserable way."[47]

The great benefit of Brace's imprisonment was that it placed him in intimate contact with the very people he had most wanted to meet: Hungarian revolutionaries. For a couple of hours every morning the cell doors were opened and the prisoners were allowed to mingle freely in the corridor. Half of Brace's fellow inmates were the "much oppressed" Bauers, or peasants, but there were also "Catholic priests, Protestant clergymen, Jewish Rabbis . . . Poles, Italians, Frenchmen, Magyar noblemen, and Honveds, and Wallachs, and Croats, and Slavonians." It comes, perhaps, as no surprise that in these assorted enemies of Austrian oppression Brace found yet more reasons to love humanity. "Of course," he wrote,

> where so many were mere soldiers, there were many thick-headed and self-opinionated, and rude enough. But their noble side was their sympathy with the people, and their real devotion to Freedom. When they spoke of that, their thoughts were grand, and I make no doubt — though some of them had been living there for years — that there was not a man among them who would have bought his freedom on the best estate in Hungary, for a betrayal of their cause.[48]

A young Hungarian countess was also imprisoned at the castle. She had been arrested about the same time as Brace and was likewise charged with being an agent of Hungarian exiles. She was also rumored to have been the lover of the Italian revolutionary Giuseppe Mazzini. Many of Brace's fellow prisoners assumed, despite his protestations of innocence, that he and the countess were part of the same organization — a notion that Brace, for more than one reason, found rather appealing.

Whenever he could during those morning sessions when the cell doors were unlocked, Brace would sneak past the guard to a window through which he could peer across the yard into the two small rooms in which the countess had been confined. He would watch her as she sat reading two old grammar texts, which were the only books she was allowed. Often she would come to the window to attend the plants that she kept there. "Poor lady!" he exclaimed in *Hungary in 1851*. "It seemed to me that she grew paler every day. It was very sad; so young and beautiful — with wonderful accomplishments, and a noble heart — to spend her fresh, young years, in that heart crushing place!"[49] Often, when she came to her window, Brace would wave through the bars of his own, hoping to catch her eye and to be able to do her some service, but she never looked in his direction.

∽

Brace was arrested on May 24 and released thirty days later, on June 21 — two days after his twenty-fifth birthday. Often he was told that he might never be released. Once it was rumored that he was going to be beaten, or worse, by prison guards. He saw other inmates given savage treatment — chiefly during what were called "street runs," in which a prisoner would be made to pass between two rows of 150 club-wielding soldiers, who would strike at him with all their might. But Brace was never subjected to physical punishment himself. His suffering consisted entirely of uncertainty, fear, humiliation, searing boredom, and the relentless itch of lice and fleas.

His release did not come about through any finding of the auditor, but only through the exercise of a superior bureaucratic power. And perhaps somewhat to his chagrin, Brace owed the intervention of that power to a Catholic priest who was being released and agreed to convey a verbal message to the American consul.

One morning, a fortnight after the priest's departure, the normally grim and impatient auditor greeted Brace with the good cheer of a host who wants to make amends to his guest for some minor slight on their previous encounter. As Brace sat down, the auditor slid a single sheet across the table and declared, "I have good news for you!" It was a letter from the American consul describing the efforts he had taken on Brace's behalf and ending with the assertion: "I expect your immediate release."[50] Five days later Brace stood on a balcony overlooking the castle yard, a free man.

He was waiting for the carriage that would take him to Pest when he saw the countess being escorted back from her afternoon stroll by the prison provost. One last time Brace attempted to catch her eye, if only to bid her farewell, and yet again she failed to notice him. Long afterward, when Brace was back at Fred Olmsted's Staten Island farm, putting the final touches on his account of his imprisonment, he heard that after many months of sham trials, the countess had finally been sentenced to twenty years' imprisonment.

After four days of travel Brace was safe, at last, in Pest, sitting down to tea on the balcony of the home of an English missionary who had been active in securing his release. "How shall I ever forget that evening," he wrote near the conclusion of *Hungary in 1851:*

> The sun was just setting, and the rich rays poured down into the whole valley of the Danube, which lay at our feet, gilding with glowing light the fine buildings of Pesth, and the summit of the old fortress of Ofen, while it left the side toward us in dark shadow. The colors changed each instant on the clouds above, becoming more and more gorgeous. And as the sun went down behind the Ofener mountains, there seemed to be almost endless vistas of splendid coloring opening beyond.
>
> We all felt the scene with an awe and happiness not to be spoken in words. And as the old missionary called us to the table, and uncovering his gray locks, thanked HIM who had made all this, for His goodness, and that He had brought their friend back again from danger and suffering, I joined with a thankfulness not to be described. And as he prayed for "the unhappy land," and that "the ends of justice might everywhere be fathered," I resolved inwardly that, God willing, my efforts would never fail, while I had strength to give them, for the oppressed in any land.[51]

PART II

Doing

TESTIMONY

JOHN JACKSON

The Runaway White-Slave Boy

ℐℐℴ January 24th 1859. This morning a boy made his appearance in
the office with a note of recommendation from Mr. O'Connor of the
Newsboys Lodging House. He appeared to be about 14 years old, and
had quite a good humored well looking face, and a merry twinkling in
his eyes. His attire was very simple, almost consisting of a primitive
garment something like a coat with long skirts — the original color
was quite gone — several greasy hues having taken its place, and it was
fastened near his neck with a piece of twine. His yellow skin appeared
through a rent or two in the sleeves, the remark is superfluous that his
linen was invisible. Before he told his story he desired something to
eat "for I han't had nothing today," said he, "an' I never likes to talk
was a hungry mouth."

The story is here set down in the very words in which he delivered
it. His name is John Jackson, he spoke in a foreign accent which he
picked up he said in Europe, and at sea.

"I am a native of America," commenced John. "Father died when I
was a year old. Mother four years ago. My troubles began before
mother was lost. We were living at Philadelphia, and I was a very little
boy. I heard the soldiers one day, as they were a goin' through Philadelphia with their music and drums. So I followed them along, and at
night I couldn't find my way back home to mother. I was so sick from
crying and so tired from walking that I lay down in Market Street
and fell asleep.

"I don't know how long I was asleep, but two policemen came
along, and picked me up. They asked me where I lived, and I could
give no correct answer, so they took me to the Station House, and kept
me there two weeks. I was treated so well that I liked this place. They
gave me candy and I could have gone away if I had any mind to it.
At the end of the two weeks I was taken to the House of Refuge. I was
told by my friends the policemen that this was a good place, and in-

deed, I hadn't much to say against it, for I was treated tolerably well. There was a certain lot of work to do for the week, and every boy had so much money given to him at the end. The good boys got 4 shillings some weeks; sometimes we got only two. There were about 280 boys in all there, and they were of all sorts, good, bad and middling. With my money I used to buy lots of cakes from the bakers who supplied the House with bread.

"At last mother heard I was there, and she came to see me twice. She was to take me out on a certain day, but 'fore that came, I wasn't present. There was a Mr. James Mitchell came to look for two boys to live with him on his farm in Delaware State, and so Henry Brown and I were bound out to him, and he was to give us maintenance and sustenance, and school in the winter besides, and we were to serve him like honest boys, and one of us tried to be as honest as he could, and to work as well as he could too.

"He carried us home to his farm in Delaware State, about 12 miles from Dover. He had some niggers, and 160 acres of land and a stingy old wife that helped him to starve us. Soon enough I was sorry that I was bound to such a man, 'till I would be of age.

"I wasn't treated right any way. I had to eat with the niggers, and to work and sleep with them. Our food was corn bread. The corn was put in a pot, some salt shaken into it, then thrown on a griddle and afterwards served round to us, or we might scrabble for it as well as we could, whites and niggers in a heap. When the Superintendent of the Refuge came for a visit everything was made to show fair. Then we had something like fine times, for we all ate at the same table, and we had meat with our corn bread. Mr. Mitchell would then tell the Superintendent (there was a new one every year, the only one I know was Mr. Alfred) how much we were improved — though we never had a chance of goin' to school or any place else, where we could improve the least. We dursn't speak a word to the Superintendent for fear. Henry hadn't the right courage, he was more afraid than I was, and when I saw he was so scared it made myself the same.

"Mr. Mitchell had very nice children but they were never allowed to speak to us. The poor niggers were beaten into jelly every day, and we were licked till we were as black as the niggers. At last I began to think 'twas time to clear out from Mr. Mitchell, and I told Henry I would quit. Henry as I said hadn't the right courage, for he was afraid he'd be killed by the savage man our master, but he didn't like to remain behind, and so he said he would run off with me, and one of the colored boys, Robert Wilson, who had been nearly killed with lickings made off with us too.

"We ran off as fast as we could 'till we got to Dover, where we told our story to the people, and they had much compassion on us, and we were taking our supper in a house when we were taken prisoners by our savage boss who came in on us like a great wild beast with another man who had joined in hunting us up. Oh! if you were to see the look he gave us, and how we shook for fear, and to hear how we cried, and how the good woman who had given us our supper cried with us. He bought a cowhide for us as he was returning, and give it to us strong. I didn't feel it much — I don't know why it was — I got great courage like, but the black boy roared like a thousand. Henry came along after us and got into the barn and was hiding in the hay. One of the men as savage as the boss, went in for some hay to feed the horses, and he stuck the pitch fork into Henry's pants, and a little farther, and he roared for mercy.

"Five times after this I ran away, and four times I was catched, and brought back.

"About a year after this, when I had been with Mitchell, about four years, he put us out to work in new ground — a clearing just planted with wheat and corn, and he put me dropping corn and told me to keep up with the driver of the plough.

"I dropped the corn as well as I could, but for all that I dropped it wrong — it was the first time I had ever dropped corn. The boss came round, and asked who dropped the corn? I answered at once that I had dropped it — and that I had done it as well as I could. Without a word more, he pulled the shirt over my head, and beat me over the back with a hickory stick, as fast as he could lick. I was all over blood. I had a bad night you may be sure, and you may think my thoughts were not good.

"He sent me the next morning to Smyrna five miles off to get the wheat and corn ground. He said I should be back in two hours, or he would flog me. I had four bushels of wheat and corn in the waggon. I did my errand straight off, and was returning, when I met another boy and he said, 'Oh! you will be all cut to pieces — master is furious about your delay.' I put the horse in the stables, and I left the grist in the waggon, and made up my mind to run off, to escape another flaying.

"I soon got to Smyrna, and from this place I ran to Johnstown without looking behind me. I then got on the cars as far as Newcastle, and safe to Philadelphia.

"After knocking round for some time, I got on a canal boat, and followed this kind of life for more than a year. In summer time I thought it good enough — at any rate 'twas better than to be flayed alive as I was by Mitchell, so I was contented enough when I remembered that I was out of his hard grip.

"I next went on board the steam-ship 'Philadelphia' as mess boy. I was washing dishes and doing the slush-work for some time, and bye and bye, came to be promoted to store keeper. I tended the lamps and kept them trimmed, and was always at the engineer's call when he wanted a hammer. I was much liked by the engineers, but not by the firemen as I wouldn't do business that didn't belong to me. The 'Philadelphia' is a U.S. Mail steam ship, and he's at the foot of Warren Street. I was 'bout five months in the 'Philadelphia,' we went first to Spain and thence to New Orleans. I left the 'Philadelphia' a week last Saturday. I slept the first night in the house of an old woman who took me in when she saw I had no other home. Next night I slept on board a ship, and since that I have been staying only at the Newsboys Lodging House — I don't know what boys would do only for that place." This strange boy related his story in the pleasantest way imaginable. The hard usage he had received from the taskmaster Mitchell, and his other reverses by "flood and field" had not made him in the least splenetic. His face was bright and varied as he told his little history in which we were all much interested.

Jan 26th 1859. The boy above mentioned went with a large company for the west this afternoon. He was the merriest of the party — all smiles and good humor, and gave three cheers and hip! hip! hurra for the Children's Aid Society in a voice that drowned every other as they entered the stage which was to take them to the ferry boat. We anticipate good news from him soon.[1]

*   *   *

The official record for John Jackson's placement is sketchy, as are almost all the early orphan train records.[2] He was picked out of the crowd of other CAS "emigrants" at a meetinghouse in Pawpaw, Indiana, by James DeHaven, a farmer. DeHaven later wrote to the Children's Aid Society that he "liked" John but the feeling did not seem to be mutual. John grew "dissatisfied," according to DeHaven, and left his farm after only a year. He stayed in the neighborhood, however, and DeHaven would see him from time to time. The final entry in the file states that John joined the Union Army in 1862 and died of wounds sustained at the battle of Shiloh in June 1863. He was eighteen years old.

✧ 3

City Missionary

CHARLES LORING BRACE spent the first twenty-five years of his life preparing to take action. He was driven by twin ambitions. One was to help humanity and the other — which he may well have hesitated to admit even to himself — was to achieve a social prominence equal to that of Horace Bushnell or Lajos Kossuth. The many references in the letters of his young manhood to social problems — slavery, Austrian oppression, urban poverty — were immediately followed by pained and impatient exclamations like, "Oh, that I could do something!" But for all of his impatience, he seemed possessed, during his early twenties, by a Hamlet-like paralysis of will. There were plenty of social and political groups in which he could have fulfilled his urge to "do something." But instead, he chose further preparation: more traveling, more touring of charitable institutions, and especially more study of the life and ideas of yet another of his role models, the carpenter's son from Galilee, whom he always represented as the greatest social reformer of all time.

Things began to change during Emma's illness, but once she had died, Brace postponed action yet again by setting off on a tour of Europe. In the end, however, it was this tour, culminating in his imprisonment in Hungary, that finally gave him not only all the motivation he needed to commence the great business of his life but also a clear sense of what that business ought to be.

Immediately upon his return to New York City in November 1851, Brace was overtaken by what he called "Kossuth fever." "I am a patented writing machine now," he declared in a letter to Fred Kingsbury. "[I] have forgotten my friends, my country, my dinner, till *The* book is finished."

"*The* book" was *Hungary in 1851,* a more than 400-page account of his travels and imprisonment that he did indeed write with astounding speed. Taking up residence with Frederick Law Olmsted at South Side, Brace worked daily from eight in the morning until midnight — "with interludes of lager beer and theological discussion" — managing to finish the book in time for publication a mere five months after his return to the United States.[1] A year later, in March 1853, his equally substantial *Home-Life in Germany* was also in print.

The publication of these two hefty volumes would have been an impressive accomplishment had Brace been doing nothing else during those seventeen months. But even as he wrote and revised his books, he was producing numerous lectures and articles on Hungary, Kossuth, the British ragged schools, and other social and theological issues; arranging for Kossuth's first visit to the United States (Brace put Fred Olmsted in charge of New York's welcoming parade); continuing his studies at Union Theological Seminary; visiting Blackwell's Island; doing extensive work with the Ladies' Methodist Home Missionary Society at Five Points; and — not incidentally — founding the Children's Aid Society.

In the spring of 1852, just as his book about Hungary was about to appear in print, Brace wrote to his father:

> If I am only a city missionary with two hundred dollars a year,[2] or anything else mean, but really doing good, you should be contented. I don't care a straw for a city pastor's place. I want to raise up the outcast and homeless, to go down among those who have no friend or helper, and do something for them of what Christ has done for me. I want to be *true* — true always. Not orthodox, or according to any one school or sect, but to follow my own convictions of truth. So did Christ.[3]

By undertaking so much "practical" work on his return to the United States, Brace was effectively deciding to give up his lifelong ambition of becoming a minister. Breaking free of such an entrenched vision of himself and of his place in the world seems to have required the buildup of tremendous emotional force. His letters during this period are filled with anger — at his father and at religion itself. "I do not think . . . ," Brace declared to his cousin, Mrs. Asa Gray, "that the Christian faith has much hold on the best young minds of the country."[4] And in another letter he pronounced churches technologically

outmoded: "Minister craft is passing away. Our papers are the pulpits."[5] Most astonishing is the opinion Brace expressed in a letter to
the abolitionist minister Theodore Parker concerning Parker's newest
book *Sermons on Theism:*

> I think much fault might be found by Atheists with your positions on
> the morality and virtue which does connect itself with a hereafter. Is it
> not the highest nobleness, which is utterly unconcerned with a future,
> which loves and sacrifices and suffers because, even if there be no God
> or Immortality, it is the happiest to do so, or because they in their pres-
> ent state of progression cannot help it?[6]

Brace's suggestion that atheists might be morally superior to the devout represents, perhaps, the absolute nadir of faith. It was certainly
an opinion he would never venture again. But however much it may
have been a part of the idol-toppling necessary to free him from his
old idea of himself, Brace's disenchantment with religion was also the
result of the many "sad and disgusting sights" he witnessed in his
work at the Five Points Mission.[7] Among other effects, these sights
made the notion of an all-powerful creator seem morally absurd:

> To start a human heart with passions like whirlwinds in it, and reason
> hardly acting, put it where everything bad would certainly grow and
> everything good dry up, and then to beat it and torture it and buffet
> and starve and so educate, and at last to send it out into Eternity, to be
> battered always there because it was so damned bad here, is *rather*
> hard, isn't it?[8]

The Five Points Mission, established by the Ladies' Methodist Home
Missionary Society in 1848, was located across a muddy, triangular
"square" from the infamous Old Brewery, reputed to be the district's
bloodiest bit of real estate.[9] The mission, under its original director,
Louis M. Pease, was a progressive institution, seeking not merely to
convert the poor to the way of the Lord but to provide them with
food, clothing, basic education, and job training. One of Pease's most
celebrated accomplishments was to convince several Broadway hotels
to provide free turkey dinners to some 500 poor people on Thanksgiving Day in 1850. But most of the work at the mission was far more

pedestrian, and almost never so clearly successful. During the day missionaries attempted to teach a constantly shifting group of children reading, writing, and elementary calculation. In the evenings adults came to learn such skills as cobbling and needlework. On Sundays there were church services for adults and families and religious meetings for boys.

The most laborious component of mission work was "visiting." Like many an urban missionary before him, Pease knew that people would not avail themselves of his services — or allow themselves to be subjected to his "improvement" — merely because he hung up a sign outside his front door. If he was going to reach a significant proportion of the residents of Five Points and of equally poor neighboring communities, like Cherry Street down by the East River, he and his staff of volunteer "visitors" had to seek out needy and potentially "redeemable" people on the streets, in taverns and shops, and even in their homes. During these encounters the missionaries would tell their prospective beneficiaries about the food, clothing, classes, and church services available to them and their children and deliver homilies on the evils of alcohol, the blessing of God's love, and the need to preserve young girls from experiences that might inflame their passions.

As one of Pease's visitors, Brace got his first glimpses of the home lives of the women and men he had ministered to on Blackwell's Island. He climbed absolutely lightless staircases, littered with garbage and stinking from spilled chamber pots, to garret rooms where a tubercular mother might be shivering under a heap of rags and old coats while her emaciated children sat silently in a corner, an otherworldly emptiness in their eyes. He descended into the basement warrens of divided and subdivided "apartments" where families of ten or twelve shared one airless room dense with coal fumes and body odors. Here adolescent girls had to conduct all their most private duties in full view of their fathers and brothers, and often of other male relatives or family friends — a situation that Brace thought was sure to wear off every vestige of the girls' modesty and make "unnatural crimes" all but inevitable. He entered the maze of alleys and catwalks linking dense villages of tumbledown shanties in the yards behind the brick or clapboard street-fronting houses. There he found free blacks and runaway slaves living in windowless rooms with no light or heat, iron-faced mothers cradling their dying babies, and old men with stinking sores on their legs, their scalps crawling with lice. And in Five Points' count-less "groceries" he met women buying bottles of gin to console them-selves because their men had run off to sea or to other women, and boys with the gruff manners of grown men gathered around billiard tables, laying bets on one another's skill and luck. On the streets in front of these shops equally precocious girls offered to sell him flowers and made it known — by somber glances — that they were willing to sell much more.

To all of these people Brace talked about hope and decency and God's love and the great promises held out by the American Republic to anyone with a little education, a marketable skill, and the willing-ness to work. Then he would return home so exhausted and depressed that all he could do was throw himself down on the rug in front of his fire. Years later he would describe his labors with the mission as "Sisy-phus-like work [that] soon discouraged all who engaged in it." And he would describe Louis Pease as "heroic," but only "one man against a sea of crime. The waves soon rolled over these enthusiastic and de-voted labors, and the waste of misfortune and guilt remained as deso-late and hopeless as before."[10]

It is possible that Brace felt the crush of circumstance even more pro-foundly when he lay on the floor in front of his own fire than when he had flung himself onto his verminous bed in the castle at Gros Wardein. He had been lucky in life. He had grown up in relative eco-nomic comfort, received an excellent education, and been blessed with intelligence and phenomenal energy — all of which had given him his almost boundless faith in his own capabilities and made it easy for him to believe in the power of discipline and self-control. On one level the despair of the poor, and the intractability of their manifold prob-lems, must have been all but incomprehensible to so dynamic a char-acter as Brace. But on another level he understood their plight far too well. After all, the great difficulty the poor had in helping themselves, and their sometimes outright refusal to be helped by him, resulted in his own failure. And, by analogy at least, the terrible difficulties of the poor represented the possibility that he too might become deprived by circumstance, that his luck might not hold, that all of his urgent ambi-tions might come to nothing. This was not a prospect Brace had much tolerance for.

His frustration and defensive impatience are visible in many of his letters from this time. "The poor become so suspicious," he wrote to Theodore Parker, "and are naturally so narrow and pig-headed."[11] In a very short time these negative feelings hardened into an animus that never really abated. More than twenty years later, in *The Dangerous Classes,* his classic semiautobiographical account of his work with the CAS, he could still describe the homes of some of his charges as "paternal piggeries and nasty dens."[12] And in this same book he quoted an unattributed journal entry (possibly his own) without a shadow of disapproval:

> The old story: "No work, no friends, rent to pay, and nothing to do." The parents squalid, idle, intemperate, and shiftless. There they live, just picking up enough to keep life warm in them; groaning, and begging, and seeking work. There they live, breeding each day pestilence and disease, scattering abroad over the city seeds of fearful sickness — raising a brood of vagrants and harlots — retorting on society its neglect by cursing the bodies and souls of thousands whom they never knew, and who never saw them.[13]

But at the same time those very things that most disturbed Brace about urban poverty only made him feel all the more urgently that he must do something to alleviate it, and especially to help that subset of the poor whom he thought most likely to benefit from his efforts: children.

Sometime during 1852, while Brace was still working at the Five Points Mission, he turned his back on adults. Although *The Dangerous Classes* is filled with moving and insightful portrayals of the hardships faced by poor men and women, in practical terms Brace was interested in parents only to the degree that they supported his efforts to help their children. He dismissed contemptuously those parents who stood in the way of what he thought were a child's best interests — including the removal of the child to a "better" home.

In *The Dangerous Classes,* Brace described his reason for shifting the focus of his efforts: "It was clear that whatever was done there [at Five Points], must be done in the source and origin of the evil — in prevention, not cure."[14] Working with children was "prevention" because they had not yet been infected by the evils of their environment — so they did not need to be "cured." But children were also more malleable than their parents and so were more likely to yield to the efforts of their would-be benefactors and at least to appear to have been helped by them. And thus the benefactors were less likely to feel frustrated and that they had failed.

To some extent this was a familiar social reform strategy by the 1850s. For centuries poor children had been forcefully indentured by civic authorities to remove them from the influence of their "vicious" parents; beginning in the nineteenth century, children had been placed in orphanages, asylums, and houses of refuge for the same reason. Also by midcentury many organizations and movements were attempting to shape the moral development of children in less radical ways. The originators of the Sunday school movement hoped especially to reach the "moral orphans" in poor homes. And Horace Mann, an early advocate of public education, asserted that the beneficent influence of teachers would rescue virtually every public school student from criminality and sin. Indeed, it was partly to ensure this beneficent influence that New York State passed its Truancy Law of 1853, which threatened poor children with incarceration or indenture if they did not attend school or have a job. In Boston the Children's Mission to the Children of the Destitute, an organization that foreshadowed, if not actually inspired, many of the CAS programs — including the orphan trains — was founded in 1850 to "rescue from vice and degradation the morally exposed children of the city."[15]

Mid-nineteenth-century anxiety about children was fed by a larger concern about the state of American society, especially in cities, many of which were suffering from repeated riots and rising crime. In New York the social disintegration that had seemed to commence with the Astor Place Riot and the cholera epidemic of 1849 had shown no signs of abatement by Brace's time at the Five Points Mission. Crimes against property rose 50 percent from 1848 through 1852, while convictions for crimes against persons rose 129 percent, with a threefold increase in assaults with intent to kill and a sixfold rise in actual murders. Public anxiety was heightened by the sensational manner in which newspapers reported atypical crimes. The *Evening Post,* for example, made big play out of a story about a gang of "killers" who, one Sunday morning, took over City Hall Park and "went about stabbing and cutting several persons without the slightest provocation."[16] New Yorkers blamed the turmoil on the usual suspects: the still relentless flood of immigration, the expanding income gap between rich and poor, and what one commentator called "a morbid sympathy for all criminals."[17]

Even as the many members of the Victorian upper classes venerated

their own children as holy innocents, they saw poor children — especially street children — as directly implicated in present and future
crime waves. As noted at one grand jury proceeding during this era, 80
percent of "the higher grades of felony" complaints were against mi-
nors. In his famous report, New York Police Chief George Matsell
described the city's vagrant children as "degrading and disgusting,"
while Mayor Ambrose C. Kingsland called them "apt pupils in the
school of vice, licentiousness and theft." Even organizations ostensibly
sympathetic to poor children tended to portray them in the most lurid terms. The first annual report of the Children's Mission to the
Children of the Destitute, for example, described sights witnessed by
the mission's chief agent on Boston's poorer streets:

> . . . scores of boys playing and gambling with props and cents, not only
> on week-days, but on Sundays; and rum-shops kept open, in defiance
> of the law, where youths were enticed to almost certain destruction. He
> has often seen boys from eight to twelve years of age intoxicated, and
> found that many of the rum-sellers received stolen goods from the
> boys in payment for the liquor they drank.[18]

It was chiefly his attitude toward poor children that distinguished
Charles Loring Brace from the other social reformers of his era. Although he thought there were some things truly "dangerous" about
this class of children (not only as future rioters and robbers but as vot-
ers who might elect presidents out of ignorant rage), Brace was one of
the first public activists to recognize their authentic virtues and their
tremendous potential for good. He truly liked the children he worked
with, but more important, he *respected* them — especially the boys —
as is evident in the following passage from *The Dangerous Classes:*

> A more light-hearted youngster than the street-boy is not to be found.
> He is always ready to make fun of his own sufferings, and to "chaff"
> others. His face is old from exposure and his sheer "struggle for exis-
> tence"; his clothes flutter in the breeze; and his bare feet peep out from
> the broken boots. Yet he is merry as a clown, and always ready for the
> smallest joke, and quick to take "a point" or to return a repartee. His
> views of life are mainly derived from the more mature opinions of
> "flash-men," engine-runners, cock-fighters, pugilists, and pickpockets,
> whom he occasionally is permitted to look upon with admiration at

some select pot-house; while his more ideal pictures of the world about him, and his literary education, come from the low theatres, to which he is passionately attached. His morals are, of course, not of a high order, living, as he does, in a fighting, swearing, stealing, and gambling set. Yet he has his code; he will not get drunk; he pays his debts to other boys, and thinks it dishonorable to sell papers on their beat, and, if they come on his, he administers summary justice by "punching"; he is generous to a fault, and will always divide his last sixpence with a poorer boy. "Life is a strife" with him, and money its reward; and, as bankruptcy means to a street-boy a night on the door-steps without supper, he is sharp and reckless, if he can only earn enough to keep him above water.[19]

Idealized as this portrait may be, it nonetheless reflects those qualities that Brace most admired in street children: their humor, their practicality, their strict — if unconventional — code of honor, and, most important, their fierce determination and energy. These two latter qualities were, after all, ones that Brace himself shared, and they must have seemed particularly admirable to him given that they flourished amid conditions that commonly threw him into despair.

Brace's use of the phrase "struggle for existence" in his description of the street boy hints at the complexity of his vision of the slums. Like many Victorians, he was an instinctive Darwinist, unconsciously understanding the genetic ramifications of competition and hardship long before the 1859 publication of *The Origin of Species*. When Brace finally read the book, it struck him as tantamount to divine revelation, the perfect illustration of how God acts on Earth to purify the nature of those creatures He has created in His own image. As Brace put it:

> The action of the great law of "Natural Selection," in regard to the human race, is always towards temperance and virtue. . . . The vicious and sensual and drunken die earlier, or they have fewer children, or their children are carried off by diseases more frequently, or they themselves are unable to resist or prevent poverty and suffering. As a consequence, in the lowest class, the more self-controlled and virtuous tend constantly to survive, and to prevail in "the struggle for existence," over the vicious and ungoverned, and to transmit their progeny. The natural drift among the poor is towards virtue.[20]

Brace would read *The Origin of Species* thirteen times during his life.

As appalled as he may have been by the conditions in Five Points and the other impoverished wards of the city, he believed that these districts where the "struggle for existence" was most fierce bred the most evolutionarily advanced individuals, not just in the city but in the whole nation — or even the world. (*The Dangerous Classes* contains numerous references to the superiority of American criminals to their European counterparts!) The problem, as Brace saw it, was that the very environment that bred these robust and most characteristically American of Americans often led them to employ their natural abilities in the worst possible manner, with respect to both their own well-being and society's. The way to save the children of the slums, then, and to allow the nation to benefit from their enormous potential, was to find a way to alter their environment so that their best qualities could thrive and become a boon rather than a curse. All of the projects of the early CAS would be attempts to modify the environment of poor children so as to replace the worst influences exerted on them with more "Christian" ones.

Brace regarded the children he attempted to help with much of the compassion, pity, condescension, and fear that was common among social reformers of his era, but everything that would be revolutionary in his work — his successes as well as some of his failures — grew out of his unique respect for the inborn capacities of poor children and his belief in their right and ability to manage their own lives.

The duty at the Five Points Mission that Brace most enjoyed and at which he seems to have most excelled was speaking at the Sunday "Boys' Meetings." His success was no mean accomplishment, given that his young audiences had been invited off the street to see, for example, a magic lantern show (a primitive slide projection) featuring the eight wonders of the ancient world only to find themselves subjected to a sermon on sin and salvation. As Brace put it, these meetings were "a kind of chemical test of the gaseous element in the brethren's brains." When an earnest theological student tried to win his disappointed audience over with sentimental or vague proclamations, he might be favored with contemptuous cries of "Gas! Gas!" or pelted with stones, or he might see his audience erupt into a spontaneous melee across the tops of the wooden benches.

As risible and sharp as such audiences could be, they were not unintelligent; nor were they uninterested in speakers who told them things truly worth knowing. "[W]ords which came forth from the depths of a man's or woman's heart," Brace maintained,

> would always touch some hidden chord in theirs. . . . Whenever the speaker could, for a moment only, open the hearts of the little street-rovers to this voice, there was in the wild audience a silence almost painful, and every one instinctively felt, with awe, a mysterious Presence in the humble room, which blessed both those who spake and those who heard.[21]

The testimony of several children, as well as surviving copies of his sermons, indicate that Brace was himself one of those speakers to whom at least some of the boys would listen with an almost painful silence. He spoke clearly and frankly to the boys about their loneliness and confusion and about the brutality of their world. But the most successful component of his sermons was his cherished insight that God's relationship to humankind was not that of stern lawgiver but of a loving father. "I suppose it is very hard for a poor boy to believe at all times, that GOD loves him," he told one audience.

> Half-clothed, cold and hungry, sleeping around in boxes, not knowing where he shall get his next meal and utterly without friends, he can hardly imagine that there is some one above him, who truly cares for him and follows and pities him. Perhaps he has had an earthly father who has been a drunkard, and has beaten and ill-treated his boy until he could not bear to live with him, so that he can not understand what a truly kind Heavenly Father can be. And yet, boys, it is just that message that we have come to give you — that God loves you![22]

Brace well understood the limitations of even the most successful boys' meetings. As he put it in a slightly different context, "Preaching sermons to the prostitute, who has to choose between starvation and the brothel, is of very little use." If he wanted to attend effectively to the moral and religious needs of poor children, he had first to attend to their material needs. Simple sermonizing also smacked too much of the "formalism" he so despised in American religion. What these children needed was not abstract consolation and persuasion, but exposure to that spontaneous, heartfelt, and deeply authentic Christianity

that he had seen in the most ordinary of German homes. As Horace
Bushnell had taught him, no overt influence could shape character
as effectively as the unconscious influence of truly virtuous people
whom one truly wants to please. The only way to really help these desperate and lonely children, Brace thought, was to place them in an environment where their most basic physical needs could be met and
their own most healthy and virtuous impulses would make them want
to improve themselves, to become the very best men and women they
could be.

With such thoughts in mind, on January 9, 1853, a month before the
publication of *Home-Life in Germany,* Brace met with a group of concerned bankers, lawyers, and ministers, including William C. Russel,
B. J. Howland, William C. Gilman, William L. King, Judge John L. Ma-
son, and John Earl Williams, to found the Children's Aid Society.

Although Brace would later say that he had been surprised that
the group chose him to lead the new organization, it is hard to imagine how they could have made any other choice. He was clearly a brilliant and dedicated young man — all of twenty-seven — and on the
strength of his two books, his journalism, and his association with
Kossuth, he was also a rapidly rising literary and political figure on the
New York scene. What is more, he was the only member of the group
not already established in a separate and demanding career.

As thrilled and flattered as he was by the offer, Brace took some days
before formally accepting it. He was concerned that it would interrupt
his writing and research, and he did not relish the idea of staying in
New York — in an era predating even electric fans — during its hot
summers. But in the end Brace agreed to take on the duties of secretary of the Children's Aid Society at least for a year, for an annual salary of $1,000 — considerably more than the $200 he had told his father he ought to be happy with.

Draining the City, Saving the Children

BRACE'S FIRST ORDER of business on accepting his new position was to invent the organization that ostensibly employed him. He started with real estate: within a week he had found an office at 683 Broadway, on the corner of Amity Street (now Third Street), and moved in a desk, chair, several record books, a stack of paper, an inkwell, and a pen. Six mornings a week he wrote and did paperwork in this office and spent the afternoons looking for more real estate (sites for classrooms, workshops, schools), meeting with prospective collaborators (clergymen and business owners), and, as at the Five Points Mission, visiting the homes of the poor, telling them about his new organization and asking them what they needed. He tried to reserve his evenings for scholarly work and pleasure but often made additional visits to slum families and gave talks to organizations (usually church affiliated women's groups) from which he hoped to elicit funds and volunteers. "The business tires me," he confessed to his father, "much more than writing and studying. . . . But the enterprise is a great one, and for a year I can stand it."[1]

At first he did all of this work on his own, but as money began to flow in from contributors, he hired an office assistant, John Macy, and a few additional "visitors," most of them Union Theological Seminary students. He also moved the office to a larger space on the second floor of Clinton House — the former Italian Opera House, at the corner of Astor Place and Lafayette Street, and the site of the massacre that had touched off the Astor Place Riot. This would be the Children's Aid Society's headquarters for the next sixteen years.

As essential as acquiring real estate and personnel may have been,

the real work of inventing the Children's Aid Society took place on paper. During Brace's first month as secretary his chief undertaking was
the writing, printing, and distribution of a three-page circular announcing the existence and goals of the organization and asking for
contributions. With shrewd elegance, this document played to the
contradictory impulses of the wealthy New Yorkers for whom it was
written — a double-barreled solicitation strategy that Brace would
employ throughout his career. On the one hand, he flattered his readers with their compassion:

> As Christian men, we cannot look upon this great multitude of un-
> happy, deserted, and degraded boys and girls, without feeling our re-
> sponsibility to God for them. We remember that they have the same
> capacities, the same need of kind and good influences, and the same
> Immortality, as the little ones in our own homes. We bear in mind that
> ONE died for them, even as for the children of the rich and the happy.

On the other hand, he appealed to his readers' fear and greed:

> These boys and girls, it should be remembered, will soon form the
> great lower class of our city. They will influence elections; they may
> shape the policy of the city; they will, assuredly, if unreclaimed, poison
> society all around them. They will help to form the great multitude of
> robbers, thieves, and vagrants, who are now such a burden upon the
> law-respecting community.[2]

It is, at the very least, strange to see Brace, so soon after allying himself with Hungarian revolution and the "oppressed of any land," talking about the oppressed of his own land as a "poison." Obviously, part
of the explanation for this apparent reversal of sentiments is simply
that Brace knew which side the CAS's bread was going to be buttered
on. So soon after the Astor Place Riot, and in the midst of a crime
wave, wealthy New Yorkers were terribly afraid of the poor as both
criminals and radicals, and Brace understood, correctly, that he could
use this fear to squeeze contributions out of those who could not be
motivated by compassion alone.

But it is also true that as strongly as Brace may have advocated revolution in Hungary, it was only so that the Hungarians might establish
an American-style democracy. Brace was a devoted patriot. He may
have despised the greed and materialism fostered by capitalism, but he

was convinced that the American political system truly did provide even its poorest citizens with the power to "influence elections" and "shape the policy of the city." He also shared his wealthy donors' fear of the under classes insofar as he worried that a misguided attempt to bring about greater socioeconomic justice might result in the discarding of important freedoms guaranteed by the U.S. Constitution. Although he would continue to speak out strongly against slavery — and earn censure for doing so from a CAS board member — Brace's heartfelt criticisms of the American economic system would never again be expressed as clearly, even in his letters, as they had been in the two books he wrote just before founding the Children's Aid Society.

The most remarkable aspect of this first circular is how precisely it outlined the work that the CAS would undertake over the next seventy-five years. In the opening paragraph, Brace said that the society's "objects" were to help "the destitute children of New York . . . by opening Sunday Meetings and Industrial Schools, and, gradually, as means shall be furnished, by forming lodging houses and reading-rooms for children, and by employing paid agents, whose sole business shall be, to care for them." Near the end of the circular he used a decidedly unhappy metaphor to describe one final "object" of the society: "We hope, too, especially to be the means of draining the city of these children, by communicating with farmers, manufacturers, or families in the country" who might give the children jobs and "put them in the way of an honest living."

Sunday meetings and industrial schools were both ideas that Brace borrowed from Louis M. Pease at the Five Points Mission, and he mentioned them first perhaps because they were widely believed to be effective and thus lent his new enterprise legitimacy. Brace seemed to believe in the merits of Sunday meetings, at least in these early days, despite their tendency to evoke "gas" and derision. He spent a great deal of time during his first weeks with the society finding places to have separate girls' and boys' meetings, and he and his staff spent several years trying to make these meetings successful. But in the end, as he put it in *The Dangerous Classes,* the primary effect of the meetings was to teach those conducting them "the fearful nature of the evils they were struggling with, and how little any moral influence on one day can do to combat them."[3] Brace and many other CAS agents would continue to give sermons and lectures to the boys and girls under their care, but only as adjuncts to more practically oriented programs. The

86   ORPHAN TRAINS

independent Sunday meetings would be abandoned after only a few
years and were the only project mentioned in the initial circular that
would not endure.

The industrial schools, however, would be much more successful, at
least for girls. Like the British ragged schools, these were intended only
for children who could not attend public schools, either because they
had to work during the day or because their clothes were too worn
and filthy. At the industrial schools, which generally met in the evenings, children received instruction in reading, writing, and mathematics and were also given basic job training. Girls learned the "needle
trades" (sewing and dress- and hat-making) and skills they could use
as domestics (housecleaning, cooking, serving). Boys were taught such
skills as carpentry and shoe- and box-making.

There was one clear failure in the initial conception of the industrial schools. Inspired by the *Rauhe Haus,* Brace wanted some of the
industrial training to take place in workshops where boys would earn
a modest living — $1.25 to $4.00 a week — and simultaneously raise
money for the CAS by selling the goods they manufactured. The first
of these workshops, a shoe-pegging operation, housed under an existing shoe manufactory owned by a Mr. Bigelow on 26 Wooster Street,
suffered from manifold problems even before it opened. Thanks to
Brace's prejudice against Catholics, who were plentifully represented
in this industry, and his inability to pay very much, he had difficulty
getting a shop manager who both knew the trade and was capable of
teaching and inspiring the decidedly independent street urchins who
worked for him. The urchins themselves were another problem. These
young Americans, Irish, English, and Germans simply could not be
counted on to show up on time or to work steadily, and thus they let
many orders languish. But the workshop was finally done in after only
a few years by the invention of a machine that pegged shoes more rapidly and reliably than the CAS's beneficiary-employees. Other workshops in carpentry and paper box– and bag-making were similarly
chaotic and unprofitable, leading Brace to conclude: "Benevolence
cannot compete with Selfishness in business."[4]

The failure of the workshops did little, however, to diminish the
success of the basic industrial schools. The first of these, the Fourth
Ward Industrial School, was established in the basement of a church
on Roosevelt Street, but only after visitors had spent several weeks
circulating in the neighborhood, telling parents about the school's

curriculum and assuring them — mostly Irish and German Catholics — that it was absolutely nonsectarian. The school was such a success that the CAS soon opened others in different neighborhoods, including some where students were taught in German or Italian, and others specifically for Jews and African Americans. By the turn of the century the CAS was operating more than twenty-five industrial schools all over Manhattan.

The fact that eventually these schools were attended mostly by girls was part accident and part design. It was accidental insofar as most of the teachers who volunteered to work at the schools (the perpetually underfunded CAS never had more than a few paid teachers during Brace's tenure) were women who knew how to sew and keep house but almost nothing about male trades. And it was by design insofar as these women had primarily felt compelled to volunteer because of their concern about the staggering number of working-class girls who, without marketable skills, had been forced to support themselves by prostitution.

With all of its remarkable prescience, the circular did misrepresent one important element of the CAS. When Brace talked about the "little ones in our own homes" and about "sowing good influences in childhood," the implication was that the children were very young — perhaps preschool age — and that the society would somehow preserve or restore something of their natural "innocence." In fact, the beneficiaries of the early CAS programs were mostly teenagers, and even the youngest were not treated as innocents as all, but as quasi-adults and fully competent independent agents. The society certainly did subject children and their families to persuasion, evangelization, hucksterism, and bribery, but participants in all CAS programs were always free to use them or not as they saw fit. For the younger children, this freedom, an essential component of Brace's philosophy, may have been more theoretical (obviously toddlers did not have much choice when their parents or a CAS agent placed them on an orphan train), but it became more real as the child grew up. Unlike asylums, orphanages, houses of refuge, and prisons, which attempted to reform poor children by submitting them to inflexible routines of training, religion, and work, the CAS primarily attempted to shape children's character through the choices it offered and the "unconscious influence" exerted by its ostensibly virtuous staff. Brace believed, in fact, that the offering of choice itself was character-building because it encouraged autonomy and independence.

The emotional force behind Brace's opposition to the rigid and coercive practices of the child reform institutions of his era came from his lifelong "dread of being dependent on others" — to borrow, once again, the words of Lydia Maria Child. Brace thought of these institutions as a "bequest of monastic days," which tended to breed a "monastic character . . . indolent, unused to struggle; subordinate indeed, but with little independence and manly vigor." In part he objected to the institutions because he believed that they eroded independence and virtue by depriving children of control over their lives. Compulsory prayer and strict discipline could not encourage real virtue but only superficial accommodations to authority that masked "a hidden growth of secret and contagious vices." Brace also objected to the practices of these reform institutions because they provided grossly inadequate and unrealistic training. Most of the institutions ostensibly prepared children for the work world by having them perform all day, every day, a single, elementary task, like stitching on buttons or carding wool. Brace believed that such training did nothing to prepare a child to handle the "thousand petty hand-labors of a poor man's cottage."[5] All of the CAS projects were antimonastic insofar as, rather than sequestering children in an artificial environment, they sought to train and morally reform them in the midst of ordinary life. The society's clearest failure — the Sunday meetings — was the program most dependent on coercion and most disconnected from the complex demands of daily existence. By contrast, the most innovative and successful of Brace's early programs — the Newsboys' Lodging House — gave children access to aid without removing them from their ordinary lives, and it not only presented children with choices but required them to make nominal payments.

For Charles Dickens, New York's newsboys represented the quintessence of American ambition, drive, and depravity. The very first thing that Dickens's hero Martin Chuzzlewit noticed on his arrival in New York City were the newsboys, who proclaim the latest scandals "with shrill yells" not only "in all the highways and byways of the town, upon the wharves and among the shipping, but on the deck and down in the cabins of the steamboat; which, before she touched the shore, was boarded and overrun by a legion of those young citizens."[6]

Had Dickens chosen to look at these objects of his satire a little more closely, however, he might easily have chosen to portray one of their number as an Oliver Twist or a Nicholas Nickleby, for the truth was that their desperation was horribly exploited by the newspapers.

By 1844, when *Martin Chuzzlewit* was published, newsboys seemed as characteristic of New York as its bustle and drive, but in fact they had been conjured into existence only a decade earlier, by Benjamin Day, the original editor of the *New York Sun*. The *Sun* was the nation's first profitable "penny paper" and during the nineteenth century had the largest circulation of any newspaper in the country. Its popularity was based on an astutely cultivated image of political neutrality, humorous crime reports, and shameless exploitation of scandals and hoaxes. But its high profit margins were generated by its use of state-of-the-art steam-powered printing presses and by Day's decision to turn the tragedy of New York's ever-swelling population of destitute children to his own advantage.

Sometime in the 1830s Day had the idea that he could boost circulation and gain an edge on his competition if he could get individual salesmen on the streets to cry out headlines and then all but push papers into already curious potential customers' hands. Poor boys would make the best salesmen, since they would not ask for much money and, despite their shabbiness, would not be as threatening as equally shabby grown men. Day would sell the papers to the newsboys at a discount from the cover price and let them keep the difference. But he would not buy back any unsold papers — an arrangement that gave the newsboys strong incentive to sell every paper they could.

Day's innovation was such a success that soon every paper in New York had newsboys of its own, and the very character of the city — and indeed, all American cities — underwent a transformation that was to last at least one hundred years.

A newsboy's day typically began at four or five in the morning, when he would rise from his night's shelter in the loft of a stable or under a ragman's cart and hurry to the back doors of the *Sun, Herald,* or *Times* to be at the front of the line to get papers. The first boys on the street not only sold their papers faster, and thus had more time for making money by other means, but were less likely to get stuck with unsold papers. The papers cost the newsboys one and a half cents each and were sold for two cents — so an average load of fifty-six papers would yield its bearer twenty-eight cents' profit. But to get that profit the boy had to race up and down the street, shouting about robbery, scandal, and war and tagging after first one gentleman and then another with all the frenzy that so offended Dickens.

By nine the morning papers were generally all gone, and the newsboy could retire to a basement saloon for coffee and pancakes — a deduction of nine cents from his morning's profit. After breakfast he would hurry to the ferry slips, where he might make another fifteen or twenty cents carrying passengers' suitcases — although twelve cents of this profit would most likely go to a lunch of corned beef and cabbage or a six-cent steak and a cup of coffee. Then, after lunch, he would be off to buy a supply of evening papers, which might yield him another twenty-eight cents in profit. Once again, twelve cents of this would go to his supper, and then perhaps another twelve for a seat at the theater — leaving him, at the end of his day, maybe thirty-one cents richer than he had been when he got up in the morning. If he chose, as many newsboys did, to spend his evening at a bar or a gambling den, then he might easily use up all of his profits and more. A bed on the second floor of an oyster saloon would cost him a quarter — but if he could not afford it, or just wanted to hang on to his money, then it was back to the stable loft or ragman's cart.[7]

More than any other variety of street child, the newsboys embodied those characteristics that Brace — and many of his era — most admired. They were independent, hardworking, and, of necessity, frugal with their scant earnings. Many of them were also charming and funny salesmen who sometimes showed glints of real intelligence. When Brace talked about the slums producing America's hardiest stock, he was primarily thinking of the newsboys. So it was natural when he set about trying to "aid" the children of New York City that this should be the population he would give special attention to.

Brace clearly had the idea for the Newsboys' Lodging House even before the foundation of the CAS, perhaps as early as when he toured the country pastor's lodging houses in Germany. During his first weeks on the job he sounded out a friend at the *New York Tribune* about the possibility of the paper contributing a space in which to establish the lodging house. But in the end, perhaps fittingly, it was the *New York Sun* that contributed the space — a loft atop its offices on the corner of Fulton and Nassau streets.

Brace opened the first Newsboys' Lodging House in March 1854, just after the society's anniversary. This new facility had some two score beds, a large washroom, a dining hall that could be converted into a school room, an office and private suite for the superintendent and his assistants, and a reading room where residents, at their leisure, could peruse newspapers, the Bible, and other publications. During its first year 408 boys spent an average of sixteen nights at the lodging house. In 1858 the CAS opened a new lodging house on Park Place that had 250 beds and sheltered 3,000 boys for an average stay of five nights during its first year.[8] And in 1862 the first Girls' Lodging House opened on Canal Street, sheltering 400 girls for an average of ten nights each.[9]

Admission to the lodging houses was not free. Residents had to pay six cents for a bed and four cents for a meal. (By way of comparison, the cheapest and most unsanitary and unsafe hotels cost seven cents a night.) These fees helped the lodging house meet expenses, but the main reason for charging them was to preserve what Brace thought of as "the best quality of this class — their sturdy independence." Giving residents shelter and food without payment would have encouraged them to be lazy and diminished their sense of the necessity of providing for themselves. Brace's strategy was to treat all CAS beneficiaries as "independent little dealers, and give them nothing without payment, but at the same time to offer them much more for their money than they could get anyplace else."[10] The residents of the lodging houses paid in pennies; for the children in the industrial schools, workshops, and, later, the orphan trains, payment was made through labor.

The very first residents of the original Newsboys' Lodging House knew it was too good to be true. A clean bed for six cents a night, a solid meal for four cents — where was the profit in it? It had to be a mission trap, no doubt about it. The soft-spoken gentleman who ran the lodging house — Mr. C. C. Tracy, a former carpenter — did not seem shrewd enough for any other sort of con. Some of the boys, at least on that opening night, were sure that he was a pushover and that they could get their own back for any sermonizing they might have to endure by turning off the gas for the lights and staging a free-for-all among the wooden bunks in the darkness. As it turned out, at least according to Brace, Tracy was not a pushover of any sort. He got wind of the plot, kept a steady eye on the valves for the gas lights, and placed the ringleaders in a separate room under the guard of a theological student. When one boy tried to start a ruckus during the night by flinging his boot at another, he was summarily lifted out from under his covers, carried downstairs, and thrown out onto the sidewalk, with no choice but to find some alley or cellar in which to escape the wintry chill. Seeing no reason to risk their comfortable beds, the remaining boys apparently spent a peaceful night, only interrupting the quiet with occasional comments like: "I say, Jim, this is rayther better 'an bummin' — eh?"[11]

Although the lodging house may not have been a classic "mission trap," Tracy and his successor, Charles O'Connor, were constantly reading to residents from the Bible and talking to them about such topics as the Golden Rule and God's love. Brace himself would come in on Sundays to deliver sermons and have discussions. But true to his original insight, the lodging house attempted moral reform mainly through providing practical services rather than religious exhortation.

In addition to a bed for the night, six pennies bought residents a bath, hair wash, and, if they had lice, a haircut and treatment with caustic lotions. If their clothes were worn to rags, they got new suits. If they were barefoot, they were given new shoes. Those six pennies also gave vagrant children the right to enjoy the reading room and, in the evenings, to receive a basic education in the three R's right in the lodging house itself. Most important of all, their modest payment connected them to a network of affluent and generous-spirited men and women who steered them into other CAS programs and were often willing to use their personal influence to get the boys permanent jobs, housing, medical care, advanced education, and, in at least one case, a cowriter and publisher for an autobiography.[12]

As Brace tells it, the education component of the lodging house program was inaugurated through a ruse that Tracy devised:

> "Boys," said he, one morning, "there was a gentleman here this morning, who wanted a boy in an office, at three dollars a week."
> "My eyes! Let *me* go, sir!" And — "*Me*, sir!"
> "But he wanted a boy who could write a good hand."
> Their countenances fell.
> "Well, now, suppose we have a night-school, and learn to write — what do you say, boys?"
> "Agreed, sir."
> And so arose our evening school.[13]

The Newsboys' Lodging House offered its residents one more option: the Six-Penny Savings Bank, which, like the lodging house itself, had been inspired by the work of the country pastor whom Brace had visited in Germany. This "bank" was nothing more than a table with several long rows of numbered, coin-sized slots carved into its top. Under each of these slots was a separate compartment big enough to hold at least a month's worth of savings. Any boy who wanted to use the bank was assigned a number, and he could drop however much money he wanted into the slot bearing that number. None of the money could be removed until the first of every month, when the superintendent would unlock the table top and disburse the coins to the eager depositors, all of whom, according to Brace, would be astonished at how much money they had accumulated. At first depositors would simply get back the money they had put in, but eventually, as an additional enticement, they were paid a generous rate of interest on their money. The purpose of the bank was to give the children "the 'sense of property,'" Brace said, "and the desire of accumulation, which, economists tell us, is the base of all civilization."[14]

With all of the services offered at the Newsboys' and Girls' Lodging Houses, they were, thanks in part to fees paid by their residents, among the cheapest of the CAS's projects: they averaged a $1.17 expenditure per child during their earliest decades, leading Brace to claim that they repaid "their expenses to the public ten times over each year, in preventing the growth of thieves and criminals."[15] In the lodging houses children were, Brace said, "shaped to be honest and industrious citizens; here taught economy, good order, cleanliness, and morality; here Religion brings its powerful influences to bear upon them; and they are sent forth to begin courses of honest livelihood."[16]

5

Journey to Dowagiac

ALTHOUGH WE ostensibly have free will, and although we can never be certain exactly what the future will bring, it is still true that anything that has happened, simply because it has happened, was inevitable.

One way in which the orphan trains appear to have been inevitable is as the consequence of a body of ideas that Brace had been developing at least since that morning in February 1846 when he listened to Horace Bushnell talk about Saints Peter and John. If Brace believed that no conscious attempt to shape a child's moral nature could compete with the unconscious shaping effected by every person with whom that child came into contact; and if he believed that during the earliest years the most powerful shaper of character was family; and finally, if he believed that many poor children were being corrupted not merely by economic hardship but also by the degenerate families into which they had been born; then getting those children away from their families and into more decent — more properly *Christian* — homes would seem the best way to help preserve their natural virtue.

There was also, however, a broader historical inevitability to the orphan trains. They were very much an idea whose time had arrived, and they may well have come into existence — and arguably *were* coming into existence — without Brace being involved at all.

Although the CAS habitually portrayed its "Emigration Plan" as a unique revolutionary innovation, the idea had numerous precedents. The most striking of these was the work of the Children's Mission to the Children of the Destitute in Boston. Beginning in 1850, the mission sent quarterly parties of thirty or forty destitute children by train to western New England and the near Midwest to be indentured to local farmers and merchants. Brace certainly knew about these trains, and they may even have been his main inspiration: the mission's original president, John Earl Williams, moved to New York in 1851 and was a founding member of the CAS. An even earlier precedent was set by a New York antiprostitution group, the American Female Guardian Society, which, beginning in 1847, found single mothers with children positions as domestics in rural homes. There were also foreign precedents: a German charity, "The Friends in Need," placed vagrant city children with country families. Brace also knew about this organization, having visited it during his European tour.[1] The only antecedent Brace ever acknowledged publicly was the French practice of placing abandoned and destitute infants with rural wet nurses, who often ended up adopting them.[2]

The most significant antecedent of all, however, not only for Brace's orphan trains but also for both of the earlier American "placing out" efforts, was simply the indenture system. Indenture even had a long history of being used for the reform and removal of undesirable or potentially criminal children. Beginning in the seventeenth century, the British routinely gathered up — or kidnapped — poor children from the slums of London and sent them to the colonies to be bound servants. For much of that same period American commissioners of the poor had sought to "reform" destitute children by placing them in supposedly "respectable" homes at great distances from their depraved parents. The Philadelphia House of Refuge, where John Jackson had been incarcerated, commonly indentured boys to sea captains and had even placed one child as far away as Peru.

By the mid-nineteenth century, however, the indenture system was in its final phase, having succumbed, on the one hand, to the looser employer-employee ties fostered by wage labor and the market economy, and, on the other, to changing attitudes toward children and — under the influence of abolitionism — bonded servitude itself. In a way, the orphan trains were an attempt to modify an increasingly outmoded system, or at least to rescue that system's best elements.

Under the standard indenture agreement, a child was "bound," generally until the age of twenty-one, to a master who, in exchange for labor, was expected to train the child in the "art and mystery" of his craft and to provide adequate food, clothing, shelter, and a "common" education. At the termination of the indenture, the master was also supposed to give the apprentice a suit of clothes and often a bit of money and a Bible.

The agreement between the CAS and prospective families was identical in its general outline but differed in ways designed to give the child more freedom and protection. The most important difference was that orphan train riders were not "bound" to the families they went to live with. Unless the child was adopted by the new family, the CAS or the child's birth parents retained guardianship. Also, the relationship between the child and the family could be dissolved at any time if either party was dissatisfied, and the CAS would attempt to find the child a new placement and arrange for the child's transportation, either to that new placement or back to New York City. And finally, the head of the family with which the child was placed was not the child's "master" but his or her "employer." This did not mean that the child was paid wages — although many children, especially the older boys, were in fact paid for their labors. The term was testimony to the looser nature of the placement, by comparison to indenture, and to the legal equality of the two parties. "Employer" also implied, of course, that the child was still expected to work, as a farmhand, domestic, or in some other capacity. But the relationship was not meant to be a cold exchange of labor for basic necessities. From the beginning the ideal consummation of any placement was held to be the child's incorporation into the family.

Brace's reinvention of indenture was, however, only one of many ways in which American society was struggling to preserve this ancient and ubiquitous institution. Indenture was nothing like an outmoded profession — blacksmithing, for example — that could disappear without a trace in a single generation. It was an essential component of American family and social organization. Long after the notion of bonded servitude (at least of noncriminal whites) had become intolerable in a democratic republic, long after payment only in room, board, and on-the-job training had come to seem exploitative and unnatural, and even long after the legal apparatus of indenture — the contracts, penalties, and terminology — had fallen into neglect, there were still families that needed work done they were unwilling to do themselves, and there were still parents who could not afford or did not want to raise their children to adulthood, and there were still adolescents who could not bear to remain in the homes in which they had been born. Throughout the Victorian era and well into the twentieth century aspects of indenture survived as a social safety valve, as a source of cheap labor, and, most important of all, as a set of assumptions about the obligations of family, of adults and children, and of the rich and the poor. By looking closely at these assumptions, we can see not only yet another way in which the orphan trains were inevitable, but how they could also seem natural, normal, and good.

ॐ

> Little Orphan Annie has come to our house to stay
> To wash the dinner dishes up
> And brush the crumbs away,
> To shoo the chickens off the porch
> And dust the hearth and sweep,
> To make the fires, bake the bread
> And earn her board and keep.
>
> — James Whitcomb Riley

Critics of the instability of modern family life are often nostalgic for the Victorian family — or for what is really an anachronistic variation of the 1950s family, but without that edge of postwar anxiety that all too soon gave rise to the social revolutions of the 1960s. There is no anxiety in the idealized Victorian family. Father is resolutely upright, Mother dutiful and content, the children bound inseparably to their parents by love and respect. This family is commonly pictured as living in a white clapboard farmhouse, or in a tall "Victorian" townhouse. In the former setting, when the family is imagined eating lunch, there might be a few extra young men — farmhands — sitting at the long kitchen table. In the latter setting, while the family sups at a mahogany table decked with silver, china, linen, and crystal, a young woman, usually dressed in black with a white apron — the maid — might be seen peeking out of the kitchen doorway.

What is left out of this ideal image is the exact relationship between the family and those extra members of the household. Presumably the maid and the farmhands were employees, but what was it really like for employers and employees to live together 24 hours a day, 365 days a year? The idealized image of the Victorian family cannot contain such information given that the main purpose of the image is to define ideals for our own very different families. We thus tend to misunderstand the Victorian family, and in particular to underplay its elasticity in terms of its capacity both for incorporating others — kin and strangers — and for dispensing with its own offspring.

At any given moment, between 20 and 30 percent of nineteenth-century rural American households contained servants, relatives, and children who were not a part of the nuclear family.[3] And since many of these extra inhabitants were living with the family only for short periods, over time a much larger percentage of households were "augmented" by outsiders whose various relationships to the family (employee, child, charity case, servant) were by no means mutually exclusive. James Whitcomb Riley's Little Orphan Annie may well have been a poor, parentless girl needing work, or even an orphan train rider, but she could just as well have been an orphaned niece who would have been expected, with all of the alacrity expressed in Riley's poem, to pay for her aunt and uncle's generosity by essentially becoming a servant. And while most servants were employees in a much more straightforward fashion, they were also often children and to some extent would be subject to parenting by their "employers."

Domestics were usually unmarried women in the transition between living with their parents and starting a family of their own. They were almost all under thirty and were commonly as young as fourteen. Farmhands were also generally unmarried and often even younger. In the nineteenth century it was still relatively easy for a laborer to become a landowner. By their early twenties, most young men in the country were renting land and, within a few years, had farms of their own. As a result, farmhands tended to be sixteen- to twenty-year-old boys,[4] and with so many new farms constantly starting up, there was a terrible shortage of people to work them — a fact that played an important role in Brace's original conception and in farmers' acceptance of the orphan trains.

As much as the presence of extra children in the nineteenth-century household shows the Victorian family's capacity to absorb outsiders, it also illustrates its susceptibility to dissolution. Little Orphan Annie or her brother would generally end up living with other families as a result of some sort of catastrophe — although that catastrophe need not have entailed orphanhood. Throughout the nineteenth century, between 20 and 30 percent of children became orphans before age fifteen,[5] but only one-third of the children living in orphanages had lost both parents. Nearly 60 percent of those children were what was called "half orphans" — only one parent dead — and 10 percent of them still had two living parents.[6] These figures illustrate the extent to which poor Victorian families used orphanages as places to park their children during family crises. A substantial proportion of children in orphanages were there only for a year or two, and then were taken back into their birth families once the crisis had passed. It was common, for example, for a father to place his children in an orphanage after the death of his wife and to bring them home when he remarried, or when they were old enough to look after themselves while he worked. It was also common for children to be placed in an orphanage simply because their parents could not afford to feed and clothe them; maybe the father had lost his job or could not work because of illness or injury. These children were usually brought back home as soon as economic circumstances improved.

But orphanages were almost always a last resort, even when a child had lost both parents. Most poor children whose mothers and fathers could not care for them were sent to live with grandparents, aunts, uncles, or family friends (just as the children of the poor often are today), or jobs were obtained for them. But none of these informal "placements" were necessarily permanent. Even when a child had been officially indentured, parents could exercise their right to bring the child home once the family crisis had passed, although they might have had to engage in some legal negotiation and/or pay the master a fee.

The stability and freedom from anxiety that many modern idealists like to impose on the Victorian family are actually artifacts of comparatively recent developments, such as the plummeting of the mortality rate (by the mid-1970s only 5 percent of children were orphans[7]) and the elaboration of the laws, programs, and institutions that we have come to call the "safety net." In the early days of capitalism and wage labor, workers were almost entirely unprotected from the expansion and contraction of the job market or from the economic consequences of illness or disability. Men and women were constantly being let go because of seasonal or cyclical dips in demand, as well as for a host of other reasons that are still common today. Fathers and sons were constantly leaving their families to find jobs in other neighborhoods, in other cities, in the country, or at sea. Pioneers and immigrants were far from the only ones on the move during the nineteenth century. They were in fact only engaging in a more extreme form of the universal migration of working people in quest of a means of earning a living.

All of which goes to say that when Charles Loring Brace publicized his intention to find places in the country for city children, many of the people who first participated in the venture saw nothing particu-

larly radical about it. For the farmers, it was just another way of getting needed labor; for poor parents, it was just another place to park
children during hard times; and for the older teenagers at least, it was
just another employment service. Similar services had long existed in
the city. In a process very like an orphan train auction, for example,
girls who wanted jobs as maids would sit together in the back room of
a domestic employment agency and wait for gentlemen and ladies to
pick them out and take them home. Young men also found laboring
jobs through such auction-like arrangements, though theirs might
take place on a street corner or at a dockside and, in the city at least,
they were not usually required to live with their employer.

These were the patterns of labor, migration, and family organization that, in a remarkably flexible and undogmatic fashion, the CAS,
through the Emigration Plan in particular, helped to facilitate during
its earliest decades.

❧

Practically from the day Brace first moved a desk, chair, paper, and
pens into the CAS's Amity Street offices, he was trying to find "places"
for poor children. On March 7, 1853, he provided a "bright lad just
down from the country" and living "in very great destitution" with
dinner at his own lodgings and then found him "a bed with a poor
family" and a job at the *New York Sun*. A day later he found a newsboy
a "place in Christopher Street with Lyons, a carriage black-smith." On
March 10 he found a job for a boy named "Dealy" at the Metropolitan
Bank, where John E. Williams, the CAS treasurer, was president.[8]

But Brace was never very happy about placing children in the city.
From the beginning his main goal was to find them rural homes.
And he seems sincerely to have maintained an almost startlingly idealized portrait of country folk. "[T]he cultivators of the soil are in
America our most solid and intelligent class," he wrote. "They like to
educate their own 'help.' With their overflowing supply of food also,
each new mouth in the household brings no drain on their means.
Children are a blessing, and the mere feeding of a young boy or girl is
not considered at all."[9] This idealized image was supported by a host
of Romantic notions about the purity of lives lived close to the soil,
but it was also based on the fact that while rural poverty could be severe, it lacked the concentration and intensity that made the nation's
still new-seeming slums so horrifically squalid, dangerous, unsanitary,

and, as Brace saw it, prone to immorality. In effect, when he finally got his Emigration Plan up and running, he would be using the grandest symbol of nineteenth-century modernity — the railroad — to send children back in time to an agrarian America where there were no slums and no throngs of harried, disheveled, and disoriented immigrants, and where human relationships, even within the nuclear family, had not been degraded by an economic system that saw profit as the only value.

Brace's campaign for rural placement began in earnest in late March 1853 when he ran an advertisement in newspapers near New York City describing the CAS and asking to hear from anyone who might have a job or home to offer an orphan or vagrant child. The response was almost immediate. His "Daily Journal" entry for April 6 begins: "Many applications from the country." And for April 9: "Business. Application for boys and girls from country."

Not every child who came to the CAS looking for work was willing to accept a rural placement. One boy turned down a "home in the country" because he thought the man he would be sent to might "*want to sell him.*"[10] Most often children refused to go to the country because they did not want to stray so far from their families and friends. Brace would not make his first rural placement until April 19, when he sent two boys to upstate New York, one to Wolcottville and the other to Woodstock.

Most of the applications from the country were submitted by people offering jobs, but many were from couples looking for children to adopt, often because their own offspring had died. The CAS also received applications from Henry Higgins types who, as Brace described one such gentleman from Delaware, "wished to make the experiment of bringing up a vagrant boy of the city."[11] During that first year Brace and his assistant, John Macy, found places for 207 children. In the second year they placed more than four times as many — 863, among whom were the first 46 orphan train riders.[12]

In the era before telephones and cars, the placement of individual children was immensely time-consuming and inefficient — especially when it had to be managed by only two men. As Brace explained it in his book *The Dangerous Classes:*

Each applicant or employer always called for "a perfect child," without any of the taints of earthly depravity. The girls must be pretty, good-tempered, not given to purloining sweetmeats, and fond of making fires at daylight, and with a constitutional love for Sunday Schools and Bible-lessons. The boys must be well made, of good stock, never disposed to steal apples or pelt cattle, using language of perfect propriety, and delighting in family-worship and prayer-meetings more than in fishing or skating parties. These demands, of course, were not always successfully complied with. Moreover, to those who desired the children of "blue eyes, fair hair, and blond complexion," we were sure to send the dark-eyed and brunette; and the particular virtues wished for were very often precisely those that the child was deficient in. It was evidently altogether too much of a lottery for bereaved parents or benevolent employers to receive children in that way.[13]

Individual placement also required an immense amount of money — for staffing, filing, correspondence, and transportation — something that was in very short supply, especially during the society's first decade.

By accepting the position of CAS secretary, Brace had put himself in exactly the position of dependency he had dreaded for so much of his life; he was compelled, time and again, in the presence of his wealthiest friends and acquaintances, to adopt the survival strategy of the very children he was trying to help. "No such disagreeable and self-denying work is ever done as begging money," he admitted in *The Dangerous Classes.*

> The feeling that you are boring others, and getting from their personal regard, what ought to be given solely for public motives, and the certainty that others will apply to you as you apply to them, and expect a subscription as a personal return, are all great "crosses." The cold rebuff, too; the suspicious negative, as if you were engaged in rather doubtful business, are other unpleasant accompaniments of this business.[14]

Despite all of Brace's groveling and enthusiasm, to say nothing of his double-barreled strategy of appealing to the compassion and fear of the wealthy, the society was only barely able to scrape by until it began to receive state aid in 1862. Then, as now, most "practical" men were convinced that there was not much return from money invested in the reformation of the children of the poor.

Brace was well aware of the limited generosity of the wealthy. He also knew that however much he may have disagreed with the theories behind orphanages, asylums, and other institutions for the care of poor children, one of the main reasons they rarely lived up to their founders' expectations was that they almost never received the funding necessary to run as they had been planned. This was why so many state almshouses put elderly and, often, alcoholic inmates in charge of their children's wards instead of paid and trained staff. This was why a New York State investigation of county almshouses in the 1850s found that "common domestic animals are usually more humanely provided for" than almshouse inmates, and that "the children are poorly fed, poorly clothed, and quite untaught."[15] Underfunding also explained why, during the same period, the Massachusetts State Reform School for Boys housed more than double its capacity; and why, at a time when New York City's child mortality rate was hovering around 20 percent, the unsanitary and overcrowded Infant's Hospital on Randall's Island lost between 70 and 77 percent of the children put in its care.[16]

Dreading that his own charity could be similarly compromised by insufficient funding, Brace took great pains from the beginning to ensure that it required as little money to operate as possible. By 1864 the number of children placed annually by the CAS had grown to over 1,000, and during the last quarter of the century placements averaged between 3,000 and 4,000 annually. Sending these children out west in groups and letting interested men and women simply pick out the boy or girl they liked best was enormously cheaper and faster than placing each child individually. Because the CAS did not have to play the role of middleman, it did not have to hire a large staff or spend a lot of money on correspondence. Transportation was also cheaper since the charity could take advantage of discounted group rates. And letting families (or "employers") pick out their own child limited the amount of time, money, and heartache spent replacing children whose eyes might turn out to be the wrong shade of blue, or who had no fondness for starting fires at six in the morning.

Brace made a point of advertising the Emigration Plan's efficiency to economy-minded potential contributors, emphasizing that in addition to being the most effective and humane method for reforming poor children, placing them in homes was also the cheapest. It cost $140 per year to keep a criminal in jail, for example, while it took only a onetime payment of under $20 to find a poor child a home through the Emigration Plan.[17]

The final factor contributing to the apparent inevitability of the orphan trains was the economics of the burgeoning railroad industry. In their early days one of the biggest problems faced by railroad companies was a destination shortage. Firm believers that America's destiny lay beyond the Appalachians, railroad entrepreneurs were extending veinlike networks of tracks westward from New York, Boston, Philadelphia, and Baltimore, and eastward from San Francisco into a vast territory where, especially west of Chicago, the few cities were really only small towns and the widely scattered settlements might be inhabited by no more than a handful of families. History was on the side of the railroad entrepreneurs, of course. The same forces that were overcrowding the great cities of the East Coast would inevitably fill up the forests, prairies, and plains of the Heartland. But the entrepreneurs could not wait that long. They had loans to repay and stockholders to satisfy — so they decided to give history a hand.

Their strategy was simple: rather than wait for destinations to emerge by themselves, the railroad entrepreneurs manufactured them. On swaths of land along their tracks that they either had been given by the federal government or had bought for practically nothing, they laid out grids of streets, built post offices, established general stores, blacksmiths, and maybe a newspaper and a church. Then they offered residential and commercial plots to settlers at bargain-basement prices.

To get a sufficient number of people interested in settling on these plots, the railroad companies employed that most venerable of American types: the huckster. Often in collaboration with the governments of western states and territories, the railroads would send agents to East Coast cities to sing the praises of their blueprint communities. These agents would come fortified with brochures, guides, maps, and street plans that often considerably exaggerated the state of development and bucolic splendor of the new communities, and of the West in general. Railroad agents, again often in collaboration with western states and territories, were also sent to Europe, where they traveled from village to village promoting their "product" in very much the same way as domestic agents, but there they also tried to attract large groups of neighbors to emigrate all at once. To sweeten their deals, both domestic and European agents would offer deeply discounted group fares — called "emigrant tickets" — not only for train travel but also for freshwater steamship trips and, for Europeans, transatlantic passage.

If not partly inspired by the railroad company policies, Brace's Emigration Plan was certainly a similarly self-conscious attempt to participate in and advance an already existing demographic phenomenon. The railroad company discounts also made it easier for Brace to put his own plan into action. And when the Children's Aid Society's first official company of "western emigrants," under the supervision of a young "visitor" named E. P. Smith, left New York City, it took full advantage of the discounts offered by the railroads.

No surviving records indicate why Dowagiac, a small town in southwest Michigan, was chosen as the destination for this first orphan train. In the future the CAS would primarily send parties of children to well-established towns situated in the midst of prosperous farm country, with 3,000 to 4,000 inhabitants, good schools, and, ideally, a college nearby. Dowagiac in 1853 had few if any of these advantages. The settlement had only been "platted," or laid out, by the Michigan Central Railroad in February 1848, and it would not be incorporated as a village for another fifteen years. Its homes, described by one traveler as "rock eggs on the desert sand,"[18] consisted mostly of cabins made of squared-off logs, although some of its finer buildings may have been built from clapboard or brick hauled in by freight trains. It had a tavern with rooms to let to travelers, a railroad station, a post office, and at least one church — Presbyterian — which doubled as a school from late fall to early spring. Its streets were dirt, its yards mostly bare. The "primeval forests" of oak, beech, and maple that once covered the land had been cleared away to build houses, make room for fields of wheat and livestock, and provide firewood to settlers and the railroad. It was not a particularly prosperous town, but no one was starving. Most farmers were able to grow or make everything they needed.

Michigan was a relatively progressive state in 1853. It was Republican, strongly antislavery, and substantially populated by immigrants from western New York, who were perhaps somewhat more disposed than other midwesterners to take in poor children from New York City. All these factors might have played a role in the selection of Dowagiac as the testing ground for Brace's reform experiment. But in all likelihood the village was chosen primarily because somebody there — the mayor, the doctor, the Presbyterian minister — knew Brace or someone else at the CAS. Especially during the early decades of the society, Brace tried to turn every meeting or social gathering to his advantage. Social reformers from all over the country — and the world — commonly dropped by the CAS offices to meet Brace and to see his operation firsthand. If one such visitor was a prominent citizen from Dowagiac, it is more than likely that Brace would have sounded him out about the possibility of sending a party of "emigrants" there, and if the visitor was well disposed, Brace would have asked him to organize a local committee to manage the distribution of the children.

Such committees were usually organized several weeks in advance of the arrival of the orphan trains. They consisted of prominent local citizens — clergymen, merchants, newspaper editors, doctors, lawyers — who would arrange the site where the children would be distributed, publicize the event (newspaper editors were particularly desired as committee members because they could print flyers and run ads for free), find lodgings for the orphan train party, and consult with the CAS agent on the merits of the people applying to take children. It is not clear whether so elaborate a committee was established for this first orphan train. E. P. Smith, the CAS agent who accompanied the children, made no mention of a committee in his detailed report on the trip. He did say, however, that he had to negotiate sleeping accommodations at a local tavern himself. At the very least, the Reverend Mr. O. of the Presbyterian church had known about the arrival of the party and had publicized it in advance.

The first orphan train company left New York by riverboat on the evening of September 28, 1854. There were thirty-seven boys and girls in the group. Nine others who had been scheduled for the trip apparently arrived at the CAS offices too late to make the boat and were sent by train to join the company in Albany the following morning. In his report, Smith said that the children ranged from six to fifteen years in age, and he summed up the life histories of thirty-six of the children in a single word: "orphans." But he went into the background of some of the ten vagrants in much greater detail:

> Two of these had slept in nearly all the station-houses in the city. One, a keen-eyed American boy, was born in Chicago — an orphan now,

and abandoned in New York by an intemperate brother. Another, a little German Jew, who had been entirely friendless for four years, and had finally found his way in the Newsboys' Lodging-house. Dick and Jack were brothers of Sara O ——, whom we sent to Connecticut. Their father is intemperate; mother died at Bellevue Hospital three weeks since; and an older brother had just been sentenced to Sing Sing Prison. Their father, a very sensible man when sober, begged me to take the boys along, "for I am sure, sir, if left in New York, they will come to the same bad end as their brother." We took them to a shoe shop. Little Jack made awkward work in trying on a pair. "He don't know them, sir; there's not been a cover to his feet for three winters."[19]

The single child given the most attention in the narrative was a twelve-year-old boy called "Liverpool," after the city of his birth. He had been found in the Fourth Ward (encompassing most of Five Points and the desperately poor Cherry Street) only hours before the boat's departure by a CAS visitor named Mr. Gerry. Apparently Liverpool had been a vagrant orphan before shipping to the United States as a cabin boy. Once he landed in New York, he supported himself by doing odd jobs on the docks and dressed in sailors' ragged castoffs, most of which were much too large for him. When Gerry found him, he had so many garments wrapped and tied about his body that he looked like a "walking rag bundle."

Gerry seems to have had no compunction about spiriting this boy out of the city on this first, experimental orphan train without even bothering to check into his claims of orphanhood; nor did Liverpool voice any objection to his sudden change of situation. Gerry took him straight to the Newsboys' Lodging House, where he was bathed and given a haircut, a new suit, and shoes, and then rushed him down to the dock to board the boat just before its departure.

In those days the boats traveling the Hudson River between Manhattan and Albany were sidewheelers with twin stacks that spewed long plumes of acrid black smoke. The children's boat was called the *Isaac Newton* — after the shipping company's largest stockholder, not the famous mathematician. The CAS had bought them "emigrant" or "steerage" tickets, the cheapest available, and the children had to sleep on rough, stinking, vermin-ridden matting on the ship's lowest deck. They were saved from this fate at the last instant by the boat's captain, who had heard them singing on the gangway and invited them to his salon. After listening to several of their sad stories, the captain let them spend the night in the mostly vacant berths of the boat's cabin.

The children also attracted serious interest from a couple of the riverboat's passengers. Smith gave one of the little boys to a woman from Rochester who thought her sister would like to take him in. And Mr. B., a merchant from Illinois, took Liverpool to work in his store. Smith made no independent inquiries into the background of either passenger. He simply trusted his first impression. "I afterwards met Mr. B. in Buffalo," Smith reported, "and he said that he would not part with the boy for any consideration; and I thought that to take such a boy from such a condition, and put him into such hands, was worth the whole trip."

The riverboat arrived in Albany at six in the morning, and the "emigrant train" to the West did not leave until noon. Smith put the stopover to good use, meeting up with the nine tardy children who had been sent up from New York by rail and adding a new boy to the expedition with all the casualness with which he had dispensed with the two others.

The new boy's name was John, but he went by the street moniker of "Smack," and his "twisted, tangled hair, matted for years," his "badger" coat, and pants so overlarge they fluttered in the breeze marked him as a vagrant or "snoozer." As Smith told the story, his decision to take the boy along was a matter of reason losing out to compassion — and to the urgings of the other children. "Here's a boy what wants to go to Michigan, sir," Smith was told by a group of his charges. "Can't you take him with us?"

"But, do you know him?" Smith responded. "Can you recommend him as a suitable boy to belong to our company?"

The children knew nothing about him, not even his name. "Only he's as hard-up as any of us," they said. "He's no father or mother, and nobody to live with, and he sleeps out o' nights." The boy also pleaded for himself, saying he wanted to be a farmer and live in the country.

Smith finally relented after a moment of meditation: "Our number is full — purse scant — it may be difficult to find him a home. But there is no resisting the appeal of the boys, and the importunate face of the young vagrant. Perhaps he will do well; at any rate, we must try him. If left to float here a few months longer, his end is certain."

After a face scrub and haircut, Smack was allowed into the company and formally interviewed. Smith's notes on the interview reproduce exactly the standard entry for orphan train riders in the CAS "Record

Books," the main filing system used during the society's first three decades: "*John* ———— *, American — Protestant — 13 years — Orphan —
Parents died in R* ——*, Maine — A 'snoozer' for four years — Most of
the time in New York, with an occasional visit to Albany and Troy, 'when
times go hard' — Intelligent — Black, sharp eye — Hopeful.*"[20]

Smith's description of the trip from Albany to Dowagiac is so vivid,
and tells so much about the conditions endured by the children and
all emigrants of the era, that I am quoting it in its entirety. This passage is also striking when considered as propaganda, in part because
Smith and Brace (Brace selected and edited the journal entry for publication) seem utterly unashamed of the hardships the children suffered — an attitude that tells us something about normal nineteenth-
century travel conditions and, perhaps, about common notions of
what treatment poor children deserved. But it also illustrates clearly
Smith's and Brace's distinct vision of such children. Whereas many
commentators of the era might have cited the children's misbehavior
as a sign of their innate criminality, Smith celebrated it as evidence of
their vitality and even innocence:

> At the depot we worked our way through the Babel of at least one
> thousand Germans, Irish, Italians, and Norwegians, with whom noth-
> ing goes right; every one insists that he is in the wrong car — that his
> baggage has received the wrong mark — that Chicago is in this direc-
> tion, and the cars are on the wrong track; in short, they are agreed
> upon nothing except in the opinion that this is a "bad counthry, and
> it's good luck to the soul who sees the end on't." The conductor, a red-
> faced, middle-aged man, promises to give us a separate car; but, while
> he whispers and negotiates with two Dutch[21] girls, who are traveling
> without a protector, the motley mass rush into the cars, and we are
> finally pushed into one already full — some standing, a part sitting in
> laps, and some on the floor under the benches — crowded to suffoca-
> tion, in a freight-car without windows — rough benches for seats, and
> no back — no ventilation except through the sliding doors, where the
> little chaps are in constant danger of falling through. There were scenes
> that afternoon and night which it would not do to reveal. Irishmen
> passed around bad whisky and sang bawdy songs; Dutch men and
> women smoked and sang, and grunted and cursed; babies squalled and
> nursed, and left no baby duties undone.
> Night came on, and we were told that "passengers furnish their own

lights!" For this we were unprepared, and so we tried to endure the darkness, which never before seemed half so thick as in that stifled car, though it was relieved here and there for a few minutes by a lighted pipe. One Dutchman in the corner kept up a constant fire; and when we told him we were choking with smoke, he only answered with a complacent grunt and a fresh supply of the weed. The fellow seemed to puff when he was fairly asleep, and the curls were lifting beautifully above the bowl, when smash against the car went the pipe in a dozen pieces! No one knew the cause, except, perhaps, the boy behind me, who had begged an apple a few minutes before.

At Utica we dropped our fellow-passengers from Germany, and, thus partially relieved, spent the rest of the night in tolerable comfort.

In the morning, we were in the vicinity of Rochester, and you can hardly imagine the delight of the children as they looked, many of them for the first time, upon country scenery. Each one must see everything we passed, find its name, and make his own comments. "What's that, mister?" "A corn-field." "Oh, yes; them's what makes buckwheaters." "Look at them cows (oxen plowing); my mother used to milk cows." As we whirled through orchards loaded with large, red apples, their enthusiasm rose to the highest pitch. It was difficult to keep them within doors. Arms stretched out, hats swinging, eyes swimming, mouths watering, and all screaming — "Oh! oh! just look at 'em! Mister, be they any sich in Mich*igan?* Then I'm for that place — three cheers for Mich*igan!*" We had been riding in comparative quiet for nearly an hour, when all at once the greatest excitement broke out. We were passing a corn-field spread over with ripe yellow pumpkins. "Oh! yonder! look! Just *look* at 'em!" and in an instant the same exclamation was yelled from forty-seven mouths. "Jist *look* at 'em! What a heap of *mushmillons!*" "Mister, do they make mushmillons in Mich*i-gan?*" "Ah, fellers, *ain't* that the country tho' — won't we have nice things to eat?" "Yes, won't we *sell* some, too?" "Hip! hip! boys; three cheers for Mich*igan!*"

At Buffalo we received great kindness from Mr. Harrison, the freight-agent and this was by no means his first service to the Children's Aid Society. Several boys and girls whom we have sent West have received the kindest attention at his hands. I am sure Mr. H.'s fireside must be a happy spot. Also Mr. Noble, agent for the Mich. C.R.R., gave me a letter of introduction, which was of great service on the way.

We were in Buffalo nine hours, and the boys had the liberty of the town, but were all on board the boat in season. We went down to our place, the steerage cabin, and no one but an emigrant on a lake-boat can understand the night we spent. The berths are covered with a coarse mattress, used by a thousand different passengers, and never changed till they are filled with stench and vermin. The emigrants spend the night in washing, smoking, drinking, singing, sleep, and licentiousness. It was the last night in the freight-car repeated, with the addition of a touch of sea-sickness, and of the stamping, neighing, and bleating of a hundred horses and sheep over our heads, and the effluvia of their filth pouring through the open gangway. But we survived the night; *how* had better not be detailed. In the morning we got outside upon the boxes, and enjoyed the beautiful day. The boys were in good spirit, sung songs, told New York yarns, and made friends generally among the passengers. Occasionally, some one more knowing than wise would attempt to poke fun at them, whereupon the boy would 'pitch in,' and open such a sluice of Bowery slang as made Mr. Would-be-funny beat a retreat in double-quick time. No one attempted that game twice. During the day the clerk discovered that three baskets of peaches were missing, all except the baskets. None of the boys had been detected with the fruit, but I afterwards found they had eaten it.

Landed in Detroit at ten o'clock, Saturday night, and took a first-class passenger car on the Mich. C.R.R., and reached D —— c, a "smart little town," in S.W. Michigan, three o'clock Sunday morning.

⁂

One element suppressed in all CAS writing is the children's suffering at being separated from their families, friends, and homes and sent hundreds of miles away to live with total strangers. Not all of the children suffered great fear or grief, of course. Some of the older ones were so used to being on their own, or had suffered such mistreatment, that they found nothing daunting in the prospect of leaving the city and living with a farm family. Younger children, especially those who had been orphaned in infancy, often had not made strong ties to anyone and so did not feel much loss; nor had they any clear idea of what it might mean to be part of a family. Other children reacted to the ordeal of transport and placement simply by shutting down emotionally, while still others became hyperactive — perhaps some of the very children whose vitality Smith celebrated. But common sense and the testimony of surviving orphan train riders make clear that there was a lot of weeping and a lot of fear at every stage of the orphan train process — and none of it was ever referred to in any CAS account.

Sometimes Brace or other CAS correspondents referred to parents weeping as they gave up their children, but the children themselves were always presented as happy, or at the very least as stalwart and resolved. The closest E. P. Smith came to showing the suffering of the children in his care was when he told about the grief of a seven-year-old boy named Peter at the disappearance of his six-year-old brother.

Having arrived at Dowagiac at three in the morning, there was nothing for Smith or his group of children to do other than try to catch a little sleep right on the railroad platform. The children were so excited to at last be in Michigan, however, that as soon as the sun rose they ran off in all directions to explore the town. Within a very short while, they were all back at the station, hungry for breakfast — all except Peter's little brother George. Smith apparently never noticed the little boy's absence, and if Peter noticed, he never brought it to his caretaker's attention.

Smith led the children to the American House (the tavern where he had negotiated their lodging and board) for breakfast, and then took them to the Presbyterian church, where they would be presented to the citizens of Dowagiac for the first time. The minister was late, so the children entertained the congregation by singing hymns, including "Come Ye Sinners Poor and Needy." When at last the Reverend Mr. O. arrived, Smith made his pitch to the congregation about the children and announced that he would himself deliver a sermon in the afternoon. It was only as the group was returning to the tavern for lunch that Smith noticed, or was informed, that Peter's little brother was missing.

George had last been seen near daybreak, heading out of town across a bridge. Smith and the children dove into the creek beneath the bridge, looking for the little boy's body, and searched the surrounding woods, all to no avail. That night when the children came in for supper, there was, according to Smith,

> a shade of sadness on their faces, and they spoke in softer tones of the lost playmate. But the saddest was George's brother, one year older. They were two orphans — all alone in the world. Peter stood up at the table, but when he saw his brother's place at his side vacant, he burst out in uncontrollable sobbing. After supper he seemed to forget his

loss, till he lay down on the floor at night, and there was the vacant spot again, and his little heart flowed over with grief. Just so again when he awoke in the morning, and at breakfast and dinner.

Smith implied great sympathy for Peter with this description, but apparently he did not feel enough sympathy to do anything more to help find George. The "morning" referred to was Monday, the day the distribution of the children had been set to begin, and Smith was not about to let the loss of a six-year-old orphan interfere with the proceedings. And by his account, the children were as resigned to George's disappearance as he was: "Monday morning the boys held themselves in readiness to receive applications from the farmers. They would watch at all directions, scanning closely every wagon that came in sight, and deciding from the appearance of the driver and the horses, more often from the latter, whether they 'would go in for *that* farmer.'"[22]

Smith seems to have occupied himself that day exclusively with interviewing prospective "parents" and "employers" and determining whether the children chosen by the adults truly wanted to go home with them. Demand was strong, and by nightfall he had placed fifteen children.

At noon, while Smith was still occupied with his work, the "citizens" of Dowagiac finally "rallied and scoured the woods for miles around" for the missing boy.

[B]ut the search was fruitless, and Peter lay down that night sobbing, and with his arms stretched out, just as he used to throw them round his brother.

About ten o'clock a man knocked at the door, and cried out, "Here is the lost boy!" Peter heard him, and the two brothers met on the stairs, and before we could ask where he had been, Peter had George in his place by his side on the floor. They have gone to live together in Iowa.

Smith would never have mentioned this near-tragedy, and the brothers' suffering, had he not thought it all ended happily. But the truth is that he had little evidence for such an appraisal. Peter and George were among the nine youngest children for whom Smith was not able to find homes in Dowagiac — in all likelihood because the local farmers and merchants thought they were too small to be much good as laborers. On Saturday, almost a week after their arrival, Smith escorted these unclaimed children as far as Chicago and placed them alone on a train to travel two hundred miles further west (at the rate of eighteen miles an hour!) to the Reverend C. C. Townsend in Iowa City.

For many years the Reverend Townsend was the CAS's sole western representative. He ran an industrial school in his own parlor and devoted much of his time to finding homes for local orphans and for CAS "emigrant companies," whom he sometimes brought west himself. Townsend did his best, but during a time when merely crossing the state required days of hard travel, he often had little idea what had happened to the many hundreds of children he had placed all over Iowa and in several surrounding states. And when he did know how the children were doing, his reports to New York were so cursory and euphemistic (the most common account was simply "doing well," even when it was clear from other evidence that the child was not well at all) that no one at the CAS, and Smith in particular, could have had any real idea of the children's well-being.

CAS contact with the rest of these first orphan train riders was even more distant and intermittent. At the end of his report, E. P. Smith announced that the Reverend Mr. O. took "several" children into his own home, that a few of the boys were "bound to trades" (probably meaning that they went to live with craftsmen or merchants rather than that they were formally indentured), but that most of the children "insisted" on being farmers. Two brothers were placed on adjacent farms. The expedition's solitary Jew went to live with a physician. A sweet little girl named Mag was, Smith said, "*adopted* by a wealthy Christian farmer."[23] (This arrangement was probably informal as well, since at that time Michigan, like most states, had no laws governing adoption.) And finally, Smack, the Albany recruit, found "a good home in a Quaker settlement."

Sketchy as this summation may have been, it was all the CAS would ever know about most of these children. In its early decades the society monitored placements almost exclusively through the letters it got from children and their foster parents/employers. John Macy regularly wrote to placements asking for information but was lucky to get a 5 percent response rate. A sizable majority of the early orphan train riders' records contain nothing after the notation of where the child was placed than a list of the dates of Macy's unanswered letters. But this paucity of information had almost no effect on the enthusiasm of Brace, or any CAS writer, for the program.

Smith ended his report by declaring, "On the whole, the first experiment of sending children West is a very happy one." One might justify this nearly baseless assertion on the grounds that Smith's account, published in the third annual report of the Children's Aid Society, was meant primarily to garner contributions from wealthy readers. But even that most mundane of bureaucratic documents, the "Company Book," which listed all the orphan train riders and was meant exclusively for internal use, commenced by declaring this first "experiment . . . successful indeed."[24] No surviving document from the early years of the CAS expresses a shred of doubt about the efficacy of the Emigration Plan.

Charles Loring Brace was a man of faith. He once explained to a correspondent that the only way he and his colleagues had been able to avoid falling into abject despair at the many "sad and lonely histories" they confronted every day was by believing in "One above this black poverty and suffering. We have faith in the promises He has given of a better time on this earth."[25]

There is much that is beautiful in this faith. It gave Brace and his colleagues the strength to go on with their terribly difficult work and enabled them to see human dignity in the most dirty, deprived, and despairing face. But it also gave them license to believe what they could not verify, and thus to promote an all-but-unproven program that would radically change the lives of a quarter million children over the next seventy-five years.

6

A Voice Among the Newsboys

IN JUNE 1854 Brace set sail from New York to tour of British ragged schools and visit the young woman who had been for him, and for whom he had been, primarily a fantasy spun over three years of correspondence. Brace intended to propose to Letitia Neill but seems to have had some doubt as to whether they would find each other as attractive in the flesh as they had in their imaginations — which is perhaps why he dallied in England before crossing the Irish Sea. In the end, however, neither he nor Letitia suffered any rude surprises, and after what their daughter, Emma, would later describe as a "short engagement," they were married in Belfast on August 21, 1854, by a clergyman who worried that this daughter of the respected Neill family did not know what she was getting into by marrying an obscure Yank.[1]

Letitia seems to have known exactly what she was getting into. No sooner had she set her bags down in their New York home than she astonished Brace's friends by going out with him to visit the Fourth Ward Industrial School. She had herself worked at a ragged school in Belfast and had strong convictions about where her husband could best apply his energies.

When Brace had accepted the job of secretary of the Children's Aid Society, he had agreed to work for a trial period of one year, which he had then extended for a second year. As the deadline approached for making a final decision about whether to continue in charitable work, he was having grave doubts. "My life," he told his cousin Mrs. Asa Gray, "has become too practical, too much outward and executive, and my intellect is rusting."[2] He wanted to continue his education, do more writing, and preach. But for Letitia it was clear that, whatever her husband's intellectual and theological potential, he could serve humanity best through the Children's Aid Society — and in the end he agreed with her.

Over the next year the habits of Brace's bachelorhood were rapidly replaced by the pleasures and responsibilities of married maturity. The couple's first child, Charles Loring Brace Jr., was born in the spring of 1855. Although the family still kept a home in the city, they moved up the North (or Hudson) River to Westchester County, where they bought a house in Hastings and began to travel in very elevated social circles. Schuylers, Livingstons, Hamiltons, and Roosevelts (families that had been the very definition of polite society since colonial days) were their frequent dinner companions.[3] Ralph Waldo Emerson and Henry Ward Beecher came regularly to the Braces' breakfast parties.[4] In his letters Charles also reported having lunch with his Westchester neighbor Washington Irving and, on a trip to Cambridge, dinner with Henry Wadsworth Longfellow.[5] The expansion of Brace's domestic life in no way diminished his dedication to his professional work. He remained a frequent contributor to the *Independent* and the *New York Daily Times,* and by the spring of 1855, having already sent several orphan trains west, he had established all the main policies and programs that would dominate the Children's Aid Society into the next century.

This was the beginning of a long, happy period for Brace. His marriage to Letitia would remain solid and loving until the day he died. They would have four children, two boys and two girls, all of whom would survive to adulthood, and none of whom would suffer extraordinarily during their youths or their own marriages. Despite Brace's anxiety about the rusting of his intellect, he would publish five hefty books, all blends of social science, history, and theology, with one, *The Dangerous Classes,* being partly a memoir. His work with the CAS would remain, however, the foundation of his public reputation. By the time Brace turned thirty he would already be the preeminent figure in American child welfare, a status he would enjoy for the rest of his life.

There is no doubt that much of the high public regard that Brace enjoyed was justly earned. The CAS was in many ways a revolutionary and truly beneficial organization. But at the same time there was much about Brace's reputation that rested on fantasy — fantasy that he was not alone in creating.

છƥ

Vagrant children lived on stories. The most talented earned pennies by telling tall tales on street corners, or declaiming Shakespeare, or reciting ballads or poems. But all poor children learned early on that, properly told, nothing had more power to garner them handouts, places to sleep, and sometimes complete changes of circumstance than the stories of their lives. Liverpool earned the favor of E. P. Smith by telling his life story "with a quiet, sad reserve, that made us believe him truthful," and the stories of his fellow orphan train riders won the whole company comfortable berths on the *Isaac Newton.*

To achieve maximum value, the stories had to be terrifically sad, but not depressing. The child's fundamental goodness could be tried but never tarnished by harsh experience, and in the end the stories had to compensate for whatever suffering they may have caused their audience by testifying to the power of fortitude, self-sacrifice, and religious devotion. They also had to appear to be told only under duress or through the spontaneous upsurge of overwhelming grief. Any child who turned a hat upside down on the sidewalk before beginning to speak, or who manifested the slightest sign of insincerity or artifice, would earn only instant derision.

Johnny Morrow was one of the most successful of storytellers ever to enter the doors of the Children's Aid Society — so successful that several versions of his life history are preserved in CAS records, in newspaper articles, and in his 135-page autobiography, *A Voice Among the Newsboys,* which was privately published in 1860 to raise money for his divinity school tuition. By comparing the various versions of Johnny's biography, we are able to get a more complete vision of his life and, by extension, the lives of many of the street children who used the CAS during this era. But we are also able to see how a child's desire to get the most out of his story led him to confirm the sentimental fantasies that CAS workers most wanted to believe. In effect, children like Johnny and the adults who worked with them often collaborated on fictions that not only made both parties feel better but influenced policies that affected thousands of lives.

This collaborative fictionalization is most apparent in Johnny's autobiography, and it begins even before the first word of text. The boy portrayed on the book's engraved frontispiece is the perfect representation of the Victorian cliché that street children were "young in body, with faces made old by woe." The Johnny Morrow of this engraving has the expression of a terribly unhappy middle-aged man. His eyebrows turn down at the sides and buckle up in the middle, conveying both sorrow and worry. There are deep circles under his eyes, and his gaze does not directly meet the viewer's but is shifted slightly to the left, as if he is lost to drear imagining. The corners of his mouth, too, have a slight downward turn, and there are puckers on either side of his chin, as if his whole face has been depressed by a mix of gravity and grief.

He is wearing a black suit, with a waistcoat buttoned nearly to his neck. A round, broad-brimmed hat, perhaps made of straw, dangles in front of his right arm from a long thong around his neck. Under his left arm he carries a small wooden box, from which he is extracting what would seem to be a wallet. A small book, or perhaps an open penknife, also juts out of the box, as do what appear to be two women's shoe stretchers.

The most striking thing about Johnny — apart from his grief — is his proportions. He has the large head and narrow shoulders of a toddler, although the two-thirds of his body that is visible seems stretched to the length of a seven- or eight-year-old. It is a surprise, then, to read that this child is sixteen years old. This information comes in the introduction, in which the book's supposed editor, "W.B.D.," asserts that the work is "a daguerreotype of fact, untouched by art," and claims that he,

> by request, performed the necessary duty of putting [the manuscript] into a somewhat more correct and attractive shape than could possibly be expected by a boy of sixteen years, which is all that [Johnny] as yet numbers. Yet in this revision, care has been exercised to leave every page as nearly as possible in its original characteristic shape.

This very assertion of authenticity only further obscures the fact of Johnny's age, for CAS records show that the very youngest he could have been when the book was written was seventeen, and that he was more likely to have been nineteen.

It is impossible to know for sure where to lay the blame for this deception. Perhaps Johnny's proportions really were as distorted as the artist rendered them. He was indeed constantly called "little" in the CAS records and journals, and he may well have been something of a midget. If this was the case, Johnny certainly had good reason not to correct anyone's misapprehension about his age. The younger people thought he was, the more innocent and precocious he seemed, and the more likely they were to help him. But by the same token, it was in the interest of both W.B.D. and the CAS (with which the editor had, at the very least, a strong sympathetic connection) to emphasize the innocence and precocity of the "child" they were aiding.

Another possible deception that clearly served the interests of Johnny, W.B.D., and the CAS had to do with his nationality. In his autobiography, Johnny claimed that he spent his earliest childhood in a "village not far from Liverpool," and that his mother was English and his father "Scotch by birth."[6] But other evidence indicates that the Morrows were in fact Irish. The CAS record of Johnny's younger sister, Annie, called her an "Irish Orphan." Johnny himself said in his autobiography that his two older brothers studied at the Royal Blue Coat Hospital in Dublin, and he told Anna Hope, an *Independent* reporter who interviewed him shortly after his arrival at the CAS, that his father had been "a foreman over the carpenters who worked for Bishop ———, of ———, in Ireland."[7]

Johnny's family immigrated to New York in 1847 or 1848, at the height of the potato famine, and at a time when anti-Irish sentiment in America was especially virulent. He and W.B.D. may have chosen to conceal his ethnicity both to escape the taint of that prejudice and to make it easier for people who might contribute toward his divinity school tuition to see themselves in his place.

For similar reasons, perhaps, the autobiography portrays Johnny's childhood as a middle-class idyll. In this account, his father is not a "foreman over carpenters" but "an architect by profession, and, in those days, a respectable man, and quite prosperous in his business; he stood well in society, and was exceedingly affectionate and indulgent to his family." The Morrows, the book states, lived in a "very nice house which belonged to my father, in front of which was a pretty little garden plot, containing a great variety of grasses and flowers, kept in order by our hired man." Johnny, born in 1841 or 1842, spent his first five years "sporting" in this garden, especially among the roses, with his sister Annie and their cat "Puss." He attended an "infant school," where he chanted "delicate childish stanzas" about clapping away rainy days, and also a Sabbath school, after which his father would instruct him in the catechism.

As the book presents it, the first of Johnny's many misfortunes was a fall from a "flying swing," which broke his left leg so severely that it healed three inches longer than the right. "Since then I have had to hobble along through life," Johnny stated humbly, and then showed true Victorian fortitude by adding: "though fortunately I can manage pretty well, without using crutches. There is one comfortable reflection in this matter, and that is, *it might have been worse!*"[8]

The second great tragedy of Johnny's childhood, the death of his mother, is so stripped of context in the autobiography that his suffering seems odd and almost beside the point. Saying nothing about the cause of her death or how he found out about it, Johnny simply declared, "[M]y own dear mother . . . was called away from her family while her children were in their tender years," and then cut straight to the morning of her funeral:

[F]ather took me into the room where she lay in silent death upon a white bed, while her face was as white as the counterpane itself. When he told me to kiss her I was afraid to do it — for all the ghostly stories which the servants had told me about the dead rushed upon my mind, and it was not until father told me that death was but a long *sleep*, and tried otherwise to soothe my mind, that I ventured, crying and terrified, to put one kiss on that cold cheek. There is something so awful in death that it impresses even a child so young as to be entirely ignorant of its true nature — and feelings with which that scene inspired me never left my mind. After leaving the room, I was dressed in my best clothes, and put in a carriage, which wheeled along in a slow and solemn way to her last resting-place; when they had covered her with the sod, we came away mournful and sad, though I could hardly comprehend the reason *why*; perhaps it was the departed spirit of my dear mother hovering over me, that impressed me so powerfully. Every new year of my life has made me more and more conscious of the extent of this my early loss.[9]

Johnny's suffering in this scene becomes much more comprehensible and horrific, and the narrative choices of the autobiography much more puzzling, when we consider what he told Anna Hope, the *Independent* reporter, of his mother's death: "My real mother would have been alive now, I think, if my father hadn't drunk so much. When he was drunk he used to quarrel with her, and beat her. When she died she was all black and sore where he had beaten her, *and she died*."[10] If Johnny was not lying to Hope, then when he stood beside the body of his dead mother, the hand of her murderer was on his shoulder. It is hard to imagine how Johnny or W.B.D. — both of whom otherwise show so little aversion to melodrama — could have chosen to pass up so potent a detail. It is also hard to imagine why they chose to suppress Johnny's father's early drunkenness and brutality when it would seem to make the whole future course of Johnny's hard life so much more credible and sad.

It is possible that Johnny and his editor thought this early brutality was too much for refined readers to take, especially if those readers were to believe in Johnny's persistent innocence. And it is certainly true that Victorian readers would not have had much difficulty believing in a man's fall from perfect virtue. This was, after all, a commonplace of sentimental literature of the time, to say nothing of being an eminently familiar paradigm from scripture. Johnny's dating of the onset of his father's drinking to his remarriage, "after remaining some years a widower," also corresponded to well-worn clichés about evil stepmothers and the sin of infidelity even to a dead spouse.

The collaborative fictionalization of Johnny's life and character in these early pages of his autobiography promoted bad child welfare policy, first of all, by reemphasizing the distinction between the "deserving" and the "undeserving" poor. The reader was encouraged to sympathize with Johnny because he maintained perfect middle-class virtue in the midst of all his troubles, and the natural consequence of the reader's sympathy was to make the poor children who were less well spoken and devout (the vast majority) seem less deserving of sympathy and aid. The whitewashing of Johnny's character also understated the severity of urban poverty by making it seem that only the constitutionally weak-willed were damaged by it. The real tragedy, and the problem most in need of redress, was the fact that children who might have been happy and productive members of society were made bitter, vengeful, and self-destructive by the dreadful conditions in which they grew up. Johnny's portrayal also oversimplified the solution to the problems of poor children. All he seemed to need was a bit of education, or an upright foster parent, and he would be well on his way to becoming a respectable member of the bourgeoisie. In reality, solving the problems of the majority of slum children required a much broader effort that supported their communities, birth families, and, when removal was unavoidable, their foster families as well. And finally, Johnny's autobiography grossly misrepresented the sort of child helped and sent west by the CAS. In various ways all of these misrepresentations — perpetrated by do-gooder adults and their favorite child beneficiaries — would provoke the criticisms and reforms that ultimately ended the orphan train era.

As much as Johnny's stepmother fits the classic fairy-tale mold, it is only after she comes on the scene that Johnny's story begins to feel compellingly authentic and offers us a vision of the harsh experiences that were all too common among CAS children.

On her first day at the Morrow house, the stepmother gave each child a shilling and seemed sincerely to want to be a good mother to them all. It was not long, however, before she became indifferent to the children, and finally — once she bore a child of her own — positively abusive.

Her relations with her husband fared little better. He was often away from home at night, "carousing with a few companions, spending in this way much of his hard-earned money." Soon the stepmother herself became such an inveterate whiskey drinker that she "neglected entirely her household duties, left the table in disorder, the cow un-milked, the children uncared-for, and indeed often entertained carousing friends against father's will."

In a desperate attempt to alleviate this situation, the father sold his house and most of his possessions for 700 guineas and moved his family (except for the two oldest brothers, who remained at Royal Blue Coat Hospital in Dublin) to New York City. He also brought along a serving girl whose passage he paid and who thus was bound to the family until she could work off the cost of her ticket.

Things did not go well for the Morrows in their new home. What with the father's drinking and the vicissitudes of the economy, he could not hold a job for more than a few weeks. The stepmother took in sewing but was barely able to cover even her own expenses. By the end of six months the family's savings were all gone and they were living on the edge of starvation.

At first Johnny and Annie were sent to a local school, but only until their father noticed a neighbor carrying in a bundle of firewood collected at the docks and decided that there were more productive ways his children could spend their time than in learning to read and write. Annie (no older than six) was set to do sewing with her mother, while Johnny (only seven or eight) hobbled around the docks, gathering up the twigs and chips left behind after piles of firewood were loaded onto steamers.

Annie's earnings and the money saved by the acquisition of free fuel did little to improve the family's situation because it all went into brandy. Every evening the father and stepmother would send one of the children to the distillery for a bottle and then spend the rest of the night drinking. On good days the brandy would lead only to carousing and lewd behavior. But with dreadful frequency the drink would result in a fraying of tempers that culminated in the stepmother or the children being beaten by the enraged father.

The family got a brief respite when the father found a job as a carpenter in the village of Yorkville, some five or six miles north of their home at Fortieth Street and Tenth Avenue. Because public transportation was so expensive and slow, the father slept five nights a week at a Yorkville boardinghouse and was only home from Saturday afternoon until Monday morning. The cost of dual lodgings left the family hardly any money to spend on food, but the children at least felt that, with five peaceful nights a week, their lives had definitely improved.

This job didn't last, however, nor did the next, and once again the Morrows were on the edge of starvation. Things became so desperate that they sold a fifty-dollar feather bed for a mere six dollars and moved from their already decidedly humble apartment to a single cellar room on Forty-fourth Street, the typical last stop before homelessness during that era, and a standard abode of CAS clientele.

Johnny described their new home in detail:

The whole of our family, seven[11] in number, were occupying the same room, for this was all that father at this time was able to rent. Its size was about thirty feet by twenty; in one corner there stood a good-sized and plain bedstead, made of hemlock by my father, and it was mounted by a bed stuffed with chaff. This had to accommodate five of us children — Annie, William, Mary Jane, Margaret Ann, and myself. To stow away so many in one bed, it was necessary to arrange it so that three slept at the head and two at the foot, packed together very much like sardines in a box. And though we sometimes had trouble in our crowded night-colony, on account of those at one end getting more than their share of the bed-clothes, at the expense of those at the other, yet, on the whole, we got along peaceably and comfortably. In the opposite corner, across the room, was a five-dollar bedstead, containing a good soft bed, in which my father and step-mother slept, together with my newly born brother, Jonathan.

In one of the remaining corners, there stood a carpenter's bench, at which my father had sometimes made little wooden stools, for the use of ladies while they were at church, or while sewing at home; and which I used to sell for from twelve to fifteen cents apiece (being several cents more than they cost), and on some days, when father had been very industrious, and had made twenty-four of them, we had done pretty well in our earnings; but now he had neglected this source of support. The rest of the room was taken up by a plain table, three chairs, two benches, and a few other very humble articles of furniture.

As Johnny indicated in this passage, he had taken up the occupation of street peddler sometime around the age of ten. This new career began one day when he attempted to steal a large board lying on the ground and was caught by the board's owner and caned on the legs until he bled.

That night he told his father that he was done with stealing but averted a second beating by suggesting that he could make more than enough money to buy the fuel by selling matches on the street. After hearing the mathematics of the deal, Johnny's father decided that he liked it and gave him twenty-five cents with which to capitalize the new venture.

The following morning, his basket on his arm, Johnny walked down to a match factory outlet on Twenty-ninth Street that was run by two Germans. At least fifty match girls and boys — and nearly an equivalent number of adults — bought their wares wholesale from this shop. With his quarter, Johnny bought ninety-seven bunches of matches to sell for a penny each.

He spent the remainder of the day walking down street after street, knocking at every door he passed and holding up his basket to display his wares to whomever might answer. Most people just shook their heads and slammed the door in his face. Nevertheless, by the end of the day he had sold all of his matches and had been given five cents besides. He bought two cakes for himself on the way home and turned over a whole dollar to his father. The old man was astounded. He heaped Johnny with praise, calling him "My big son!" and "My best and most dutiful son!" He even sent Annie out for brandy that he made into a punch so that he could treat Johnny to a celebratory glass.

If Johnny thought that his success as a peddler would mark a turning point in his relations with his father and in his family's finances, he was due for disappointment. At least half of the money he brought in was spent, not on fuel, but on drink. And it was a rare night that he would escape a scolding or a beating for not having brought home more. Most days he got neither breakfast nor supper and ate only if his customers were charitably disposed.

Shortly after the commencement of Johnny's new career, word came that his elder brothers, James and Robert, had arrived from Dublin. James, who was seventeen, had gotten a job in a grocery store paying $4 a week, and Robert, fifteen, was working in a brass foundry for $2.50 weekly. As soon as their father heard the news, he went out looking for them in the hope that he could induce them to move in with him and help support the family. Both boys knew their father well enough to resist his pleas and threats, and he returned home furious, declaring that Johnny had to work extra hard to compensate for the income that would not be coming in.

After about a month Robert lost his job and joined the family in their cramped abode. He and Johnny went into partnership, selling picture books in addition to matches, and bringing home between one and two dollars a day. Although Annie and their stepmother were still stitching shirts for a tradesman downtown, it was only, at least on the stepmother's part, in the most desultory fashion — and even in the best of circumstances, needlework earned women little more than pocket change. Because their father, it seemed, was now entirely incapable of holding a job, for most of a year Johnny and Robert were virtually the sole support of the family. After a while, William and Jane, who were only seven and five, also began peddling. But then, finally, James rescued the family by moving in and paying for his board. While this extra money eased the Morrows' hardship, it also allowed the father and stepmother to indulge more heavily in drink, which only made the atmosphere within that one room — now shared by ten — more intolerable.

One Sunday morning a few months after he had come to live at home, James was sitting by the fire reading a dime novel entitled *Claude Duval, the Dashing Highwayman.* In what Johnny described as "a sudden streak of morality," their father leaped out of bed, snatched the book from his son's hands, and berated him for reading such trash on the Lord's day. That was the end of it for James, who, calling his father a drunken sot, paid his board in full and left the house, never to return.

Shortly before this, Robert had apprenticed himself to a machinist. He would begin work early in the morning and did not come home until late at night. At the end of every week he would give his father his entire salary. One week, however, he stopped on his way home to buy a much-needed pair of shoes. When his father saw the shoes and noticed that seven shillings (roughly eighty-eight cents) was missing from the pay envelope, he flew into a rage and kicked Robert out of the house. For a while Robert lived quite happily at a boardinghouse where he paid a weekly rent of $2.50. At the end of the week he went to collect his wages, only to be told by his master that his father had already claimed them — an act that, by law, was the right of a father whose child was not yet of age.

Without his wages, Robert had no money with which to pay his rent or buy food, and no choice but to move back in with his hated father. In despair he wandered down by the docks, where he happened to see a schooner just casting off. At the last instant Robert jumped on board and asked the captain whether he didn't want an extra hand. The captain simply told Robert to "fall to" — and thus began a new career on the sea.

Johnny was very lonely without his older brothers. He would see each of them only one time more during the remainder of his life. But their escape began to give him ideas.

One day Johnny and Willie's father sent them out to steal carrots from the docks. "[W]hen we were getting them," Anna Hope quoted Johnny as saying, "we saw a Dutchman coming after us with two dogs. We threw down the carrots and ran as fast as we could, and got away. That night we didn't go home."

They spent two or three nights away, sleeping in a parked stagecoach, and lived by peddling and begging. Then one day when they were bathing in the Hudson River, they were spotted by their father. Johnny, who could barely run, was caught instantly, but Willie got away. His father promised Johnny that if he could convince Willie to come back, neither of them would be punished. Johnny called out to his brother, and the three returned home, where the promise was immediately broken. "[S]tripping our backs of clothing," Johnny reported in his book, their father beat them

> with a piece of clothes-line till the blood came trickling down. We promised him that if he would leave off this punishment, we would not

run away again, but that if he did *not*, we would seize the first chance to escape from him. But this declaration only irritated him the more, and increased the weight of the blows. We kept our word. We ran away at the first good chance that we found.

That chance came a few days later when they were sent to collect money from a woman who had bought some chairs from them on credit. Their father had told them not to come home without the money, and when the woman would not pay up, they took him at his word. They spent the next few nights sleeping on the seats in the gentlemen's cabin of the Fulton ferry, which made a three-stop run between Manhattan, Brooklyn, and Jersey City and cost them only four cents each to get on. Having accumulated a fair sum through begging and by selling matches, illustrated books, pocket knives, and purses, they decided to see whether they could stay at a boardinghouse run by a Mrs. Moore on Thirty-eighth Street. The landlady was apparently quite astonished to have two such young (or at least small) children asking to board with her (Johnny was about thirteen and Willie was nine), but she agreed, provided they gave her seven dollars in advance — enough to cover three weeks' residency. As this was nearly all the money they had, they gave it up reluctantly but managed to abide quite contentedly at the house until a Sunday evening, three days after their arrival. They were sitting in the parlor in the middle of their tea when their landlady opened the door and their father rushed into the room. Apparently she had sent for him in secret, seeing a way to turn a tidy profit as well as do what was only right, considering their age. In scant seconds, crusts of bread still in their mouths, the boys found themselves out on the street, being hurried home to another flogging.

Two or three weeks later Johnny and Willie were once again on the Fulton ferry, heading to Brooklyn where they hoped they might have better luck with their peddling and begging than they had had in Manhattan. During the ride a gentleman took pity on them because they were barefoot and gave Johnny a $2.50 gold piece. Having never seen such a coin in his life, Johnny assumed it was only a brass dime and thanked the gentleman accordingly. It was only later that night, when the coin was rejected by the ticket collector on the Eighth Avenue streetcar, that Johnny began to understand his mistake.

Their father was utterly delighted when the boys brought the coin home and celebrated by immediately sending round to the distillery for a gallon of brandy. The following morning man and wife were dead drunk in bed and Johnny went out to purchase breakfast with five cents of the other money he had gathered the previous day. While the children were eating, their father woke up and asked where they had gotten the food. On hearing Johnny's explanation, he said, "It's a nice thing of you to be spending *my* money that way!" When Johnny insisted that the money was his own, his father grew so enraged that he had what was called a "brandy fit."

In his autobiography Johnny described his father as flying into an astonishingly violent tantrum, during which he not only beat Johnny and the other children but kicked and smashed everything in the room that crossed his path. Johnny didn't actually employ the term "fit" in his autobiography. The term comes from Anna Hope, in whose rendering of the events — which ostensibly only reproduced Johnny's words — this "fit" seems something close to epilepsy: "[H]e went around the room like a top, and then he fell on the floor, with his teeth tight shut together. His hands were clenched, and he shook all over, and then he looked up as if he were dead." Whatever actually happened, the enraged man did finally fall back into his bed and, exhausted and still drunk, was instantly unconscious.

Some weeks before this, Johnny had run into an urban missionary on the street who had asked him to attend his Sunday school and had given him a three-cent piece as an incentive. With his father's permission, Johnny had gone to the school and heard the story of Lazarus and the rich man, which fascinated him. But he was more impressed by the gentleness and refinement of the missionaries and got the first inkling of the notion that would soon take hold of him so powerfully: that through studying the Bible and emulating the *gentle*men, he might find a way to escape his miserable poverty.

He soon grew to see attendance at Sunday school as his deserved reward after a week of hard work. On the Sunday of his father's brandy fit he asked his stepmother — who had, of course, been awakened by the fit — whether he might go to Sunday school, and she told him, "You're a pretty looking fellow to go to Sunday school, with such clothes!" Permission was denied and none of Johnny's arguments made a difference.

He contained his fury at that time, but that evening, when Annie was being mocked by some boys on the street as she washed the ashes out of a pail of cinders in order to save everything burnable, and his

stepmother asked him why the boys were being so cruel, all of his in-
dignation poured out.

> I am sure I don't know; *you* ought to know better than *I,* for you are in
> the house all the year round, and do nothing but sit at the fire helping
> father to drink all that we earn! You don't care *where* or *how* we get it,
> so long as we bring you this money, for which we have to slave from
> morning till night! You need not hope that it will be *always* so; for I am
> going to run away, and shall go where you will not be able to find me!
> Once every three weeks you carry to an office down town some shirts,
> made for you mostly by sister Annie; you get the money for them, and
> call it *your* earnings, and while you continue to scold us, you never
> cease to talk of *your earnings,* even after you have used up in drink all
> that you can possibly call yours, and then, for the next three weeks,
> have to depend on our little daily sales for your support and your
> *drink!*[12]

At this point Johnny's father reared out of bed, shouting, "I have
heard every word!" He picked up a stick, slammed it down hard on the
table, and declared, "I will teach you how to use your tongue towards
her, sir!" He flew at Johnny with the stick, striking, kicking, and
punching him, until the boy begged to be murdered so that he would
no longer have to endure the pain. Relenting at last, his father threw
him into bed and left him alone.

The following morning William, Janie, and Johnny ran away. In the
evening Janie went to the station house to sleep, while her brothers
spent a couple of nights in a grocery man's coal box, and yet another
on the Fulton ferry, where a kindly deckhand let them sleep in the en-
gine room. But on their fourth night away from home Johnny decided
to follow through on a plan he had had in mind for some time.

In all likelihood, Johnny and Willie had passed the *Sun* building many
times on their trips to and from the Fulton ferry, and perhaps had
seen the sign announcing the existence of the Newsboys' Lodging
House. Or perhaps Johnny had noticed clusters of ragged, barefoot
boys "chaffing" one another on the sidewalk outside or consuming
their griddle cakes and coffee in the Nassau Café in the *Sun* building's basement. Or maybe it was his Sunday school teacher who told
him about this nonpenalizing refuge for homeless boys. In any event,

after dark on their fourth night away from home, sometime in late 1854 or early 1855, Johnny and Willie climbed five flights of stairs until they came to a wooden door with a large, frosted-glass panel, through which they could detect the ocher flicker of a solitary gas lamp. "Opening the door," Johnny wrote:

> I walked up to the desk, and inquired of the gentleman who seemed to preside, "Is this the place for boys to sleep who haven't got a father or mother?" Mr. Tracy (for that was the name of the gentleman whom I addressed), answered, "Yes." Then I told him that we had neither father nor mother, and asked whether we might sleep there. I think that if he had looked hard at my face he could have seen that I was telling a lie, for I felt my guilty cheeks burn with shame! But he only inquired where we had been sleeping lately, and then gave us the permission which we wanted, on condition of our paying six cents apiece for the privilege, according to the rules of the establishment.

Johnny and Willie seem to have taken instantly to the lodging house and to the people they met there — both the staff and the other boys. They were so happy, in fact, that as Johnny described it, they began to feel uneasy: "There was a constant sense of guilt and shame resting on our minds; we had got a comfortable home, and the kindest of friends, but to acquire these we had made use of a very wrong story, and the more cordial our new friends, the deeper did this arrow of guilt sink into our hearts."

The morning of the third or fourth day after their admission, Johnny finally summoned up the courage to confess.

> I went to Mr. Tracy's desk; he was writing, but in a moment or two laid down his pen, and looked at me inquiringly; I then said to him at once before my resolution should fade out: "Mr. Tracy, when I came here I told you a *lie*, and now I am sorry for it; I said that I had not any father or mother, but *I have*, and they drink so much brandy, and beat us so often that we could not live with them!" I went on to tell him the whole story. Mr. Tracy, instead of getting angry and driving us from the building with a command never to return, as we expected he would, said that he was sorry that we had deceived him, but was very glad we had confessed it; and from that day forward seemed a better friend than ever before.

This scene figures prominently in every document relating to Johnny (it even inspired the title for Anna Hope's article, "The Boy Who Confessed His Sin") and thus provides an excellent opportunity to see how CAS record keepers, even in their most private documents, wove in little fictions designed to prove to themselves as much as to others that their difficult work was truly good and effective. In most of the reports of Johnny's confession, the variations are only minor. Brace implied that Johnny resolved to confess only after hearing "some religious remarks" by Tracy. (Johnny never mentioned such remarks, although that doesn't mean he didn't hear them. Tracy was constantly sermonizing to the boys.) The most exaggerated and significant variation occurs in a May 30, 1855, entry in a Children's Aid Society "Record Book," the only one of the documents relating to Johnny absolutely *not* intended for public consumption. This passage is from the file of Johnny's sister, Annie, and represents more than half of the most extended comment made about her:

> Ann Eliza Morrow 12 Irish Orphan a sister of little Johnny, who has been staying at the Newsboy's Lodging house, and in whom Mr. Tracy and many others take such an interest. When he first appeared there, he told Mr. Tracy that he was an orphan, but a short time afterward he said laying his cheek to Mr. Tracy's, that he had told a lie, and was sorry for it. This ingenuousness, and frankness, endeared him the more.[13]

"[L]aying his cheek to Mr. Tracy's" — none of the other accounts of the confession include this detail, which not only makes Johnny seem considerably younger than his likely age of thirteen years but also makes his relationship with Tracy seem much more intimate and filial than it really was.

On their own, little fictions like this may seem insignificant, but when hundreds and thousands of them are considered together, they amount to an enormous fantasy that helped keep CAS workers from recognizing and eliminating the weaknesses of their program.

At six-thirty every morning one of Tracy's assistants marched through the dormitory of the Newsboys' Lodging House calling, "Up, boys, up!" and the forty or so residents rolled and clambered out of their bunk beds and headed straight for the washroom. Here, in several long sinks, they scrubbed their faces and hands and sometimes doused

their heads. And then, without so much as a crust of bread for breakfast, the boys were sent out onto the streets with their baskets to make
their livings as they could. The boys were not allowed back into the
lodging house until supper time. After the meal the tables and benches
were all turned around to face one side of the room and the dining
hall became a school, although boys who did not want to participate
in lessons were free to lounge in the dormitories.

Johnny was one of the newsboy scholars and, according to Brace,
"learned to read and write rapidly."[14] He also regularly attended
Sunday school at the Five Points Mission, where he was taught by a
theological student named Mr. Coffin.

Even before Johnny had consented to be interviewed by Anna Hope,
his "story" had earned him money on the streets and a warm place in
the hearts of those at the CAS. It was not until Anna Hope's article was
finally published, however, that Johnny's story began to dramatically
improve his life. Whatever its factual accuracy, the article could hardly
have been more flattering, portraying Johnny as industrious, frugal,
truthful, and calling him "good" and even "beautiful." He brought
the article to Coffin, who was so impressed that he offered Johnny a
bed in a corner of his own dormitory room at Union Theological
Seminary. Although Johnny made no mention of this fact, Brace reported that Coffin charged Johnny a dollar a week for the room and
board (considerably more than the seventy cents Johnny would have
spent weekly at the Newsboys' Lodging House). Brace presented the
move as part of Johnny's desire to be self-supporting and to get an education.

Johnny did not, however, have tremendous luck supporting himself
during his stay at the seminary. The impoverished students apparently
managed to get many of the items he sold from his own wholesalers,
and so he never did more than middling business.[15] But his education
was a whole other matter. No longer restricted to an hour or two of
classes in the evening, he now attended public school every weekday
from nine until three and afterward would not only sell his wares on
the quadrangle but also discuss with the students what Brace called
"abstruse theological questions," some relating to his own experience.
For example: "Which is a greater sin, to lie or to steal?"[16]

The Newsboys' Lodging House journal offers several glimpses of
Johnny during this period, one of which is particularly interesting be-

cause of what it shows both about his intellectual aspirations and about the condescending admiration of its author:

> I saw Johnny Morrow today at the Seminary. He looks very delicate, and his cheeks have a transparent appearance which gives him an angelic likeness. His soft gentle voice sounds so sweetly too, that the accents sink into the heart. "Are you getting better Johnny?" "Oh! yes — but I am sick today, and I am going to take a walk while the sun shines — my foot is bad yet, but I am not so lame as I was." "Why don't you come see us at the Lodging-House — Mr. Tracy loves to see you." "I don't have time or I would — I like to see Mr. Tracy too — had ye a good anniversary"[17] "Yes — a very good time of it" — "I have a nice room here, and I can read when I have a mind. I am reading the Pilgrim's Progress. That is a very good book, and it reads nice. I followed Christian all the way along, and I thought it was very entertaining about the giants and the enchantments — that Milton was a great author wasn't he?" — "Yes Johnny, but he was not the author of the Pilgrim's Progress" — "Well I thought he was; — and as the author's life wasn't at the beginning of the book I couldn't correct the mistake — and who was the author?" "Have you never heard of John Bunyan?" "Oh! yes, now I recollect — and it was John Bunyan composed that book — Milton couldn't do it better — it reads like the bible — wasn't John Bunyan a tinker?" — "Yes, and wrote his great work under great disadvantages — his own life you will find as deeply interesting as the Pilgrim's Progress." "I will get it from one of the students," said Johnny — "I will walk about the square[18] now while the sun shines — what a pity it is one can't see much green about the fields or trees yet. How I long for the warm sunshine of Spring; but this is a pleasant day, and I feeling like Christian when he was drawing near the happy land, the sun is shining so brightly."[19]

There is no question that Johnny Morrow was a remarkably determined, intelligent, and perhaps even good young man. However much the chroniclers of his life — including Johnny himself — may have slanted their portrayals to make him seem the ideal self-reliant and devout street boy, he would never have attracted so much attention had he not possessed real virtues and had he not seemed truly to justify his chroniclers' fondest hopes. The fantasies that supported the CAS's work were never wholly spun from the imagination.

Willie, on the other hand, never inspired the admiration and affection of CAS employees that his older brother did. When he was referred to in CAS journals, it was only as "a brother of little lame Johnny."[20] Nothing bad was said of him, but no one at the CAS seemed to find anything to praise either. Willie remained at the Newsboys' Lodging House after Johnny moved to the seminary, and he seemed to have no other aspirations than to keep himself fed and in pocket money.

One morning, after Johnny had been at the seminary about a month, Willie came by to stock up on books to peddle. Johnny gave him five dollars' worth. The younger lad went off to try his luck — and had precious little.

At eleven o'clock that night Willie was still out on the street trying to dispose of his stock when, as Johnny described it, he was "pounced" upon by the Metropolitan Police. The police charged Willie with vagrancy, but Johnny believed that they really arrested him as a favor to a man for whom Willie had refused to sell pen-holders. Being only nine or ten years old, he was taken first thing the following morning to the Nursery Department of the House of Refuge on Randall's Island.

Johnny found out his little brother was missing only when, after not seeing him for two or three weeks, he went to the lodging house to check up on him. No one there had seen Willie for at least as long as Johnny, and no one had a clue as to what might have happened to him. After several days' search, Johnny finally met a street kid named "Yankee" who had seen Willie being transferred from one station house to another. On this evidence, Johnny took the Third Avenue streetcar uptown and caught the ferry to Randall's Island where, at last, he was reunited with his younger brother.

Apparently on the advice of Coffin, Johnny decided that it was neither safe nor good for Willie to remain on the streets of New York, and he asked his friends at the Children's Aid Society to secure Willie's release and put him on a train west. On October 23, 1855, Willie left in the company of Reverend C. C. Townsend and managed to attain, the CAS told Johnny, "a comfortable situation with a barber" in Iowa City.

Shortly after Willie's departure, Johnny was studying geography in his room at the seminary when he heard a knock at the door. Coffin's roommate answered, and then told Johnny that his stepmother had come to tell him that his father was dying. Assuming that she was trying to trick him into returning home, Johnny had the roommate send her away. But when she returned the next day with Annie, Johnny believed her story and agreed to return with her, but only if Coffin was allowed to accompany him.

They found Johnny's father lying desperately ill in the cramped and completely lightless cellar room. Johnny sent Janie out for candles, and when these had been lit, the ill man held out his hand. "Is that Johnny?" he asked. Johnny nodded, but could think of nothing to say. Finally Coffin asked Johnny's father what he wanted his son to do. "Whatever he thinks best for himself."

Seeing that the ill man was indeed not long for this world, Coffin performed the duties for which he was being trained. He and Johnny left the cellar room in the late evening, and by three in the morning the old man was dead. He had no funeral and was buried by convicts in Potters Field.

Shortly after their father's death, Annie came again to Johnny's room at the seminary. Confessing that their stepmother "did not use her exactly right," she asked whether he might arrange for her to be sent west. Johnny brought her into the CAS office, where the entry already quoted was made on May 30, 1855, but before she could be placed, her sister Janie was severely beaten by the stepmother and Johnny spirited her out of the house and put her straight onto an orphan train. For reasons that remain unclear, Annie did not go west for nearly a year after her first contact with the CAS.

In his autobiography Johnny said that Annie "succeeded in finding a place in a good family, where she is now living happily, and with improvement to herself." But CAS records show that Johnny was, at the very least, vastly oversimplifying his sister's fate. Although he implies that Annie had simply been sent west, she had in fact first been placed with a Geo. H. Nelden in Newton, New Jersey. The only notation in the CAS "Record Book" regarding this placement is: "Jan 7 1856 Arrived safely gives satisfaction." The next notation, dated eight months later, says simply: "Has since returned and found a good home in the city." No explanation was given as to why she left her previous home, and nothing whatsoever was said about her new placement, other than that it was a "good home" — which only makes the next entry more puzzling: "Has been sent West by C. C. Townsend see No 5 Page 412."

The reference to the fifth volume of the "Record Book" tells us that, for some reason, when Annie was to be sent west, she was processed as if she had never had anything to do with the CAS. Double- and even triple-entering of children into the record books was fairly common in the early days of the CAS, and makes it quite difficult to track down some children — no doubt for CAS workers in the past as well as for present-day researchers. The bleak entry on page 412 gives no indication that anyone knew Annie was Johnny's sister, nor that there was already a record started for her:

1857
Nov 18
Ann Eliza Morrow 14 years of age American Protestant Shirt maker and all plain sewing can do housework cant cook or wash has a step-mother at No 707–47 Street can read & write cant pay any part of her fare will work it out.

Once again, we find no explanation of what happened at her previous placement, although there is a nearly illegible scribble reading: "Brought to [or "by"?] Mr. Knight[ly?]."

As it turns out, however, the CAS *had* recorded an explanation of how Annie came to leave her supposed "good home" in the city, but no one looking at her official record would have had any idea that it existed. It can be found — not insignificantly — in an entry about Johnny from William Colopy Desmond's CAS office journal:

July 10th 1857. I was returning from the Boy's Meeting on Sunday afternoon, and was passing the Seminary, when I was hailed by "Little Johnny," who was sitting on the steps, enjoying the freshness of the evening in the shade. He was not so pale as when I had before seen him. His features were animated, and his health is evidently improved. He inquired after Mr. Macy very warmly.

"Well how do you get along Johnny?" "Pretty well now — I have given up much study for awhile as I think it is better to make money. I'll tell you why. When I have gathered some money I can then go in for educating myself — that's what I am thinking of," and his countenance grew brighter while he spoke with the gentle voice for which he is so remarkable. "And how are you making money, Johnny? What is the means you use to pile the quarters?" "O, I can do many things — you must know I work as a carpenter — I do all the mending about the seminary. When the furniture is broken, I have my hammer, and my chisel, and my saw. There are a few ways of making a few dimes that I try — Beside those I keep boarders." "In the seminary?" "Yes, you must know some of the students patronize me very kindly. I want to make money so that I may educate myself.

"I went to see little Annie a few days ago," continued Johnny. "I went to the woman in ———— street with whom she lived. I couldn't rest from thinking of Annie for I was always fonder of Annie than of anybody else. Mrs ———— met me with a very angry face, and when I asked after little Annie, she burst out crying, and said bitterly, 'I wish the d—— had her before ever I saw her the nasty slut. I have a sad heart on account of her this day.' I was frightened at this and I cried out, 'Oh! I hope nothing has happened to poor Annie,' and she shouted, 'I wish I could lay my ten fingers on her. I'd pay her for killing my child.' I trembled all over when I heard her speak this way.

"The woman went to Brooklyn or New Jersey to see some friends, and in her absence, Annie let the child out of her sight, and one of the cars[21] ran over her, and she was killed. Annie cleared out, as soon as she heard of this frightful accident, and I was in great trouble about it. I went to the house to look for her for I longed very much to see her, but my troubles were only increased by this step.

"As soon as mother[22] saw me she flew at me, and drove me away, calling out to the neighbors all round to have a care of their children; for that I was coming to kidnap them. She would have struck me if I wasn't quick. A crowd got together, and they looked surprised that a small boy like me should be such a dangerous body. Some of them spoke to me half kindly, half scoldingly, so I got away as quietly as I could. They shan't have Annie though. I will have her away out of that place, for I din't want to have the poor girl ruined. I will call on Mr. Macy in a day or two," he said as I bade him good bye, "to consult with him about it, and to know from him if he has heard anything from my brother. I intend to go West very soon."[23]

Annie Morrow's entries show clearly how haphazard a record-keeping system the Children's Aid Society had in the early days. Detailed records were kept about certain favorites (like Johnny), whose stories it was thought would provide engaging reading in the society's annual reports. But even these records were not particularly coherent, since they included only the most entertaining, sad, or inspiring stories about these children and there was no cross-referencing of any sort. Run-of-the-mill children, as Annie had certainly become by her second record, received only cryptic, telegraphic entries that seemed designed to jog the memories of people already concerned with their cases rather than to give new workers a clear sense of what had happened to the child, and what the child needed.

Both of Annie's entries are, in fact, exceptionally long. The first, with its adoring description of Johnny laying his cheek against Tracy's, goes on to detail the family's situation — the father's drinking and death, and Johnny's bringing Annie to the society. The second, with its catalog of Annie's capacities, or lack thereof, is one of several entries in a row made in a handwriting that never appears in the "Record Books" again; all of these entries are equally gloomy and portray the children only as job prospects. Indeed, most of the entries from this era do little more than note how the child came to the CAS (for example, "from Brooklyn," or, "from Randall's Island") before devolving into a list of placements and the responses, if any, to letters.

This system, which assumed that CAS staff would easily remember the most important things about the children whose cases were recorded, was devised by a man who was antiformalist and believed that personal relationships mattered most in charity. It was a system that was already overwhelmed by its fourth year of operation. In 1857, when Annie was sent to Iowa, 741 other children rode the orphan trains and a total of 2,748 children had been placed by the CAS since its founding.[24] This volume was way beyond what a staff of twenty (which had already experienced turnover) could be expected to keep track of without detailed records, especially when the workers often had not known much about the children under their care in the first place.

The system was slow to change for a few reasons. First, there was no precedent for detailed record keeping. Prior to the massive population expansion of the nineteenth century, charities had rarely had to deal with such large numbers of people, and those that had done so primarily doled out aid on a case-by-case basis and had not entered into a long-term custodial relationship with their beneficiaries. Like other emerging social work institutions, it took the CAS a while to figure out what information about the children it cared for was truly necessary. When communication and transportation restrictions made it impossible to micromanage even placements a few miles away, there seemed to be little purpose in keeping track of the vicissitudes of a child's emotional state. The assumption was that the CAS would intervene only in a crisis; otherwise, it would devote itself to the necessary work it was actually able to do, like finding homes and jobs for more children.

Money entered into the question too. It was hard to justify spending scant funds on a large staff of field agents to gather detailed information when it was not clear that such information was necessary.

And finally, the Children's Aid Society did not see itself as having a parental or nurturing relationship with its charges. Parenting was the preserve only of birth and foster parents. When an institution tried to be nurturing, it not only would be inefficient but would encourage pauperism and dependency. From the beginning, Brace saw the CAS as simply providing a chance at a better life to independent contractors, no matter how young they might be. The assumption was that if children got into trouble, it was up to them either to contact the CAS or to take care of the problem themselves — often by running away. That was what independence was all about.

The result of all these beliefs and limitations was an incoherent filing system that was prone, on the one hand, to treat emigrant companies as if they were merely shipments of widgets and, on the other, to include irrelevant anecdotes about endearing brothers and the like. In its inefficiency as much as its sentimentality, the system well served the hard-pressed CAS staff's need to believe the best about its work.

The reluctance of the record keepers to recognize the significance of the facts they themselves recorded is positively dumbfounding at times. The first notation after Annie's western placement, for example, was a February 22, 1858, report from the Reverend Mr. Townsend stating that Annie's "employer" represented her as "having taken an unprofitable course." No explanation was given as to what this "unprofitable course" might have been, or whether Townsend thought there was any merit to the man's assertion, or what ought to be done about it. The next entry, a month later, said only that Annie was "doing well." And the next, nine months after that, said that *"Anna is at the Home of Industry and much improved."*[25] No mention was made of why she had to leave her placement, or why she ended up in what was either an almshouse or juvenile prison. The record keepers were so fixated on writing only *good* news that they seem incapable of recognizing the obvious fact that orphan train placement was *not* serving Annie well. And as a result of this blindness, the CAS was less likely both to give Annie the help she really needed and to modify the Emigration Plan so that it served all children better.

The last entry under Annie's name in volume 5 of the "Record Book" is an utterly noncommittal jotting that on August 28, 1861, she was living in Tipton, Iowa. Then, for no clear reason, we are referred back to Annie's original entry in volume 4 for the final notation in her file: on March 22, 1865, Townsend wrote saying that she had married. Despite the fact that the lives of Annie's own mother and stepmother, to say nothing of thousands of other battered and abandoned women with whom the CAS came into contact, were not significantly improved by marriage, matrimony was always seen as the ultimate proof of success for female orphan train riders.

Johnny did not follow through on his intention of going west for nearly a year. Instead, he moved from New York to New Haven, where he attended public school and lived with a friend from Union Theological Seminary who was studying at Yale's Divinity School.

By the summer of 1858, however, Johnny had run too short of money to continue his education and decided to make his trip west, both to visit his siblings — especially Willie, whom he had not heard from in nearly nine months — and to raise cash by peddling his wares at a substantial markup to all those affluent and generous farmers he had been reading about in CAS propaganda. Interestingly, he chose to travel with an orphan train party from the Five Points Mission rather than the CAS — which may indicate that he already had an inkling of what would happen when he finally saw his brother.

By accompanying the Five Points party, Johnny was able to get to Chicago for seven dollars — half the regular fare. From Chicago, he traveled one day and one night by train to Iowa City, where the first thing he did was visit Annie. This was during the period when, according to the CAS file, she was "doing well," but was still with the man who thought she had taken an "unprofitable course." In his book Johnny confirmed that she was in "a very comfortable home" and, like the CAS file, gave no indication of why she would end up in the House of Industry only six months later.

To find Willie, Johnny had to travel a mile or two out of town to visit the Reverend C. C. Townsend. The house was deep in the woods and not easy to find. When Johnny finally arrived on the doorstep, he was led by a servant into a tiny office where Townsend was sitting at his desk. The Children's Aid Society's lone western agent greeted Johnny enthusiastically but gave him the bad news that his brother was no longer with the barber in Iowa City, but 120 miles further west, in what he called "Fort Desmoines." Despite being the state capital, Des Moines was not yet on a railroad line and could be reached only by a three-day stagecoach ride.

Traveling by stagecoach in the mid-nineteenth century was a lot like tumbling down a bluff inside a trunk. When the roads were not rivers of mud, they were deeply rutted and full of rocks, and the coaches had no real suspension. Wheels were constantly slamming into or out of sudden declivities, and passengers were constantly ramming their heads against the coach's lightly padded walls. Matters were not helped by the fact that the drivers made frequent stops for refreshment at the taverns arrayed at regular intervals all along the way. Also, the stages did not stop at night, so passengers had somehow to cling onto sleep while periodically being propelled into one another's laps.

Johnny spent two nights and three full days in the coach. Among his four traveling companions was a Mr. D——, who had heard him tell his life story at the hotel in Chicago and asked him to repeat it for the benefit of their fellow passengers. Johnny agreed with obligatory humility — amplified within his published retelling of substantially the same tale by the assertion that he had succeeded in interesting his companions only because "the driest original thing told to a weary stage-traveller is acceptable even when it would not be elsewhere; — as it helps to while away the time."

In Des Moines Johnny found out just how little Townsend had known about his brother's situation. Willie was not living with the man Townsend had sent him to, but this man was able to direct Johnny to his brother's new abode two miles out of town — a journey that Johnny, lame and carrying his luggage, had to make through heavy rain and deep mud.

When at last Johnny saw Willie, for the first time in two years, he found him "much taller than when I had seen him last, much darker in complexion, and very scantily clothed, showing marks of having had a rough time of it; but he was strong and healthy in appearance." Willie was now thirteen and, as Johnny put it, had "changed employers a number of times." He had lived mostly in Iowa, but also in Kansas and Wisconsin, and had worked as a *"peddler,* newsboy, errand-boy, farmer-boy, servant, and then school-boy again." This list of occupations is quite at variance with how the CAS portrayed the typical orphan train rider's experience. Only three of his jobs — errand-boy, farmer-boy, and servant — actually required an "employer," and only the latter two seem likely to have provided Willie with room and board, to say nothing of clothing. And the jobs of newsboy, peddler, and even errand-boy were just the sort of thing Willie had done back home in New York, and by no means justified his removal by the orphan trains. Perhaps this was what he and Johnny were thinking when they decided he should return east.

After making stops at the tailor and shoemaker to improve Willie's scanty attire, the two brothers went to catch the early stagecoach. Along the way they ran into Mr. D——, who "kindly slipped a dollar into my hand to help me on my journey." Thanks to heavy rain and a baby who had to have a still stagecoach for a few hours' nap, the return trip to Iowa City took the better part of four days. From Iowa they journeyed to Canton, Illinois, to visit Janie, telling their story to conductors who rewarded them with free passage.

In his book, Johnny reported that Janie was happy in her new home, and in this case he was probably telling the truth, if for no other reason than that this was the only one of his siblings' placements he bothered to describe in more than a single euphemistic phrase. "Jane was staying with a nice old lady," he wrote,

and was treated very kindly. This lady made our visit quite pleasant, by introducing us to a little party of young girls, in whose company we had quite a frolicsome time of it, swinging, singing, picking apples, and engaging in many other sports that carried me back in memory to my early happy home, and furnished many pleasant thoughts to my mind. When the time came to leave this pleasant place, we felt sad, and almost wished that we could take up our abode in Canton with such good friends; but we bid Jane good-bye, . . . leaving her in tears at our departure.

The only disconcerting thing about Janie's placement is that the CAS seems to have known nothing about it. Her entry in the "Record Books" states only that she had been placed with a Mr. J. S. Langdon in Montrose, Pennsylvania. There is no mention of an old woman, or of

Canton, Illinois, or of any further placement, and no indication that any of John Macy's several letters to her were answered.

Johnny and Willie spent some time in Peoria replenishing their funds by peddling penknives, then went on — once more riding free through the charity of conductors — to Chicago, where they made the acquaintance of a Captain P—— and several of his friends. Not only did these people put them up in their homes and show them around the city, but when it was time to go they gave the brothers seventeen dollars and a railroad pass that ensured their free transportation back to New Haven.

&

On their way home Johnny and Willie passed through New York City and stopped to visit their mother and youngest sibling, Jonathan. No doubt because of a failure to pay her rent, she had moved yet again and was living in a garret on Seventeenth Street between Ninth and Tenth avenues. When the boys opened the door to these digs, their mother was, in Johnny's words,

> lying on the floor of a small room and was covered with an old shawl; we could not make out whether she was drunk or only tired. The only furniture in the room consisted of two chairs and a stove, while the floor was the only sleeping-place. My little brother Jonathan, now five years old, was living so wretchedly in this miserable place — half-fed, and not half-clothed — that I resolved to take him to better quarters.

In essence, Johnny kidnapped yet another of his siblings. But this time he did not take Jonathan to the CAS to be put on an orphan train. Rather, he and Willie bought him clothes and took him to live with them in New Haven.

This semireconstituted family moved into a room on Chapel Street, which they furnished with a bed, bedstead, table, chairs, and stove. While Johnny went out to earn their rent through peddling and begging, Willie stayed at home taking care of little Jonathan. Sadly, Willie was neither by experience nor disposition a competent baby-sitter. One day, only a week after their arrival, he grew tired of trying to keep his little brother in good spirits and decided that what Jonathan really needed was a nap. Jonathan did not share this opinion, however, and after he had escaped from bed several times, Willie tied him in with the sheets. Needless to say, Jonathan did not appreciate this stratagem and showed his displeasure by shouting at the top of his lungs, drawing tenants from every room in the house. Once they saw what was happening, they untied Jonathan and gave Willie a severe beating.

When Johnny got home about an hour later, the crowd outside his door would not let him in and accused him of cruelty. He ran off and got his friend the divinity student, but even in such company, he had difficulty making his case, "principally because of the presence," he said, "of a narrow-minded busy-body in the shape of a woman, who got the idea into her head that Jonathan was the son of respectable parents in some part of the country, who had been stolen by us and was being abused."

Although it seems that he and Willie were ultimately left alone with their little brother, it was now clear that their attempt to reconstruct their family was doomed to failure. They struggled on for an indeterminate amount of time, but in the end Jonathan was put into the New Haven Orphan Asylum, and Willie went back out west with a new orphan train.

The sales of *A Voice Among the Newsboys* brought Johnny enough money to pay off $300 worth of tuition at the New Haven Theological Seminary and meet some of his living expenses, but his royalties provided no lasting security. At the time of his death in early June 1861, a year after the book's publication, Johnny was found to have only a few pennies and an IOU for three dollars from a newsboy in a purse under his pillow.[26]

Johnny died in Brooklyn, where he had recently undergone an operation on his knee. According to all observers, Johnny's leg kept him in constant pain — a fact that, characteristically, he never mentioned in his autobiography. When Anna Hope first caught sight of him, he was standing in front of a map, supporting himself on a cane, while Tracy showed him how to get to the office of a doctor who might take an interest in his leg.[27] When Johnny finally had his operation, in May 1861, he instructed the doctor to be "very thorough." No sooner had the operation finished than he asked whether he would still be lame. The doctor answered that in all probability he would. Brace reported Johnny's response: "'Well,' he said, his natural cheerfulness running over, though his body was yet quivering with the surgeon's knife, "taint so bad after all, for now when I want, I can limp and pass for half price on the railroad, or I can stretch up and be a big man!'"[28]

Johnny died, says Brace, because of "the very self-reliance, which had secured his success."[29] One morning he decided to save his doctor trouble by changing his bandage himself. In the process he accidentally opened his wound and bled to death.

Johnny Morrow ended *A Voice Among the Newsboys* with a description of a return visit to the Newsboys' Lodging House. He found it much changed, but chiefly by the absence of his old friends and Tracy, who now spent most of his time escorting the emigrant parties west. Just as he walked in the doors, he heard

> the well-known voice of Mr. Brace; he is making the boys a speech, and is telling them, for their encouragement, of a senator who was once a newsboy, and showing them that perseverance and industry can accomplish almost everything. The speech is through; I open the door and walk in; Mr. Brace gives me a friendly shake of the hand, and a kind word or two of encouragement; then taking his hat, leaves the room.

One of the most striking things about Johnny's little book is its ambivalence. On the one hand, it is potent testimony to the limits of what even the most industrious and persevering boy could do, and it provides ample evidence that the orphan trains were, at the very least, no sure solution to the problems of poor and vagrant children. On the other hand, Johnny seems to have had no hesitation about backing up Brace's claims — surely bogus if he was implying that his, at most, seven-year-old organization had produced a senator — by speculating that his absent friends from the lodging house will be heard from "one of these days, as great men who are helping to steer the SHIP OF STATE, or sitting behind judges' desks, or filling honored pulpits with heaven-blessed talent." By the end of this section of the book Johnny's advocacy of the orphan trains had reached heights of eulogistic delirium to which even Brace would have been hesitant to ascend:

> As the Indian vanishes toward the West, at the sound of the woodman's axe, and before the march of civilization, so vanishes the newsboy at the sound of the voices of good men, and before the march of intellectual culture, and although fresh newsboys rise up to take the places of the departed, still their numbers are growing less and less. Not less in the same way as the Indian, but "beautifully less"; not dying out as the

poor freedom-loving and slavery-hating Red man, but dying out of sin and wickedness; dying to the temptations of a large city, and going to enjoy a gentler life in the Western prairie, and a happy rural home.

It is tempting to believe that such passages and sentiments were purely the work of W.B.D. — the book's supposed editor. But while it is true that this last passage in particular hardly sounds like the work of a relatively untutored street kid, I think it would be a mistake to assume that Johnny's apparent faith in the works of the Children's Aid Society was all a sham perpetuated either by W.B.D. or by Johnny himself. Certainly Johnny's faith in the goodness of his friends and even in his own ability to transcend fate was exceedingly unusual, and this was part of the reason why it was attractive to the do-gooders at CAS, who — like do-gooders everywhere — often had difficulty believing they were in fact doing, or were themselves, good. But that does not mean that Johnny's faith was only deception or even self-deception. Although Johnny's life must be examined with a critical eye, it would be too easy to say cynically that such faith, sustained by so little, was only illusion and not also good, and a force for good. That would not do justice to the authentic virtues and victories of a former street kid whose hard life ended too soon.

𝒥𝒫 7

Happy Circle

Wherever we went . . . we found the children sitting at the same table with families, going to the school with the children, and every way treated as well as any other children. Some, whom we had seen once in the most extreme misery, we beheld, sitting, clothed and clean, at hospitable tables, calling the employer "Father!" loved by the happy circle, and apparently growing up with as good hopes and prospects as any children of the country.

— Charles Loring Brace, 1859[1]

IN TERMS OF scope and influence, the Emigration Plan of the Children's Aid Society was an enormous success. Throughout the second half of the nineteenth century the society alone placed an average of 2,500 children a year, and an ever-growing number of other organizations were following its example. By the 1870s the Five Points Mission, the New York Juvenile Asylum, the New York Foundling Hospital, and the New England Home for Little Wanderers in Boston all had orphan train programs of their own. At first such programs were confined to East Coast cities, but as western cities grew they too followed Brace's example when dealing with the problems of their poor. The Illinois Children's Home Society and the Boys and Girls Aid Society of San Francisco were among many organizations that found country homes for orphans and slum children. Indeed, the idea of rescuing "friendless" children by finding homes for them became almost fashionable. For many years *The Delineator,* a women's magazine edited by Theodore Dreiser, carried brief, heartbreaking descriptions of poor and parentless children in every issue and asked readers to take them in by indenture, outplacement, or adoption.

Brace's Emigration Plan may have been even more influential in Europe than in the United States. Several European nations, including

Germany, Norway, and Sweden, set up orphan train–like programs, but none so enthusiastically as the English. The largest of the British programs directly inspired by Brace's work was Dr. Barnardo's, which alone exported more than 80,000 English slum children to the commonwealth.

It is impossible to determine the exact number of children transported by all orphan train programs. None of these organizations kept very exact records. Many of them would enter the same child two and three times on their rosters. Not all of the organizations, including the CAS, bothered to sort out clearly which children were benefiting from which programs. And some, like the New York Foundling Hospital, have still not opened their records to public scrutiny. Estimates of the number of children the Children's Aid Society placed range between 32,000 and 300,000.² Victor Remmer, the current CAS archivist and a former director of the society, says that by his count the CAS placed approximately 105,000 children between 1853 and the early 1930s. The most widely quoted figure for the total number of children placed by all orphan train–like programs in the United States is 250,000 — although that figure is little more than a guess.

The true test of the orphan trains' success is not, of course, their extensiveness or their adoption by other organizations, but the degree to which they actually helped the children who rode them — and here the facts are decidedly more ambiguous and obscure. Approximately 20 percent of CAS records made under Brace's stewardship are so incomplete that it is impossible to get any idea of how a child fared in his or her new home, and most of the remaining files are so fragmentary that conclusions based on them can only be educated guesses at best.

Calibrating the degree to which the Emigration Plan satisfied the needs of children is also made difficult by the fact that during the nineteenth century children's needs were conceived of very differently and in fact were very different (in certain significant particulars at least) from the needs of children today. To mention only one obvious example: during the 1800s not only was it thought to be good and right that children should work long hours, but the economic structure of the entire society dictated that if lower-class children did not work, they and their families were going to end up hungry and homeless. Although it is perfectly true that any modern-day program that aimed to help twelve-year-olds by getting them full-time jobs would be barbaric, any mid-nineteenth-century program that did not consider child labor normal and beneficial would have been a nonsensical pipe dream. It is very difficult in an era when child labor is thought to be almost as abhorrent a crime as slavery to consider that in an earlier era decent, even admirable, people saw nothing wrong with children doing what we think of as adult work. But this is precisely the sort of leap our moral imagination must make if we are to understand the orphan trains.

The final factor complicating any evaluation of the Emigration Plan's effectiveness is the paradox that the orphan trains look worst when they are judged by some of Charles Loring Brace's own publicly elaborated standards, particularly in regard to the desirability of adoption.

Although Brace frequently talked about the Emigration Plan as a means of getting children jobs, in his annual reports and other promotional writings he tended to present its typical and ideal result as adoption. This was the implication of all his arguments about the importance of removing poor children from bad families and all the anecdotes of the orphan train riders' happiness in their new homes. The ideal of adoption was even implicit in the verbal agreement that the CAS had with the children's employers: the child would be treated exactly like the employer's own birth children and kept until age twenty-one.

Anyone who accepted adoption as the ideal goal of the orphan trains would have been deeply disappointed by their actual results, and anyone who believed that the typical orphan train rider ended up adopted would have felt equally betrayed, because the truth is that only a minority of orphan train riders ever experienced anything like what we would call adoption today. In a comprehensive statistical analysis of 280 placements made by the Children's Aid Society during its first year of operation, sociologist Bruce Bellingham found that a mere 20 percent of the children stayed in their placements for sufficient duration and had enough familial involvement to approximate the modern understanding of adoption. He also found that an additional 24 percent stayed at their placements because they found them satisfactory as jobs. But fully 56 percent of the placements expired before the terms set in their verbal agreements, many in only a matter of days. Sixteen percent of placed children ended up returning on their own to New York or to their families. And 11 percent were retrieved by their kin.[3]

The first independent analysis of CAS records, conducted in 1922 by Georgia G. Ralph of the New York School of Social Work, would seem to indicate that as time passed the Emigration Plan made some progress toward fulfilling Brace's publicly stated ambitions. Although Ralph made no attempt to distinguish placements that were adoptions from those that were merely jobs, she found that 56 percent of the placements made in 1865 (the first year she studied) lasted at least as long as their verbal agreements stipulated, and that in 1875 that number rose to 60 percent. Eight percent of the children placed in 1865 returned to New York or their families, and 5 percent ended up in jail. For 1875 those figures were 10 percent and 4 percent, respectively.[4]

Bellingham, who conducted his study in the early 1980s, did not categorize placements as successes or failures on the basis of duration, but Ralph accepted Brace's claim that adoption — or at least long-term placement — should be the ideal goal of emigration. Thus, she labeled those placements that endured for their expected term as "favorable" and those that did not as "unfavorable." Although this interpretation would seem to present the majority of placements as successes, it would also give the early Emigration Plan a failure rate upward of 40 percent — a rate that hardly seems to justify the extravagant claims so often made for the plan in CAS literature.

Ralph did her study at a time when Brace's arguments about the desirability of removing poor children from their homes were far more widely accepted than they are today. Nowadays, when a child is taken from his or her family, adoption is not a primary goal but a last, best hope. The first priority is family preservation. Only when a family is so troubled that a child's safety or healthy development is at risk will the child be removed from the home and placed in foster care. The hope is that the child's stay in foster care will be as brief as possible and last only as long as it takes the family — ideally with the help of social service agencies — to get over whatever crisis led to the child's removal. Only when the child is orphaned or the parents are deemed permanently unable to provide adequate care does adoption become a primary goal. In general, only a small proportion of children who are removed from their homes end up being adopted. The vast majority go in and out of foster care in a matter of days or weeks.

From the modern perspective, then, Bellingham's finding of a 20 percent adoption rate might seem not at all low but excessively high, and Ralph's 56 percent and greater "favorable" outcome rates would seem to be even worse. By the same token, it is the roughly 10 percent of children who ultimately returned to their families who would seem to represent the orphan train program's greatest success.

It is not, however, truly fair or meaningful to compare the orphan trains to the whole spectrum of modern foster care. Although the orphan trains are the direct antecedent of foster care, the typical foster child today is probably more similar to the boys and girls who stayed briefly at the CAS lodging houses than to the average orphan train rider. The children the CAS sent west tended to be its hardest cases. They were more likely than the beneficiaries of other programs to have been incarcerated in jails or asylums, and more likely to have been abused or neglected by their families. If we look only at today's hardest cases — those children in foster care for more than eighteen months — we find that roughly 25 percent of them end up being adopted,[5] a proportion fairly close to Bellingham's figure. Although it would be a mistake to place too much weight on a comparison of two such different mechanisms in two such different eras, the rough correspondence between orphan train and present-day hard-case adoption rates suggests at the very least that, when it came to helping children become part of new families — Brace's publicly stated ambitions aside — the Emigration Plan may have succeeded as well as could reasonably be expected.

Another way in which Brace misrepresented his work was by portraying the CAS as an *active* agency, "saving" children, "reforming" character, "draining" the city of its poor, rather than as the more *passive* agency that it actually was. One of the most important differences between the CAS and the other major child welfare organizations of the era — the houses of refuge, juvenile asylums, and orphanages — is that it did not impose a mandatory program of moral reform on children. Whatever reform the CAS effected was achieved by offering children help in getting what they most needed to become happy and productive members of society — jobs, homes, shelter, education. At least in theory, no child was ever required to accept this help — though obviously, young children did not have a choice when their parents or guardians put them on the orphan trains, and any child who came into contact with the CAS was subjected to heavy persuasion. But even so, however Brace may have represented the CAS to wealthy contributors, he had designed it to be a tool of the working — or "dangerous" — classes, and this was in fact how it succeeded best.

The Morrow family's experience was typical. Johnny was subjected to an intense campaign promoting western migration — a campaign he ended up abetting in his own writing — but no one at the CAS ever thought the worse of him for choosing not to ride the orphan trains. On the contrary, every reference in CAS records to Johnny is radiant with affection and respect. And likewise, no one at the CAS decided what should happen to Johnny's siblings as their home life became intolerable or they got into trouble on the streets. It was Johnny himself who decided — as de facto head of the family — to put his siblings, one by one, on orphan trains. And when Johnny went out to Iowa and found that Willie had not remained with his original placement but had traveled on his own from employer to employer and state to state, going as far away as Wisconsin, Johnny never saw this as a failure of the Children's Aid Society. On the contrary, Willie had been doing precisely what the Emigration Plan was primarily designed for: he had been trying to take advantage of the supposedly greater opportunities open to him in the West — something he could never have done had he been required to stay with his original, less than satisfactory employer. Thus, when Willie returned to New Haven with Johnny, it was the West that had failed, not the orphan trains.

And no one at the CAS seems to have seen anything particularly worrisome in Willie's case. Although the CAS record keeper was clearly perturbed that Johnny had "smuggled" his brother home, his or her account of Willie's travels from placement to placement across four western states includes no harsher comments than "doing well" and "getting along finely."[6] A similar complacency colors John Jackson's record-book entry. His original employer, James DeHaven, seems to have felt no shame in reporting that John had grown "dissatisfied" on his farm and had left to work for a neighbor. He claimed to still "like" John and to be in touch with him. And the CAS seems to have found nothing about the situation that merited investigation or even concern.[7] Drifting was a perfectly normal and acceptable consequence of the Emigration Plan as actually managed by the CAS, if not in how the CAS presented the program to the public

Georgia G. Ralph would have placed these two cases in her "unfavorable" category, but this was clearly not the way CAS workers viewed them. With all of Brace's rhetoric about children finding better families and homes, the CAS workers well understood that a placement might succeed even if it was not permanent, and that even children had a right to determine their own lives. CAS workers also understood that transportation west did not diminish children's obligations or bonds to their birth families. The record books from the early decades of the Emigration Plan commonly mention that a child returned to New York "to care for mother," or because "the family's situation improved." Neither the record keepers nor the employers seem to find anything improper about this. In their autobiographical writings, in fact, some orphan train riders mention that their employers paid for their transportation home. Bellingham finds only one case in which a birth parent was prevented from retrieving his or her child, and only a handful of cases in which the society or the child's employer even attempted to prevent retrieval by birth parents.[8] The records also show almost no evidence of children being taken directly from unwilling parents, although there are countless cases of the CAS not bothering to contact the parents of children who came to their offices on their own, or not bothering to substantiate children's claims to be orphans. (Again, Johnny Morrow's and John Jackson's cases are perfect examples.)

The Emigration Plan had many grievous faults, in particular its failure to provide adequate screening of and assistance to foster parents and employers, adequate monitoring and supervision of placements, and adequate help to birth families so that they could remain intact. But the program also provided children with many real and important benefits. At a time when it was necessary for poor children to work, the Emigration Plan got children jobs, and at a time when even very young children would travel great distances to find work, the CAS not only provided them with free transportation but, if things did not work out with one employer, sent them a ticket to another or back to New York. The Emigration Plan also helped runaways escape difficult or abusive families. Like orphanages, the orphan trains provided a service to parents who temporarily or permanently were unable to care for their children — although it was certainly more difficult to retrieve a child from out west than from a New York orphanage. For children who truly needed new and decent families, the orphan trains offered the chance, although by no means the certainty, of finding such families. The orphan trains also gave homeless children an alternative to jails, juvenile asylums, and traditional indentured servitude. And finally, the CAS treated poor children (if not their parents) with more respect, and had more faith in their capabilities, fundamental goodness, and future prospects, than any other organization that preceded them — as well as many that followed. And the orphan trains represented the very pinnacle of the Children's Aid Society's optimism.

ɔʃ

In the first circular by which Charles Loring Brace announced to the world the existence of his new organization he made sure to assert: "We do not propose in any way to conflict with existing Asylums and Institutions, but to render them a hearty cooperation, and, at the same time, to fill a gap, which of necessity, they have all left."[9] Although it may have been politically wise for Brace to avoid presenting his fledgling effort as competition for the city's biggest and very well established institutions for the management of street children, his assertion was almost entirely disingenuous. Not only would the CAS compete directly with the New York Juvenile Asylum and the House of Refuge for a never very substantial pool of tax money and charitable contributions, but Brace stood firmly on the opposite side of a philosophical fence from the managers of the two institutions. This disagreement did not consist only of differing opinions about the effectiveness of caring for children in large groups, or about subjecting them to military-style discipline, but extended all the way down to the most fundamental understanding of heart, mind, and soul.

Brace was a proponent of a decidedly optimistic view of human nature. He saw human beings as fundamentally good, and evil as largely exterior to our essential character. Although Brace certainly acknowledged the role of biological inheritance in behavior, he believed that moral character was shaped primarily by the environment. The vast majority of children raised in decent homes and coherent communities, he believed, tended to grow into good men and women. This belief provided the whole rationale for the Emigration Plan. All human beings, under all circumstances, had the potential to do evil, but the general tendency was nevertheless very much in the direction of virtue — how else could a just, all-knowing, and father-like God arrange things?

The asylums, juvenile prisons, and much of the legal establishment took a decidedly more pessimistic view of human nature, seeing people — especially the poor — as, if not intrinsically evil, at least having a strong tendency toward wrongdoing, a tendency that could be restrained only by rigid discipline and unequivocal punishment. Much of the most ferocious criticism that the orphan trains were to receive during Brace's lifetime came from adherents of this pessimistic view of human nature. To their minds, the children of the poor were strongly disposed to be criminal by birth and needed rough treatment to be set on the straight and narrow.

As shall be seen, because Brace rejected outright any criticism based on this pessimistic view of human nature, the CAS made only the most grudging and superficial accommodations to it. Thus, the criticism persisted in various forms well into the twentieth century and ultimately made the operation of the orphan trains legally impossible. But these legal obstacles did not arise until philosophical objections of a very different order had made them all but unnecessary. Although Brace and his successors would always be resistant to critics who saw poor children as guilty in advance of the fact, they were extremely vulnerable to, and ultimately were most deeply affected by, critics who, like them, saw the children as innocents in need of aid and protection. And it was this friendlier criticism that ultimately ended the Emigration Plan even before the legal restrictions were fully in effect.

Animosity between Brace and the directors of congregate care institutions like the Juvenile Asylum and the House of Refuge built up slowly. Outright hostility was initiated by Brace himself in 1857 at the First Convention of Managers and Superintendents of Houses of Refuge and Schools of Reform, which was held in New York City.

This convention took place during a period of intense turmoil in American cities. The nation was in the midst of a severe recession, and urban crime was rising to unprecedented levels, with murder rates doubling over the previous decade and, by some reports, rising sixfold. All categories of street crime were undergoing similar rises, and a substantial proportion of the perpetrators were juveniles. Mob violence was also rife in poorer neighborhoods. In July 1857 alone, one policeman was killed and several other people were wounded in the Kleindeutschland riot in New York's German district, and a street fight between a Protestant gang, the Bowery Boys, and a Catholic gang, the Dead Rabbits, resulted in the loss of twelve lives.[10]

These were just the sort of circumstances to set off fierce debates between the adherents of optimistic and pessimistic visions of human nature, with the former attributing the violence to the economic and social environment, and the latter blaming the corrupt souls of the perpetrators. In his 1857 annual report, Brace argued forcefully from the optimistic-environmentalist camp:

> Is not this crop of thieves and burglars, of shoulder-hitters and short-boys, of prostitutes and vagrants, of garroters and murderers, the very fruit to be expected from this seed so long being sown? What else was to be looked for? Society hurried on selfishly for its wealth, and left this vast class in its misery and temptation. Now these children arise, and wrest back with bloody and criminal hands what the world was too careless or too selfish to give. The worldliness of the rich, the indifference of all classes to the poor, will always be avenged. Society must act on the highest principles, or its punishment incessantly comes within itself. The neglect of the poor and tempted and criminal is fearfully repaid.[11]

Given the prevailing social chaos, juvenile penal institutions ought to have been in a strong position in 1857, but in fact they were very much on the defensive. By the end of the 1850s the belief that children were better cared for in families than institutions had received considerable attention, and many experts on the treatment of dependent and criminal children had come to believe that the "cottage" or "family" system, as innovated by the *Rauhe Haus* in Germany, was the best model for congregate care. In response to this growing current of opinion, the seventeen institutions represented at the 1857 convention were eager to portray themselves as, in essence, big families — an image that was made ludicrous, however, by the information provided in their own reports.

The "families" of the institutions attending the convention consisted of, on average, 216 inmates, with the oldest and most influential of these institutions, the New York House of Refuge, having 477 inmates.[12] Such figures were simply too much for Brace to resist. Having piloted the CAS through four years of steady growth in prestige, funding, and social service, and, at thirty-one, being as much possessed of drive and enthusiasm as he ever would be, Brace felt no need to tiptoe in front of the competition. In his own address at the conference, he declared,

We hear, in these Reports from the Institutions, of one person presiding over five hundred children, and it is asserted that he manages this family on the purest parental principles. . . . I hold that it is impossible for a man to feel towards them in any degree as a father feels towards his own offspring. . . . The poor boy in the great house can never become to us like the child of our flesh and blood; in some degree he must be a stranger; and my observation has been, that where you have large numbers of children together, you cannot have that direct sympathy and interest and personal management which make the family so beneficial to children.[13]

This criticism, which bore the weight of common sense, was substantially reinforced by the fact that the alternative Brace advocated, his Emigration Plan, was so much cheaper than institutional care. In 1857, for example, the year of the convention, it had cost the House of Refuge $85 per annum to care for each of its 477 inmates, while the CAS sent 742 children into the country for a onetime payment of a mere $10 each.[14] In addition, despite the rise in every category of juvenile crime, and perhaps in part because of CAS competition, both the Juvenile Asylum and the House of Refuge had fewer inmates than they were set up to handle and thus were having financial difficulties — a condition that only made them more sensitive to Brace's charges.

The congregate care institutions — whom Brace labeled collectively as "the Asylum-Interest" — retaliated forcefully during the next convention, held two years later in 1859. "Shall we take these children as they are brought to us," asked R. N. Havens of the New York Juvenile Asylum, "thieves, liars, profane swearers, licentious, polluted in body and soul, and put them into your families in that condition?"[15] To expect that these "little vagabonds" should be "clasped in the arms of the heads of families and cared for, and protected as their own offspring," was, Havens maintained, "all very poetical and imaginative" but hardly realistic. "I would have you pluck out the *vagabond* first, and then let the boy be thus provided with a home, and not before."[16]

To this attack Brace responded with a considerably less rosy image of both the orphan train riders and the families who took them in than was normally featured in CAS literature:

I do not draw any imaginary picture of a Christian family in the West. I do not suppose that the Christian family there or here is always so wonderful, but I believe that it is the change of circumstances, and the new family and Christian influences bearing upon the child [that reforms him].[17]

If there is a good family in the West, that is willing to take in a poor boy from the city, to give him social and Christian instruction, why in God's name, should they not do it? What if the boy is bad, they know his character and associations. If they are willing, from Christian and business motives (because his labor is useful), to take that child in and train him, why should they not be permitted to do so? If enough families can be found to serve as reformatory institutions, is it not the best and most practical and economical method of reforming these children to put them under the charge of such families?[18]

The Juvenile Asylum attempted to defuse the conflict by assigning each of the major New York organizations caring for criminal and dependent children a separate portion of the population. The House of Refuge would take the most serious criminals under fourteen, and the Juvenile Asylum the beggars, vagrants, petty thieves, and other "morally degraded and vicious children." The CAS would be left only those poor children "who had been measurably well cared for, . . . but who, through the misfortune of parents, stood in need of assistance from the benevolent."[19] In the fullness of his enthusiasm, Brace saw no reason to read this compromise as anything other than a humiliating sop. He responded by cutting the Juvenile Asylum out of the picture entirely, proposing that the House of Refuge care for those boys and girls who had crossed that "narrow line of distinction" from merely destitute or vagrant to truly criminal, and that the CAS handle all the rest, chiefly through its Emigration Plan.[20]

As confident as Brace may have appeared at the two conventions, he understood full well that "the Asylum-Interest" would not be the only party accusing him of "scattering poison over the country" as long as he continued to send children west who had not been officially "reformed," "corrected," or "purified" through a period of institutional incarceration.[21] To head off such criticism, he conducted a not entirely disingenuous but by no means exhaustive or unbiased inquiry into the results of his own work. This inquiry had two parts. One was a series of letters sent to placement committee members, clergymen, law officers, heads of reform schools, and other potentially knowledgeable authorities in the West, asking whether they knew of any CAS children who had been imprisoned or abused, or who had stolen, run away, returned to New York, or otherwise "turned out badly." For the second part of the inquiry Brace journeyed west himself during the spring of 1859 to talk to orphan train riders and local authorities.

Claiming to have "visited personally, and heard directly of, many hundreds of these little creatures," Brace pronounced in a field journal entry that:

> The results — so far as we could ascertain them — were remarkable, and, unless we reflect on the wonderful influences possible from a Christian home upon a child unused to kindness, they would seem incredible.
>
> The estimate we formed from a considerable field of observation was, that, out of those sent to the West under fifteen years, not more than *two percent.* turned out bad; and, even of those from fifteen to eighteen, not more than *four percent.*

It was in explaining the foundation of these estimates that Brace first presented the "no news is good news" defense with which he would respond to criticism for most of the remainder of his career: "[I]t may generally be assumed that we hear of the worst cases — that is, of those who commit criminal offenses, or who came under the law — and it is these whom we reckon as the failures."

Brace adopted a similar defense in response to accusations that orphan train riders suffered abuse:

> It is also remarkable, as the years pass away, how few cases ever come to the knowledge of the Society, of ill-treatment of these children. The task of distributing them is carried on so publicly by Mr. Tracy, and in connection with such responsible persons, that any case of positive abuse would at once be known and corrected by the community itself.

He continued:

> On this journey . . . we heard of but one instance even of neglect. We visited the lad, and discovered that he had not been schooled as he should, and had sometimes been left alone at night in the lonely log-house. Yet this had roused the feelings of the whole country-side; we

removed the boy, amid the tears and protestations of the "father" and "mother," and put him in another place. As soon as we had left the village, he ran right back to his old place![22]

The modern reader cannot help but be taken aback by passages such as these. It is hard to imagine how a man of Brace's intelligence, moral rectitude, and compassion could have dared to justify his entire life's work with such weak and — at the very least — self-deceiving arguments. It is true that the CAS "Record Books," like the records of most child welfare organizations of the era, were so incomplete that they could give him little insight into the true experiences of the children he had placed. But even so, Brace had visited countless tenement basements where he had seen evidence of every sort of physical, sexual, and emotional abuse. How could a man who could be so outraged by the parents of slum families remain so apparently innocent of the abuses that occurred unseen in farm kitchens and outbuildings, especially when he had also heard so many children — John Jackson being only one of them — tell of their bestial treatment at the hands of farmers, country shopkeepers, and mechanics?

It is impossible to know exactly what sort of blind spots and evasions might have enabled Brace to carry on his work with so little apparent doubt as to its merit or efficaciousness, but it is important to remember that everything he wrote about the CAS was intended primarily to woo supporters and contributions and did not necessarily represent his honest opinions. In a more considered report written upon his return to New York, Brace's claims for the Emigration Plan were considerably more modest and sober: "Under any discipline, a certain number will turn out badly; we only claim for this method fewer failures than under any other, and a work much more economical and extensive."[23] What this shows is that Brace was prepared to practice a fairly grim calculus. Like many Americans of his era, he perceived, perhaps with perfect justice, that a staggering number of slum children were living in absolutely desperate conditions. He knew that, especially given the limited funds available for helping the poor, it would be impossible to save every child, and so he considered failure (children suffering abuse in solitude and silence; children running away in fear or homesickness; children whose anger and pain turned inward, driving them to drink, violence, and worse) to be an inevitable component of his humanitarian labors. That he may have knowingly overlooked failures and exaggerated his rates of success does not mean that he did not sincerely believe that his work was thoroughly justified and good.

In any event, Brace emerged the clear victor over "the Asylum-Interest" in the battle of images, especially in his own city. He followed his 1859 report about the "remarkable" results of the Emigration Plan with an 1861 report based on figures provided by the City Prison that showed an 88 percent decline in petty larcenies committed by children under ten over the preceding decade, and a 50 percent decline in vagrancy, even as the population of the city continued to increase.[24] Brace presented these figures as evidence of the effectiveness of CAS programs, neglecting to mention that crime had actually risen substantially during most of the 1850s and had only begun to fall as the city's economy improved in the final years of the decade. But the coup de grâce in Brace's struggle with the congregate care institutions came with what he termed "indiscreetly" published figures that showed that the longer a child was kept in the House of Refuge or the Juvenile Asylum, the more likely he or she was to commit a crime upon release.[25]

Even as Brace triumphed over "the Asylum-Interest," his nation became embroiled in the worst cataclysm of its history, one that he first celebrated as the answer to long-held prayers but that soon caused him deep disillusionment.

♉

> Freedom to the slave! The words sound as might the songs of angels amid the curses and groans of battle. We cannot believe them. What! This curse and burning shame at length, after so many years of hopeless prayers and tears to be taken away! . . .
>
> Another result of our final victory must be the full justification of the American Idea. . . . Now, in the hour of our peril . . . we find the foreign-born rising, if possible, with more enthusiasm and patriotic self-devotion to defend the Republic than our own citizens. The brave Irish, the gallant French, the well-drilled Germans, Poles, Hungarians, and English are hurrying to stand by or die for the capital of their country. Henceforth, the blood of the foreign dead on this soil consecrates universal suffrage, while the American nation endures.
>
> — Charles Loring Brace, May 1861[26]

When South Carolinians fired on Fort Sumter on April 12, 1861, Brace rejoiced, believing that the now-inevitable war between the North and South was God's way of enabling the United States finally to fulfill its promise. Only through a crisis as dire as war could patriotic instincts become fervid enough to "override the selfishness which free institutions so rapidly develop" and make a true nation out of many peoples divided by class and ethnicity. And most important, only a war could inspire the leaders of the nation to, at last, end slavery — "the greatest sin which a nation ever committed."[27]

Although Brace was only thirty-five at the outbreak of the war, and he publicly lauded "professional men who have abandoned all civil honors to take place as privates,"[28] he did not enlist himself — perhaps believing that he could do more good by remaining at his labors in the city, or that he could not abandon his wife and small children. He did, however, rush to aid the cause in more discreet efforts, first as a journalist.

Within two weeks of the shelling of Fort Sumter, Brace went to Washington as a correspondent for the *Independent* and the *New York Times*. His first reports from the front primarily concerned the massing of troops to defend the capital and mount an attack on the Confederates.

For the most part Brace painted a flattering portrait of the bravery of Union soldiers and their leaders, but he did write with some concern about a "tide" of drinking, gambling, and swearing and an "unmanly dodging of religious responsibilities" that was running through the army.[29] Then, on July 12, 1861, following 30,000 Union troops on their march toward the Confederate capital of Richmond, Virginia, Brace saw action for the first time and described it in a letter to Letitia:

Yesterday I was *in a battle*. Don't be frightened; we escaped all right, and I suppose the danger was trifling. We stood on the hill above Bull's Run, and saw the whole affair, and suddenly had the cannon-balls flying among us. I tell you, the first experience of a round shot, whirring over one's head, is a sensation. Every one ducks and *whirr!* they go right over you. A number were killed on our side. I have written a long account for the "Times." Our men did not act very well, and the enemy were well posted. It was a trap for us. We go to the same point today, and will attack them with a larger force. It was the most exciting day of my life, yesterday, and I could hardly sleep, tired as I was.[30]

The renewed engagement with the Confederates at Bull Run resulted in a terrible defeat for the Union forces and drove home to northerners that the war would not be won as easily and quickly as so many had expected. Brace's articles and letters did not again display such complacent optimism about the Union troops or their campaign until the very end of the war. Indeed, the war provided Brace with a series of disappointments, both personal and political.

One of the personal disappointments came to pass when he tried to aid the war effort by joining the Sanitary Commission, an organization devoted to implementing the latest theories about hygiene and disease prevention within the army. The commission was headed by his old friend Frederick Law Olmsted, who had already completed the bulk of his work on Central Park.

Brace and Olmsted had grown distant over the years. Although they would remain friends until Brace's death, their letters never again exhibited the easy affection and solidarity of their early correspondence. Olmsted's response to Brace's offer to help out at the Sanitary Commission was couched in humor but showed clear hostility:

> *Dear Charley:* I employ three classes, surgeons, nurses, and women — the first and last of two grades, but in neither of either would you yoke. For nurses, I find that any not very sick common soldiers, Yankee, Irish, or German, are better than any volunteers; also mercenaries are better than gratuitous volunteers. I have therefore abandoned volunteers. Don't want them. Consequently, in the way of business, I don't want you; for any man without a clearly defined function about the army is a nuisance, and is treated as such. . . . I have seen enough of it, and it is not an entertainment to which I would invite a friend.[31]

In the end, Brace would do some work for the Sanitary Commission, but primarily as a publicist. His main involvement in the war effort, apart from serving as a correspondent until the summer of 1862, was to work as a chaplain for the Christian Commission, "distributing sherry and spiritual consolation"[32] to patients in field hospitals.

Brace's political disappointments centered on the nation's failure to achieve that solidarity transcending all boundaries of class and ethnicity that he had considered all but inevitable in the heady days following the shelling of Fort Sumter. Even after the Yankee defeat at Bull Run, Brace had maintained a powerful certainty of the impending "overthrow of slavery and the restoration of liberty." But once he had experienced battle, he began to conceive of that overthrow in terms that were not merely less celebratory but uncharacteristically brutal:

> The smothered indignation of years, now that at length there is a practical vent, bursts forth. If they speak of the subjugation or extermination of the slave holders, *as a class,* it is not in the spirit of revenge or personal bitterness, but because such seems the Divine Providence or retribution, and because they feel the wrongs done to the helpless and the unbefriended.[33]

Despite this alleged grim resolve of Divine Providence, the U.S. government seemed decidedly reluctant to make the just and inevitable proclamation of the emancipation of slaves, and the American people, including even some prominent abolitionists, were slow to demand it. Brace's impatience with anyone not demanding freedom for the slaves was so extreme that he concluded one *Independent* column by speculating that "a nation whose teachers and priests were such" might deserve "extermination."[34]

One of the "teachers" who particularly frustrated Brace was Horace Greeley, a longtime abolitionist and the editor of the *New York Tribune,* then the most respected paper in the North. When Brace wrote urging that the *Tribune* be more assiduous in its promotion of emancipation, Greeley responded with advice that Brace could only have found disgraceful:

> [T]rust the Divine Disposer . . . to do the needed work, with little help from you or me. If every Abolitionist of three months' standing were to die to-morrow, the war could not continue two years without ending in (or involving) emancipation. It may be well for the "Tribune," as you say, to say more on this point. But I doubt that it is well for the cause, and feel sure it is unnecessary.[35]

Brace's letters and articles on abolitionism, as well as his avowal of controversial religious and scientific opinions and, especially, his support of "old John Brown," raised the concern of the new chairman of the CAS board as to his fitness to run the society. In a letter responding to the chairman, William A. Booth, Brace asserted that he strenuously avoided making controversial statements whenever he spoke or wrote as a representative of the CAS, but that he had to be free to speak his mind in all other contexts: "Any other principle would strip an agent of his individuality."[36] Although the relationship between Booth and Brace would never be more than cordial, the chairman seemed to accept Brace's reasoning and did not interfere with his activities outside the CAS again.

Even as Brace was campaigning for emancipation of slaves, writing on the war, and serving as a chaplain, he was not only still running the CAS but lobbying government on behalf of poor children. In 1862 the CAS opened its first Girls' Lodging House, and New York City appointed its first two truant officers. Brace had argued for many years that compulsory education was the best means for combating the twin evils of poverty and the exploitation (primarily in factories and mines) of child labor. New York already had a law requiring all children under the age of fourteen to attend school, but no mechanism for enforcing it. It was Brace's urgent campaigning that finally convinced City Hall to appoint those first two truant officers, with the result that, according to Brace's daughter, within two months' time more than 500 former truants had become full-time students.[37]

Brace's 1861 assertion that the war would heal the bitter divides between ethnic groups, and in particular that the "brave Irish" were "hurrying to stand by or die for the capital of their country," was proven sorrowfully inaccurate by the New York draft riots of 1863.

For years New York employers had been playing off African Americans and Irish immigrants against one another to keep wages low. Whenever one group started to get obstreperous, they would be fired and replaced by the other. Thus, many Irish were singularly uninterested in fighting a war for the emancipation of slaves (whom they saw as only more competition) and were outraged in July 1863 when a new law subjected them to a draft for the first time. They were especially indignant over a provision in the law allowing the rich to evade military service by paying $300.

What began as a protest against the draft and Lincoln's policies soon turned into an attack on the people those policies were thought most to benefit. The rioters went from ransacking draft offices to trashing the homes and places of business of prominent Republicans and abolitionists. Horace Greeley's office at the *New York Tribune* was attacked twice. But the worst of the immigrant fury was vented in the "colored" neighborhoods between Five Points and the present-day

West Village. At least eleven black men were lynched and horribly mutilated by the rioters, and the Colored Orphan Asylum at Forty-third Street and Fifth Avenue was burned to the ground. During the three days before the Union Army finally quelled the rioters on July 16, 105 people were killed — making these riots one of the bloodiest urban disturbances ever to take place in the United States.

Although Brace was horrified by the savagery of the draft riots and feared for the survival of the nation, they provided him with an absolutely irresistible fund-raising opportunity. "The rioter of 1863 is merely the street-boy of 1853 grown up!" he declared in a special circular issued shortly after the riots.

> No other fruit from so much ignorance and poverty and heathenism, as exist in the degraded quarters of New York could be expected than such rioters and such mobs. A boy or girl left to drift about on the foul currents of New York street-life, without moral influence, or common education, cunning and ignorant, making a living by all sorts of devices and trickery, exposed to the worst company and the most depraved associations, must inevitably grow up, as by a fixed law, into such young men and women as recently fired dwellings, sacked orphan asylums, and murdered unoffending and Christian men and women for mere brutal thirst of blood.

Although Brace referred to incidents of racist barbarity in this document, he chose to present the riots to his affluent readers and potential contributors as "a grand attack against Property . . . an insurrection of the irresponsible and outcast classes against the well-to-do and the rich." He concluded with an appeal to guilt, fear, and common sense:

> [T]hough great numbers have been saved [by the CAS] during the last ten years, it must be remembered how small the efforts are, compared with the evil, and how little expense and trouble have been incurred by our citizens in comparison with the property in danger from these neglected children, or the vast multitude of the degraded classes.
>
> Many there were, without doubt, engaged in this riot who were simply very poor and ignorant laboring people. Yet we cannot question that the bitterness shown by these against those well-off and rich, would have been much lessened had more been done by the upper classes to fill up the great gap between them.[38]

Brace's implication that the CAS had been working with "great numbers" of the Irish poor who had been responsible for the riots was by no means inaccurate. For most of the nineteenth century the Irish accounted for 20 percent of the orphan train riders and were the largest single ethnic group served by the CAS, apart from the Americans, many of whom were of Irish extraction. The high proportion of Irish on CAS rosters did not mean, however, that the Irish universally welcomed the society's efforts. Many Irish, and Catholics in general, saw the CAS as a key element in a Protestant plot to destroy their faith.

ᴊᴘ

There had been no significant Roman Catholic presence in New York City until the century of exponential growth that began with the building of the Erie Canal in 1826. By 1865 New York's 400,000 Catholics made up half of the city's population and were by far its largest denomination.[39] Some of them were Italian, German, and French, but the vast majority of New York Catholics were Irish who had fled the famine in the 1840s, '50s, and '60s.

Throughout the famine years the main object of the New York Catholic church was simply to keep up with the explosive growth of its congregation. The deep poverty of most New York Catholics kept the church perpetually short of funds to finance the building of new churches and schools, and all such institutions, once established, tended to operate on the very edge of financial insolvency. Up until the Civil War, apart from an orphanage built in 1817, there were no substantial Catholic urban aid or reform organizations. As a result, when the church's poorest parishioners needed help, they had no choice but to turn to Protestant charities, which many believed were primarily, if covertly, intended to lure Catholics away from their church. Up until the 1840s even the public schools were run by a semiprivate Protestant society that promoted a markedly anti-Catholic curriculum and insisted on the use of the Protestant King James Bible in class. (It was in fact a dispute between the city and Catholic Bishop John Hughes that led to the removal of the Bible from the classroom and — much to Hughes's dismay — to the gradual secularization of New York public education.)

Practically from its foundation, the Children's Aid Society was one of the Protestant relief organizations most hated by Catholics, largely because of its Emigration Plan, which was commonly seen as little more than institutionalized child snatching. A multipaneled cartoon in an Irish American newspaper portrayed one of the society's agents as a dour ghoul who only smiles when a westerner gives him $20 for a frightened Catholic newsboy. The agent is shown lecturing the boy on the "iniquities of popery." And the CAS's success at accomplishing what "England failed to effect by the sword" is illustrated by the cartoon's final panel, which shows the boy, fully grown, a "Baptist Preacher," and a near twin of the ghoulish agent who "rescued" him.[40]

At first Catholic opposition to the CAS was purely ad hoc. An anecdote often repeated in the Catholic community during the nineteenth century told of a priest who intervened at the last minute to stop the departure of an orphan train and restore a group of Catholic children to their mothers, who had been "wild with grief."[41] And Brace himself, in *The Dangerous Classes,* told of an Italian priest named Rebiccio who in 1855 "flung ferocious anathemas" from the pulpit on all who permitted their children to attend the society's first Italian School. To Brace's immense satisfaction, however, the "whole opposition scheme exploded" when Rebiccio absconded with funds he had collected from his Five Points parishioners on the pretext of building a church and starting a school of his own.[42]

The earliest program aimed at countering Brace's influence — the Catholic Protectory, founded by Levi Silliman Ives in 1863 — could hardly have been more opposite to the Children's Aid Society in philosophy, or more directly confrontational.

Levi Silliman Ives had been raised an Episcopalian and had so devoted himself to his church that when he visited Rome in 1852, at the age of fifty-five, he was bishop of North Carolina. Under the influence of the grandeur and poignant beauty of Italian churches, however, as well as his conversations with devout Catholics, Ives came to feel that he had lived more than half a century in tragic error. He resigned his post, converted to Catholicism, and, on his return to the United States, joined the faculty of Saint John's College in New York, a Jesuit institution that later became Fordham University.

Ives believed that the CAS orphan trains were truly charitable, at least in intent, for Protestant children. But when the children "differed from their benefactors in their religion," charitable intentions yielded to a "temptation . . . to place a bar between these children and their parents; to sever the precious tie which binds them to the parental heart and the parental influence." The cutting of these ties was accomplished, Ives maintained, in subtle stages:

> Concealment is first resorted to, a veil of secrecy is drawn over the proceedings, parental inquiries are baffled, the yearnings of the mother are stilled by tales of the wonderful advantages to her children, and promises of their speedy restoration to her arms. Yet all this while they are undergoing a secret process by which, it is hoped, that every trace of their early faith and filial attachment will be rooted out; and, finally, that their transportations to that indefinite region, "the far West," with changed names and lost parentage, will effectually destroy every association which might revive in their hearts a love for the religion of which they had been robbed, — the religion of their parents. Here, then, a new principle has been at work. What charity commenced, fanaticism has grossly perverted. . . . We had looked for a great benefit, and behold a great wrong, a foul injustice, has been practiced.[43]

With all of his distaste for the orphan trains, Ives began his career in charity by attempting to duplicate them. For some years before founding the Society for the Protection of Destitute Roman Catholic Children in New York, the organization that managed the protectory, he had been finding, informally, "good homes in the country for untrained and destitute Catholic children," and it was this experience that most determined the protectory's goals and methods. Ives did not simply disapprove of the CAS for kidnapping good Catholic children; he found the entire practice of outplacement "perfectly preposterous." In the protectory's first annual report he explained that although he had found homes for many children, "I can call to mind only a single instance where the child either did not abscond or prove to be utterly ungovernable and worthless."

Ives fell securely within the camp of those who took a pessimistic view of human nature and thus believed that children, especially poor children, could be saved from their vicious impulses only by being subjected to strict control. As he saw it, the prime reason for the utter failure of outplacement was that the practice alienated children from "the religion of their parents," by which phrase he meant not merely Catholicism but the inculcation of religious values through parental authority. As he explained it:

Charles Loring Brace in 1853, the year he
founded the Children's Aid Society

An orphan train publicity flyer from the 1860s

A card given to foster parents of orphan train riders during the 1890s

An orphan train bound for Texas in 1904

THE WORK OF THE CHILDREN'S AID SOCIETY

Illustrations commonly used as a frontispiece in Children's Aid
Society annual reports between 1873 and 1890

A cartoon from an 1874 edition of the *Irish World* newspaper, showing a widely held Catholic vision of the true nature of the "work of the Children's Aid Society"

John Brady, the governor
of Alaska, and Andrew
Burke, the governor of
North Dakota, who rode
the same orphan train to
Indiana in 1859

A party of "emigrants" in front of the CAS offices on East 22nd Street, circa 1910. From the left, the adults are Robert L. Neill, Clara Comstock, and Anna Laura Hill, agents of the society.

Charles Loring Brace in the 1880s

Teach children to put a low estimate upon the parental claim to their obedience, and you give them the most effective lesson of insubordination to all rule and all government. Take away from them proper reverence for those who are the instruments of their being, and who nourish their infancy, and whom Almighty God has made their first and essential spiritual guides, and you take from them a vital principal, a controlling power, which can never be restored.[44]

For Ives, "saving" poor children and keeping them Catholic were both accomplished by the same mechanism: preserving parental ties. Thus, in its work with destitute children, the protectory did everything it could to keep families together.[45] When it was deemed necessary, by the protectory or by the parents themselves, that a child should be removed from home, it was understood that the separation would only be temporary. All children who were taken from their families were boarded at the protectory's industrial school, where they were subjected to strict discipline and religious — as well as vocational — training. Although some of the children were indentured, they were never sent far from home. Parents were encouraged to visit their children frequently and to make some contribution toward the cost of their upkeep at the institution. This payment served two purposes, apart from the obvious one of helping the protectory meet its bills: it helped preserve the parents' sense of responsibility for their offspring; and it kept parents from simply dumping unwanted children at the protectory and then running off, never to be heard from again.

With all of its antipathy to the CAS, the protectory's emphasis on the importance of family shows the influence of Brace — but with a major difference. The families that Ives and his successors thought most important were the very ones that Brace turned his back on: the poor families in the slums. It was this emphasis on helping poor children by helping their families that was the strongest part of the Catholic Protectory's work, and the element that ultimately would have the strongest influence on the evolution of child welfare.

The most significant of the domestic imitators of the CAS orphan trains was the New York Foundling Hospital (originally called the New York Foundling Asylum), which was started by the Sisters of Charity of Saint Vincent de Paul in 1869. As indicated by its name, the hospital was intended to help children far younger than the street arabs and job seekers served by the CAS.

New York had a dreadful problem of infant abandonment throughout the nineteenth century. Every year thousands of illegitimate and unwanted babies were left on the doorsteps of hospitals, orphanages, and other charitable organizations all over the city — including the CAS. During the latter part of the century Bellevue Hospital alone had to care for an average of four abandoned infants a day.[46] And of course, then as now, there were many disturbed young women who could imagine no other alternative for disposing of unwanted babies than cramming them into trash cans or tossing them into the East River. The Sisters of Charity hoped their new hospital would diminish all of these practices, especially by members of the Catholic community.

The Foundling Hospital kept a white-curtained bassinet in its vestibule so that mothers, generally at night, could turn their children over to the Sisters' care in complete anonymity. In this manner, the hospital took in forty-five babies during its first month of operation.[47] But the Sisters also encouraged mothers to care for and breast-feed their babies at the hospital for at least the first few months of the child's life. Such care might cause at least some of the mothers to decide to keep their babies, they reasoned, but it would also increase the infants' chances of survival.

Nineteenth-century hospitals and orphanages commonly had infant mortality rates of between 60 and 80 percent, with the most common killer being intestinal ailments. But institutions that encouraged breast-feeding, like the Foundling Hospital, saw their rates plummet to — and even below — the 26 percent mortality rate that prevailed in the city at large.[48] When the Sisters could not convince mothers to feed their own offspring, they would employ the French system of sending the infants out to paid wet nurses. From the boarding of newborns for breast-feeding it was only a small step to in-city foster placement, and then to CAS-style orphan trains.

Although it is perfectly true that Brace and many of his coworkers were deeply prejudiced against Catholics, and that most Catholic children who were sent west did in fact end up being raised Protestant, their conversion was never an overt aim of the charity and came about primarily because there were very few Catholics living outside the major East Coast cities. These were the demographics the Foundling Hospital had to contend with when it decided to set up its own orphan trains. CAS-style "auctions" simply would not work, since even in areas with a fairly dense Catholic population, non-Catholics would still be likely to make up a substantial portion of the people who would come to such auctions. What the Foundling Hospital did instead was work through a nationwide network of priests, who informed their parishioners when a party of children would be coming and helped to match each interested family with a particular child. Although the Foundling Hospital did occasionally send unclaimed children west, the vast majority of its orphan train riders never had to endure the anxiety and humiliation of being scrutinized and picked — or not picked — by a group of unfamiliar men and women. The children wore tags inscribed with the name or identification number of the family who had agreed to take them. All they had to do when they arrived at the station was wait for the man or woman they would be living with to spot them and take them home.

Another way in which Foundling Hospital orphan trains differed from those of the CAS was that their children were *indentured* until age eighteen (girls) or twenty-one (boys). Brace believed that a placement would be beneficial only as long as it was desired by each of the parties involved, so he saw no point in "binding" children to their "employers." The foster parents or employers in a CAS placement were given a card stating their obligations toward the child and the child's toward them, but during Brace's lifetime no one was required to sign any documents. If either party wished to end the arrangement for any reason, the CAS would either find the child a new placement or bring him or her back to New York. The Foundling Home indenture papers contain most of the same provisions as the CAS verbal agreement. The child would both "live with, and be employed" by its foster family, who would clothe, educate, and otherwise treat the child as if he or she were their own by birth. But whereas CAS "employers" only promised to send the child to church and, if possible, Sunday school, the signers of the Foundling Hospital papers agreed to bring the child up "in the Catholic faith." The indenture papers also said nothing about what would happen if the placement did not work out and treated that possibility only as a breach of contract. Finally, the Foundling Hospital papers attempted to fill the place of an adoption contract by stating that if the child had not been "returned to" the hospital by age twenty-one, the parents would "be deemed to have elected to keep, treat and maintain such child as if it were *their* own natural and legitimate child," which, as far as it was specified within the papers, chiefly meant that the child would inherit the parents' property just as their natural offspring would.[49]

The Foundling Hospital's network of parish priests was so effective that by the late 1870s the Sisters' placements were rivaling those of the CAS. While the hospital, like the CAS, placed children throughout the Midwest and West, it placed a far larger proportion of its orphan train riders in states with substantial Catholic populations, such as Louisiana and Texas. Whereas, all told, the CAS made only a score or two of placements in Louisiana, the Foundling Hospital sent a single party of 300 children to that state in 1906. In fact, the Sisters placed so many children in Louisiana that it is generally thought to be the western state that received the most New York children of all. By 1919, the hospital's fiftieth anniversary, it claimed, nationwide, to have indentured 24,658 children in "free homes" — as opposed to "boarding homes" (the present foster care standard) where the parents were paid for taking care of the children — and to have had 3,200 children legally adopted.[50] The last Foundling Hospital orphan train went west in 1923.

The eagerness of the Sisters of Charity to serve not only abandoned children but also the Catholic faith resulted in some controversial practices. First, perhaps in an attempt to compensate for all the children the CAS ostensibly had stolen, the hospital commonly changed the surnames of Jewish children and passed them off as Catholic. One former Foundling Hospital orphan train rider had lived well into adulthood believing that her name at birth had been Ryan, only to find, after confronting the hospital regarding forged baptismal records, that her real name had been Rubin and that she was Jewish.[51] In another case a Jewish girl with a German last name was placed with a non-Jewish German couple. When the deception was uncovered, the couple placed the girl in a Kansas orphanage. The biggest scandal of the Foundling Home's orphan train venture, however, was rooted not in the Sisters' prejudices but in those of the surrounding community.

In 1904 the hospital placed forty children of European extraction with Mexican families living in Arizona territory. This so outraged the local Anglos that a party of men forcibly removed the children from their new homes. The men also threatened the nuns who had accompanied the children with violence and nearly lynched the priest who had arranged the placements. Ultimately these men allowed the Sisters of Charity to resettle twenty-one of the children in other parts of the country but kept the other nineteen in their own families. When the hospital sought to regain custody of the children, the Arizona Supreme Court held that the Anglos had been justified in removing them from the Mexican homes and should be allowed to keep them. Not only did all of the boys and girls involved have to endure the agony of multiple placement and the threat of violence during this episode, but the Foundling Hospital was subjected to national humiliation. The *Los Angeles Examiner,* for example, ran a story about the incident under the headline "Babies Sold Like Sheep," and the *Boston American,* in a similar article, characterized the hospital as a "notorious institution."[52]

Despite competition and criticism, Brace's reputation only became steadily more elevated during the Children's Aid Society's first two decades of existence. For the most part, the public and the press were entirely uninterested in the fine points of methodological controversy. All they cared about were results, and up through the mid-1870s the results of Brace's labors certainly appeared to be impressive.

When he first began reporting police arrest records in 1861, Brace neglected to mention that juvenile crime had in fact risen during the first six years of the CAS's tenure before beginning to make an impressive decline. That decline continued, however, for more than a decade, even as the city's population grew by 13 percent. Arrests of female vagrants declined every year, from a high of 5,880 in 1860 to 548 in 1871. The decline in arrests of male vagrants was not quite so dramatic but was still impressive, going from 2,708 in 1860 to 934 in 1871. Over the same period, petty larceny arrests of females dropped from 890 to 572, and of males from 2,575 to 1,978. Although these vagrants and thieves were by no means only children, these were nevertheless the categories of crime for which children were most often arrested. There were also drops in the number of children under fifteen who were in prison. In 1864 there were 295 girls in New York City prisons, and in 1871 there were 212. The equivalent figures for boys during those same years were 1,965 and 1,017.[53]

Although arrest and imprisonment rates are obviously affected by such factors as police policy, the presence or absence of serious epi-

demics, and the vigor of the economy, it does not seem unreasonable
to attribute some portion of these declines to the work of the CAS and
similar charities — and not just because of the orphan trains, which
indeed "drained" the city of thousands of poor children over the periods covered by these statistics, but also because of the many thousands
more who received job training and basic education at industrial
schools or were given clean, safe places to sleep as well as other services at the Girls' and Newsboys' Lodging Houses. The newspapers of
the time had no trouble crediting the CAS with diminishing the misery of all New Yorkers — not just of the children who might otherwise
have become the perpetrators of crimes but of the people who might
have been their victims — and with saving taxpayers hundreds of
thousands of dollars in incarceration expenses. Brace estimated that
the decline in female vagrancy saved taxpayers $125,000 in one year
alone.[54] And such apparent successes in the city only made it easier for
New Yorkers to believe the CAS's heartwarming reports about its rural
placements as well.

8

Almost a Miracle

BRACE'S AMBITIONS for his Emigration Plan were always contradictory. On the one hand, he wanted to provide children with a home,
but on the other, he was getting them a job. Rural placement was
ostensibly for the children's benefit, but it was also a way to provide farmers with labor and to "drain" the cities of their "dangerous
classes." Brace had great admiration for orphan train riders' slum-
born drive and resilience, but he wanted to transform them into para-
gons of middle-class restraint and discipline. And finally, he believed
— with more passion than he ever stated publicly — that by removing children from the modern "materialist" city and placing them in
good families in the country, he was encouraging the development of
a humbler, more old-fashioned, and more Christian morality than
that which dominated his ambitious and dynamic era. But at the same
time he believed that the hard work and discipline of farm life would
turn orphan train riders into future statesmen and captains of industry — which is to say, into some of the most ambitious, materialist,
and, as it often turned out, morally corrupt of modern Americans.

This last was a contradiction not simply of Brace's philosophy but
of the entire Victorian era. Even though the pulpits were still dominated by Calvinist notions of human fallibility, much of the rest of society was delirious at the new and, many thought, all but unlimited
freedom of individuals to shape their own destinies and of humanity
to perfect the world. And so it was no accident that these contradictions determined not only the way the CAS treated orphan train riders
but also the roles that at least some of these children would lead in
their adult lives — and no one more so, perhaps, than the child whose
Horatio Alger rise would turn out to be the Emigration Plan's single
most dramatic success.

John Brady's early life could hardly be more typical of the stories commonly featured in the Children's Aid Society annual reports. He was born on May 25, 1848, in a tenement east of Five Points. His parents, James and Catherine, were Irish Catholics who had fled the famine. James was a stevedore and a drunk. Catherine died when John was so young that all he remembered of her were her attempts to keep him from scratching at his smallpox blisters — a futile effort, it would seem, since inflamed blisters would leave him scarred for life.

John's father beat him. At first the beatings had a semirational justification. He was once punished because he ran off to play on the streets when he had been left to care for his infant stepsister. But after James Brady lost his job, the beatings were motivated mainly by alcoholic rage. When John was eight, he ran away from home, staying for a while with his father's sister. But he was, in his own words, "a very bad boy, having an abundance of self-will."[1] When his aunt married and moved to Boston, she did not want to take him with her, and so he had no place to live but the streets.

John may have been homeless for as long as a year. Like most street kids, he survived by a mix of begging, thieving, and doing odd jobs. Some days he got his food by pilfering from the Fulton Market. Other times he would go down by the docks early in the morning when the steamboats jettisoned their refuse. He got his best meals when he could pay for them and earned the money by ripping the lead out from around chimneys and selling it at junk shops, or by running errands for the patrons of taverns and saloons. He also garnered pennies by singing Irish ballads on Broadway, Park Row, and other streets heavily trafficked by affluent New Yorkers. And sometimes he would simply hold out a filthy hand.

One night shortly after Christmas in 1857, when John was nine years old, he was standing in front of the Chatham Street Theater hoping to make a meal out of the half-eaten cobs of hot corn that playgoers were apt to cast onto the sidewalk before taking their seats. After a while he grew tired and cold and sat down on a window grate warmed by an updraft from the theater's basement. The next thing he knew a man was shaking his shoulder and asking whether he wouldn't like to have three solid meals a day.

In his unpublished autobiography, "Zigzags of a New York Streetboy," John identified this man as Theodore Roosevelt Sr., the father of the president. But in a letter to Charles Loring Brace, John described him only as "some kind person from your Society."[2]

Later in life Brady may well have had an ulterior motive for claiming to have been rescued from the gutter by a president's father, but Roosevelt did indeed have a long history with the Children's Aid Society. In 1854 he provided a substantial portion of the original funding for the Newsboys' Lodging House and was a trustee of the society from 1867 to 1878.[3] He also had a tradition of taking his Thanksgiving and Christmas dinners at the lodging house, sometimes with his eldest son and namesake in tow. Given this history, it seems odd that Roosevelt would have recommended that John go, not to the Newsboys' Lodging House, but to the Nursery Department of the House of Refuge on Randall's Island. "His voice was so wonderful," John said in his autobiography, "that he soon won me."[4] Escorted by his rescuer, John went to a nearby police station, where he spent the night. The following morning he was transferred to Randall's Island.

During his year and a half at the refuge, John acquired a couple of tattoos — a cross on his wrist and a "JB" on his elbow (inscribed by rubbing ash into needle wounds) — and hardened into what he would remain, in many ways, for the rest of his life: a bandy street tough, always ready to win his way with his wit or his fists. Photographs taken of him in old age show that he never lost his back-alley cockiness, and even during the last years of his life he was prone to show his displeasure by calling out, "Put up your dukes!"[5]

In July 1859, shortly after his eleventh birthday (although, because of a records mistake, John thought he was only ten), an agent from the Children's Aid Society, H. Friedgen, came to Randall's Island to talk about the Emigration Plan. Friedgen was not a terribly well-educated man. His letters to Brace are filled with gross spelling and grammatical mistakes. But he was deeply committed to the children, and the day he spoke in front of the Randall's Island inmates he was filled with an infectious enthusiasm. He concluded his talk by asking, as John wrote to Brace many years later, "how many boys who have no parents would love to have nice homes in the West, where they can drive horses and oxen, and have as many apples and melons as they should wish?"[6] John had no idea whether his father was alive or dead, but he was so tempted by those horses and melons that he promptly proclaimed himself an orphan and signed up for a trip west. And since no one at the Children's Aid Society or, it would seem, the House of Refuge ever bothered to look into his parentage, he left New York on August 2, 1859, with twenty-seven other children and Friedgen, bound for Indiana. Before leaving New York, however, John met Brace, who gave him and the other children in the party personally inscribed Bibles.

During his first day on the train John looked out at the passing rural cabins and houses, most of them separated by wide stretches of unpeopled fields and forests, and began to feel that the country was a terribly large and lonely place. At one point the train passed a grove of trees, each of which had a pile of wood around its base and tongues of flame licking at its bark. Knowing nothing of "girdling," a common land clearance practice, John could only marvel that the scant citizens of this empty land could be so perverse as to set fire to beautiful trees. His tears began to flow and would not stop until he had fallen asleep.

For much of his weeklong journey west he sat beside Andrew Burke, a boy his own age, whom he recognized from the Randall's Island nursery but had never gotten to know. The two boys had a great deal in common, not only their Irish Catholic backgrounds, their institutionalization, and their shared anxieties and hopes about what would happen to them in their new homes, but also unusual intelligence and determination. They became fast friends on their ride and would stay in touch throughout their lives. Perhaps partly by mutual influence, they would also end up fulfilling startlingly similar destinies.

On the last day of their journey the train stopped at Tipton, Indiana, and John Green, a farmer, judge, and state senator, got on board. During the thirty-mile journey south to Noblesville, Judge Green became curious about the crowd of boisterous young New Yorkers and wandered into the car where they were riding. John Brady would later remember seeing a man standing for some time in the doorway, wearing a dark suit and a soft black hat and holding a cane. As the train pulled into the Noblesville station, however, the man disappeared.

Friedgen took the children off the train and escorted them over to Aunt Jenny Fergusson's hotel, where they had lunch. While they ate, interested adults were allowed into the dining room to observe them and ask questions. It was at some point during this meal that John saw the man in the dark suit again, looking at him from across the room. Years later Judge Green also described this moment: "It was the most motley crowd of youngsters I ever did see. I decided to take John Brady home with me because I considered him the homeliest, toughest, most unpromising boy in the whole lot. I had a curious desire to see what could be made of such a specimen of humanity."[7]

Green had other motives than Henry Higgins–style curiosity for taking the city orphan back to his Tipton farm. His eldest son had left home to run a farm of his own, his next son was on the verge of doing the same, and the judge needed someone trustworthy to keep up the family's original farm while he attended to his other labors.

Despite an early attempt to milk a bull named Augustus Belmont (after the New York financier), John felt right at home from the moment he came to live with the Greens. Although he never particularly took to farm labor, finding it stultifyingly repetitious, he performed his chores dutifully and won the respect and affection of the entire Green family. It was the judge's labors outside the farm — in his law office, the courts, and the state capital — that most intrigued John. He also read the literary and philosophical books that the judge kept on a row of shelves in the family sitting room. An entry in the CAS "Record Book" from not long after John's placement reads: "Mr. John Green writes 'John Brady is still living with me. He is a very attentive boy to his books, is a good arithmetician and is learning grammar and Algebra. He is posted in national affairs and seems to be disposed to make a man of himself.'"[8] After a year on the farm John was enrolled in the local school — where, during his very first week, he demonstrated considerable prowess, both by his academic performance and by knocking the class bully flat on his back.

Although never activists, the Greens were Republicans with abolitionist sympathies. Sometime in 1860 or 1861 they took in an ex-slave named Jim who had come north on the Underground Railroad. John and Jim worked side by side on the farm, the only difference between them being that Jim got paid for his work while John was rewarded by the privilege of quasi-family membership.

In April 1861, near the end of John's second year with the family, South Carolinians fired on Fort Sumter and the judge's second son joined the Union Army. Now nearly fourteen, John also wanted to enlist as a drummer boy, but his foster parents would not hear of it. He was too young, the war was too brutal, and besides, he was needed on the farm.

It was obvious, however, that John was not developing much of a taste for farm life. Thinking that the labor might be sweetened by a taste of its economic rewards, the judge sold John some unfattened stock at a reduced price. John seems to have taken full advantage of the opportunity. When Friedgen visited the farm in August 1865, he reported to the CAS office: "John has grown up to be a fine young man respected by everyone. Has $200 in cash a horse and 7 acres of land."[9]

In the end, however, the profit motive turned out not to be enough to bind the boy to farm life. As soon as Lee surrendered to Grant at Appomattox in April 1865, John began to look for ways to get out into the wider world. One day, on a visit into town, he saw a group of men and women waiting in line to enroll in a teacher training program. He joined them and a short while afterward was appointed master of the Mud Creek Public School in Sharpesville, Indiana, nine miles from Tipton.

During his two years at the school the community suffered a cholera epidemic that infected the entire farm family with whom John was boarding and killed two of them. For an extended period he was the only healthy person in the household and had to nurse the family in addition to carrying on with his duties as schoolmaster.

In a final attempt to persuade John to stay with him, Judge Green made him a proposition: "By continued application," he said during one of John's visits, "you can become a lawyer in my office, or you can take full charge of the farm. I will pay taxes, make the improvements and give you half of what the farm produces."[10] For an era in which the common understanding was that a foster child was infinitely beholden to the family who had taken him in, this was an extraordinarily generous offer. But teaching had only made John more adverse to resuming the life of a farmer, even if he might also practice law. His rejection of the offer brought a look of disappointment into the judge's face that pierced John to the heart. "I was so overcome with emotion," he wrote, "that when I went out on the road I fairly fell on my face and rolled in the dust with agony of tears. I felt that I had lost my best friend in making my decision."[11] Although John had certainly not lost Judge Green's friendship, his decision would make it increasingly difficult for him to visit Tipton over the remaining years of his foster father's life.

Not only had John Brady been placed with what Brace might have thought of as the ideal family, but he himself seems to have been Brace's ideal orphan train rider. At Randall's Island he had listened carefully to visiting missionaries — many of them graduates of the Yale Divinity School and/or Union Theological Seminary — and he seems to have taken them as role models. At Tipton he had similar feelings regarding his Sunday school teacher, about whom he says in his autobiography: "There was a graciousness in his face and manner which won me at once."[12] (Although Brady had been born into a Catholic family, once he came to live with the Greens he attended a Presbyterian church and a Methodist Sunday school and, like most Catholic orphan train riders, seems never to have given a second thought to the religion of his parents.) But it was not until he had gone to Mud Creek that Brady decided to become a minister himself — a decision he made, once again, while under the influence of a clergyman: the Reverend Isaac Montfort. In the fall of 1867, aided by a $100 scholarship that Montfort had obtained for him from the Presbyterian Board of Education, Brady attended the Waveland Collegiate Institute, a preparatory school dedicated to "the intellectual and religious training of pious youth for the gospel ministry."[13] After three years at Waveland, Brady moved on to Brace's own alma mater, the Yale Divinity School.

Brady's journey to New Haven, in the fall of 1870, brought him east for the first time since he had left on his orphan train. Although he made no attempt during an extended stopover in New York City to discover whether his father was still alive, he did visit the offices of the Children's Aid Society and spent some time with John Macy. One result of this visit was that the CAS provided him with money to help defray the cost of his education — although he still had to work to meet expenses: as a janitor during the school year and at a Pennsylvania sawmill during the summer. In October 1871, at Brace's request, Brady wrote a letter telling his life's story and including the pronouncement, "I shall ever acknowledge with gratitude that the Children's Aid Society has been the instrument of my elevation. To be taken from the gutters of New York City and placed in a college is almost a miracle." He signed the letter with the name he had taken shortly after moving to Tipton, "John Green Brady."[14]

While this letter had been requested and written for use in CAS publicity (it appeared in both the society's 1872 annual report and *The Dangerous Classes*), the whole future course of Brady's life attests to its sincerity. After graduating from Yale in 1874, Brady, like Brace, moved to New York to study at Union Theological Seminary. During his three years at Union, Brady worked in city missions and frequently gave inspirational talks to the residents of the Newsboys' Lodging House. And on graduation he decided that he too would devote his life to doing for poor city children what had been done for him.

The problem was that after his years in Indiana Brady no longer had much liking for city life and felt a powerful urge to return west. As it happened, Brace was then struggling with the question of what to do with "large boys" (fourteen years and older) who were turning out to be less than ideal placements, often making trouble for their employers and running away. During a long night at the Children's Aid Society, Brace and Brady came up with a means of solving both of their problems. They decided that John should move to Texas and start an industrial school where boys fourteen to nineteen years old could get a year of basic agricultural training and then be found a job on a farm.

Brady devoted the summer of 1877 to pursuing this plan. In quest of financial support, he visited Theodore Roosevelt, Sr., but got no certain promise of help. He had far better luck with a "lady friend," apparently a major donor to the CAS, who promised him $9,000 if he found a suitable site for his school. He promptly set off for Texas and did find a 1,700-acre plot on the Brazos River that could be purchased for $7,000. But 1877 was a year of great economic upheaval and labor unrest, and during his absence the "lady friend" experienced such severe losses on her investments that she no longer had any money to spare. The industrial school was not to be.

John Brady spent his whole life looking for a father, or at least for an older man whom he might trust to guide him. He had found that man in a series of ministers at Randall's Island, at Tipton, and at Sharpesville, Indiana. He had found him, most especially in Judge Green, and perhaps for a time in Charles Loring Brace. But the man who was to become the single most important influence in Brady's life was Dr. Sheldon Jackson, the remarkably energetic superintendent of the Presbyterian church's missions in eleven western states — a district that covered more than half of the nation's total land mass.

Brady had gotten in touch with Jackson through the intercession of a Yale classmate even before cooking up the Texas industrial school with Brace. Jackson seems to have taken to the young minister almost immediately. On the basis of an exchange of letters and perhaps a meeting, he pegged Brady as a smart, driven man not unlike himself, and he invited Brady to assume a pastorate in Colorado's silver mining district. By that point, however, Brady had committed himself to the industrial school project, so he put Jackson off. When the project collapsed, Brady told Jackson he would be interested in the pastorate after all, but by then the elder evangelist had an entirely new proposition in mind.

Like many a missionary before him, Jackson was an immensely ambitious and skillful power broker who was never able to abide within
the strictures of his church's hierarchy. Shortly before establishing
contact with John Brady, and without the approval of the Presbyterian
Home Missionary Board in New York City, Jackson had opened the
first Presbyterian mission in the newly acquired U.S. possession of
Alaska, expanding the territory over which he had jurisdiction by
nearly 50 percent. But this move also brought Jackson an entirely new
sort of power, since, for the next few decades, missionaries would
make up a substantial portion of Alaska's de facto government. The
other top members of the Presbyterian hierarchy, both in New York
and the West, resented Jackson's end-run around their authority, but
he was too wily and powerful to be removed from office, and they had
no choice but to live with his fait accompli. Jackson, for his part, was
eager to consolidate his holdings, and so when Brady got back in
touch, he invited him to found a second Alaskan mission. The first
had been in the panhandle village of Wrangell. The new mission
would be in Sitka, another panhandle village, and the only other settlement of any importance in that enormous, wild land. Not insignificantly, Sitka was also Alaska's capital.

In 1878 no more than 200 white Yankees lived in Alaska — almost all
of them in the forested archipelago of the southern panhandle. The
panhandle settlements were also occupied by about 2,000 "Creoles,"
the mostly Russian-speaking descendants of fur traders and native
women. The overwhelming majority of the Alaskan population —
more than 30,000 people — were members of four Native American
groups: the Eskimos in the northwest, along the Bering Sea; the Aleuts
along a trail of islands arcing westward toward Siberia; the Athapascans in the Yukon Valley, which roughly bisects the Alaskan main-
land in an east-west direction; and finally, the Northwest Coast Indians in the panhandle.[15]

When nearly thirty-year-old John Brady marched down the gangplank of the SS *California* on Saint Patrick's Day in 1878, Sitka was little more than a settlement of two or three score white clapboard
houses clustered between a row of jagged hills and the rocky coast. Its
grandest buildings were the onion-domed Saint Michael's Church and
the Baranov Castle, a multilevel, hotel-like structure that occupied the
highest promontory near the harbor, both of which had been built by
the original Russian settlers.

At the time of Brady's arrival, one hundred or so white Yankees occupied the highest strata of Sitka's social hierarchy. Some of these were
the customs and naval officers who had been posted to Alaska — virtually all that existed of government. But the majority were transients
— men mostly, attracted by Alaska's great emptiness and tales of its
extraordinary natural resources. They were trappers, fishermen, lum-
berjacks, carpenters, blacksmiths, coopers, and shopkeepers, and most
of them did not stay for more than one of the territory's dark, intermi-
nable, gut-freezing winters. The next level down from the whites were
the Creoles, permanent residents who plied many of the same trades
as the Yankees and also served as translators between them and the local Tlingit-speaking natives. Below the Creoles were a smattering of
Chinese, Turks, and other non-Europeans, many of whom had been
imported to perform menial, quasi-slave labors. And finally, at the
very bottom rung of Sitka society were the Tlingits, who lived in a separate, desperately poor section of town called "the Ranche."

In his early visits to the Ranche, Brady was struck by its resemblance to the slums of New York City. Here too stinking open sewers
ran along the streets; here too were drunken, brutal husbands and
drunken, beaten wives and children with shut-down faces who lived
by begging and thievery, and "fallen women" who had been forced
to "surrender their virtue," often to white trappers and sailors, and
had no place in either culture. Like Brace before him, Brady knew that
preaching and prayer were not enough to solve the problems of the
Ranche. So he decided that the first major project of his mission
would be the founding, at long last, of his industrial school.

Brady's career is fascinating not only for how it illustrates the influence of Brace's work and personal magnetism but for the way Brady's
own work reveals hidden aspects of Brace's. Brady's efforts to duplicate elements of the CAS in Alaska show the cultural limitations of
Brace's ideas and illustrate how, even in New York, the CAS unwit-
tingly worked to suppress the values of one culture (or class) in favor
of another.

Everybody in Alaska despised the missionaries. The natives hated being forced to submit to their humiliating rituals and nonsensical ideas
about clothing, sex, home life, and the spirit. The whites hated the
missionaries because they "loved" the natives — and supported prohibition.

When Alaska was purchased from Russia in 1867, Congress decreed that the territory's entire 586,000 square miles should be off limits to "spirituous liquor," a policy meant in part to prevent Alaskan natives from succumbing to the ruinous alcoholism of Native Americans in the "Lower Forty." Not surprisingly, liquor smuggling was a major Alaskan industry, as was the distillation of a local concoction called, in the native language, *hoochinoo* (from which we derive the word *hooch*). The very boat that first dropped Brady off at Sitka also carried twenty-two barrels of molasses, which were hurried straight from the docks to illicit distilleries.[16]

By law, local customs officers and a minute naval force (two single-stack steamships) were responsible for enforcing the liquor ban, but in practice the most visible opponents of alcohol consumption were the missionaries. They were constantly preaching against drunkenness and liked nothing so much as to overturn a vat of hoochinoo onto a muddy street. Although never a teetotaler himself, one of Brady's very first acts as a missionary was to get all of the merchants of Sitka to sign a document saying that they would import no more molasses for use in illegal distillation. The merchants kept their word. They ordered brown sugar instead, and hoochinoo production went on without interruption.[17] Brady soon realized that prohibition in Alaska was a total failure and he would become a strong campaigner for its suspension.

Yankee Alaskans also despised missionaries for their role in U.S. education policy. Although building schools was always presented as quasi-charity for the benefit of natives and whites alike, education was the primary means by which the federal government hoped to pacify Alaska's enormous population of "ignorant savages" — yet another "dangerous class" who needed serious retrofitting if they were not to become a burden or a threat to American society. Education was such a high priority that for twenty-one years after the establishment of civil government in 1884 Alaska's sole representative in Washington — the man who advised presidents on all territorial matters, including the appointment of governors — was the general agent for education. It did John Brady's career no harm that this all-important bureaucrat was none other than Dr. Sheldon Jackson.

According to the prevailing theory, Indians and Eskimos had lifted themselves out of primal "savagery" but were stuck in the phase of "barbarism" that preceded "civilization." Many whites, including Brady and Jackson, who styled themselves as sympathetic to natives,

saw education as the mechanism that would at last enable these be-
nighted peoples to achieve civilized enlightenment. As early as 1819 the
U.S. government designated an annual appropriation of $10,000 to a
"Civilization Fund" for the purpose of educating Indians. Soon after
the purchase of Alaska from Russia, the U.S. commissioner of education urged the creation of a similar fund to educate Alaskan natives.
And shortly after Jackson's appointment, he and Brady were able to
win $15,000 specifically for Brady's industrial school.[18] Some years
later they managed to raise the federal contribution to Alaska's total
education budget from $30,000 to $145,153 per year. What infuriated
many white Alaskans was Brady and Jackson's stipulation that this
money be spent without regard to race — which, as the Yankees saw it,
meant less money and learning for their own children. Most whites
believed that every dollar spent on the Indians was wasted. If the natives became a problem, there were much simpler ways of civilizing
them.

Brady may have served the federal government's interest in native pac-
ification, and his own church's interest in conversion, but he did so for
profoundly personal reasons. Sounding the urban missionary, he told
a gathering of church women early in his career, "To Christianize the
Indians without helping them to new industries and new methods of
earning money is to impoverish and to make them more wretched.
The work of the church is only half done in giving them the gospel;
she must also assist them in their efforts to live a Christian life."[19]
    Although Brady founded a maternity hospital for native women,
and an all-Indian police force that kept the peace in the Ranche, his
industrial school, the Sitka Training Institute, was the absolute center of his missionary labors. The school was constructed entirely by
skilled native carpenters. (Woodworking — the construction of totem
poles and large, plank lodges — was an ancient part of Northwest
Coast Indian culture.) The students were taught how to do needlework, to weave and to fish with nets, and to operate cannery and sawmill equipment. They were also taught the four R's of all mission
schools. But for Brady, the last R — religion — was less a matter of
church doctrine than the values of bourgeois liberalism.
    Brady had considerable respect for Indians and their culture. Dur-
ing the course of his career he frequently asserted that native Alaskans
were "a hardy, hardworking and industrious people, and have always
been self-supporting."[20] He was one of the only white officials in Sitka

to learn to speak Tlingit, and he amassed a substantial collection of
Tlingit art that he ultimately put into a museum open to both natives
and whites. With all of his respect, however, there were certain traits of
Indian culture that Brady could not abide and felt that native Alaskans
must transcend if they were ever to achieve dignity and contentment
within American society. And it was to these traits that he was referring when he declared that the church must assist the Indians in their
"efforts to live a Christian life."

Prime among those traits, of course, was native religion, which
seemed mere superstition to Brady. He also strenuously objected to
the Tlingit practice of slavery. But he was most a man of his era when
he condemned communal living and property. Echoing Brace's anxiety about overcrowded tenement basements, Brady believed that the
custom of large extended families living under one roof (in one large
room, really) corrupted the morals of girls and was thus the main reason for the Ranche's large population of "fallen women." And communal property, he thought, deprived Indians of a major incentive to
adopt the Protestant work ethic, as well as to develop self-reliance, individuality, thrift, and that most mercurial of virtues, ambition. Communal property also made it difficult to punish natives, since they
could not be fined or deprived of assets if they did not own anything.
Thus, Brady attempted to help natives in their "efforts to live a Christian life" by encouraging them to move into single-family homes, by
attempting to pass laws sanctioning native ownership of land, and
finally (in a variation of the strategy that had transformed his own
life) by separating children from their parents.

Children could not attend the Sitka Training Institute unless their
parents agreed to let them live there for at least five years. Expressing Brace's own "environmentalist" beliefs in more naked and global
terms, Brady asserted that only through such an extended separation from their families could native children be cleansed of the most
pernicious elements of their culture. He sometimes subjected particularly promising or troubling students to even more profound separa-
tions by sending them to the Carlisle Indian School in Pennsylvania.
Founded by Richard Henry Pratt, the Carlisle school had adopted the
motto: "Kill the Indian and save the man."[21]

Although Brady may well have modeled his career on Brace's, he
would never so wholly devote himself to laboring "among the poor,
the weak, the forgotten." He had been poor himself, after all, and knew

far more intimately than Brace what a fragile privilege it was to have good and wholesome food on the table and a warm coat on his back. Also, however high-mindedly he may have lectured his students about the importance of hard work and the acquisition of property, he was living at a time and place in which such virtues were far more — and less — than moral ideals. This was the era when Carnegie, Morgan, Rockefeller, and others were building up the nation's first great fortunes. And in spite of its extraordinary beauty, the Alaskan frontier was a place where most people came only for one reason: to get rich quick.

Soon after his arrival in Alaska, Brady went into partnership with an ex-liquor smuggler, Amos T. Whitford, to open the Sitka Trading Company, a one-room store selling everything from oil lamps and canned food to underwear and native art. The store did so well that Brady and Whitford soon opened a second branch in Juneau. The two partners were never wholly compatible, however, especially on moral and social issues. Brady particularly objected to Whitford's desire to institute a Jim Crow policy, which would have required natives to enter the store by a back entrance. But when Brady finally sold his share of the company to Whitford in 1891, it was not for moral reasons, but because he wanted to put more money into his second business, the Sitka Sawmill Company.

This profitable venture grew directly out of his missionary work. In 1882, capitalizing on what he had learned working at a Pennsylvania sawmill during a summer vacation from Yale, Brady bought a primitive, steam-driven saw with the idea of providing vocational training for his industrial school students while at the same time generating income for the school. Apparently Brady's mill was considerably more profitable than Brace's cobbling and box-making businesses. In 1889 he built a new mill with an up-to-date saw and planer, and by 1891 Brady had spun the venture off as a wholly independent business with himself as the sole owner. Even after the mill had become independent, Brady drew on native apprentices from his industrial school to operate it and, for this reason, was charged with slavery by his enemies.

Brady was certainly not one to pass up a bargain, but as he saw it, while he may have profited from the students' free labor, they were getting on-the-job training — just exactly the sort of exchange on which the apprentice system had been founded. He also had paid native mill hands, mechanics, and engineers working for him — some of them Sitka Training Institute graduates. One of these natives, Peter Simpson, eventually capitalized on what he had learned working for Brady by founding Alaska's first all-Indian business: a sawmill on Gravina Island.

Brady's store and sawmill earned considerable money and helped transform him into one of the pillars of Alaskan Yankee society. But the true engineer of his fate remained Sheldon Jackson. In 1884, shortly after his appointment as general agent for education, Jackson persuaded President Chester Alan Arthur to designate Brady one of Alaska's four commissioners. As a commissioner, Brady was, in essence, a justice of the peace; he adjudicated in assault, petty larceny, liquor smuggling, probate, and other similar cases. Long after rejecting Judge Green's offer of a partnership in his law business, Brady finally did study law, and on May 6, 1885, he officially became known as Judge Brady. He was the fourth person admitted to the bar in Alaska.

When Benjamin Harrison was elected president in 1888, Jackson saw an opportunity. Harrison was both a Republican, like Jackson and Brady, and a Presbyterian. Jackson hoped that the new president might be inclined to help solidify what the press called the "Presbyterian hierarchy" — a group of missionaries and fellow travelers, including Brady, that, thanks to Jackson's efforts, was coming close to dominating the political establishment in Alaska. On January 22, 1889, shortly before Harrison's inauguration, Jackson wrote him a letter that was addressed: "Dear Brother," and read, in part, "It gives me great pleasure to transmit to you the action of the Presbytery of Alaska, and also of the Missionaries and teachers of the Southeastern Alaska recommending to your favorable attention Mr. John G. Brady of Sitka, as Governor of Alaska." Jackson went on to remind Harrison that the governors appointed by his predecessors, Rutherford B. Hayes, James Garfield, and Chester Alan Arthur, had been "Godless, drinking" men, and that eight-tenths of Alaska's population were "Indians or natives just emerging from barbarism," whose interests could be served by no one better than John Brady.[22] Jackson also had dozens of congressmen, ex-Alaskan officials, religious leaders, and members of the Women's Christian Temperance Union deluge Harrison and his secretary of the interior with similar letters.

On the basis of this campaign and Brady's reputation, the *Juneau City Mining Record* newspaper considered him almost a shoo-in:

He is the unanimous choice of the better element in Alaska. . . . He is a Christian gentleman of high intellectual abilities, and has used every effort to aid the missionaries in reclaiming Indians from barbarism. As a businessman he has been successful, and has gained an almost un-limited knowledge, through long residence, of the habits and customs of the Indians. . . . Mr. Brady is a staunch Republican. . . . [T]he only opposing faction in either party consists of those who ridicule mis-sionary efforts and are engaged in the sale of intoxicating liquors, ille-gally in Alaska.[23]

In the end, however, not wanting to appear prejudiced in favor of his own denomination — or so Jackson theorized — Harrison chose a *non*-Presbyterian for governor. Jackson and Brady had to wait for the better part of a decade — until another Republican, William Mc-Kinley, was elected to office — before they could launch a second campaign. And this time Brady took a much more active role in work-ing toward his own appointment.

In February 1897, the month before McKinley's inauguration, Brady headed south to Seattle, Portland, and San Francisco, where he gained the support of prominent western politicians, religious figures, and businessmen. Then he journeyed east, to New York, where he visited Charles Loring Brace Jr., who had assumed leadership of the Children's Aid Society on his father's death in 1890. The younger Brace gave Brady a letter of introduction to C. N. Bliss, the secretary of the interior, and the man who would become Brady's immediate superior should he be appointed governor. Brady then headed south to Wash-ington, where he stayed with Jackson's family, met with Bliss, and, in April, had a meeting with President McKinley. The new chief execu-tive was pleasant, but noncommittal. Brady returned home in early June, certain that the brewing war with Spain would cause McKinley to delay making appointments to crucial posts. But on June 25, Brady received a letter from Interior Secretary Bliss: "There is transmitted herewith, under separate cover, a commission from the President for your appointment to the office of Governor of Alaska . . . you have been so nominated to and confirmed by the Senate."[24]

*

John Green Brady served as governor during the wildest and most corrupt period of Alaska's history. On August 16, 1896, an American prospector named George Carmack struck gold on Bonanza Creek, a tributary of the Klondike River in Canada's Yukon Territory. News of the strike did not leak out until the fall, and because of the territory's long harsh winters, the Yukon Gold Rush did not begin in earnest until just about the time of Brady's appointment.

While the gold strike had been in Canada, the two main routes for traveling to the Klondike passed through Alaska. The easiest of these routes was to travel up the Yukon River from the Bering Sea, right across the center of the territory. A route that seemed much shorter but was far more arduous was to travel across the coastal mountains from the panhandle. During the warm months of 1897 and 1898, tens of thousands of often ill-prepared prospectors traveled across Alaska in quest of riches. Some would walk away from the Klondike with hundreds of thousands of dollars in their pockets, but most did little more than bankrupt themselves financially, physically, and morally. In scant weeks whole cities rose up where there had been only tiny settlements — cities that stank, buzzed with flies, and were infested with rodents and every variety of human vermin: gamblers, thieves, prostitutes, claim jumpers, drunks, and con artists. Rising crime rates also brought a rise in vigilante justice. In the aptly named boomtown of Skagway, where it was reported that "at least every other house is a saloon or a dance house,"[25] a Frenchman caught midrobbery by a group of miners was shot to death while he screamed for mercy. As a warning to others, the Frenchman's body was then hung from a tent pole for three days — not a sight that encouraged much respect for the law.

The gold rush also caused many less colorful but nonetheless serious problems. A huge escalation in demand for goods and services led to a steep rise in inflation and considerable hardship for the poorest Alaskans, especially the town natives. As winter approached, public concern arose that droves of greenhorn prospectors might starve or freeze to death. So Brady amassed food and sent out troops along the major gold rush routes to hunt — in vain as it turned out — for potential victims. While few if any greenhorns succumbed to starvation or cold, the long, lightless, frigid winter during which prospectors sometimes spent weeks isolated in their cabins apparently caused so many to go mad that Brady had to order the construction of an insane asylum to house all the lunatics who descended on the cities and towns with the spring thaw.

The intensity of the Klondike Gold Rush diminished considerably with the start of the Spanish-American War in April 1898. The sure pay offered by the army, as well as the chance of glory, was more than many of the exhausted and penniless prospectors could resist. But by the autumn of 1898 the war was all but over and gold had been struck again — this time in Nome, on the southern edge of the Seward Peninsula, not far from the Bering Strait. The following spring a whole new crop of prospectors came north with their picks and pack mules and their lust for lucre and liquor.

As a result of the two gold rushes, Alaska's white population doubled in the last half-decade of the nineteenth century, reaching an estimated 24,000, and coming close to parity with the 31,000 natives and Russian Creoles — whose population actually diminished in some places.[26]

Governor Brady was deeply troubled by the effect of the gold rushes on the native populations, especially the Eskimo, whose situation he described in his annual report of 1902:

> We have invaded his country and have killed and driven off the whale, walrus, seals, and caribous, and in places have made fish scarce. We have gone along the shores of Bering Sea and have burned up the driftwood on the beach, set fire to the tundras, have driven off the birds, and in our mad hunt for gold we have burrowed under his rude barrabbara and allowed it to tumble, even when the inmates were sick and dying.[27]

Brady had been a strong advocate for native Alaskans from the very beginning of his administration. His first annual report in 1898 asserted that Alaskan Indians and Eskimos should "be admitted to the enjoyment of all the rights, advantages, and immunities as citizens of the United States, and . . . be maintained and protected in the free enjoyment of their life, liberty, and property."[28] Much of his work as governor focused on improving conditions for the native populations — although always with an eye toward aiding the progress of "civilization." He imported herds of Siberian reindeer, for example, for two reasons: to give the Eskimos and Athapascans a new source of meat and fur to compensate for what the prospectors had eaten and driven away, and to keep them too busy maintaining reindeer herds to succumb to the lure of the white men's saloons.

He employed a similar rationale in his drive to win Alaskan natives the right to federal "homestead" claims. In 1862 Congress had passed the Homestead Act, a law designed to speed white migration into the Midwest and West. Under that law, for a $10 fee, the government would give 160 acres of land to anyone who farmed or otherwise improved it for five years. Although the Homestead Act clearly accomplished its goal of drawing crowds of settlers west, its application had been so full of conflict and corruption that Congress would not extend it to Alaska. For much of his tenure as governor, Brady had to fight for the homestead rights for any Alaskans — red or white — but in asserting that natives also had a right to homestead claims, he argued that land ownership would naturally tend to "civilize" them by breaking down their communalism.

In the pursuit of these and other causes, Brady traveled frequently to Washington to lobby Congress. On one such trip he stopped off at the Indian School in Carlisle, Pennsylvania, where he shared the stage with the former governor of North Dakota, a robust and good-looking man of forty-nine with a weighty, dark mustache and receding hairline. Brady too was forty-nine, and entirely white-haired, with a full, closely trimmed beard, but still possessing the compact, wiry body and defiantly lifted chin of a street tough. These two men had looked decidedly different the first time they had sat beside one another, nearly forty years before. The former governor of North Dakota was none other than Andrew Burke, Brady's fellow inmate from Randall's Island whom he had befriended on their orphan train.

While Brady had moved north to Tipton, Andrew Burke's first placement had been with a man who lived right in Noblesville, the town where, during lunch in Aunt Jenny Fergusson's hotel, the children had first been on display. Although Burke would live with three different families during the time that he was tracked by the CAS, he claimed to be happy and "doing well" in each one of them.[29] After serving as a drummer boy in the Union Army during the Civil War, he attended college at Ashbury (now DePauw) University in Greencastle, Indiana, but dropped out as a result of a breakdown attributed to "over study."[30] There is no way of knowing how often he and Brady

communicated with each other over the years, but Burke's CAS file
does mention a letter from Brady stating, "Andy is attending College
in Greencastle," and it may well be that Burke's military service was
what had made Brady so eager to be a drummer boy during the Civil
War.

After trying his hand at various businesses in Indiana, Illinois,
Ohio, and Minnesota, Burke became a cashier at the First National
Bank of Casselton, Dakota. (The territory had not yet been divided
into north and south.) He was elected treasurer of Cass County, Dakota, three times and became the second governor of the new state of
North Dakota in 1891, after being elected by a substantial majority on
the Republican ticket. Like his predecessor and successor during those
turbulent first years of statehood, Burke lasted only one term and left
office in January 1893. He failed in a go at the grain business back in
Minnesota and finally got himself appointed inspector of the U.S.
Land Office by President McKinley, a position he held until his retirement. At the time of his reunion with John Brady, he was living in
Colorado but would soon move to New Mexico, where he would remain until his death in 1918.[31]

Like many street kids before them, these two men of state were
making the best of their stories. Indeed, Andrew Burke's Horatio Alger
rise in society is featured prominently in many contemporary accounts of his career[32] and must certainly have played a role in his cam-
paigns. Brady does not seem to have made much of his origins until
after his election, but then he was frequently feted as he was at the
Carlisle School. In 1900 C. P. Vedder, a former state senator from New
York, presented Brady with an award at the Waldorf Astoria Hotel,
proclaiming, "Alaska's Governor illustrated the possibilities open to
any American boy. Grander victories than those of Napoleon are on
the common field of life."[33]

Brady and Burke were not, of course, the only ones using their stories. Everyone who celebrated, toasted, awarded, or merely praised
them did so to glorify any number of causes, from the Children's Aid
Society to American democracy. Typical of such eulogies are the remarks of the *Wall Street Journal* reporter who, not long after Brady's
award at the Waldorf, wrote: "The Governor's life is all wrapped up in
the country. The story of his own life is so remarkable, and his rise to
distinction so unique, that he naturally is in great love with American
institutions, and naturally is using his present power to extend them

fully over Alaska."[34] What none of these commentators (nor perhaps Brady and Burke themselves) seem to have recognized was that the very uniqueness of the two orphan train riders' rise in society said at least as much about what was wrong with the world in which they lived as it did about what was right.

Brady exploited his own story most blatantly at a meeting of western governors in Portland, Oregon, in 1900. The meeting had been called to honor the governor of New York, Theodore Roosevelt Jr., who was William McKinley's new running mate in his bid for reelection. When candidate Roosevelt walked into the room, the western governors lined up to greet him, with Brady bringing up the rear. Roosevelt and Brady's conversation was transcribed in Corinne Roosevelt Robinson's memoir of her brother:

> BRADY: Governor Roosevelt, the other governors have greeted you with interest simply as a fellow governor and a great American, but I greet you with infinitely more interest, as the son of your father, the first Theodore Roosevelt.
>
> ROOSEVELT (*while shaking John's hand warmly*): In what special way have you been interested in my father?
>
> BRADY: Your father picked me up from the streets of New York, a waif and an orphan, and sent me to a western family, paying for my transportation and early care. Years passed and I was able to repay the money which had given me my start in life, but I can never repay what he did for me, but it is through that early care and by giving me such a foster mother and father that I gradually rose in the world, until today I can greet his son as a fellow governor of a part of our great country.[35]

With all of his phenomenal success, in the presence of this up-and-coming patrician Brady instantly reverted to street-boy beggar, hustling Roosevelt with the most battle-proven Victorian clichés about the noble benefactor and the deserving and grateful waif — most of it sheer fantasy. If the elder Roosevelt actually was the man who picked Brady up from the street, he certainly never contributed a penny directly toward the boy's expense, and far from paying him back, when they met again, Brady only asked for *more* money. It is not clear how the candidate responded to this overture. Although it is true that Brady scored many of his most important Washington victories during Roosevelt's administration, Roosevelt had no hesitation about casting Brady aside the moment he became inconvenient.

Within a year of this first meeting the newly reelected William Mc-Kinley was assassinated at the Pan American Exposition in Buffalo, New York, and Roosevelt became the twenty-sixth president of the United States. For a while Roosevelt was Brady's firm ally, strongly seconding his opinion that Indians should be granted citizenship and the right to equal treatment with whites under the law, and helping to bring about the legal recognition of Creole Alaskans' "natural-born" rights of citizenship. (Full-blooded Indians and Eskimos would have to wait until some years after Brady's term of office to be granted equivalent rights.) It was also during Roosevelt's administration that Brady and Jackson were able to quintuple federal education expenditures in Alaska and Brady himself finally succeeded in getting Congress to pass legislation granting native Alaskans the right to homestead 160 acres of government land — although this happened only after whites had been granted the right to homestead twice that acreage.[36]

Brady was least successful during the Roosevelt administration as an advocate for Alaska itself. Like many of his constituents, he worried that competition from Cuba, the Philippines, and the other islands the United States had acquired during the Spanish-American War would drain federal funds and programs away from Alaska. He took advantage of every opportunity to tout the territory's economic and strategic importance to the United States but on several occasions ended looking the fool. One time, for example, when he had made extravagant claims about Alaska's agriculture, a senator told a story about a mule who had been made so miserable by the territory's harsh climate that "he walked down into the ocean, waited for the tide, and committed suicide."[37]

Despite such occasional missteps, Roosevelt had enough respect for Brady to appoint him, in 1905, to an unprecedented third term as governor. In the end the relationship between the two men would not sour over Brady's performance of his official duties but over his pursuit of his own financial advantage.

Roosevelt took office during the Progressive Era, a period of heightened public intolerance of governmental corruption, and thus he was eager to stay clear of any appearance of impropriety. One of Brady's

great assets as a presidential appointee was that everyone, even his enemies, considered him thoroughly honest. If anything, Brady was opposed for being *too* good, for being naive and not supportive enough
of business interests — for being a "damned missionary." All of this
began to change in the summer of 1902, when, for the first time in his
life, he surrendered himself to the influence of a man who was something of an evangelical — but decidedly not a missionary.

H. D. "Harry" Reynolds was a flamboyant, big-talking businessman
from Boston, the very embodiment of the profit-oriented utopianism
that Brady had sought to inspire in Washington. He walked down the
gangplank onto the Sitka pier spewing gorgeous visions of an amal-
gam of railroad, mining, and real estate ventures that would combine
business and community development into a mutually reinforcing cy-
cle of growth. The problem was that Reynolds was less interested in
actually creating the reliably profitable business ventures (primarily
mining) on which all of his other schemes depended than in the
beauty of his vision. His main goal seemed to be to convince people
that he was an up-and-coming captain of industry, a man whom they
could trust with their money and their hopes. He was, in short, a consummate con man — the nineteenth-century entrepreneurial spirit's
revenge against itself. Investors all over the East and in Alaska believed
his hype about the arm-in-arm progress of business and frontier settlement and poured their money into his paper corporations. Brady
himself turned over, to the horror of his wife, Elizabeth, all the money
he had saved for their children's education. His biggest mistake, however, was to allow Reynolds to name him as the "resident director" of
the Reynolds-Alaska Development Company, and to attach his signa-
ture to at least one promotional letter.

Reynolds's use of Brady's office to lend an air of legitimacy to his
decidedly shady operations provoked an investigation by the U.S. Department of the Interior. Although, in the end, Brady was found guilty
of nothing more than bad judgment, his reputation for honesty was so
thoroughly tainted that President Roosevelt compelled him to resign
the governorship on March 2, 1906.

Even after his relationship with Reynolds had cost him his job and
his good name, Brady still professed faith, both in the man and in his
business. Elizabeth Brady was astonished by her husband's continued
fascination with someone she had recognized early on as a shyster. Her
only explanation was that Brady had been "mesmerized" — which to

some extent must have been true, even if it was only by the beautiful dream that Reynolds represented, and perhaps by the ghost of a father's love. Brady also had more pragmatic reasons for sticking by Reynolds: to rescue his own savings and the money he had convinced friends to invest in the partnership. Sadly, all of his efforts were in vain. Reynolds-Alaska staggered for a year and a half after Brady's retirement before finally collapsing into bankruptcy in the fall of 1907.

Now nearly sixty, Brady was jobless and all but broke. He and his family left Alaska for Brookline, Massachusetts, where his children could go to good schools and he could employ his "old boy" connections from Yale to look for work. The family lived extremely frugally and had to sell much of their collection of native Alaskan art to meet expenses. Finally, in 1911, Brady got a job at the General Manifold and Printing Company in New York City, and the family moved to Manhattan, where they lived for five years.

During this period Alaska was never far from Brady's thoughts. In the seclusion of the New York Public Library he wrote articles for popular journals both on his experiences and on Alaskan political issues. In one series of essays for *Commerce and Industries,* Brady extracted revenge by attacking Roosevelt's conservation policy as "a knockout blow to the coal business in Alaska."[38]

It was also in the library that Brady attempted to write his autobiography, but somehow he never managed to get past his Union Theological Seminary days. When he thought about his "story" — his rise from the gutter to the university — he could rest assured that almost no one had accomplished the like, and he could feel justly happy and proud. But when he compared his life after Yale and Union with the lives of his fellow students, his accomplishments must not have seemed nearly so remarkable, especially given his present state of impecunity and disgrace in the very city he had fled so many years before.

In August 1916, Brady, his wife, and his eldest daughter at last returned to Alaska for good. He was sixty-eight years old and still carried himself with the pluck of a street tough. But he was not in good health, having suffered from diabetes since before leaving office. His eldest son was waiting for the family at the Sitka docks and was at Brady's side when, midway down the gangplank, he stopped, staggered, and fell, having suffered a stroke. Brady survived, only to deteriorate steadily for another two years. He died in Sitka on December 17,

1918, a month after the armistice ended the First World War, and during the same year that his fellow orphan train rider, Andrew Burke, died in New Mexico.

♪

Although John Brady and Andrew Burke were certainly the most dramatic successes of all the orphan train riders, they were not the only ones to hold government office. James Richards, who had been placed by the CAS in Philadelphia, Ohio, became a congressman. Thomas Jefferson Cunningham became mayor of Chippewa Falls, Wisconsin, and was the oldest delegate at the 1940 Democratic Convention, which renominated Franklin Delano Roosevelt. And the orphan train rider Henry L. Jost was mayor of Kansas City, Missouri, from 1912 to 1916 and later served in Congress.[39]

A list of "Noteworthy Careers" published in the CAS annual report for 1917, the year before Brady's and Burke's deaths, reads:

> a Governor of a State, a Governor of a Territory, two members of Congress, two District Attorneys, two Sheriffs, two Mayors, a Justice of the Supreme Court, four Judges, two college professors, a cashier of an insurance company, twenty-four clergymen, seven high school Principals, two School Superintendents, an Auditor-General of a State, nine members of State Legislatures, two artists, a Senate Clerk, six railroad officials, eighteen journalists, thirty four bankers, nineteen physicians, thirty-five lawyers, four civil engineers, and any number of business and professional men, clerks, mechanics, farmers, and their wives and others who have acquired property and filled positions of honor and trust.[40]

Does the existence of these 180 enumerated "Noteworthy Careers" among the approximately 100,000 children whom the CAS had placed in rural homes by 1917 constitute significant evidence of success?[41] Certainly not — and not only because the people who accomplished these careers represent only .0018 percent of all orphan train riders up until that time. To truly measure the success (or failure) of the orphan trains we would have to come up with some means of comparing each orphan train rider's level of happiness, modified by each one's level of moral decency (since a contented psychopathic murderer could not be counted a success by any sane measure), with the happiness–moral decency quotient they would have had under any of the other possible treatments, including no treatment at all. All pipe dreams, of course. How are we to agree even on a definition of happiness, let alone moral decency?

The Children's Aid Society's oft-made claims of 87 to 90 percent success rates were founded on little more than wishful thinking.[42] The records for most orphan train riders simply are not complete enough to provide any realistic evaluation of the success or failure of the placements. Still, what evidence exists, both inside and apart from the files, would indicate that many of the orphan train riders did find happy placements, or at least went on to lead rich and satisfying lives. And there are even cases where the record indicated that the placement had been an unmitigated disaster whereas in fact the child ultimately did quite well.

When all is said and done, however, even if we make the most generous interpretation of the available evidence, it would seem that a substantial majority of orphan train riders did *not* find the happiness or the loving homes that everyone associated with the Children's Aid Society hoped they would. Many of these children were deeply troubled, psychologically and physically, and probably would not have found happiness under any conditions. But even so, as the years passed and the number of orphan train riders mounted into the tens of thousands and then the scores of thousands, and particularly as attitudes toward children and poverty began to evolve, it became increasingly clear that the Children's Aid Society and its imitators were not doing all that they could to help the children under their care find whatever portion of happiness and decency that might be theirs in life.

PART III

Redoing

TESTIMONY

LOTTE STERN

ℐℛ Nov. 2. [1853] — Mrs. Forster, the excellent matron of the female department of the prison, had told us of an interesting young German girl, committed for vagrancy, who might just at this crisis be rescued. We entered these soiled and gloomy Egyptian archways, so appropriate and so depressing, that the sight of the low columns and lotus capital is to me now inevitably associated with the somber and miserable histories of the place. After a short while the girl was brought in — a German girl, apparently about fourteen, very thinly but neatly dressed, slight figure, and a face intelligent and old for her years. . . .

Her eye had a hard look, but softened when I spoke to her in her own language.

"Have you been long here?"

"Only two days, sir."

"Why are you here?"

"I will tell you, sir. I was working out with a lady. I had to get up early and go to bed late, and I never had rest. She worked me always; and finally, because I could not do everything, she beat me — she beat me like a dog, and I ran away. I could not bear it." . . .

"But I thought you were arrested for being near a place of bad character," said I.

"I am going to tell you, sir. The next day I and my father went to get some clothes I left there, and the lady wouldn't give them up — and what could we do? What can the poor do? My father is a poor old man who picks rags in the streets, and I have never picked rags yet. He said, 'I don't want you to be a rag-picker. You are not a child now — people will look at you — you will come to harm.' And I said, 'No, father, I will help you. We must do something now I am out of place'; and so I went out. I picked all day, and didn't make much, and I was cold and hungry. Towards night a gentleman met me, a very fine, well-dressed gentleman, an American, and he said, 'Will you go home with me?' and I said 'No.' He said, 'I will give you twenty shillings' [$2.50], and I told him I would go. And the next morning I was taken up outside by the officer."

"Poor girl!" said some one, "had you forgotten your mother? and what a sin it was!"

"No, sir, I did remember her. She had no clothes and I had no shoes, and I have only this (she shivered in her thin dress), and winter is coming on. I know what making money is, sir. I am only fourteen, but I am old enough. I have had to take care of myself ever since I was ten years old, and I have never had a cent given me. It may be a sin, sir (and the tears rained down her cheeks, which she did not deign to wipe away), I do not ask you to forgive it. Men cannot forgive, but God will forgive. I know about men. The rich do such things and worse, and no one says anything against them. But I, sir — I am poor! . . . I have never had any one to take care of me. Many is the day I have gone hungry from morning till night, because I did not dare spend a cent or two, the only ones I had. Oh, I have wished sometimes to die! Why does God not kill me!"

She was choked by her sobs. We let her calm herself a moment, and then told her our plan of finding her a good home, where she could make an honest living. She was mistrustful. "I will tell you, Meine Hern; I know men, and I do not believe any one, I have been cheated so often. There is no trust in any one. I am not a child. I have lived as long as people twice as old."

"But you do not wish to stay in prison."

"Oh, God, no! Oh, there is such a weight on my heart here. There is nothing but bad to learn in a prison. These dirty Irish girls! I would kill myself if I had to stay here. Why was I ever born? I have such Kummerniss (woes) here (she pressed her hands on her heart) — I am poor!"

We explained more, and she became satisfied. We wished her to be bound to stay some years. "No," said she passionately, "I cannot; I confess to you, gentlemen, I should either run away or die if I was bound."

We talked with the matron. She had never known, she said, in her experience, such a remarkable girl. The children there of nine or ten years were often as old as young women, but this girl was an experienced woman. The offense, however, she had no doubt was her first. We obtained her release; and one of us, Mr. G. [Mr. Gerry, an early CAS visitor], walked over to her house or cabin, some three miles on the other side of Williamsburg, in order that she might see her parents before she went. As she walked along, she looked up in Mr. G.'s face and asked thoughtfully why we came there for her? He explained. She listened, and after a little while said in broken English, "Don't you think better for poor little girls to die than live!" He spoke kindly to her, and said something about a good God. She shook her head. "No, no good God. Why am I so? It always was so. Why much suffer if good God?" He told her they would get her a supper, and in the morning she should start off and find new friends. She became gradually almost ungoverned — sobbed — would like to die — even threatened suicide in this wild way. Poor girl! to her there was only one place where the wild embittered heart could rest. Kindness and calm words at length made her more reasonable. After much trouble they reached the home or the den of the poor rag-picker. The parents were very grateful, and she was to start off the next morning to a country home, where perhaps finally the parents will join her.[1]

*   *   *

Lotte Stern was placed as a domestic in New Hampshire. Her parents never came to live with her, and she returned to the city after four months. There is no subsequent record of her fate.

✑ 9

Invisible Children

THE CAS WAS unique among mid-nineteenth-century child welfare organizations for seeing poor children as a potential benefit rather than an unmitigated burden to society. But not all children were illuminated equally by Brace's optimism. White Protestant boys always stood at the radiant center of his regard, with Catholic boys just beside them. African Americans and Jews lingered near the edge of obscurity, and girls drifted through a dusky middle ground occasionally brightened by rose-colored spotlights. Children's problems and needs also did not get equal attention. The loneliness that evoked so much sympathy on city streets became beneath consideration once a child was placed on a farm. Love for a foster parent was eulogized, while love for a birth parent was denigrated. All too often problems that could not be ameliorated by education, work, religion, or outplacement simply disqualified a child for assistance or sympathy.

The CAS cannot be blamed for all of its failures. The hard truth about social work is that the most earnest and well-conceived efforts often come to nothing. People generally do not attract a social worker's attention until fate has turned against them in numerous ways — and fate is notoriously indifferent even to the most prodigious acts of human resistance. CAS workers can be blamed, however, for those times when they recognized suffering and did nothing within their power to alleviate it, and for those much more frequent occasions when prejudice, laziness, or the desire to maintain a virtuous image caused them not to recognize suffering in the first place.

✑

In 1863, the year of the Emancipation Proclamation and the New York draft riots, Brace published a cobblestone-sized opus, *The Races of the Old World,* upon which he had been working for ten years — since the founding of the CAS, in fact. In this book he attempted to devote equal attention and respect to all races, both in the interest of scientific impartiality and as a model for discussion of all issues related to race — including America's slavery question. In an essay entitled "Ethnological Fallacies," published in the *Independent* during the final years of his labor on the book, he declared:

> It is a shame that now, all through Europe, American science in ethnology has become identical with perverted argument for the oppression of the negro, and an American's conclusions upon the black races are as certain *a priori* as a Brahmin's on the origin or rights of his caste in India. . . . [T]he only method for philosophy is to divorce the whole subject from sympathy, whether for slavery or freedom, and stand on the solid basis of facts and inductive reasoning.[1]

Unfortunately, *The Races of the World* falls comically, and at times infuriatingly, short of fulfilling these laudable intentions. The book shows Brace to be an odd mix of abolitionist and white chauvinist, Darwinist and Lamarckian, scientist and crackpot. He states his opposition to racial prejudice frequently, and with emotion, but is inclined to present Europeans, especially the English, as "noble" and Africans as "low" and even "hideous." His prejudices are in full (if unconscious) display, for example, when he establishes the antiquity of races by describing their representation in Egyptian artifacts: "The negro had his black skin, his thick lips, protruding jaw and curved legs; the Semite his bent nose; the Egyptian his bronze complexion and voluptuous lips; the Aryan, his white skin and noble features before the time of the Pharaohs."[2] When explaining the darkness of African skin, he never presents it as beautiful, or even as a desirable accommodation to climate, but only as a sort of deformity that he attributes to a number of causes, including African soil and scenery and miasmatic, electrical, and moral influences. He seems to grant particular credence to the theories of "a distinguished physiologist, Dr. Draper," who maintained that the black skin and "thick skull" of "the most degraded negro type" stem from the liver, which is "quickly disturbed in its duty by a high temperature."[3] The foulness of such reasoning is only slightly diminished by the ranking of one northern European group — the Irish — on more or less the same low level as the Africans. The following is just one of many examples: "The difference between the average English and Irish skull is nine cubic inches and only four between the average African and the Irish. The largest African skull in his [a Dr. Bachman's] collection measured ninety-nine inches, and the largest Irish ninety-seven inches."4

It is difficult to understand how a man laboring under such crude racial stereotypes could at the same time be so devoted a campaigner against prejudice. But Brace had a strong sense of the self-sufficiency of moral imperatives. "The inferiority or superiority of a given race," he wrote in his book,

> the question of justice to the weak, and of Human Brotherhood, have no connection whatever with the scientific problem of Origin. The strong are equally bound to be merciful to the weak: men are equally under obligations to follow the Law of Love, and Slavery is equally wicked and damnable, whether mankind have one parent or twenty parents. The moral Brotherhood of man does not depend on community of descent, but on a common nature, a similar destiny, and a like relation to their common Father — God.5

Even with this passage's implicit legitimization of the possibility of racial superiority, there is no question of Brace's sincere desire to discount it, nor of his fierce abolitionism. Thus, it is puzzling that the CAS did so little for African American children prior to the draft riots. Blacks made up 4 percent of New York's population, and a considerably larger proportion of the poor, during the mid-nineteenth century but were scarcely mentioned in CAS office journals and annual reports. Partly this was because New York's African community had many self-help and charitable organizations of its own. The nationally celebrated Colored Orphan Asylum, in particular, duplicated some of the services offered by the CAS, including the orphan trains. But nothing explains the scarcity of black children as thoroughly as simple racism, within and outside the CAS.

With the lynching of eleven blacks and the torching of African American homes and institutions (including the Colored Orphan Asylum), the draft riots were a horrific example of racist violence. But Brace makes only passing mention of race in the CAS 1864 annual report and says nothing about it at all in his special draft riots circular. Given his long history of using the specter of the "dangerous classes" to scare money out of the "fortunate classes," portraying the riots as the first skirmish in a potential class war may have been irresistible to Brace. But he also understood, if only because of the reluctance of the American elite to back emancipation, that his charity would suffer financially if it became too closely identified with African Americans. Indeed, after the Second World War, as Protestant child welfare organizations, including the CAS, became the first to have a largely black client base, they saw a substantial decline in contributions as compared to their more ethnically homogeneous Catholic and Jewish counterparts.

Racism also frustrated the few attempts the CAS did make to give black children the same treatment as whites. The one black boy sent west during the society's first year was promptly returned by his farmer employer as "unsuitable."[6] And in the fourth CAS annual report, an unsigned letter from a Michigan clergyman averred that the only child ever to return to New York from his state was a "colored boy" whom C. C. Tracy brought back in 1856.[7] This claim was utterly untrue, and Brace knew it. One of his own letters, written in 1863, told of two sisters, seven and nine years old, who left their Michigan placement in 1854, after only two weeks, and made their way back to New York all by themselves.[8] The fact that he allowed the "colored boy" to be labeled Michigan's only failed placement at the very least says something about which population he thought it most permissible to fail.

This boy, however, was something of a darling at the CAS, and other passages about him illustrate the society's "friendlier" strains of racism. He was the child whose question about a guardian angel statuette in the CAS office inspired William Colopy Desmond to write a poem as well meant and as sabotaged by its own rhetoric as Brace's *Races of the Old World*:

> There stood a white robed angel,
>   Within a fair recess,
> With guardian hand extended,
>   Dear little ones to bless;
> And near a boy was musing —
>   Of Afric's hapless race —
> His dark eyes on the statue,
>   And tears upon his face.

Oh! tell me, little brother,
　So favored in your hue,
Have I a Guardian Angel
　To watch o'er me like you?
When I would wander darkly
　From God and truth astray,
Have I a Guardian Angel,
　To turn me on his way?

The "little brother," a "boy with golden hair" and "tears within his blue eyes / And on his cheeks so fair," responds, in part:

We both have guardian angels,
　For both to God are dear —
And brother while we love him,
　Our angels will be near.
Those guardians hither led us,
　And all this little band,
Where kindly friends protect us,
　And take us by the hand.[9]

The black child is "hapless," confused, a victim. The white child is "favored" and "fair," wise beyond his years, compassionate and condescending. It does not take a great deal of imagination to see how such a vision of the races and their relations could sap the self-esteem of the very African American children whom Desmond, Brace, and the other CAS staff believed themselves to be helping.

But black children were also subject to much more direct racism within the CAS, including from other beneficiaries, as is illustrated by the following extract from the journal of the Newsboys' Lodging House's first year:

A little negro boy lately applied for lodging, but with no money. The question was, whether to trust him; after some delay, one of the large boys, Mick, spoke up, "I say, Mr. Tracy, there's three cents to Jimmy's lodging!" Mr. T. thanked him; and the evening passed quietly, but when the time for settling came, just before bed-hour, "Mick" repented, "Mr. Tracy! I ain't agoin' to pay that nigger's lodgin'."

"Very well," said Mr. T., and then told him, of course, he could do as

he chose with his money — but said he, "this little colored boy is a respectable, well-behaved boy, as much as you — and you have no right
to speak about him in that way." "I have taken you in, a good many of
you, when you were much worse off than he — some of you were ragged and dirty and hungry — and you hadn't anyone to care for you,
and I was a father to you — and now you will talk in this way at the
boy, because his skin is not so white as your's."

One tall boy, who had been once a regular loafing hard boy, was
seen to wipe his eyes at this. Mick looked terribly ashamed. And,
"Here's a cent, Mr. Tracy, for Jimmy!" came from one of the boys,
and "here's another!" and "here's another," until the six cents were
made out. "Ye'll have bad luck!" said the boys, pointing at Mick, as they
went in to bed. "Ye will, 'cause you didn't give nothin' to Jimmy's
lodgin'."[10]

Much as Brace downplayed race in his writing on the draft riots, they
were the catalyst for a significant escalation in aid to black children.
The change began even as the rioters were battling Union troops in
the street. With the destruction of the Colored Orphan Asylum, hundreds of black children were left homeless, and Brace felt that the most
pressing task was to help the asylum's managers to find them shelter.
One of the places he put the children up was at the Cottage Place Mission, which had been founded in 1859 by his second-in-command,
John Macy, and Macy's two sisters. According to Brace, when the mission's school opened following the riots and word got around that
there were now black students in attendance,

> a deputation of hard-looking, heavy-drinking Irish women, the moth-
> ers of some twenty or thirty of the children, waited on [Miss Macy] to
> demand the exclusion of some colored children. In the most amiable
> and Quaker-like manner, but with the firmness of the old Puritan
> stock from which she sprung, she assured them that, if every other
> scholar left, so long as that school remained it should never be closed
> to any child on account of color. They withdrew their children, but
> soon after returned them.[11]

In the months following the riots the CAS opened a "colored
school" on Spring Street, which, as Brace claimed in an annual report,
had "a high reputation" and attracted students from "distant parts of

the city,"[12] and the Saint John's Park School on Hudson Street, which served "utterly destitute" children of "various nationalities, Jew, Irish, German, Italian, and colored."[13] More black children also began to attend the CAS's regular industrial schools.

African American children never made up more than a smattering of orphan train riders, largely because the CAS did not have an extensive enough network of connections among black farmers and Brace felt that black children placed with white farmers were less likely to establish a family-like relationship and more likely to be used as slave labor. On the whole, he considered their placement better left to the Colored Orphan Asylum, which reopened in Harlem in 1867. Most of the black CAS orphan train riders were placed in the early twentieth century — after Brace's death — and were primarily found homes with African American farmers near New York City, many of them in Maryland and in Delaware, where, according to Charles Loring Brace Jr., the society placed its "less promising boys."[14]

Although the racist elements in the CAS treatment of black children are fairly obvious from the perspective of the present day, during the entire orphan train era no one — not even Brace's most bitter enemies — ever criticized the CAS for its handling of black children. According to the standards of the time, the society seemed only admirable. The same was true for the CAS handling of girls. Although the inadequacy and injustice of their treatment seems blatant today, it was never commented on during the nineteenth and early twentieth centuries. In many ways girls, like blacks, were invisible children. No one saw who they really were, so no one understood what they really needed.

჻

In July 1879 Emma Brace made her first solo voyage to Europe and her father sent her a letter of advice:

> I want you to be very ambitious and eager for the best of things; to learn a great deal and get the best. Even the constant consideration required on such a trip will be a great gain for you. . . . Try to learn about each city something of its history and politics. Ask yourself why you like certain pictures, and choose the best before you know the artists. Analyze the architecture you like best, and try to recognize different schools of art. You should take a little pains with your letters to us. First

give us a brief journal, then describe the things which strike you most in the most condensed form, and the small things; — use no conventional language, but the true expression.[15]

Brace was the son of a male feminist. All of his life he had known and respected brilliant, forthright women: the Beechers in his youth, George Eliot and Emma Lazarus, among many others, in his maturity. He had great respect for his wife's intellectual abilities and wrote that he had learned a lot from her. He also set high standards for his daughter. He wanted her to be ambitious, to analyze and to learn, not just about art and architecture but about history and politics as well. But the feminism of the male Braces was limited by the cultural assumptions of their era. Charles wanted women to achieve the most in life, but only according to what he believed to be their nature. Women could and should be brilliant and strong, but Brace never considered for a moment that they could achieve a "manly" force of intellect or independence of will, nor that marriage was anything but the epitome of feminine achievement. With all of his respect and deep affection for Letitia, his letters to her could be as condescending as those to his daughter. Like the majority of Victorian men, Brace simply did not take women seriously — a fact that had disastrous consequences for many female orphan train riders.

Girls were so beneath consideration during the nineteenth century that CAS journal and record keepers — including Brace — referred to the orphan train riders almost exclusively as "boys" and "lads" even though 39 percent of them were girls.[16] More significant was Brace's difficulty recognizing girls' successes. All of the cases cited in the brief section labled "Our Failures" in *The Dangerous Classes* related to girls, even though, in her retrospective study of 1922, Georgia Ralph determined that, according to Brace's own standards, girls (with an average "favorable" placement rate of 74 percent) succeeded more often than boys (only 54 percent favorably placed).[17] And, while Brace happily declared the Newsboys' Lodging House an agency "of pure humanity and almost unmingled good," the Girls' Lodging House was written off as having "cost" the society "more trouble than all our enterprises together."[18] Brace's opinion was forcefully underlined by the lodging house matrons, whose reports were often little more than catalogs of the misbehaviors they dealt with daily. What neither these women nor Brace understood was the degree to which that misbehavior and the "failures" of the lodging house were the result of a self-fulfilling prophecy.

In *The Dangerous Classes*, Brace maintained that the street girl "feels homelessness and friendlessness more [than boys do]; and she has more of the feminine dependence on affection; the street trades, too, are harder for her, and the return at night to some lonely cellar or tenement room, crowded with dirty people of all ages and sexes, is more dreary." Girls had a natural aversion to these crowded tenements, Brace believed, because their instinct was "more toward the preservation of purity."[19] But such assertions of feminine weakness and virtue were frequently followed in CAS literature by directly contradictory claims. In the first circular, for example, no sooner had Brace described girls as "more pitiable" than boys than he summed up their typical fate in two blunt sentences: "They grow up passionate, ungoverned; with no love or kindness ever to soften their heart. We all know their short, wild life; and the sad end."[20] And many of the behaviors that the lodging house matrons complained of revealed anything but feminine weakness, dependence, or preference for "purity."

The primary complaint of Mrs. E. Trott, the first matron of the Girls' Lodging House, was that her charges, especially those who worked in shops or factories, were *too* independent. "Her work through the day," Trott asserted, "entirely unfits her for spending evenings as every true woman ought. She is neither inclined to sew nor read, but seeks some place of amusement. Again, she is unstable in business, and seeks to better her condition by changing her employment."[21] Trott's successor, Mrs. E. S. Hurley, complained of "saucy, impudent, independent [girls,] who, though often smart, clean, industrious, and virtuous, are from their tempers and dispositions frequently thrown out of employment, and thus come to want." Hurley especially despised

the wicked, designing, and dishonest girls who come [to the lodging house] to mislead or steal, and the vain silly, idle ones, bright and pretty, who go fluttering around trying to make life a holiday, but are so often caught in the net of the destroyer, and drawn down to misery and death. Restive under restraint, confident in their power to guide themselves, they can only be influenced through the affectionate natures they generally possess.[22]

Boys were almost never subjected to such categorical condemnation. On the contrary, their low morals, criminal associations, dishonesty, violence, and carelessness often inspired only a wink-and-nudge celebration, as in Brace's previously quoted description of the typical street boy:

> A more light-hearted youngster than the street-boy is not to be found. He is . . . merry as a clown, and always ready for the smallest joke, and quick to take "a point" or to return a repartee. His views of life are mainly derived from the more mature opinions of "flash-men," engine-runners, cock-fighters, pugilists, and pickpockets, whom he occasionally is permitted to look upon with admiration at some select pothouse. . . . His morals are, of course, not of a high order, living, as he does, in a fighting, swearing, stealing, and gambling set. . . . [H]e is sharp and reckless.

Boys had to sink very low indeed to be seen as "failures," whereas girls had only to act like boys and they were dismissed as "passionate," "ungoverned," "wild," and doomed to a "sad end." The fact that so many girls were as high-spirited and independent as boys seems to have had no effect on CAS (or Victorian society's) notions of femininity. Such girls were simply held not to be, in Mrs. Trott's words, "true women." And, whereas the CAS sought nothing so much as to encourage boys' independence, they attempted to make "true women" of girls by encouraging them to be subservient.

Trott considered domestic service far superior for girls to working in a shop or factory, because as a domestic, a girl "is surrounded with home comforts, and with a considerate mistress is well cared for; has one to take an interest in her welfare, advise and assist her when she needs it. She has also a true friend; for what girl that is honest, truthful, and studies the interests of her mistress is not highly valued?"[23]

The fact that the unequal relationship between a mistress and a self-sacrificing servant should be designated as "true" friendship says a lot about the CAS's lack of respect for a girl's more spontaneous and authentic affections. Brace, in fact, wanted girls to be sent west for domestic placement precisely so that their choice of friends would be limited:

> [A] poor girl — a domestic — in one of our city or suburban families, though greatly raised above her former condition, does not improve to

anything like the same degree as one in a country family. The great reason being in the power . . . of social influences, which here are entirely those of the kitchen and the servant class, while in the West they are those of the family and the American community.[24]

When a girl resisted her benefactors' attempts to limit her freedom, rein in her passions, and control her friendships, she was not seen as independent or strong, but as manifesting the most dangerous form of female weakness — a fascination for what Brace called "the strange and mysterious subject of sexual vice."[25] Despite their supposed instinct "toward the preservation of purity," girls were considered far less capable of resisting the promptings of the flesh than boys. Brace claimed that one of the "most dark arrangements of the world" was that

a female child of the poor should be permitted to start on its immortal career with almost every influence about it degrading, its inherited tendencies overwhelming toward indulgence of passion, its examples all of crime or lust, its lower nature awake long before its higher, and then that it should be allowed to soil and degrade its soul before the maturity of reason, and beyond all human possibility of cleansing![26]

It is no exaggeration to say that the primary goal of all CAS work with girls was to prevent them from becoming prostitutes. This was especially true at the Girls' Lodging House. In her reports, Mrs. Trott often bragged about winning girls "from the streets,"[27] and her husband, the lodging house's "superintendent," described their mission as "to rescue, hold up, and keep from falling every virtuous, industrious girl that applies to us."[28]

The CAS was absolutely obsessed by female sexuality. The erotic life of boys was almost never mentioned in the society's publications or records, but *all* extended discussions of girls contained at least one veiled reference to the perils of sex. This obsession was due not only to the notion that girls were too weak to resist their libidinal urges but to the belief that the consequences of indulging those urges were vastly worse for girls than boys. "[T]here is no reality," Brace claimed, "in the sentimental assertion that the sexual sins of the lad are as degrading as those of a girl." By offering "for sale that which is in its nature beyond all price," he added, a girl loses self-respect, without which every human being soon sinks to the lowest depths; she loses the habit of industry, and cannot be taught to work. . . . [B]ecoming weak in body and mind, her character loses fixedness of purpose and tenacity and true energy. . . . If in a moment of remorse, she flee away and take honest work, her weakness and bad habits follow her; . . . she craves the stimulus and hollow gayety of the wild life she has led; her ill name dogs her; . . . the world and herself are against reform.[29]

The Victorian propensity to condemn girls for not meeting standards that were never applied to boys was particularly horrific because sexual disparities in earning power left many single women with little choice but to turn to prostitution. The needle trades paid so meagerly that it was all but impossible for a woman to support herself, let alone her children, on her earnings. During an era when the humblest two-room apartment rented for $2.50 a week, the average woman made only $1.50 stitching shirts or suits. Domestic service had the advantage of providing room and board but was generally available only to young childless women. A working-class mother who had been widowed or abandoned and had no male relative to support her would be terrifically tempted to at least supplement her earnings by catering to male desire. A prostitute with a working-class clientele could make in a single hour what she would earn in a day for stitching shirts, and more affluent johns commonly paid five and ten dollars for each sex act. Partly because of the Victorian notion that virgin blood cured venereal disease, girls earned ten dollars for their maidenhead at Five Points brothels and were sometimes paid as much as fifty dollars.[30]

Given the alternatives available to working-class women (to say nothing of the chafing of Victorian repression), one might be tempted to applaud their desire to profit from and, at least in some instances, enjoy sex — except for the fact that Brace's description of a prostitute's decline to the "lowest depths" was far from only a moralistic fantasy.

In 1855 Dr. William W. Sanger, a resident physician at Blackwell's Island, interviewed 2,000 New York prostitutes between the ages of fourteen and sixty-two. The statistics he compiled showed that, as a result of disease, drinking, and the brutality of pimps and johns, the average prostitute did not live more than four years after commencement of her career,[31] and her lifestyle could be just as hazardous to her offspring — a sad irony given the fact that many women only began selling their bodies so that they could keep their children. At a time when the mortality rate for New York City children five and under was 18.5 percent, the mortality rate for prostitutes' offspring exceeded 60 percent.[32] The truncated lives of prostitutes and their children were partly the result of the city's wildly misguided attempt to restrain the sex trade. New York doctors were forbidden by law to treat prostitutes for venereal disease. The only way a woman could get treatment was to declare herself a pauper and go to the Charity Hospital on Blackwell's Island. But since going to the hospital amounted to imprisonment, many women refused treatment until their disease was so far advanced that they could not practice their trade and were in danger of starvation.

But even before prostitutes reached such grim extremes, they were subjected to all the humiliation and ostracization that Victorian society reserved for "fallen women." The working class and poor, of necessity, understood the inexorable pressures that drove some women to prostitution. They also were not immune to the glamour of fast-living dancehall girls. But even so, the poor, like the rich, often felt tainted by and shunned their "fallen" friends, sisters and daughters, especially once these women's best earning years had passed, or they had succumbed to the degradations of alcoholism and opium addiction. Prostitutes were also looked down upon because many of them were pathetic victims. Although nearly one-third of Sanger's subjects claimed they had taken up the sex trade by "inclination" or for the "easy life,"[33] many actually had little choice in the matter. It was not uncommon for desperate and unscrupulous parents to auction off their daughters' virginity for what could amount to a year's earnings. Pimps and the mistresses of "low" boardinghouses often tricked, drugged, or bullied unprotected women into sexual slavery. Many women were brought to the city by supposedly loving men who then abandoned them, leaving them penniless and with stained reputations. And many, many others — like Lotte Stern — had been so broken by circumstance that they saw little reason to resist the tendency of men, and of society, to judge them as "disreputable" simply by virtue of their class.

The Girls' Lodging House was the idea of William A. Booth, who took over as president of the CAS board in 1861 and was the man who criticized Brace for his abolitionist writing. During 1862, its first year of operation, the lodging house took in roughly 400 girls, and during its second, nearly 800, most of them eighteen years old and younger. By 1877 the Girls' Lodging House had moved from Canal Street to larger quarters on Saint Mark's Place and had sheltered more than 14,000 girls for an average stay of ten nights each. Because the CAS was so afraid that financial pressure would only make young women more likely to walk the streets, lodging house residents were allowed to pay the eight cents total charge for their beds and meals by mopping floors, cooking, doing laundry, and especially by stitching dresses and suits for orphan train riders. This needlework was a major operation. During 1864 alone the girls made 2,500 garments.[34]

The lodging house's mission was to rescue those girls who were "[n]ot yet corrupted or ruined, but just on that line"[35] — a goal that Brace and the matrons believed required excluding girls who had crossed the line. As was typical of the CAS in this era, however, the lodging house matrons did not apply this policy of exclusion rigidly, but they complained bitterly about the exceptions they made. "Occasionally some kind missionary brings in a penitent Magdalen," wrote Mrs. Hurley,

> who will not consent to go to the Homes for the fallen, and prevails on us to make an exception to the rule, and take her in; but, as far as our experience goes, over this class may almost be written *"hopeless";* no matter how seriously they are cautioned not to reveal their past lives, the first night in the dormitories rarely passes without a recital of it, and in a few days they tire of restraint, make some excuse, and are off to their old haunts again.[36]

There are many things to object to in this quote. For one, it seems unreasonable and unrealistic to forbid residents from discussing what may be the most troubling aspect of their lives with girls in similar positions. For another, it seems absurd to drive these residents back out onto the streets and, presumably, into grievous sin, merely for talking. Hurley's sanctimonious condescension also seems guaranteed to do anything but allow her to make a strong connection with young women who badly needed her help. And finally, the main effect of excluding prostitutes and sexually active girls was to reinforce the grim fate that the CAS ostensibly sought to ameliorate.

Brace well understood the role of self-respect in keeping human beings from "sinking to the lowest depths." The most revolutionary component of his work with boys was his respect for them — his assumption of their competence and fundamental goodness. This respect was so much a part of institutional culture at the CAS that the superintendents of the Newsboys' Lodging House were all but indifferent to how the boys spent their days or came up with their rent. Had the Girls' Lodging House matrons been half so respectful of their residents' abilities and privacy, it might have been a much happier and more successful institution. The girls might have felt they had found true allies in the CAS matrons and been more inclined both to take their advice and to believe themselves capable of profiting from it. But, sadly, this was never really possible. Life on the streets truly was vastly worse for girls than boys — far too miserable for Brace and his colleagues ever to feel they could relax their vigilance against it. The sexism and prudishness that had created this miserable situation had also created their own justification.

The "rescue" of the girls admitted to the lodging house had two phases. While the girls were actually in residence, the CAS sought to instill in them habits of cleanliness, punctuality, and religious devotion and to teach them all the skills they would need to be domestics. And when it came time for the girls to leave, the CAS sought to find them decent "employers." Much to Brace's regret, however, the overwhelming majority of girls were "indisposed to go to the West."[37] During 1863, 111 Girls' Lodging House residents accepted placement with employers in or near New York City, while only 22 went west.[38] In 1876 the contrast was even more stark: a mere 29 girls accepted western placement, while 818 were placed in the New York area.[39]

The reasons girls would not go west were not recorded, but it is highly likely that the very ties Brace thought best to sunder were what kept them close to home. According to Bruce Bellingham's statistical analysis of the CAS's first year, the stronger a child of either sex's ties to family and friends, the more likely she or he was to be placed close to home.[40] It is also very possible that these Victorian girls did not want to go far from the people they could trust because they, no less than Lotte Stern, *knew men.*

Brace and the lodging house matrons saw domestic service as girls' best hope of escaping prostitution, but William Sanger found that half of the women he interviewed began selling their bodies after having been domestic servants.[41] There is no way of knowing how many of these women were driven into prostitution after yielding to or resisting the sexual advances of their employers. Although there was an elaborate mythology about foreign aristocrats impregnating serving girls and fleeing overseas to escape scandal, Victorian Americans were largely silent about the possibility of similar events occurring in their own homes. When such events did come to light, they were generally dealt with by outright denial or by placing all blame on the sluttish, lower-class servant. The effectiveness of such repression mechanisms is clearly demonstrated in CAS policy and writing. As obsessed as Brace and the lodging house matrons were by the sexual dangers their female charges faced in the slums, they seem never to have even considered that such dangers also existed in "respectable" homes. The only problem Brace saw for serving girls who remained in the city was the persistence of their relations with their lower-class friends and family, and he portrayed the West as nothing less than a paradise of sexual decency, where a female orphan train rider need only anticipate the happy fulfillment of marriage.

The CAS records during Brace's era are all but silent on the sexual abuses endured by girls in their placements, never being more explicit than references such as "she was not well used by her employer." The records, however, do contain numerous references to girls being "of low morals" or "unsuitable" or otherwise at fault for whatever misfortune occurred during their placements. It seems reasonable to suspect that victims' fear of being blamed and punished was another reason for the paucity of reports of sexual abuse in the CAS files.

The silence imposed by shame and fear was so pervasive that it is only within the last few years that some surviving female orphan train riders have begun to talk about unwelcomed sexual encounters. Marguerite Thomson, who was placed in Nebraska by the New York Foundling Hospital in 1911, reported that she had to leave four out of the five homes where she worked as a housekeeper during the 1920s because the men made sexual advances toward her. When she turned one man down, he raped her and fired her the next morning. Thomson also had sex forced upon her when she was twelve years old by the husband of a woman who had given her refuge after her original placement had become too much to bear. "I'd wake up in the night-time," Thomson said, and he would be in bed with me. I'd holler to her, and she'd come and get me and tell him to go back to bed. She'd tell me to lock the door, but it didn't do any good. One time he drilled a hole in it so he could watch me undress, and another time I caught him watching me through the window. They had a daughter too, and she got married at sixteen. I think it was to get away from him. He had been in a mental institution at one time.[42]

Alice Bullis Ayler was one of the very last orphan train riders. The CAS slipped her into Kansas in 1930 (the year placement from out of state became illegal) on the excuse that she was visiting her previously placed twin younger brothers. Ayler was only ten when she arrived and lived in three different homes before finally finding one that was tolerable. In two of those homes, she said, she had "to run from every man involved." One of these men "couldn't find his own bedroom," she said, and another would accost her in the corner every time his family went into town on errands.

"None of those people took me in because they wanted someone to love," Ayler said. "They didn't know what love was. They just wanted me for work, and for whatever those old men wanted. The wives took me in knowing what their men wanted. They didn't want to mess with these men! It wasn't like modern days where you have to chase the women off. Women had headaches all the time. And this was just a way of getting the husbands off their back."

Ayler believes that children placed by the CAS and the Foundling Hospital were easy targets for abuse of all kinds because, as she put it,

the orphan kid couldn't tell anybody. They'd say he or she was lying. That was our big problem. We didn't have an advocate. We didn't have anybody who would say, "That kid is all right, I'm gonna stand up for him come hell or high water." Except I had Georgia. Georgia was a person who could listen, and every kid wasn't a liar. Afterward Georgia became my friend.[43]

Georgia Greenleaf, the CAS agent in charge of Ayler's case, had a strikingly different relationship with her than the Foundling Hospital's western agent had with Marguerite Thomson. To some extent the difference was a function of time: Ayler was placed nearly twenty years later than Thomson, after laws and attitudes regarding foster children had undergone significant evolution. But the difference also reflected the contrasting values of the two agencies.

Both Ayler and Thomson suffered several unhappy placements as children. All of Ayler's were arranged by the CAS, but after her first placement, Thomson had to shift for herself. This first placement was with the Larsons, who ran a boardinghouse and dairy farm in Bertrand, Nebraska. Although the house had five bedrooms, Thomson had to sleep on the living room couch. She was constantly humiliated by her foster mother for her New York accent, for being an orphan, and for clumsiness, and she was beaten with a rawhide whip for minor infractions like breaking a toy or eating jam. Although the Larsons made their living from the sale of milk, Thomson was not allowed to drink any, ostensibly because it was too valuable, but everyone else in the house could have as much as they wanted. The result was that Thomson's teeth never developed properly and had to be pulled out and replaced by dentures when she was a teenager. She was also deprived of food, getting one helping when the Larsons' natural children got two, and being made to go without supper on the slightest pretext — as, for example, when she passed gas at the dinner table.

Once a year the Foundling Hospital's agent, Mr. McPhealy, came to the Larsons' home, and Thomson would dance an Irish jig for him and sing songs like "Looking on the Bright Side." But she was never allowed to talk to him in private, nor did he ever ask for a word with her. The result was that he never took any sort of action to improve her situation. Finally she took matters into her own hands by moving out when she was eleven and going to live with a family who needed help caring for a new baby. When the baby was a year old, Thomson moved in briefly with the woman whose husband molested her, and finally she had no choice but to return to the Larsons.

At fifteen Thomson ran away, hoping to become a dancer with a vaudeville troupe that had recently passed through town. She caught up with the troupe in Broken Bow and was put up in a hotel room by the managers, whom she knew from the Larsons' boardinghouse. But the very next day, through a mix of bad luck and Mrs. Larson's ill will, a sheriff arrived at the hotel's front door and took her back to Bertrand. The sheriff had come to Broken Bow only because another girl from Bertrand had run off there independently of Thomson. When Mrs. Larson heard about the sheriff's trip, she asked him to pick up her foster daughter as well, not because she wanted the girl home again, but only, Thomson believed, to frustrate her dreams of independence and success. As soon as Thomson was back in Bertrand, Mrs. Larson wrote to Mr. McPhealy asking him to take the girl off her hands. McPhealy came to visit and offered two choices: Thomson could either go back to New York or be put in a convent. Naturally, Mrs. Larson chose the more repressive of the alternatives: the convent — and McPhealy never bothered to ask Thomson about her preference or experiences.

At the Good Shepherd Convent in Omaha, Thomson, like all of the other inmates, was given a new name and forbidden to say one word about her life outside, not just about the supposed misbehavior that had led to her commitment, but about any aspect of it. She was taught typing and shorthand for two hours a day, and the rest of the time did piecework for the Beau Brummel Shirt Factory.

McPhealy did not come to see her until she had been at the convent for two years; when he did, he had his first solitary conversation ever with her. He was shocked by what she told him of her treatment at the Larsons and her other homes. He said that if he had known he would have taken her away with him. But he also told her that he could do nothing to get her out of the convent now. She could be released only to the custody of the person who had put her in — Mrs. Larson.

A year later elderly former neighbors happened to visit the convent and run into Thomson. When they heard her story, they went straight back to Bertrand and threatened to call the authorities if Mrs. Larson did not obtain her foster daughter's release. When Thomson finally walked out through the convent's five locking doors, she was eighteen and had lost three years of her youth. No longer welcome at the Larsons', she began her career as a housekeeper.

Although Alice Ayler had a far more sympathetic and effective agent than McPhealy handling her case, in the end her experience was not that different from Thomson's. Georgia Greenleaf clearly worked very hard on Ayler's behalf, always talking to her in private when she visited, never doubting her complaints, and always acting on them immediately. But there were limits to what she could do. Potential foster parents were screened so hastily that, even by 1930, orphan train riders had no guarantee about the quality of care and affection they would find in their new homes.

Ayler's initial placement was with her twin brothers' foster parents. The mother seems to have been a fine woman, but the father was a bootlegger and embezzler. When Greenleaf heard that this man kept creeping into Ayler's bed, she took the girl away but left her two brothers. Ayler's next placement was with a deaf-mute couple who had taken another of her younger brothers. This couple seemed to have had little interest in their foster son. They made no attempt to teach him sign language, and they kept him in an empty bathtub much of the day. By the time he was three, he still could not speak, even though there was nothing wrong with his hearing or comprehension. The deaf couple were apparently even less interested in Ayler, and she was moved after only a very short stay. Her brother remained with the couple until the woman, after years of trying, finally got pregnant and did not want him anymore. Then he was placed with an extremely elderly man and woman who, according to Ayler, were equally unable to give him an adequate upbringing.

When Georgia Greenleaf heard about the farmer who kept accosting Ayler in the corner, she moved the girl to her fourth and final placement — which was only marginally better than the others. Her new foster mother humiliated her in very much the same way as Mrs. Larson had Thomson. She told her that her nose was too big, that her birth parents had been bad people, and that she was just like them. She let her own children take Ayler's toys and penny collection and constantly accused her of things she had not done. (She was particularly paranoid about sex.) The abuse got so bad that, at seventeen, Ayler started to have severe headaches and blind spells. Finally she went to Greenleaf, who moved her out of the family and into town, where she got a job at J. C. Penney and lived in an apartment with another young woman. Within three years Ayler was married, and then, she says, she never felt an orphan again.

As vulnerable as both Ayler and Thomson were to male predation, they were both far better protected by their placement organizations than the average female orphan train rider of the nineteenth century. To a large extent, their safety was a product of technological innovations, such as the telephone and automobile, that made it easier for their agents to keep in touch with them. But they also benefited from shifts in social attitudes. By the early 1900s, people had become much more sensitive to the risks of foster care and convinced of the obligation of placement agencies to watch out for their charges. And by the 1930s, as Ayler's case illustrates, this sensitivity to risk had developed to such an extent that it had begun to encompass the taboo subject of sexual assault. A growing number of placement agents were willing, like Greenleaf, to believe both in the pervasiveness of sex crimes and in the innocence of the victims, whereas during the nineteenth century many female orphan train riders had no choice but to endure repeated sexual abuse because, often isolated miles from the nearest village, there was no one to whom they could tell their stories.

⅌

When Brace stated that there was "no reality in the sentimental assertion that the sexual sins of the lad are as degrading as those of the girl," he made one exception: the practice "of some Eastern communities which are rotting and falling to pieces from their debasing and unnatural crimes. When we hear of such disgusting offenses under any form of civilization, whether it be under the Rome of the Empire, or the Turkey of to-day, we know that disaster, ruin, and death, are near the State and the people."[44]

Brace was referring to "the sin that dared not speak its name" — homosexuality. The obliqueness and ferocity of his language were typical of his era. Even though it may not have been permissible in polite society to discuss those acts and desires that caused so many women to "fall," their existence was universally recognized and the object of intense fascination. Homosexuality, on the other hand, was so forbidden that for the most part it could be referred to only through irony and code words (a "sunflower knight," a "gilded youth"), and when addressed directly, it had to be presented as grossly beyond the limits of human normality or, at least, of Western civilization.

Homosexuality's namelessness (the term was coined by Richard von Krafft-Ebing only in 1869 and did not enter English until the 1880s, through the work of Havelock Ellis) did, however, give Victorian gender identity a certain flexibility we do not have today. Even in socially conservative circles, it was perfectly normal for men and women to declare love for members of their own sex, or to sleep in the same bed with them. There were strict limits, of course. Sodomy was a grave crime, and suspected perpetrators could suffer severe punishments both within and outside the law.

Despite Brace's location of homosexuality only in "Eastern communities," it thrived in the United States, perhaps even more so than in Europe. In 1872, the very year Brace published the quoted passage in *The Dangerous Classes*, a young man wrote from Germany that in

America "the unnatural vice in question is more ordinary than it is here; and I was able to indulge my passions with less fear of punishment or persecution. . . . I discovered, in the United States, that I was always immediately recognized as a member of the confraternity."[45]

Then, as now, New York City was a refuge for homosexuals. There were gay beer gardens on the Bowery that were protected by the police, and male prostitution in City Hall Park and on Cedar Street. The very street boys served by the CAS were an integral part of the city's gay community, and many runaway teenage boys made their living as male prostitutes. Adult male vagrants often traveled with "prushuns" — homeless boys, ten to fifteen years old, who performed many of the duties of wives. Although the existence of homosexuality among street boys was almost never referred to directly, it was nonetheless widely understood, as is implied by an 1882 cartoon from the *National Police Gazette* showing Oscar Wilde followed by a procession of newsboys and bootblacks imitating his flamboyant gestures. In the accompanying article these boys are referred to as the "precocious set," and a later piece describes Wilde as "permeating society even to its lower strata."[46]

Brace certainly knew that some New York street boys, happily or unhappily, had sexual encounters with men, or he would not have referred to the practice in his book. But the ferocity of his language makes it clear that any boy who confessed to such experience could expect little sympathy or aid — perhaps less even than the most confirmed female prostitute. Her activity would have been, to Brace's mind, in accordance with her nature, whereas the boy's could hardly be more "unnatural" or "disgusting."

The Victorian taboo against acknowledging the existence of homosexuality also made it harder to protect boys from sexual assault. Girls may have chafed under the assumption that their virtue was everywhere in danger, but at least it offered them real protection, whereas an untold number of boys suffered dreadful consequences from the assumption that they were everywhere safe. The very absence in the CAS records of even the most indirect reference to sexual assault against boys shows how utterly isolated the inevitable victims of this crime must have felt — whether they encountered their abuse on lonely western farms or within the ostensible safety of the CAS itself.

In 1868 Horatio Alger published *Ragged Dick,* the story of a plucky New York street boy, and the first of his enormously successful rags-to-riches tales. Brace knew that the book had been based on research that Alger did at the Five Points Mission, and sensing a possible fund-raising and publicity opportunity, he asked the celebrated author to visit the Newsboys' Lodging House. Alger was so inspired by his con-versations with the newsboys that he soon took up residence in the lodging house himself. For several years he had a bed reserved for him there, and a desk where he could jot down notes on the boys' stories and characteristics while they were still fresh in his mind. Just as Brace had hoped, these notes led to dozens of novels illustrating the virtues of street boys. Some of Alger's heroes even made their fortunes by em-igrating west.

But Alger's relationships with vagrant boys were not confined to the lodging house. He also brought them to live at his West Twenty-sixth Street apartment, where he seems to have found them equally inspir-ing. According to a profile in *Argosy*, he did his best writing with some half-dozen boys "making the liveliest kind of music" in the back-ground.[47]

Neither the *Argosy* reporter nor Brace seems to have known that Alger had been forced to resign as minister at a Unitarian church on Cape Cod in 1866 (the year before he wrote *Ragged Dick*) after having been charged with the "abominable and revolting crime of unnatural familiarity with boys."[48] Alger admitted his guilt grudgingly at the time and later talked quite openly with Henry James, Sr., about what he called his "insanity."

There is no evidence that the celebrated author ever had a sexual re-lationship with any of the boys he befriended inside or out of the Newsboys' Lodging House, nor even that he had a homosexual en-counter of any kind after leaving Massachusetts. But he cannot have been the only male visitor to or employee of the CAS with a sexual in-terest in boys. And his story cogently illustrates yet another way in which the Victorian aversion to even recognizing homosexuality left boys in danger of, at the very least, unwanted advances.

Brace's invitation to Alger naturally evokes the question of his own in-terest in boys — a question that I have often been asked and can only answer with a few ambiguous facts and an educated guess.

Brace's admiration for boys is apparent throughout his work. He clearly took delight in their physical appearance, as well as their gumption and wit. Although modern notions of sexuality and propri-ety would preclude most male social workers from expressing such delight in the physical nature of their juvenile male clients, men in the nineteenth century were allowed much greater freedom to express strong emotion — one reason why Victorians can seem so sentimental to our tastes. Also, Brace's admiration for boys was never couched in particularly sexual terms. His sexual interest in adult women, by contrast, was expressed both overtly and implicitly in his letters, in many passages in his books, and, of course, in the fact that he married and had four children. Given the complexity of the human psyche, none of this evidence is particularly conclusive, but if Brace did harbor some degree of sexual interest in boys, it was probably unconscious and never acted upon.

♪ 10

Neglect of the Poor

BRACE WAS A MAN who could believe that God would murder his beloved sister, Emma, to teach him humility. He had a similar response one morning in April 1865 when his eldest son, Charles, burst in upon the family at their prayers to shout that President Lincoln had been shot. This tragedy too, which came just days after Lee's surrender at Appomattox, Brace believed to be a message from God: "In the height of our exultation and consciousness of our power, with victory flaunting in every banner, we are taught that we are but drifting weeds on the great eternal currents of Providence."[1]

All of his life Brace struggled to restrain his prodigious pride and to remain mindful that he and his ambitions were nothing more than such "drifting weeds." Often, as in the following letter to Letitia that he wrote from Stockholm, he chose to express his desire to master his vanity in strikingly masochistic language:

> I have been so impelled lately by the expression, "Bring every thought into captivity to Christ." It is so sweet to have them chained, captured to Christ. I have lately been so ashamed and struck down. . . . I say, O God! that I should think of wealth or honor or fame or friendship as my aim and Thou and Eternity all near me since a child. . . . However, I have good hope. God is a friend to the poor soul. Perhaps the best way to him is through disappointment and humiliation.[2]

Brace returned to the theme of being "captured" by the deity in another letter written during this same European trip. He had gone to London to attend the International Reformatory Union Exhibition. During his stay he had met some of the pioneers of the British "Home Children" movement and had been put up by Lady Byron. He had also had dinner with one of his idols, John Stuart Mill, who became a friend and regular correspondent. After these heady experiences he traveled to the Continent, and eventually to Switzerland. To his wife's sister, he wrote:

> How can I ever tell the sublime visions I have had in the mountains, of the unseen! The lesson of the Alps is worship and purity. "Oh, to be like this forever! to see God as only the pure can see!" have I often said on the great heights, in the presence of the Unapproachable One. From the vast peaks above cloud and earth, one peers into Eternity with such intense desire to know. Our individuality sinks away so, and the realities seem goodness and God. "Oh, make me thine!" is the cry of one's heart continually in the solitary mountains.[3]

The truth is that when Brace felt he had come close to God, the experience was never one of "disappointment and humiliation"; he never felt any sinking or diminishment of his "individuality." For Brace the experience was all ecstatic expansion — especially during this era, when political events had finally taken so favorable a turn, his work was going so well, and his reputation was undergoing a meteoric rise. In another letter written not long after this one, Brace declared, "Probably few human beings ever had a more real sense of things unseen than I habitually have," and he confessed his belief, not only that he was doing "God's work," but that God had his (Brace's) goals "far more in heart" than he did himself.[4]

❧

The absolute apogee of the CAS's reputation came between 1870 and 1875, when Brace was in his middle forties, still possessed of his phenomenal energy, and working to improve the lot of poor children on a number of fronts.

Although Brace thought labor, especially farm labor, was a good thing for children, he was alarmed by the plight of boys and girls who worked in factories ten hours a day, six days a week, with no time for education or even play. In 1871 he had the CAS attorney draft a law limiting the amount of time that children could work in factories. Brace went up to Albany every year for three years to campaign for this law, and finally, in 1874, the New York State legislature passed a slightly watered-down version of it, one of the first laws to limit child labor in the United States.

In 1872 Brace published his classic account of his life's work, *The Dangerous Classes,* to wide acclaim in America and Britain, winning praise from the likes of Florence Nightingale and Charles Darwin. That summer Brace and Letitia were invited to spend the night at Darwin's home in Kent, an experience Brace considered one of the high points of his life.

In 1873 he was awarded a medal by King Humbert of Italy in appreciation for his efforts to end the pernicious *padrone* system, under which a Fagin-like master (the *padrone*) would buy children from their parents in Italy, transport them to New York, and make them work the streets as beggars and musicians and take all of their earnings.

That same year the CAS commenced what would evolve into pioneering work in public health and hygiene by opening a "Summer Home" at Bath, a beachfront community in Brooklyn, midway between Coney Island and the Verrazano Narrows. Each year, up to 4,000 girls from the CAS industrial schools got to spend six days at the Summer Home and have a taste of some of the benefits — fresh air, good food — that children in the Emigration Plan were thought to be enjoying all the time. After a while, however, it became clear that the fresh air did not benefit the girls nearly so much as what they learned about personal hygiene and nutrition. The girls were encouraged to bathe frequently and were required to wash their faces and hands daily. They were also taught to avoid infection by sleeping between clean sheets rather than their normal bedding of rarely washed blankets and a filthy mattress. They ate three solid meals a day — a great luxury among the city's poor. But perhaps most important, they were encouraged to drink milk rather than only coffee or tea. On the basis of what he saw at the Summer Home, Brace came to think that drinking milk was the easiest and most effective and inexpensive way of improving the health of both children and their mothers.

Brace also advocated vigorously, along with many other New York reformers, for the passage of the 1875 Children's Law, perhaps the most significant piece of child welfare legislation passed in the latter half of the nineteenth century. The law forbade committing children between the ages of three and sixteen to county almshouses, the underfunded and poorly run institutions that had been the subject of severe criticism by child welfare advocates for many years. In 1856 state-sponsored investigators had condemned the almshouses as "the worst possible nurseries" and "the most disgraceful memorials of public

charity."[5] Critics asserted that children — who might have been incarcerated along with their parents, or on their own for vagrancy — were
often mistreated by adult inmates and were always subjected to their
"vicious" influence. Critics also condemned the lack of competent
staff. There were no teachers at most almshouses, and as a cost-cutting
measure, children were generally cared for only by unpaid elderly female inmates. Most of the law's advocates — who, like many on the
right today, believed that poverty was a prima facie disqualification
for parenthood — hoped that the children excluded from the almshouses would be placed with foster families. But the vast majority
of them ended up in orphanages and other institutions. That said, in
1875 the CAS placed more children — 4,026 — than in any year before
or after.[6]

As well as things were going during this half-decade, Brace did suffer several major losses and setbacks, the most severe of which was the
death of his father in October 1872.

John Pierce Brace had been ill for some years, suffering from rheu-
matism that kept him confined to a wheelchair, and from a dementia
that left him unable to remember the names of close friends and family. When he had grown too ill to take care of himself, he had retired to
Litchfield, to live in his aunts Mary and Sarah Pierce's old house,
which had been left to him on Mary's death. Right until the very end
he spent almost all of his time in his library, reading and attending to
his naturalist's cabinets. Charles made regular visits to Litchfield but,
as a result of a delayed telegram, was not able to attend his father on
his deathbed. He wrote to his old friend Fred Kingsbury of his "intense disappointment. . . . No father ever did more for his son. He was
a man of vast acquirements, and he sacrificed everything for his children. . . . Every time I left him I expected his departure. He has left a
sweet and noble memory, and I only pray that I may do one-tenth as
much for my children."[7] John Brace also left behind a respectable estate of some $70,000, mostly acquired during his tenure as editor of
the *Hartford Courant*. Charles used his share of the money to build a
house he called Ches-knoll on a steep hillside overlooking the Hudson, just above the village of Dobbs Ferry.

Even as Brace was being celebrated as both author and reformer, he
and the CAS were subjected to a series of vexing public humiliations.
In 1871, at a time when the society was $90,000 in debt owing to the

construction of a new lodging, $30,000 in state appropriations was put at risk by accusations leveled by H. Friedgen, the earnest if ill-educated CAS agent who had escorted John Brady and Andrew Burke to Indiana.

Friedgen had left the CAS to work for the Commissioners of Charity, only to be fired shortly afterward for writing what the *New York Times* called "an abusive letter." When the CAS refused to rehire him, Friedgen apparently sought revenge by exposing the society to a committee headed by the state senator William "Boss" Tweed, the infamous leader of Tammany Hall, who was himself on the verge of an exposure that would send him to jail and end his career. Friedgen mostly made already familiar accusations: that the society commonly placed Catholic children with Protestant families who then changed the children's religion and names; that Protestant clergymen frequently spoke at lodging house meetings; and that "large boys" (over fourteen) often came back to the city from western placements — all charges that were manifestly accurate, but that Friedgen mysteriously withdrew under cross-examination.

The only new charges, ones that both the *Times* and the *Tribune* called "severe" but did not specify, were made against Mr. E. Trott, the superintendent of the Girls' Lodging House. When called upon to testify, Brace flatly dismissed the accusations as "slander" and "hearsay," utterly unsupported by the facts, and said (echoing the "blame the victim" responses to sexual assault in the "Record Books") that the charges against Trott "had come from girls of bad character and had never reached the ears of officials of the Society." The newspapers all gave absolute credence to Brace's defense and painted disparaging portraits of Friedgen; the *Tribune* went so far as to label him "a most extraordinary scoundrel."[8] The Tweed commission apparently agreed in the end and, after a frustrating bureaucratic delay, granted the CAS its appropriation.

In 1872 an angry father sued the Brooklyn Children's Aid Society for "abducting" his eighteen-year-old son. Like many other orphan train riders, the boy, William Nash, had taken advantage of the society's semi-willful credulity to run away from home. He had given the Brooklyn CAS agents a false name, told them he was an orphan, and in short order found himself on a train headed west. The Brooklyn City Court refused to sustain the father's complaint against the CAS, in part because the agents had not known the boy's true identity, but also because, as the judge put it, "the enticement to travel and find new homes which is held out by a children's aid society, and sanctioned by the statute incorporating it, is not an unlawful enticement or solicitation."[9]

Despite the favorable decision, both the New York and the Brooklyn societies became much more careful about where and how they got their orphan train riders. They entirely gave up the practice of sending "visitors" into poor neighborhoods to garner emigrants and increasingly took children only from the Randall's Island nursery, the Juvenile Asylum, the New York Orphan Asylum, and other congregate care institutions. Those children who came to the CAS through its lodging houses and schools were scrutinized more thoroughly than ever before. But the fact remains that, in an era of scanty and inaccessible public records, there was often no way to tell whether a poker-faced child was telling the truth or lying. And despite these precautions, the CAS suffered many similar suits and complaints from parents in the ensuing years.

The charges made by the former agent Friedgen and the suit by Nash's father did little, however, to damage the CAS's reputation. It was Brace's own behavior that, in the winter of 1874, caused the New York newspapers and a substantial portion of the city's reform establishment to turn against him. During a period of great economic uncertainty and severe cold, Brace wrote an article criticizing the "Soup Kitchen Movement" for "pauperizing" its beneficiaries by giving them something for nothing. This harsh stance outraged journalists and many members of the public who had grown used to thinking of Brace as the very model of charitableness. The campaign of "violent abuse" put such a "bitter strain" on him that it was remembered in eulogies occasioned by his death a decade and a half later.[10]

None of these hardships, however, seemed to diminish Brace's enthusiasm or satisfaction in the least. Even in the midst of a letter referring to his villainization in the press, Brace could still declare: "My life has been exceptionally happy, especially in my profession and home enjoyments."[11]

❧

Ten years have now tested the soundness and wisdom of our plan of operations. . . . If the objection had been well founded, that we were "scattering the seeds of vice and crime" through the West, in sending out these unfortunate little creatures, there would have arisen from the whole West, an united groan of opposition to our movement. The fact is, however, that . . . the West has never contributed so liberally to our charity, or has called for so many children, as during the last year.

— Charles Loring Brace, 1864[12]

At the 1874 meeting of the National Prison Reform Congress, Brace was forced once again to confront criticism he thought he had put behind him. A delegate from Wisconsin, probably Hiram H. Giles, responded to a report by Brace on "preventive and reformatory work among children" by declaring that as a result of the CAS's transport of "criminal juveniles, . . . vagabonds and gutter snipes," the people of Wisconsin would be better off "building cheap jails, instead of so expensive churches; or State Industrial schools for boys instead of State Universities." He continued: "[I]t is a misdemeanor to scatter and sow noxious weeds on the prairies and in the openings of Wisconsin, but it is 'Moral Strategy' to annually scatter *three thousand* obnoxious, 'iron-clad orphans,' juvenile criminals among the peaceful homes and in the quiet neighborhoods of the state."[13] At a meeting of the National Conference of Charities and Correction (NCCC) in Detroit the following year, Giles made clear that western resentment of eastern political and economic dominance played a role in the reaction against outplacement: "[W]hile we cannot resist the bringing among us of these street waifs, we can and do most earnestly protest against it."[14]

Although Brace had always presented the placement communities as universally eager to share their bounty with New York's neediest children, many western politicians and editorialists had objected to the Emigration Plan, its beneficiaries, and its agents from the very beginning. The Reverend C. C. Townsend, whom Johnny Morrow had visited in Iowa City, had been required by the county board to put up a $5,000 bond to "indemnify the county against any loss it may sustain, by supporting any of the orphan children or foundlings which he has brought, or may hereafter bring into the county." And perhaps because Townsend never paid the bond, the board forbade him, in June 1867, to bring any more "street outcasts of large cities" into the county.[15]

The Emigration Plan was also attacked in the West on considerably less selfish grounds. In 1858 an Illinois editorialist portrayed the orphan trains as little more than slavery:

If some Missionary Agent had taken that many little negroes from the plantations of Louisiana to Springfield or Jacksonville, and should have prepared to do the very thing with them that everybody knows will be done directly or indirectly with these poor children from New York, our good abolitionist friends . . . would all have fainted at the horrid thought.[16]

Prior to Giles's address, Brace had, for the most part, been able to ignore such protests because they had remained a local matter and had not been given serious hearing at the highest levels of the charity and social reform establishment. He responded to Giles's criticisms as he had to those of 1858 — by ordering an in-house investigation, this one conducted by Charles Fry, a CAS agent based in the West. Brace did not attend the following year's meeting of the Conference of Charities and Correction. Instead, Moore Dupuy, a CAS representative, read a paper by Brace and announced Fry's findings. In the paper Brace contradicted Giles's assertions by saying the vagrant children sent west were not "the children of criminals, but of honest people made suddenly unfortunate [who had been] nursed by care and want and poverty [but had only] picked up the external bad habits of the street."[17]

Fry had investigated three states: Indiana, Illinois, and Michigan. Of the 6,000 children who had been sent to Indiana over the previous twenty years, Fry found only five who had been incarcerated in reform schools. One of these children was a girl who had been released several times but had always gotten into trouble again and was, he concluded, "no doubt the source of many charges against the 'placing out' system." As for Illinois and Michigan, which had received 5,000 and 4,000 children each, not a single child had turned up in any of the states' penal or reform institutions.[18]

Although Brace concluded, at least for public consumption, that the Fry report proved "the charges made in the Prison Congress were almost baseless,"[19] his critics argued that the report — and Brace's "no news is good news" defense — were invalid because prison records said nothing about where inmates had lived, but only about where they had happened to be living at the moment of arrest. So any CAS child who had left his or her placement could not be detected. The controversy was far from settled, but it quieted down for most of another decade. And when the controversy did resume, it would be in association with a wholly new line of argument, one that Brace would find particularly difficult to resist.

&

It is a curious fact of history that substantial cultural shifts can build slowly over generations, without being recognized, and then spring full-blown into the public consciousness, as if out of the blue. The Gay Liberation Movement, for example, had been building unnoticed, underground, at least since the era of Marcel Proust and Oscar Wilde, and had gathered steam during the "sexual revolution" of the 1960s, and then exploded onto the streets with the Stonewall Riot of 1969 and permanently changed the American social landscape.

During the very year when Brace first had to deal with the criticism of Hiram H. Giles, a similar sea-change took place in American attitudes toward children, a change that would permanently diminish Brace's stature before his peers and the judges of history. The catalyst for this sea-change was a case of child abuse not unlike countless other incidents of cruelty to children throughout history — except for the attention it garnered.

In April 1874 eight-year-old Mary Ellen Wilson was escorted into a New York City courtroom by an Officer McDougall of the New York Police Department. Despite the chill in the morning air, she wore only a calico dress and was barefoot, but someone had given her a carriage blanket to hold around her shoulders. Her eyes were darting, observant, and showed intelligence, but in the words of a *New York Times* reporter, she also seemed "care-worn, stunted and prematurely old."

When she took the stand, Elbridge Gerry, legal counsel to the recently established American Society for the Prevention of Cruelty to Animals (ASPCA), asked her about a partially healed wound that ran across her face from forehead to cheek, just beside her eye, and she explained that one day when she had been attempting to help her "mamma" with some quilting, the woman had grown dissatisfied and slashed her with a pair of open scissors. The little girl also testified that as far back as she could remember she had been kept locked up in her family's two-room apartment all day long and had been allowed into the backyard only at night. Her bed was "a piece of carpet stretched on the floor underneath a window." She could remember having only one pair of shoes in her whole life. Her mother had beaten her "almost

every day" with a whip or a cane, and the welts, scabs, and bruises on
her legs and arms were plainly visible to the court audience. In answer
to Gerry's final questions, she said:

> I have no recollection of ever having been kissed by any one — have
> never been kissed by mamma. I have never been taken on my mamma's
> lap and caressed or petted. I never dared to speak to anybody, because
> if I did I would get whipped. I have never had, to my recollection, any
> more clothing than I have at present. . . . I have seen stockings and
> other clothes in our room, but was not allowed to put them on. When-
> ever mamma went out I was locked up in the bedroom. I do not know
> for what I was whipped — mamma never said anything to me when
> she whipped me. I do not want to go back to live with mamma, be-
> cause she beats me so. I have no recollection of ever being on the street
> in my life.[20]

Like many of the children who come to the attention of child welfare authorities, then and now, Mary Ellen had a complicated history.
Her "mamma" was not her biological mother but the widowed wife of
her father, Thomas MacCormack. For several years during his marriage MacCormack had had an affair with a woman named Wilson,
who had borne him three children, and given them all over to a "baby
farmer."

Baby farmers were a particularly unscrupulous form of entrepre-
neur who took advantage of Victorian working-class women's lack of
financial independence and terror of appearing "unrespectable" or
"fallen." Most baby farmers were women who, for a monthly fee,
would take in unwanted infants and care for them. Baby farmers
would claim to seek adoptive parents for their charges, but such adoptions almost never happened. If the monthly payments stopped, the
most pernicious baby farmers would simply let the infant die, although it was also common for baby farmers to continue to collect
payments for children even after they had died of natural (or less than
natural) causes. There is nothing on record about the fate of Mac-
Cormack and Wilson's other two children, but when the eight-dollar
monthly payments for Mary Ellen ceased shortly after the little girl's
first birthday, the woman caring for her simply dumped her at the Department of Charities.

MacCormack also had three children by his wife Mary, but each of these had died as an infant. So when he heard, somehow, that Mary Ellen had been dumped by the baby farmer, he and his wife went to the Department of Charities to collect her. Mary knew just who the child was and presumably agreed to take her in as some sort of substitute for her own lost children.

No one at the Department of Charities ever asked the couple about those children, or how they had died. No one knew of Thomas's relationship to Mary Ellen — or of Mary's for that matter. No one looked into their background in any way. The MacCormacks were simply given indenture papers to sign, and they walked home with the little girl in their arms. And then Thomas MacCormack promptly died, leaving his widow with little more than the responsibility of raising another woman's child. She does not seem to have grieved overlong, however, for she married Francis Connolly when Mary Ellen was too young to remember ever living without him.

Under the indenture agreement that Mary had signed with her first husband, she was supposed to report annually to the Department of Charities on Mary Ellen's condition. Under examination by Elbridge Gerry, however, Mary Connolly admitted that she had filed no more than two reports during the six years she had the child in her keeping, but no one from the Department of Charities seems ever to have bothered to investigate.

Mary Ellen's plight only came to the attention of the authorities through the efforts of a charity worker named Etta Angell Wheeler, who was with the Saint Luke's Mission. Wheeler had happened to visit a terminally ill woman living in the same tenement building as the Connollys. This woman told Wheeler that she was afraid to die because she did not have a clean conscience. Every day for years, she confessed, she had heard through her bedroom wall a child's sobs and the sound of a lash and she had done nothing to stop it. Wheeler talked to other tenants in the building and, hearing more grim details about the beatings, decided to visit the Connollys herself. She knocked on the door and no one answered, although she did hear someone stirring inside. On her next visit to the building she knocked again, and this time Mr. or Mrs. Connolly opened the door wide enough for Wheeler to get a clear glimpse of Mary Ellen and see the lash marks on her legs and arms.

Wheeler went to several asylums to ask whether they could take the poor girl. All of them said that she first had to be legally removed from

her foster parents. Wheeler then approached several charities and lawyers about handling the removal but was told only not to meddle in
other people's family affairs. Finally, at the suggestion of a niece,
Wheeler contacted Henry Bergh, the founder of the ASPCA. Although
afterward Bergh would make a big display of the role he and his society played in Mary Ellen's rescue, at first he was reluctant to handle the
case. He had no great fondness for children and often depicted them
in his promotional literature as the tormentors of dogs and horses.
Also, he worried that focusing public attention on this case of cruelty to a child would ultimately make people less concerned about animals. In the end, however, he was swayed by Wheeler's argument
that a child was, after all, an animal, and he asked Gerry to look into
the matter — but purely on a private basis, not as a representative of
the ASPCA.

Gerry's prosecution of the case could hardly have been more successful. Mary Ellen was permanently removed from her foster parents
and taken in by Etta Wheeler's relatives, who lived on a farm in upstate New York. Mary Connolly was given what the *Times* called "the
extreme penalty of the law" — one year in the state penitentiary at
hard labor.[21]

Just months before Mary Ellen's rescue, the case of thirteen-year-old
John Fox, who had been beaten to death by his father, had been given
only passing mention in the *New York Times*. By contrast, Mary Ellen's
trial and abuse, and Bergh and Gerry's efforts, received extravagant
coverage from newspapers all across the country. There were even two
popular songs written about the case, "Little Mary Ellen" and "Mother
Sent an Angel to Me." What was it about this girl's story that made it
such a sensation when so many similar cases had been all but ignored?

Certainly one reason for its prominence was the fact that Etta
Wheeler's husband was a well-connected journalist. Bergh and Gerry
too were both savvy publicists who drew as much attention to Mary
Ellen and themselves as they possibly could. But it is also clear that
Mary Ellen's suffering would not have provoked nearly so powerful a
response if the public had not already been well primed, not only to
have its heartstrings plucked but to countenance a vast escalation of
the right of public authorities to intrude on the sanctity of family.

Before 1874 people had seen cruelty to children as an inevitable and
unremarkable fact of life. Beatings and other physical and emotional

punishments were considered an essential and effective means of in-culcating virtue. When punishments went too far, or were clearly sa-distic, they might result — but only rarely — in prosecution. More often neighbors — like Johnny Morrow's in New Haven — would simply take matters into their own hands. But equally commonly — like Mary Ellen's neighbors — they might not have felt justified med-dling in other people's private business. Mary Ellen's case was a land-mark, not merely for its celebrity, but because it evoked an outpouring of demand for public intervention — as is illustrated by the spectacu-lar growth of child protection societies.

The first of these, the New York Society for the Prevention of Cru-elty to Children, was founded in December 1874 by Elbridge Gerry. By 1914 there were 494 societies dedicated to eradicating child abuse, although some of these, called "humane" societies, aimed to protect both animals and children. By 1890 Gerry's New York society was handling 15,000 cases in the city alone; and the state legislature made obstruction of the society's work a crime and gave the society's agents the right to arrest abusive parents.[22] Whereas in its early years the Children's Aid Society had been compelled to rely primarily on persuasion and intimidation to get children away from parents, agents of the Gerry Society, as it was commonly called, could march into a home and wrench children out of their parents' arms with complete impunity.

The reappraisal — or *discovery* — of child abuse occasioned by Mary Ellen Wilson's case has certainly saved countless children's lives over the last century and a quarter, but the utterly unprecedented in-trusion of public authority into private lives that it brought into being often did more harm than good. The agents of the NYSPCC, no less than those of the CAS, tended to confuse the inescapable effects of poverty with true cruelty and thus sometimes subjected the very chil-dren they were trying to save to unjust, unnecessary, deeply disturb-ing, and just plain cruel treatment. This was especially true with cases of neglect. Sometimes Gerry Society agents, confusing inability to provide food with intentional deprivation, would rip a malnourished child away from perfectly loving but very poor parents and put him or her in an orphanage, never thinking that a better alternative would be to help the family and the child get more food.

As a result of such injustices, the residents of poor neighborhoods — the only places then, as now, that were truly subject to child welfare interventions — usually had profoundly ambivalent feelings about the Gerry Society. On the one hand, they saw it as a last resort in cases of intolerable abuse like Mary Ellen's; on the other, they spoke of it as "the Cruelty." They shouted warnings down the block when they saw an agent coming and threatened their enemies by saying, "If you don't watch out, I'll report you to the Cruelty!"

Mary Ellen Wilson's celebrity and the founding of the Gerry Society were far from the only evidence of a major shift in public attitude toward children in the mid-1870s. The New York Children's Law of 1875 also represented heightened intolerance of juvenile suffering, as did the state's 1874 restrictions on child labor. The mid-1870s were, in fact, the period when the anti–child labor movement really began to gather momentum. This was also a time of growing concern about baby farms, institutions that previously had been allowed to function in discreet silence but that now became the subject of editorials and exposés, as well as lurid tales in the penny press.[23] And finally, 1875 was also the year when the Prudential Company began marketing life insurance for juveniles, a curiously ambiguous product that capitalized on the new and growing tenderness toward children (it was meant to give them "decent" rather than "paupers'" funerals), even as it put a price on their heads. Critics of the insurance asserted that parents would bump off their children so that they could use the funeral money to buy a new house, or just throw a big party.

Although an increased sensitivity to the suffering of children may have been the most visible aspect of the era's cultural shift, it both grew out of and enhanced a developing sense of the dangers the world held for children. The Gerry Societies played a pivotal role in this phenomenon through the grim tales and images in their promotional literature, and in press stories about their work. That most sacred of Victorian institutions — the family — was under attack. Mothers and fathers were routinely shown to be capable of previously inconceivable atrocities. And if these icons of domesticity could be so evil, what did that say about the rest of the human race?

Whereas once upon a time people had thought little of sending their children off to live with and work for total strangers, or even make transatlantic voyages on their own, now such ventures seemed perilous, unwise, and even immoral. This new sense of danger only encouraged and was encouraged by a greater need for control. People had once been willing to take a more ad-hoc approach to dealing with cruelty and injustice, but now they wanted to protect children and protect themselves by tightening the reins, passing laws, constructing supervisory bodies, and building elaborate bureaucracies. Ultimately it was this intensified need for control that would do the most to make Brace's Emigration Plan seem antiquated, ineffective, and cruel. The younger generations simply did not share his optimism about human nature or his tolerance for risk and adversity.

﹏

In the years following Hiram H. Giles's 1874 assault on the CAS, Brace came under frequent attack as well from representatives of the "Asylum-Interest" and the western states. Lyman P. Alden, superintendent of a Michigan reform school, objected to family placement on the grounds that "the majority of even respectable well-to-do families [were] unfit to train up their *own* children," and he proposed that New York build a monument to Brace for "relieving" the city "of so many incipient criminals."[24] It was not until the 1882 meeting of the National Conference of Charities and Correction, however, that a younger generation of child welfare workers began to criticize the Emigration Plan for endangering the child rather than the community in which the child was placed — a line of attack that Brace could not help but take seriously.

J. H. Mills, from North Carolina, focused his attention on the CAS's lax supervision and screening. "About once a year," he said, "a man comes to North Carolina and brings a large company of children and gives them out to the farmers of a certain district without asking any questions or obtaining any information regarding them, or any security for their proper care or protection." Mills asserted that the children were taken in only for the most mercenary motives: "Their slaves being set free, these men needing labor take these boys and treat them as slaves [and force them] to associate with the lowest Negroes we have."[25]

Mills's charges were seconded by E. W. Chase of Minnesota, who said that children were frequently abused in their placements, and that nearly every month boys who had been placed with Mennonites ran away because they were not given enough to eat. Even CAS supporters like Andrew Elmore of Wisconsin, who was presiding over the meeting, could not refrain from joining the criticism: "I do not doubt but the intentions of the Society are good. . . . But when they have placed these children in the West, do they look after them a moment? Not any. They get them off their hands and that ends the story. . . . [I]t would be as well if you cut their jugular veins in the first place."[26]

Brace had his defenders at the meeting. Some representatives talked about orphan train riders who had done well in their states, while others commended the Emigration Plan in principle but said that placements had to be selected and monitored more carefully. Franklin B. Sanborn, the secretary of the Massachusetts Board of State Charities, gave Brace backhanded support by saying that the CAS had grown too big for him to control and that he was being deceived by his agents.

Most of these charges were not new. Editorialists and critics had compared outplacement to slavery practically since the departure of the first orphan train, and these were far from the first examples of abuse that had been brought up in a public forum. What was different was that so many joined so vocally in the criticism, a signal both that a new consensus was emerging among a mostly younger class of child welfare professionals and that Brace's power and prestige had begun to erode.

Brace was being attacked partly because of his prominence, especially after the publication of *The Dangerous Classes*. The sins that the CAS was being accused of were, after all, true of virtually every organization that placed orphaned or vagrant children in families. The New York Department of Charities relied on correspondence from foster parents to monitor even children placed in the city and, as Mary Ellen Wilson's case demonstrated, did not do a much better job than the CAS of checking up when required reports did not come in. In-city placements by a well-regarded Philadelphia agency were visited only once a year, while children placed by the Catholic Protectory were visited once every two to five years. Those children placed by the Randall's Island House of Refuge were never visited at all. The attacks on Charles Loring Brace were clearly part of a much-needed self-correction of the entire American child welfare system. And he was singled out for attack because he was the exemplar of the old consensus — the main idol who had to be toppled.

வ

Brace had not attended the 1882 conference because he had been in Europe recuperating from what he believed to be the strain of overwork. At fifty-six he was still in excellent physical shape, strong enough to row his family more than a mile across the Hudson, to the cliffs just south of his home in Dobbs Ferry, and then back against the current. What he seemed to lack, however, was the stamina to endure his normal workweek. He was frequently so exhausted at the end of the day that he would become dazed and depressed. In the year 1882 he also suffered a series of personal losses. One was the death of his hero and friend Charles Darwin. Far more severe a loss, however, was the death of his partner from the earliest days of the Children's Aid Society, John Macy, who, toward the end of his life, was almost totally blind. But the hardest death to bear was that of his youngest sibling, James, who succumbed to a severe fever while on a long journey fulfilling his duties as a western agent for the CAS.

Brace returned from his travels in England, France, Hungary, and Transylvania reinvigorated and excited about the publication of his latest book, *Gesta Christi: A History of Human Progress Under Christianity*. The book was well received by the Christian clergy and press but was given a sharp review in the *Sun* by Emma Lazarus, the young poet now best known for having written the sonnet inscribed on the base of the Statue of Liberty ("Give me your tired, your poor, your huddled masses / yearning to be free"). Lazarus faulted Brace for his tendency to see the lives of the wisest and most saintly Christians as the very definition of Christian society, while portraying equally virtuous men and women during the classical ages as exceptions in their cultures. She also criticized him for not acknowledging the degree to which Christianity was an outgrowth of Judaism.

Brace was so profoundly influenced by Lazarus's review and by his subsequent correspondence with her that the questions she raised ultimately dictated the subject of his next and last book, *The Unknown God*, a survey of all the major non-Christian religions. Although, in the book, Brace portrayed these faiths as stepping-stones toward the ultimate truths revealed by Christ, he nevertheless treated them with uncharacteristic openness and respect. He wanted so much to be truly democratic and fair, but he was hamstrung by his utter inability to question the moral and metaphysical superiority of Christ.

Although Brace would prove to be equally responsive to the criticism he had received at the NCCC meeting, he began with some serious damage control, publishing a pamphlet in which he attributed disapproval of the CAS's work to false charges leveled against one boy placed in Iowa. In regard to the charges of slavery in the South, he said that the CAS's southern placements were "usually large boys, perfectly

able to take care of themselves, and not indentured" — a claim that
did in fact reflect established CAS policy. Long suspicious of the former slave states, Brace had sent only the oldest and least adoptable
(usually because they were mildly retarded or somehow deformed)
children to the South. And finally he declared: "As to stories of ill
treatment of our children, whether in the West or South, we hold
them to be bosh."[27]

Major changes in CAS policy had begun long before the 1882 NCCC
meeting. Ten years earlier the society had established its Summer
Home for industrial school girls on the Brooklyn shore. What made
this institution a remarkable departure from previous policy was that
for the first time the CAS was giving without taking. Unlike the Newsboys' Lodging House, where residents had to pay nominal rents, or the
industrial schools, where students had to work, the Summer Home
residents neither paid for their stay nor were required to do anything
during it other than relax and eat well. Apparently satisfied that the
girls had not been pauperized by the experience, the CAS launched
other programs that gave without expecting a return. In 1879 the society commenced a "Sick Mission," under which visitors brought medicine and good food to ailing tenement dwellers, and the decidedly less
vital "Flower Mission," under which the CAS brought "the sunshine of
bright flowers to the miserable rooms."[28] These programs differed
from previous CAS efforts in that they represented a slight softening
of Brace's utter rejection of the communities where children he chose
to aid were born and brought up. Although CAS industrial schools
had, of course, always given something back to the communities, their
immediate beneficiaries were only the children who attended them.
The medicine, food, and flowers provided by these "missions" benefited not just children but whole families.

The most effective and forward-looking of the projects to grow out
of this new policy was the "Health Home," or sanitarium for sick infants, that the CAS opened on Coney Island in 1884. Having discovered how little industrial school girls knew about basic hygiene, and
how fortified they were by a balanced, milk-rich diet, Brace thought
he might best help improve the health of poor children by making it
possible for them to have these benefits available to them from birth.
In the summer of 1884 alone, 2,200 mothers and ailing infants stayed
at the Health Home for periods of one to several days. During their

residence mother and child were both given healthy diets that included pasteurized milk. The mothers were also instructed in the role
that clean bodies, clothing, and bedding could play in disease prevention and were encouraged to spend as much time as possible sitting
with their children on the home's deep verandas partaking of the fresh
and invigorating sea air. Although none of these benefits could do
much for truly diseased children, the "immediate revival of apparently
dying babies was," as Emma Brace put it, "a striking proof that in
many cases their desperate condition was merely from lack of proper
food and fresh air."[29] Her claim is substantiated by the fact that decades later community health stations, which also provided infants
with milk and gave mothers hygiene instruction, made substantial
contributions to the decline of infant mortality. The Health Home was
very expensive to operate, however, and not as popular among donors
as other CAS programs, and so it often had to shut down early in the
summer because of lack of funding.

༄

> I was myself a witness of the distribution of forty children in Nobles
> County, Minnesota, by my honored friend, Agent James Mathews, who is a
> member of this Conference. The children arrived at about half-past three
> P.M., and were taken directly from the train to the court-house, where a
> large crowd was gathered. Mr. Mathews set the children, one by one, before
> the company, and, in his stentorian voice, gave a brief account of each. Ap-
> plicants for children were then admitted in order behind the railing and
> rapidly made their selections. Then, if the child gave assent, the bargain
> was concluded on the spot. It was a pathetic sight, not soon to be forgotten,
> to see those children and young people, weary, travel-stained, confused by
> the excitement and unwonted surroundings, peering into those strange
> faces, and trying to choose wisely for themselves. And it was surprising
> how many happy selections were made under such circumstances. In a lit-
> tle more than three hours, nearly all of those forty children were disposed
> of. Some who had not previously applied selected children. There was lit-
> tle time for consultation, and refusal would be embarrassing; and I know
> that the committee consented to some assignments against their better
> judgment.
>
> — Hastings H. Hart[30]

Shortly after the 1882 meeting of the National Conference of Charities
and Correction, the chairman of the Committee on Child-saving
asked Hastings H. Hart to conduct an inquiry into the work of the
Children's Aid Society. Hart was then secretary of the Minnesota

Board of Corrections and Charities but would soon move to New York to assume the directorship of the Department of Child Helping at the Russell Sage Foundation, where he would become a major figure in the development of child welfare policy.

Hart's report, presented at the 1884 NCCC meeting, was both the first comprehensive independent analysis of the Emigration Plan and a rhetorical tour de force. It eschewed the traditional hyperbole and sentimentality of nineteenth-century social welfare writing and derived its power instead from balanced, well-reasoned, and factual argument. It was by far the most powerful assault against Brace's work to that date, not because it was harsh, but because it was incontrovertible — at least by the standards of the time.

Beginning by saying that he was going to speak on "the work of the most extensive and important children's charity in the United States," Hart mainly had good news for the CAS. On the question of whether orphan train riders were "vicious and depraved," Hart found that of the 340 individuals sent to Minnesota over the preceding three years, only six were "known to have committed offenses against the laws," and nine were sent back to New York by local committees as "incorrigible." He also found that three or four "depraved" adults had been sent to the state by the society. None of these numbers seemed high enough to substantiate the claims of western representatives like Hiram H. Giles that the Emigration Plan was flooding the states with "criminal juveniles, . . . vagabonds and gutter snipes." Nor did Hart find the least evidence that the society intentionally, through some "Moral Strategy," sent New York's worst cases west.[31]

As for the charge that the CAS, after having "disposed" of its children in the West, left them "to shift for themselves without further care," Hart once again found the society innocent, at least in regard to its handling of younger children. When the cases of "incorrigible children" were reported to the society, Hart observed, they received "prompt attention": the children were either transferred to a new local placement or "removed from the state." He also pointed out that the CAS answered letters promptly and selected its local committees "judiciously."

On one point, however, Hart's approval of CAS practices rested on assumptions that appear highly questionable today. He stated that, while CAS agents did return to the counties where they had placed children, their trips, "being hurried, have not permitted visits to all the children, special attention being given to urgent cases." In regard to the placement of children under twelve, at least, Hart apparently did not feel that agent visits were necessary because he believed that "younger children are taken from motives of benevolence and uniformly well treated." Also, although he did take into account incidents of criminality by placed children, he, like Georgia Ralph, primarily judged the success of placements on the basis of their endurance. Thus, the fact that 90 percent of the children under thirteen remained at their placements, as opposed to only 52 percent of the children thirteen or older, seemed clear evidence that all was well with the younger children. It was only when Hart discussed the cases of older "intractable" children that he documented the inadequacies of CAS supervision that in fact applied to all of its placements.

Although Hart complimented the CAS's efforts to act promptly when orphan train riders got into trouble, he pointed out that instructions mailed from New York often arrived too late to be of any use. This was especially a problem because, although the local committees were meant to stand in loco parentis to the placed children, they did not have legal guardianship of them — that was retained by the New York office — and so could do little on their behalf. He was also concerned by the fact that employers were not legally bound to educate or keep the children they had taken in, and he cited cases where children had never been sent to school or had been worked hard all summer only to be kicked out in the fall because the farmers did not want to pay their expenses over the winter. And finally, Hart felt that the CAS proviso that children were free to leave their employers merely if they felt "ill-treated or dissatisfied" encouraged too many children to run off because they did not like justified character-building punishments or work assignments. On the basis of these arguments, Hart said that, in essence, he concurred with Brace's own statement in *The Dangerous Classes* that the Emigration Plan ought to be applied only to children under fourteen, although Hart himself thought twelve was a better cutoff age.

In many ways Hart's most damning finding was that the society was indeed "guilty" of the charge that it placed its children too hastily and without "proper investigation." He cited five cases of abuse that the society — or in one case the boy himself — dealt with adequately after the fact but that obviously should never have happened in the first place. He also said that while younger children were taken for motives

of "benevolence," the majority of older children were "taken from motives of profit, and . . . expected to earn their way from the start." This
sort of exploitation was all the more likely to occur because, he said,
children were routinely placed in homes that were no more affluent
than the ones they had come from:

> The farmers in these counties are very poor. I speak within bounds,
> when I say that not one in five of those who have taken these children
> is what would be called, in Ohio or Illinois, well-to-do. To my personal
> knowledge, some of them were taken by men who lived in shanties and
> could not clothe their own children decently. A little girl in Rock
> County was placed in a family living on a dirt floor in filth worthy of
> an Italian tenement house. A boy in Nobles County was taken by a
> family whose children had been clothed by ladies of my church, so that
> they could go to Sunday-school.

Hastings Hart's report may have been steeped in the class and ethnic
prejudices of his time. It may also have been shockingly naive about
the safety of younger foster children (especially given the revelations
of Mary Ellen Wilson's case), but it did represent the maturation of a
long-developing opinion that outplacement, as it had been practiced,
was all too often only another form of cruelty to children. The fact
that this opinion was predicated on a sympathy for poor children and
an optimism about human nature very like Brace's own made it particularly difficult to dismiss as "bosh."

In fact, the CAS radically altered its policies after the 1884 meeting.
The notes in its "Record Books" immediately became much more detailed. Before 1884 most of the CAS's records had consisted primarily
of the dates of the inquiry letters sent to the employer or child, and
one- or two-line summations of the rare answers to those letters and
the almost equally rare visits by agents. From 1885 on, no child's "Record Book" page was mostly blank, as the majority of them had been
before. They all contained descriptions, admittedly brief, of the placements and evidence of more frequent agent visits. Many records now
had two and three pages of commentary affixed atop the child's original page. Also, letters were no longer summarized but actually inserted
into the books along with photographs and news clips.

The western agent A. Schlegel testified to the new imperatives the

CAS was placing on its agents, as well as to the difficulties of fulfilling them, in the annual report of 1885:

> As our emigration work increases, the importance of visiting the children in their homes becomes more and more manifest; but it is an immense undertaking. These children are often in homes ten or twenty miles from town or railroad, and can only be reached by long drives, and often a whole day will be consumed in visiting a single child. Sometimes changes are made without notifying the Society, or a child may leave the home provided for him, and seek another for himself, and much time and labor is thus expended in following him up.
>
> The plan adopted is for agents to revisit, at the end of six weeks, the company taken out by them on their previous trip. By this means, if an error should possibly have been made in the locating of a child, there is an immediate chance to rectify it.[32]

But even these minimal visitation plans proved impossible to realize, at least for Schlegel. Although on one trip he did gather information on a number of the children he had placed, he did not visit them, because (directly contradicting Hart's beliefs) "these large boys are well able to look out for themselves, and I desired to devote as much time as possible to the smaller children." But Schlegel did not manage to visit the homes of all of the smaller children and — astonishingly — chose to bypass one because he felt his visit would be "unwelcome."[33]

Although Schlegel's failure to visit this last child was indefensible, it was certainly true that until automobiles became readily available in the 1920s, visiting many of the orphan train riders was extremely difficult if not impossible. The invention of the telephone, which became common in rural homes during the 1890s, helped agents keep better track of their charges but was still no substitute for visits. Harry Morris, who was placed on a farm in DeWitt, Nebraska, in 1897 and received frequent and severe beatings from his employer, was never visited by the CAS agent in charge of his case — a man he called "Mr. Titus." In Morris's account of his experiences on that farm, he described the one time his agent called on the telephone: "I asked the farmer if I might talk to him. I got such a stern look that I held my tongue. If he had given me the chance I would have asked Mr. Titus to come to the farm and let me speak with him personally, and then I would have had a chance to make the situation clear to him."[34] An indication of how distant the contact between Morris and his agent was is that the agent's real name was not Titus but Tice.

Marked, if incomplete, improvements in screening foster families and monitoring placements did not insulate the CAS from further criticism. At the 1885 NCCC meeting, Lyman P. Alden, the Michigan reform school superintendent who had suggested that New York build a monument to Brace for ridding the city "of so many incipient criminals," renewed his attack by declaring that the "best families do not want to assume the responsibility and risk" of caring for street children fresh from the "slum holes of society." Once again Alden asserted that only specialists in institutions could and should provide such care. And at the 1886 meeting Hastings Hart repeated his critique of the Emigration Plan, adding that he thought the main reason for the CAS's failures was that it had tried to accomplish its work at too little expense. In 1889 a report by the Indiana Board of Charities declared that the state had become "a dumping ground for dependents from other states,"[35] and an attempt was made there to pass a law regulating the resettlement of children from out of state. Michigan, in 1895, became the first state to pass a law limiting the placement of children from other states. Indiana, Illinois, and Minnesota instituted restrictions of their own in 1899, and two years later Missouri and Nebraska followed suit.

But as much as this tide of criticism and anti–orphan train legislation constituted a defeat for Charles Loring Brace, it was also, in important ways, a victory. Much of the criticism was, after all, based on his own argument that the children of the poor and of the streets were as deserving of love and consideration as the children of the more affluent classes. And even as many critics attacked the CAS for the way it handled family placement, they by no means rejected family placement itself. On the contrary, by the 1880s family placement was decidedly the most favored form of treatment for any dependent child, with institutional care being only a last resort. One participant at the 1881 NCCC meeting was only exaggerating slightly when she declared, "So general has become the expression of sentiment of preference for a system of family life for deserted children, over one of institutional life, that it is unnecessary to dwell largely upon it in this paper."[36]

Although institutions — predominantly orphanages — did continue to handle the vast majority of children until the passage of Roosevelt's New Deal legislation in 1935, the huge, factory-like orphanages, reform schools, and juvenile prisons of the mid-nineteenth century were almost entirely out of favor by the 1880s and were being replaced by cottage-style institutions that sought to reproduce a family environment in smaller, semi-independent units. Even the states that banned the CAS and other eastern charities from sending their children did so not because they rejected family placement but because they did not want to run the risk of their taxpayers having to support children they thought should be the responsibility of other states. As, one after another, the western states developed large populations of dependent children of their own, they all instituted varieties of family placement. In 1883, for example, an Illinois minister named Martin Van Buren Van Arsdale founded what was to become the Children's Home Society with the prime purpose of finding homes for orphaned and abandoned children. By 1892 the National Children's Home Society had member societies in ten midwestern and western states. By 1903 there were member societies in twenty-five states that had a total of 12,000 children under their care.

Unlike the CAS, the Home Societies and the many other child placement organizations that arose in the 1880s and afterward tended to screen foster families and monitor placements carefully. They also did not send their children so far from home but rather operated primarily within the boundaries of their own states. And, especially after the turn of the twentieth century, the average age of the children they placed became younger and younger. Ultimately the CAS would adopt nearly identical policies, but not until after the death of Charles Loring Brace, and not until after the most notorious of all the orphan train riders had begun to make headlines across the nation.

The Trials of Charley Miller

ON SEPTEMBER 27, 1890, at the tiny settlement of Hillsdale in the high prairie of eastern Wyoming, a railroad brakeman named George Manafield was checking the coupling between two boxcars when he heard a weak moan. As he stepped out to the sloping edge of the gravel rail-bed, Manafield heard the moan again, coming through the narrow gap of a boxcar door that was not quite closed. Pushing the door open, Manafield discovered a young man of about twenty, lying on a heap of railroad ties, blood seeping from a bullet wound in his temple. Manafield shouted down the tracks for help, then climbed inside the car to see what he could do for the bloody, pale, moaning young man. It was not until another brakeman and a conductor had crouched around the body that Manafield stood up and noticed a pair of bare feet jutting over the edge of a stack of railroad ties that reached nearly to the ceiling. Climbing the stack, Manafield found a second young man wedged face down between two of the creosote-soaked timbers — "like a traitor in his coffin," as a newspaper would put it — a bullet in his temple and a cheap, nickel-plated, thirty-two-caliber revolver lying beside his face. This young man's body was still warm, but he was no longer breathing.

The Hillsdale stationmaster telegraphed the news of the wounded man and his dead companion to Cheyenne, twenty miles to the west, where there was both a hospital and a sheriff. By the time the train had arrived in the city scores of curiosity seekers were waiting at the station, debating whether the injured man and his dead companion had been the victims of a suicide pact or a Clan-na-Gael assassin, or were just a couple of tramps crushed by a collapsing stack of ties.

Also waiting at the station was a teamster named Thomas J. Shaugnessey, who had been delegated by County Commissioner Hoyt to transport the two young victims. Shaugnessey seems to have had an odd, but decidedly firm, sense of protocol. Once the two bodies had been placed side by side in the back of his wagon, he insisted, over the objections of the crowd, that before he could go to the hospital, both victims had to be inspected by his boss, the county commissioner.

While Shaugnessey's wagon proceeded down the street at a slow walk, impeded by the crush of curiosity seekers, several members of the crowd rushed ahead and pulled Commissioner Hoyt from behind the counter of his dry goods store. By the time the wagon pulled up, Hoyt was already out on the wooden sidewalk in front of his store, explaining impatiently that he had not asked for the two men to be brought to him. Once presented with the bodies, however, some combination of professional duty and curiosity caused him to clamber up onto the back of the wagon, pull back the bloody blanket from the face of the dead man, and then squint at the seeping wound in the temple of his weakly breathing companion.

Hoyt looked at the victims long enough to see that they were hardly more than teenagers and that, from their clothes, they probably came from respectable families. The dead man was dressed particularly well, in a brand-new, ankle-length, tan overcoat. With a heavy sigh, Hoyt turned around, clapped Shaugnessey on the back of his head, and said, "I didn't mean for you to bring them here. This boy belongs in the hospital and the other in the morgue. Get along now, and do what you should have done in the first place." With that, he hopped off the wagon and went back to his customers, leaving Shaugnessey to engage in yet another dispute with the crowd — this time over what order the bodies should be delivered to their destinations. Since the shortest route to the hospital passed right by the morgue, it seemed only a matter of common sense to Shaugnessey that he should stop there first. This time the crowd was adamant, and the bullheaded teamster finally surrendered to its will, but only after a ten-minute shouting match during which his wagon did not budge from in front of Hoyt's store.[1]

The living man, who, on the basis of papers found in his pocket, was determined to be Ross Fishbaugh of Saint Joseph, Missouri, died at 7:00 P.M. without ever regaining consciousness. By 9:00 P.M. he had joined his companion, Waldo Emerson, also of Saint Joe, on twin enameled tables at the Mercantile Undertakers. Lamps burned late that night at the Mercantile as the bodies were readied for the morning train to Saint Joseph, and also at the offices of the *Cheyenne Daily Leader,* where the story of the killing was being prepared for the general public. Shortly after dawn, as the ice-packed bodies were being loaded into a boxcar, newsboys hurried out into the streets carrying papers that, under the headline "A Bullet in Each Brain," declared the double murder to be "the most dastardly crime ever committed in the west."

Over the next couple of weeks the *Daily Leader* ran regular articles about Emerson and Fishbaugh and the progress of the investigation into their deaths. Much was made of the apparent affluence of the two young men. The newspaper remarked on the softness of their hands and the fineness of their clothing, which was such as "a young man roughing it might choose from a fair wardrobe." Fishbaugh, twenty years old, was said to have been the only child of, and sole means of support for, his widowed mother. Emerson, eighteen, was the son of a relatively well-educated factory foreman who, having little faith in the local authorities, had hired a private detective to investigate the case. The young men had been on their way to Denver in search of employment. Emerson's father had assumed that they would be traveling first-class, but apparently they had chosen to save money and have a bit of adventure by riding the boxcars. Emerson's father had also been under the impression that his son was a teetotaler, but he and Fishbaugh had been seen in at least one bar and had a bottle of whiskey on them when they died.

Both the police and the detective hired by the Emersons assumed that the motive for the double murder had been robbery. The boys were said to have left Saint Joseph with a silver watch and $140 between them and were rumored to have won $100 at a crap game in Grand Island, Nebraska. But the police had found only twenty-five cents and two diamond shirt studs (worth ten dollars) on the bodies. Suspicion centered on William Frantzell, a thief who had been let out of jail in Saint Joseph the day the boys departed and who had been seen leaving the train in Hillsdale.

One of the investigators, however, had a different theory: John Martin, the Laramie County sheriff, was intrigued by a story told by John Brooks, the water pump engineer at Hillsdale.

At the very moment when Manafield had discovered the two bodies on the stopped train, Brooks and his family had been sitting down to their midday meal. Answering a knock at their back door, Brooks found a slight sixteen- or seventeen-year-old tramp standing on the step, clutching his canvas sack of belongings against his chest. The boy wanted to know whether Brooks could spare some food. He seemed a little anxious but didn't look like a troublemaker, so Brooks invited him in and had his daughter put another chair at the table.

Brooks had not yet heard about the bodies on the train, which was still waiting on the tracks within sight of his house, but as the meal progressed he became increasingly suspicious of the odd, young tramp he had let into his home. The boy told Brooks that he came from New York, but when he talked about where he was going, he said Cheyenne one time, Kansas another, and Omaha a third. When Brooks asked the boy why he did not just get back on the waiting freight train, he answered that he wanted to "get a good feed" first — but for most of the meal he just pushed his food around his plate with a fork and hardly ate a mouthful. Brooks also noticed that, every now and then, the boy would steal a glance at a silver watch that he kept under the table. The boy paid for his meal with a quarter, which he said was all the money he had, but later at the station Brooks saw him purchase a ticket on the next passenger train to Cheyenne with a silver dollar. When Sheriff Martin spoke to the Hillsdale stationmaster, he learned that the boy had first asked about a ticket to Manhattan, Kansas, and then abruptly changed his mind. On the hunch that this confused lad might eventually make it to Kansas, Sheriff Martin telegraphed the boy's description to his colleagues in Manhattan.

On October 15, 1890, two and a half weeks after the murder, sixteen-year-old Fred Miller walked into the office of the *Republic,* a weekly newspaper in Manhattan, Kansas, and asked to speak to the paper's editor, Albert Stewart. Fred was accompanied by his brother, Charley, a wiry, hollow-chested boy who was only five feet four inches tall, with a bulging forehead, ghostly gray eyes, and a long, thin beak of a nose. Although Charley looked several years older than his brother, he was in fact more than a year his junior, having just turned fifteen.

Albert Stewart knew Fred as the adopted child of his colleague J. L. Loofboro, the editor of a weekly paper in nearby Leonardsville. Fred had come by train from New York with a party of orphans some four years earlier. He was a good worker, a quiet, considerate boy, and Loofboro had been so happy with him that, the winter before last, he had agreed to take in Fred's youngest brother, Willy, who was now fourteen years old. Stewart did not know the third brother, Charley, but recognized the family resemblance even before being introduced. He also saw that both boys looked pale and uneasy, so he invited them into his private office, where he offered them chairs in front of his desk. Once the door was closed, Fred told Stewart that his brother had something important to say.

"It's been weighing on my mind," Charley began.

"Yes," said Stewart with an encouraging nod.

For a long time Charley seemed unable to talk. But then, drawing a deep breath and speaking in a voice that betrayed no other emotion than a slight relief, he confessed that he was the one who had killed the two young men on the train in Wyoming.

Stewart was not much of a journalist. His paper mainly ran wedding and death notices, puff pieces about local merchants and politicians, slightly reworded transcriptions of national stories from the Kansas City papers, and the occasional oddity about a two-headed pig or a sleepwalker's near-brush with death. But he was enough of a professional to realize that he had just been handed the biggest story of his career. He picked up a pen and a notebook, pulled his chair around beside Charley's, and, for the next two hours, grilled the boy, not only on the double murder but on his whole life.

Charley was to tell this story dozens of times, to other journalists, to the police, and finally in court. Everyone who heard it remarked on the odd alacrity with which he described both the killing and his own suffering, loneliness, and frustration. The disjunction between his grim tale and the easy, almost charming voice in which it was told led to his frequent description in the press and, more significantly, in legal documents as "morally irresponsible" — as, in effect, a "sociopath," although the term was not in use at the time. Given the apparent oddness of Charley's emotional responses, it is surprising, at least to the modern sensibility, that no attempt was made to look into them. He was virtually never asked about his motives or about how any of his experiences had made him feel. The result was that, with all of its detail, Charley's story was strangely hollow, dream-like, and open to wildly varying interpretations.

⁂

Charley was the third of four children born to a German immigrant couple living in New York City. His father owned a bar, much of the profits of which he drank up himself. When Charley was four, his mother died of consumption. A year later his father, who had long talked about suicide, finally killed himself by drinking Paris green, an insecticide. The bar and about $1,000 passed into the possession of a man the Miller children had always called "uncle," with the understanding that it was being held in trust for them. All four children were sent to the New York Orphan Asylum, which, founded in 1806, had been the city's first large institution for the care of orphans. Originally, the asylum had occupied a broad swath of rolling meadowland running above what is now Seventy-third Street, from Broadway down to the Hudson River. But by the time Charley and his siblings stayed there, the asylum's brownstone house had been cut off from the river by Frederick Law Olmsted's Riverside Park and the cream-colored granite pinnacles of the financier Charles Schwab's seventy-five-room mansion. To the east the asylum was dwarfed by the twelve-story turreted mass of the Ansonia Hotel.

The Miller children remained at the asylum until their twelfth birthdays, when they were placed in foster homes by the Children's Aid Society. Carrie, the oldest child and only girl, went to live with a family in Rochester, New York. Fred went to Mr. Loofboro, and so, ultimately, did the youngest of the Miller children, Willy.

Charley left New York, in a company of eighteen children, on March 27, 1888. Some days later he and the other children were led into a meetinghouse in Saint Charles, Minnesota, to be examined by a crowd of farmers, mechanics, and merchants. Charley was chosen by a farmer, W. R. Booth, who was looking not so much for a foster child as for cheap labor.

Booth's farm was in Chatfield, some twelve miles from Saint Charles. As the sun rose on Charley's first full day with his new family, Booth led him to a barn and taught him how to hitch a horse to a plow. The old farmer was annoyed when Charley told him that, having spent all of his twelve years in a city, he had never seen a plow before, or ridden a horse, or even held a pair of reins. Saying, "Well, it's time you learned," he told Charley to get behind the plow, and then he led the horse and the boy out to a field. Booth walked Charley through the first few furrows, but then left him alone until it was time for lunch. After the meal, it was back out into the field, where Charley plowed entirely on his own until the sun was down. The next day this routine was repeated, and again the day after, and so on until all the plowing had been finished. Then Charley was set to other tasks, which he also worked from sun to sun. Booth gave Charley food and a place to sleep but never made him feel welcomed into the family and never provided him with adequate clothing, even after the two suits the CAS had given him had been reduced to rags by hard labor.

In May 1888, Charles Fry, the CAS western agent who had conducted Brace's 1874 investigation, visited Charley at Booth's farm and sent the following report back to New York: "a good boy and has an excellent home — goes to school and is doing well."[2] One can only assume that Charley, like John Jackson at Mitchell's farm and Marguerite Thomson with the Larsons, had been forbidden to breathe a word of his true condition during Fry's visit, and that Fry had been so eager to see the placement as a success that he did not pick up on whatever evidence there was to the contrary. But Charley had no hesitation about confessing in regular letters to his brothers and sister that he was being worked too hard and that Booth frequently whipped and beat him. These letters were the main reason that, when it came time for Willy to leave the orphanage, Fred Miller begged Loofboro to take the little boy in.

When Charley was asked in court why he had been beaten, he said that it had mostly been for "a certain disease" that he could not control, a disease for which he had also been regularly beaten at the orphan asylum. Only when it became obvious to him that the district attorney and probably everyone else in the courtroom assumed this "disease" was masturbation did Charley confess that it was bed-wetting, and that he had only stopped for the first time in his life since his incarceration. At another point in the trial Charley did confess that he masturbated as often as four times a day, and that he had been circumcised while at the orphan asylum. A physician, verifying that Charley had indeed been circumcised, said that the operation was often done to discourage both bed-wetting and masturbation.

Under the terms of the CAS agreement, Booth was required to give Charley a "common education." At that time public school in rural Minnesota ran from the beginning of December through the end of March, but for reasons that were never made clear, Booth did not send Charley to school until February 1889.

The teacher at the Chatfield one-room schoolhouse seems to have recognized that Charley was in trouble from the moment he walked into her class. During the two months that he was her student, she wrote letters to the New York Orphan Asylum and the Children's Aid Society describing his situation with the Booths and asking that he either be placed with a different family or sent a ticket so that he could join his brothers in Kansas. She was so concerned for him, in fact, that when school let out at the end of March she took him home to the small farm just outside of town where she lived with her parents.

The Booths had no idea where Charley had gone but probably thought that, with the planting season coming up, he had run away to get out of work. Then one morning after he had been gone about a week, the Booths' eldest daughter drove past the teacher's farm and caught sight of Charley in the yard. That afternoon, in a scene strikingly reminiscent of John Jackson's capture by Mr. Mitchell, Booth and one of his grown sons burst into the teacher's home and dragged Charley away, telling him that they ought to tie him to a tree and give him a cowhiding.

Charley never found out whether they would have made good on this threat because, when they got back to the farm, Mrs. Booth handed her husband a letter that had just arrived from the CAS. The letter, prompted by the teacher's accounts of Charley's condition, simply reminded Booth of the terms under which he had agreed to take the boy and told him, among other things, that Charley had a perfect right to leave whenever he wanted.

This was the last straw for Booth. He put Charley back into the wagon and drove him, not to the teacher's farm, but twelve miles in the opposite direction, to Saint Charles. Pulling up in front of the meetinghouse where he had first picked the boy out of the crowd of orphan train riders, Booth told him to get out of the wagon, and then drove away without giving him a word of explanation or a penny of money.

Charley's courtroom description of his abandonment by Booth contains one of the very few indications of the state of his emotions to be found anywhere in any of his autobiographical accounts. Significantly, however, his feelings are not described explicitly but are only the implication of an incidental detail. The district attorney asked Charley what he did after Booth drove away, and Charley answered: "I started out into the country looking for work. The sun was just going down. I got about two miles from town, or one mile, and a farmer met me and he asked what I was crying about, and he gave me a job."

That was all. Charley was always very specific about time, distances, and other such facts. He corrected two miles to one mile. But when it came to describing what any of his experiences meant to him, or how they made him feel, he never got more explicit than "a farmer . . . asked me what I was crying about." And nobody ever asked him to elaborate.

Charley stayed with this farmer for a couple of months and, for the most part, seems to have been treated well enough, although the farmer did have a habit of periodically getting drunk and driving his whole family out of the house. Throughout his stay Charley kept in contact with his old teacher. One afternoon in late May she drove out to the farm waving a letter from the CAS. Inside was a five-dollar bill and his long-awaited ticket to Leonardsville, Kansas.

Despite months of anticipation, Charley's reunion with his brothers lasted only a few weeks. In a letter to the *Cheyenne Daily Leader,* Loofboro explained that although he had come to regard Fred and Willy as "members of the family," he simply did not have room or work for yet another Miller boy. Loofboro did find Charley a job, however, with a Mr. Colt, who was the editor of a weekly newspaper in Randolph, Kansas, about twenty miles northeast of Leonardsville.

In effect, Charley was an apprentice at Colt's paper. He got no salary other than room and board but was taught typesetting. His main complaint was that his new employer, like Booth, refused to buy him new clothing. Charley had no choice but to continue to wear the same two ragged and outgrown suits that he had been given by the CAS.

After about four months at the paper Charley, now fourteen, be-came, as he put it, "restless." Early one autumn morning he went down to the Randolph train station and slipped into a boxcar on a train heading north. In Omaha, Nebraska, he spent several fruitless days looking for work in stockyards and meatpacking plants before climb-ing aboard another boxcar and "beating" his way eastward, living by begging and doing odd jobs. It was not until he reached Chicago that he finally got a real job, on a Great Lakes steamer. During the seven days it took the steamer to reach Buffalo, New York, Charley made $3.50 — enough to pay for a train ticket to Rochester, where his sister, Carrie, was living with a minister's family.

He stayed in Rochester longer than he was ever to stay anyplace else — except prison — after leaving the Booths. Through the influence of Carrie's foster father, he got a job as a galley boy on the *Rochester Ad-vertiser.* This was the best job he had ever had, and it was not long be-fore he had earned enough money to buy himself (at last!) a new suit of clothes. But after eight months he apparently got "restless" again and decided to visit his "uncle" in New York City, whom he hoped would give him an advance on his inheritance and help him find a new job.

This visit must have been very strange for Charley, if for no other reason than that, according to an article in the *Daily Leader,* the "uncle" was still operating the Miller family's bar and living in the very same upstairs apartment where Charley had been born and where both of his parents had died. The article said nothing about how Charley felt being back in his old home and meeting this only dimly familiar man. In court testimony, all Charley himself had to say about the visit was that his "uncle" told him that he was not, in fact, a blood relative, and that he did not consider himself under obligation to help any of the Miller children until they had turned twenty one. On June 17, 1890, Charley went to the office of the CAS but was only told to go see a Mr. Sherman at the New York Orphan Asylum. Whether he actually made the visit, or got any help from Mr. Sherman, is not known.

Two weeks after his arrival in New York Charley was riding the rails again, this time in the company of a young printer who had told him about an ad for temporary typesetters placed by a shop in Orange, New Jersey. Charley and the printer were hired by the shop and each earned $4.50 for three days' work. When that job was finished, they were told that there were openings for printers in Philadelphia — but all Charley and his friend found there was trouble. No sooner had they hopped out of their boxcar than they were arrested for nonpayment of fare and thrown into an adult prison.

Six weeks later, on August 11, 1890, Charley and his friend were released onto the streets of Philadelphia. They had each earned a couple of dollars boring holes in rocks while in prison, but they had no friends in town, no place to stay, and no job prospects. Eventually they found their way to a bar, where Charley's friend got so drunk that he picked a fight with a policeman and was promptly thrown back into jail. Alone again, and deciding that he had had enough of the City of Brotherly Love, Charley took his chances by "stealing" a ride on a train heading west. He spent the next month begging, doing odd jobs, and riding the rails. He arrived in Kansas City, Kansas, on September 10, 1890 — three days before his fifteenth birthday.

This was all Charley had to tell the court about his stay in Kansas City: "I was there about a week. I got a job in a hotel washing dishes, but I was too slow so I lost that job after only one day. I couldn't find any other work, so I left." No word about his birthday. No word about why, with a whole country open to him, he had ended up within one hundred miles of his brothers on so emotionally freighted an occasion. No word about why he never journeyed that last one hundred miles. And, perhaps most significantly, no word about the fact that he had just spent a year traveling some 4,000 miles only to wind up almost exactly where he had started — except that he had no job and no money and had rejected or been rejected by every person in the country who might have offered him help. For Charley, Kansas City was just a place where he had gotten and lost a job in a single day and had not been able to find any other work. End of story.

Or not quite. Under further questioning, he did provide the court with two additional details. First, it was during his stay in Kansas City that he started calling himself "Kansas Charley" — the moniker that, like other bums, he would scrawl onto the sides of water towers as he drifted from town to town during his remaining month of freedom. And second, the day before he left the city he went to a pawn shop and bought a nickel-plated, thirty-two-caliber pistol for $1.25.

Having reached the end of the line in Kansas City, Charley seems to have felt he had no better option than to start his journey all over again. So early one morning he went down to the rail yards and caught the first train north to Omaha. The train traveled a pleasant route through cottonwood groves and along grassy bluffs overlooking the Missouri River — a route that took him through Saint Joseph, Missouri, some two or three days before his future victims were to make their departure. In Omaha he went a second time to talk to the meatpackers, men with blood-soaked clothes and knives in their hands who worked in barns that stank of fat and flesh and feces, but he fared no better than on his first trip. Returning to the rail yards, he heard from a fellow tramp that there was work on Gleason's ranch, near Cheyenne, Wyoming. So, on the morning of September 23, the day after Emerson and Fishbaugh left their hometown to seek their fortune, Charley climbed aboard a boxcar heading west along the Platte River valley.

He did not run into the two young men until Julesburg, Colorado, where they all spent the night in the same hobo camp and boarded the same train at dawn, but rode in separate boxcars. At a fairgrounds just outside Sydney, Nebraska, a conductor threw all three tramps off the train, and they walked back into town together. Once in town, however, Emerson and Fishbaugh told Charley that they did not want to be seen with him because he was so raggedly dressed. Going off on his own, he found work carrying coal for a baker, who paid him with a pie and some bread.

After leaving the baker's shop, Charley wandered down Sydney's main street, looking for a place to savor the fruits of his labor, and came upon Emerson and Fishbaugh standing on a corner. They asked him what he was carrying in his paper bag. When he held it out to them, they took the pie and left him the bread. In court Charley testified that the two friends had been drinking and carried a gun. After they finished their meal, they told him to wait on the corner while they went off, hinting that they had important business to attend to. A short while later, when he saw a blue-coated man running down the street, he assumed that they had been arrested.

Around dusk Charley spotted a freight train about to pull out of town. He climbed on board a stock car, buried himself in hay, and fell asleep before the car was moving. When the train stopped at dawn in a town near the Wyoming border, Charley decided that he had had enough of the smell of cow excrement. He gathered an armful of hay and moved down to the nearest boxcar. Throwing the hay through the door, he grabbed on to the floorboards and hauled himself inside. He was still belly-down, with his legs sticking out of the car when he heard a voice: "Hello, kid." Looking up, Charley found himself lying at the feet of Ross Fishbaugh.

Here we enter a realm of almost pure speculation. Charley said in court that as soon as he got into the car he put his pile of straw in the corner, lay down upon it, and pretended to go to sleep. When asked how long he was with Emerson and Fishbaugh before the shooting, he said, "I don't know. Five minutes. I did it right after the train started moving again. I waited until I knew they were asleep." But a Mrs. Kaufman testified at the trial that Emerson and Fishbaugh had eaten breakfast in her hotel in Pine Bluffs, Wyoming, some three hours after Charley got into the boxcar. The coroner who examined both bodies in Cheyenne concurred that they had probably been shot after the train pulled out of Pine Bluffs.

Charley's motives were also decidedly unclear. He said in court that he was afraid of Emerson and Fishbaugh because of the way they had treated him in Sydney, and because he knew they had a gun. He also admitted to robbing them right after the killing. But when the defense attorney asked him what he had been thinking when he fired the two shots (this being one of the very few times Charley was ever asked about his feelings), he said only: "I thought I was far away from my folks, and wanted to get back, and didn't know how; and I was all ragged, and cold weather was coming on, and [I had] nothing to eat, and no money and I didn't know what to do."

That is all that is known about the killing, except that the two young men probably had been asleep. They were both barefoot when Manafield found them, and their shoes were resting side by side in the middle of the boxcar floor.

By contrast to his account of the murders, Charley was extremely forthcoming about the robbery, admitting that once he had shot both men, he went through Emerson's pockets first, taking his silver watch, knife, and revolver, and left his own revolver beside Emerson's head — although he did not say why. Then, while Fishbaugh writhed and "foamed at the mouth," Charley also went through his pockets, extracting forty-five dollars in paper money and two silver dollars.

Charley stayed on the train with his victims another two hours (or six — depending on whose account we accept) until Hillsdale, where he got off, had his distracted lunch with Engineer Brooks, and bought his ticket for the next passenger train to Cheyenne. While waiting for the train, he threw Emerson's gun and knife underneath the railroad platform. On reaching Cheyenne, Charley spent the night at the home of a young man he met at a saloon. In the morning it is more than likely that he picked up a copy of the *Cheyenne Daily Leader* and found the following headline on page three:

A BULLET IN EACH BRAIN
The Awful Fate of Two Young Men
Who Were Tramping

If Charley finished the article, he would have read about how the bodies had been discovered, and about Fishbaugh's prolonged suffering. He also would have read various theories about how the two young men had met their death. The one propounded at greatest length was that Emerson had been toying with his revolver, which, because he was "fresh from a town where the most exaggerated ideas of the land of the Rockies prevail," he naturally considered "the most important portion of their equipment." When the gun accidentally went off, killing Fishbaugh, Emerson put a bullet in his own temple out of remorse and despair. A second theory was that a quarrel had led to a murder-suicide. But the theory that seemed to have the strongest support was that the boys had been killed by a robber.

Without even taking the time to buy breakfast, Charley walked straight out of town that morning, heading south. Some miles out in the country, he met a shepherd with whom he traveled for four days — stopping along the way to spend his stolen money on a new hat and gloves, into which he scratched his moniker, "Kansas Charley." Parting from the shepherd in Grover, Colorado, he threw Emerson's watch into a gopher hole and caught a train to Manhattan, Kansas.

On October 6, just before closing-up time, Fred Miller was sweeping dust out the front door of the *Leonardsville Monitor* office when he saw his little brother walking down the street in a ripped-up jacket and a brand-new brown hat with a shiny black band. Fred was so astonished that he could not speak until Charley had drawn up right beside him and said, as if they had only seen each other yesterday, "Hello, Fred."

It was several days before Charley finally confessed the secret that had been weighing on his mind, and several more before the two boys finally made their journey to the office of the *Manhattan Republic.*

ॐ

Only after Charley had finished his story did Albert Stewart send for the Manhattan sheriff. Charley spent the night in jail, and the following afternoon was interrogated by Sheriff John Martin, who came down from Cheyenne. On their return to Cheyenne a day later, Martin and a team of deputies had to shove their way through a jeering crowd to get Charley from the train station to the county jail. Journalists lined up outside Charley's cell. Others shouted questions to him through jail windows. Newspapers across the country carried stories about the "boy murderer" — and it was by this epithet, rather than "Kansas Charley," that he would be known until the day he died.

Charley's trial commenced less than two months later, at nine in the morning on December 8, 1890. At noon on December 11, after a scant fifteen minutes of deliberation, the jury found him guilty in the first degree of both murders. At a separate hearing a few days later he was sentenced to death by hanging.

Charley's lawyer, Frank D. Taggart, had hoped to get him off on the grounds of insanity and at one point during the trial tried to imply that Charley's habit of masturbating as often as four times a day had so deprived him of his sanity that he could not tell right from wrong. The prosecuting attorney, a prominent local lawyer named W. R. Stoll, argued that "no case can be produced in any medical book written, or by any man posted upon the subject of insanity showing that a practice of that kind leads to homicide." And the experts called in the case — both local physicians — testified that while Charley might be a little "eccentric" and possibly "slow" (although other witnesses thought him "exceptionally shrewd"), he had never been unable to distinguish between "right" and "wrong" and so had never been criminally insane.

Taggart's backup strategy had been to try for conviction on the lesser charge of second-degree murder, on the grounds that the double murder had been impulsive rather than premeditated — an act of extreme desperation and fear. But this defense fell apart when Mrs. Kaufman and the coroner made it seem that Charley had lied under oath about when he committed the murders.

It was the three hours or more that elapsed between the time Charley boarded the boxcar and the train departed from Pine Bluffs that, when combined with the robbery, caused the jury to conclude that he had premeditated the murders and therefore deserved the first-degree conviction. His apparent lie on the witness stand did not, of course, help him with the jury or anyone else. It was referred to again and again, along with other more minor inconsistencies in his story, by the newspapers and in the decisions of the appeals court judges as evidence that Charley was a "hardened criminal."

Charley escaped from prison twice, both times simply taking advantage of jailbreaks engineered by other inmates. After his first escape, all he did was wander eastward down the Union Pacific railroad tracks until he came upon two tramps sitting by a campfire in a field outside of Hillsdale — the town where he had gotten off the train after the killings. As he sat beside the fire, sharing the tramps' breakfast, he confessed with apparent pride that he was the famous "boy murderer" Charley Miller. Later that morning, when the tramps were themselves arrested a couple of miles down the track, they told the police that they had left Charley sleeping in a haystack. One of the police told reporters later on that he was in "great anxiety" as he approached the hiding place of the dreaded killer, and so was astonished when, at the sound of their footsteps, Charley rolled out of the stack and held his hands out to be cuffed, saying matter-of-factly, "I guess you're looking for me." After only forty-eight hours of freedom, Charley returned to prison on the exact anniversary of the shooting of Emerson and Fishbaugh.

His second escape was in the company of a notorious cattle rustler named William Kingen, whom newspapers held to be a far more nefarious criminal than Charley, even though he had never killed anyone. Having been smuggled a gun by his lawyer, Kingen overpowered the jail's only guard on New Year's Eve, took his keys, and let Charley and a black man named Johnson out of neighboring cells. Under cover of darkness, Kingen led Charley and Johnson across the open prairie, avoiding all population centers and railroad tracks. His plan was to meet up with his gang at a remote barn some twenty miles from Cheyenne. But despite his six-foot-four stature and reputation for enormous physical strength, Kingen proved to be far less fit and resistant to the subfreezing weather than either Charley or Johnson. He could hardly go a mile without having to stop and rest for long minutes. The three escapees were supposed to arrive at the barn by the afternoon of New Year's Day, but thanks to Kingen's sluggish progress, they did not reach their destination until nearly dawn of the following morning, by which time the gang members had given up and fled to Nebraska.

The weather was getting worse and worse. The three men knew that they would freeze to death if they remained at the barn, so they set out again, hoping to make it across the Nebraska line to the ranch of one of Kingen's friends. But as they progressed across the windy, vacant prairie, Kingen's condition deteriorated rapidly. Soon he could not go more than a couple of hundred yards without having to sit down on the frozen earth and rest. Finally, when they were about five miles from the barn, he fell to his knees and said he could not go any further. Johnson, who had been the most fit of the trio, maintained that Kingen was a "goner" no matter what happened, so there was no reason why he and Charley should stick around and die with him. Kingen's only response to this eminently rational assertion was to draw Charley down beside him, place a five-dollar bill into the palm of his hand, and say, "Stick with me. I'll see you through." For reasons that Charley never confessed to anyone, he decided to cast his lot with the ailing, white cattle rustler and let Johnson walk off by himself.

Once they were alone, Charley and Kingen huddled together in a slight depression, which offered them protection from the wind's full ferocity, and soon fell into a deep sleep. Charley awoke in the night to hear Kingen groaning with pain. Awaking again at dawn, Charley found that Kingen was dead and that his own feet and legs were completely numb. When a rancher came upon the two men a couple of hours later, Kingen was frozen solid and Charley was unconscious.

Charley lingered on the point of death for some hours but was finally revived and returned to prison with severely frostbitten feet. A month later his appeal was heard and denied by the state supreme court, and he was sentenced to die by hanging in just slightly over two months' time, on April 22, 1892.

"Miller is an enigma to everyone who has watched the proceedings," wrote a reporter for the *Cheyenne Daily Leader* on the last day of the trial, and indeed, as a character, the Charley Miller who appeared in court and in newspaper accounts simply did not add up — especially according to the notions by which most people would have judged him in the nineteenth century.

He was a mass of contradictions. He had confessed of his own free will because, as he said, his deeds weighed on his mind, yet every time he told his story his voice and manner revealed not the slightest remorse or awareness of the severity of what he had done. He seemed to have no trouble admitting that he had killed Emerson and Fishbaugh, but when asked at what point he had made the decision to commit the murders, he seemed to become evasive, saying only, "I don't remember ever making it." He also admitted freely that he had robbed the two young men immediately after killing them, but when asked about his state of mind at the time of the murders, he said not a word about material gain, but talked only of loneliness and desperation. Perhaps the most striking contradiction of all was between his prosecution and press image as a ruthless, "hardened" killer and the facts of his youth, his slight, hollow-chested frame, his inoffensive manner, and his obvious desire to please.

The contradictions that made Charley "an enigma to everyone" also made him the center of a passionate national debate about the degree to which such factors as youth or prior abuse reduced criminal responsibility. This debate reached its peak after the state supreme court turned down Charley's appeal and his only remaining hope was that his sentence might be commuted to life imprisonment. Over the next two months Wyoming's acting governor, Amos Barber, was deluged by letters, petitions, and editorials urging both sides of the issue.[3]

The vast majority of those advocating clemency were ministers, lawyers, congressional representatives, and other prominent figures in New York City and Washington, although Charley also had an energetic ally in the head of the Kansas chapter of the Women's Christian Temperance Union, Mrs. C. K. Smith. Almost all of these people made the same two points. First, that Charley deserved some moral credit for having voluntarily turned himself in and confessed. And second, that his youth, his low intelligence, his hard life, and his desperation at the time he committed the crime had all diminished his capacity to make a true — and therefore fully culpable — choice between good and evil. Many of these letters and petitions also placed an extremely high value on Christian mercy, often asking Governor Barber to imagine how Jesus would judge Charley. Most of these people seemed to value mercy simply for its own sake, but some also urged it for the benefits it might bestow. Mrs. C. K. Smith, for example, maintained that contemplation of the state's generous forgiveness might enable Charley to "grow spiritually and make some progress before being sent a drift [*sic*] into the world of spirits."

Another common characteristic of the arguments for clemency was their tendency to present Charley's case as part of a complex dynamic. These advocates did not think that justice could be arrived at by isolating his crime from his past and possible future. Rather, they were constantly asking Governor Barber to consider the double murder as partially the product of past suffering and to bear in mind Charley's potential to redeem himself morally, "grow spiritually," or benefit from modern institutions and techniques for treating the insane and "incapable."

The opponents of clemency saw Charley's sad history as morally irrelevant and his possibly bright future as only a sentimental illusion. He had committed a crime, so he had to suffer the prescribed punishment — and that was all there was to it. The only mercy this group advocated was that of the classic Puritan God, who shows his goodwill toward his inherently sinful creations by meeting their transgressions with sure punishment.

Another significant fact about the opponents of clemency (at least about those who left some paper record of their opinions) was that they were all from Wyoming or Nebraska. To some extent this is indic-

ative of classic east-west and urban-rural divisions. Charles Loring
Brace sent New York City children back in time, not only to an agrarian America, but to a more antique or, as he would have put it, a more
"orthodox" moral view — one that he himself had rejected vehe-
mently. He worshiped not the stern Old Testament God as "Lawgiver"
but the New Testament God as a "Father seeking our happiness," a deity whose most distinguishing characteristic was His ability to forgive
sin and recognize true repentance. The local opponents of clemency,
very much in the pessimist camp, saw the human race as fundamentally immoral and needing fierce and exact punishment to be kept in
line. But their rationale was not only theological. When these merchants, editorialists, and common citizens demanded that the state
carry out the judgment of the jury, they were responding to a long-developing conflict about the relation between power, justice, and the
law — a conflict that resulted in the loss of two lives and the jailing of
some of the state's most prominent citizens even as Governor Barber
was making his decision about granting Charley clemency.

Although the death penalty had been on Wyoming's law books from
the earliest days of settlement, it had rarely been put into effect. Before
1884 there had been only two legal executions in the territory, both of
"half-breeds," one in 1871 and the other in 1874. As the *Laramie Times*
put it in an editorial deploring the failure of the legal system to impose
the maximum punishment, there had in those years been "scores of
murders, cold blooded and atrocious," but juries had simply been unable to impose the death penalty on anyone who claimed, as all the defendants did, that he had killed in self-defense or to preserve his
honor.[4] Partly as a result of growing public outrage, two white men
were executed in 1884, for two separate murders. And in the six years
before Charley's arrest, there had been three other executions, all of
white men, the last occurring in Laramie in February 1890.

   Most of Wyoming's executions, if that is not too fine a word for
them, had occurred outside the legal system. During the decade prior
to Charley's arrest ten people had been lynched. The last two, James
Averell and his girlfriend, Etta Watson, alleged cattle rustlers, had been
hung side by side on July 20, 1890, just ten days after Wyoming officially became a state. The year and four months during which Charley's death sentence was under appeal, however, saw a substantial increase in "vigilante justice" or "mob law." In June 1891 another reputed

rustler was lynched; a second was attacked, but managed to escape, in November; and later that same month two other rustlers were "dry-gulched" — shot to death by a stock detective and a former sheriff.

It was no accident that nine of these vigilante lynchings, all of which went unpunished, were of cattle or horse thieves. As elsewhere in the West, there was fierce antagonism between the big ranchers — derisively called "cattle kings" — whose herds numbered in the thousands and grazed on several thousand acres, and the small homesteaders, many of them former cowboys, who typically grazed a handful of cattle on one or two hundred acres. Although there were plenty of true rustlers, like William Kingen, who stole ranchers' cattle, altered their brands, and sold them for high profits, the vast majority of so-called rustling consisted of the homesteaders simply incorporating their cattle king neighbors' strays into their own herds. This small-time rustling was by no means unconscious or unintentional. The antagonism between the big ranchers and the homesteaders was true class war, with each side feeling justified in its assaults against the other. But when one considers what a tiny portion of their enormous herds the big ranchers lost to rustling of any kind, it is hard to understand the ferocity of their feelings. Certainly a contributing factor was their frustration with the legal system. All but two of the nineteen rustling cases that came before the courts in Johnson County between 1886 and 1890 were dismissed, largely because the sentiment against the cattle kings was so pronounced in the public at large, and in the juries.

In the winter of 1891–92, several leaders of the Wyoming Stock Growers Association (the big ranchers' trade group), including its vice president, former governor George Baxter, decided that since they could get no help from the courts, the time had come to take independent action. On April 5, 1892, less than two weeks before Charley was scheduled to be hanged, a special train provided by the Union Pacific Railroad arrived in Cheyenne carrying twenty-five Texas gunmen, who had been brought in because the ranchers could not count on locals to do their dirty work. A short while later, having taken on supplies and twenty-four "regulators" (mostly ranch owners and managers but *no* cowboys, who were not considered loyal enough to the cause), the train set off again for Caspar in Johnson County, where the rustling problem was thought to have been most fierce.

What this group, which called itself "The Invaders," actually intended to do in Johnson County is in dispute. Some say that they carried a "dead list" of seventy men, including Caspar's sheriff and mayor; others maintain that they intended only to give suspected rustlers twenty-four hours to get out of the county. What they actually *did* is the following. After arriving at the Caspar stockyards at four in the morning, they rode more than seventy-five miles to the KC ranch, where they had heard a group of rustlers was hiding. As it turned out, only two rustlers were there, and they were both killed after a daylong siege. The Invaders then set off to track down another group of rustlers but two days later were cornered at a ranch near Buffalo by an army of 200 "deputies," led by Red Angus, the sheriff on the "dead list."

It is suspected that Acting Governor Amos Barber, along with Wyoming's two senators, Warren and Cary, had known of the big ranchers' invasion plans in advance and had at least tacitly approved of them. But Barber was certainly not in close touch with the Invaders and did not hear that they were under siege until he received a telegram from Buffalo on April 12.

Barber had already earned wide praise in his own time and condemnation by history for his role in Wyoming's most infamous conflict. He had not been elected governor but had taken over when the state's first governor, Francis E. Warren, resigned after only two and a half months to become a senator. Just over a month later Barber was told that 350 Indians, grieving over the murder of Sitting Bull by Lakota police officers, had come together near Pine Ridge. Fearing that the Indians might be planning an attack, Barber sent a cavalry detachment to observe and contain them. On December 29, 1890, partly through misunderstanding, the cavalry surrounded and fired at the Indians, killing at least 250 men, women, and children in what is now known as the Wounded Knee Massacre. At the time Barber was celebrated in the newspapers and saloons for having quelled an Indian "uprising" so efficiently. So when he heard about the troubles in Johnson County, he decided to employ the same strategy. On April 13, a detachment of federal cavalry arrived at the ranch where the Invaders were under siege and brought them back to Fort McKinney, both for their own protection and to answer charges for the murder of the two alleged rustlers killed at the KC ranch. On April 23 the forty-three Invaders were delivered to Fort Russell to be held for trial.

Governor Barber did not decide whether to commute Charley's

death sentence until April 21, the eve of his execution date. Right up until the last minute, most people, including the editors of the *Daily Leader,* had assumed that Barber would not be able to resist the strong urgings in favor of clemency from back east. One particularly persuasive petition had been signed by twenty-five congressmen and lawyers.

The acting governor thought long and hard about the case, but in the end, although he tried to come down on both sides of the fence, he seems to have been moved primarily by his fears about the effect that yet another apparent failure of the legal system to follow through on a clear mandate might have on a populace already so prone to take the law into its own hands. In a brief letter to Charley's lawyer, Frank Taggart, Barber declared that, however much his "feelings as an individual" may have prompted him to interfere with the sentence issued by the court, his thorough reexamination of the evidence led him to conclude that commuting Charley's sentence would have been "yielding to mere sentimentality." Surprised as the editors of the *Daily Leader* may have been by this decision, they roundly supported it, declaring in their April 23 edition that Charley's hanging "will do more to discourage mob law than any event which has ever happened in Wyoming."

Despite the encouragement he was given by Taggart and the many other people campaigning on his behalf, Charley seems never to have held out much hope that he would be spared, or even to have particularly desired it. In an interview granted several hours before Governor Barber issued his decision, Charley told a *Daily Leader* reporter, "I think the die is cast, that I am to be hanged tomorrow, but I want here and now to say that 'Kansas Charley' will walk to the doom that cruel fate has made necessary with as much firmness and composure as he would go to a wedding." Charley then gave the reporter a copy of the following song, which he claimed he had written himself and would sing as he stood on the gallows.

1.
The jury found me guilty
  The judge to me did say,
I sentence you to hang, Miller,
  March the 20th day.
I took my case to a higher court,

There I met the same fate.
Refused me a new trial
   And fixed the execution date.

2.

It's fixed for the 22nd of April,
   In the year 1892.
And I expect it to take place
   'Less the governor carried me through.
But that he will not hardly do
   Because I am a boy
And not very hard to manage
   But hard to destroy.

3.

Remember this life, e'er so young
   Is soon to fade away,
Fade when it has been hung
   April the 22nd day.
My life in this world is not long,
   It hangs by only a thread,
Soon forever I'll be gone,
   When to the gallows I'll be led.

4.

My blood in my life will soon cease,
   When Kelly leads me to my doom.
Then forever they will release
   Me, when I meet my doom.
I had four days trial,
   Which seemed to me long,
But time now is precious,
   I'll end my dear old song.

This song was never sung upon the gallows. When Sheriff Kelly asked Charley for his last words, he answered only, "God have mercy on me." A little later, as the sheriff examined the noose to make sure it had been tied properly, Charley asked, "Should I step onto the trapdoor?"

"Not yet," said Kelly.

While the sheriff completed his inspection, placed the noose around Charley's neck, and finally covered his face with the black mask that would shield the audience from his death grimace, Charley remained completely silent. Only when the sheriff and his deputy had each taken one of his arms and guided him forward so that he stood directly over the trapdoor did Charley say, "You're choking me a little."

"What's that, Charley?" asked Sheriff Kelly.

"You're choking me."

Kelly loosened the noose slightly. "There, is that better?"

"That's all right now."

As Kelly and his deputy descended from the platform, Charley, now standing on the trapdoor, said one last time, "God have mercy on me."

The trapdoor fell open and Charley dropped five feet, suddenly rebounding as the rope snapped taut. His body swung around backward, then slowly turned forward again. Not a quiver passed through it.

◈

Had Charley Miller not gone west on the orphan trains but remained in New York, where the legal age of "accountability" was sixteen, he could not have been tried as an adult and therefore would not have faced the death penalty. Today in New York, and in fifteen other states, including Wyoming, no one can be executed for a murder committed before the age of eighteen, and the Supreme Court has declared that applying the death penalty to anyone who committed a murder before the age of sixteen is unconstitutional. As of this writing, thirteen states and the District of Columbia do not impose the death penalty for any crime.

In this context then, the validity of Amos Barber's assertion that commuting a fifteen-year-old killer's death sentence to life imprisonment would be "mere sentimentality" is not, to say the least, self-evident. His decision was commended by the *Daily Leader* for the effect it would have on curbing "mob violence." But when it came to prosecuting the Invaders, whose severe punishment ought to have done the most to quell "mob violence," the Wyoming legal system was totally ineffective.

The trial of the Invaders for the murder of the two rustlers killed at the KC ranch was set for August 22 — exactly four months after Charley's execution. W. R. Stoll, the attorney who had prosecuted Charley's case, crossed over to the other side of the aisle and now worked as one of the Invaders' four defense attorneys. As it happened, however, he never got the opportunity to argue his case. Shortly before the trial date, Judge Richard H. Scott, who had presided over Charley's case as well, learned that Johnson County was not paying the Cheyenne jail for the cost of keeping the Invaders locked up, so he ordered them all set free. The ranchers were released on their own recognizance, and the Texans on bonds paid for by the ranchers. Apparently the twenty-five Texans stayed in town only long enough to pop a few bottles of champagne with their former cellmates and employers before catching the first train home. On the basis of purely bogus technicalities, Judge Scott managed to postpone the trial to January 21, 1893. And then, after fruitlessly examining more than 1,000 people to choose twelve jurors, the Johnson County prosecutor became so discouraged that he gave up the case, and all the defendants were discharged. In the end, the only person punished for the crimes of these wealthy cattlemen and their hired guns was a lonely, emotionally disturbed teenage orphan who had never gotten a fair chance in life.

It is not clear who organized the campaign on Charley's behalf. None of the letters sent to Amos Barber's office referred to any individual advocate or organization that was lobbying on his behalf. Whoever conducted the campaign, however, seems to have been well connected, as is evident not only from the petition signed by so many senators, congressmen, and jurists but also from the letters sent by individual New York lawyers, legal publishers, and businessmen. It is also interesting to note how many of the people expressing support came from places where Charley had lived. Eleven of the twenty-five signatures on the petition were of residents of Rochester, where Charley's sister lived, and where he had worked for eight months. His most ardent supporter of all, Mrs. C. K. Smith, who wrote several long letters on his behalf, was head of the Women's Christian Temperance Union in Kansas, and two other letter writers were Kansans. Charley also had many supporters in New York City, including the New York Orphan Asylum, which sent a petition to Governor "Barker" signed by eighteen people, including the asylum's superintendent.

Conspicuous in its absence among Charley's supporters was the Children's Aid Society. No petition or letter signed by anybody connected with the CAS appears in the file of Amos Barber's papers relating to the case. It is obvious why, in 1890, the CAS might want to dissociate itself from an orphan train rider who so confirmed the accusations of the likes of Hiram Giles and Lyman P. Alden. But it is also true that at the very moment when Charley Miller — ragged, cold, hungry, and so far from his "folks" — shot Waldo Emerson and Ross Fishbaugh, the CAS was undergoing the most severe trial of its thirty-seven-year history.

ᴊᴘ 12

The Death and Life
of Charles Loring Brace

I shall never forget a scene at sunset on the Stelvio Pass, some two miles high, where as a foot-traveller I was incautiously belated, miles from any house. Up from the Italian valleys marched, with threatening rapidity, a phalanx of dark thunder clouds, crowding one upon another, filling every vale and gorge which reached down to the plains of Lombardy, and giving warning of their approach by a continuous mutter of artillery. Their light advance had already crossed the ridge on which I stood, separating Italy and Germany, and had filled the deep gorge of the Stelvio with whirls and eddies of white mist. The sun was soon darkened, and as I turned to descend toward the Tyrol in haste and anxiety, I seemed to be plunging down by the narrow zigzag of the road into a white, boiling sea, from which gigantic icebergs were rising, — the glaciers of the Alps, — while every now and then a blinding flash of lightning would reveal an Arctic vista of white snow-peaks, and the thunder reverberated among a hundred mountains. Perilous and difficult as was the descent, it was a scene one would not for any consideration have lost. It is a relation for an instant of that which seldom visits the mortal, the unseen, the infinite and unapproachable. Man shrinks away before the gigantic forces of Nature. He is purified by a glimpse of the Temple of Deity itself.

— Charles Loring Brace, 1865[1]

IN JANUARY 1867, Brace returned home from "visiting among the poor" with what his family believed to be an ordinary cold but which turned out to be a serious case of typhoid fever. He was felled by the disease for a solid three months, and then spent another seven months recuperating in California — where he wrote his fourth book, *The New West*, a travelogue and celebration of West Coast vitality.

Typhoid fever is a gastrointestinal infection that causes high fevers, headaches, sore throats, and joint and abdominal pain. Today it is treated with antibiotics, but during the nineteenth century there was no choice but to let the disease run its natural course. In 1 to 2 percent of untreated cases, the intestine can become perforated as a result of severe bleeding, and the infection can spread through the abdominal cavity, attacking, damaging, or destroying vital organs — a condition known as peritonitis. Brace ultimately died of Bright's disease, a form of kidney failure, and it is possible that this subtle and slowly progressing illness commenced with damage done to his kidneys during his bout with typhoid.

By October 1867, however, Brace believed himself fully recovered and returned to his demanding labors at the Children's Aid Society. It was not until the winter of 1881–82, when he was fifty-six, that he once again became so ill that he had to take time off from his work. His younger brother James had just died, and the Emigration Plan was under attack. Brace seems only to have felt extremely tired (exhaustion being the most noticeable early symptom of kidney disease) and believed that his work was to blame. Once more, after a summer in London and a visit to a sanitarium at Saint Moritz, he felt fully restored to his normal vigor and fitness.

By 1886, however, he believed, once again, that his reform and literary work had taken so heavy a toll on him that he needed another summer in Europe. He and Letitia spent June in London and went on to the Alps for three months of hiking and recuperation. But this time his health was not completely restored. His letters increasingly featured meditations on death ("If one cared for last looks at death, I should pray that mine might be of the glorious Hudson in autumn"[2]), and he began to devote much more time to his literary efforts — in particular his final book about humankind's long march through ignorance to the "truth" of Christ, *The Unknown God*.

In May 1888, Letitia and Brace went abroad again, to England and Germany, with an extended stay at Marienbad, "the town of fat women and men too," as Brace described it in a letter to his daughter. "Each one is patrolling around, cup in hand, and some sipping through a glass tube. Your father appears with a red crackled-glass cup, and is very distinguished(?). We sip and listen to a lovely band, and walk up and down, — all this between six and eight, — then home, half-starved, to the best coffee in Europe."[3]

After a couple of months Brace and Letitia returned to the Alps for a walking tour and a view of the Matterhorn. But once again this trip failed to restore him, and his letters are filled not only with references to his mortality but with decidedly retrospective appreciations of life.

While on a trip south to investigate the treatment of boys sent to Virginia, he wrote to Letitia of his response to the death of his sister's husband:

> *Dearest Wife:* ... J's sudden death gives me many serious thoughts. I often think of what a happy life we have had together, and how much good you have done me, and I suppose I have you, intellectually. God bless you, ever! I feel more easy about death now the children are pretty well cared for. It will be well with us in the unseen, I am persuaded. Life has been very pleasant, and the unseen life must be more and better. I want my last days to be better. God keep you, and make us both true servants! I love you more than ever![4]

On June 19, 1889, his sixty-third birthday, he wrote to his old friend Howard Potter:

> Both of us must now feel that a very slight cause may call us away to the Unseen. I think of the Future with wonder and curiosity, but not feeling that we can know much. One can only trust. The great anxiety is to make the remaining days the best and to "finish up." ... Strange what happiness there is in life! How grateful I am for it to the Giver! My sixty years with hardly a pain or ache (except in one sickness), a freshness now as of full life, the happiest home and married life, perfect comfort; saved thus far from death in my family; a work where I never tire; and unceasing interest in intellectual things; a love of man and of Christ which grows with years. Now this has been my lot, far beyond all possibility of desert.
>
> I am so grateful to wife and children and friends, and, above all, to the *Pronoia* or Providence! It shows that happiness does not depend on money or position.
>
> Two things I want still to do, — to put the Society on a firmer base (which can be done in three or four years), and to make my last sermon to the world in a book . . . "the Unknown God, or Inspiration among Pre-Christian Peoples."[5]

The latter of these two goals Brace accomplished unequivocally. *The Unknown God* was published to respectful reviews in January 1890.

Whatever precisely he had intended to do about bolstering the society, however, had to be left to his eldest child.

In May 1890, Charles Loring Brace Jr., called Loring by the family, returned east from Colorado with his wife and children. Loring was forty-five, and a civil engineer. Ostensibly he had only come home to provide his father with temporary relief from some of his duties at the CAS and allow him to take yet another European excursion.

Brace had felt well enough the previous summer to forgo a trip to Europe and spend August at the family's summer home beside Big Tupper Lake in the Adirondacks. But by the fall he was feeling worse than ever and now knew that he was not merely tired but seriously ill. He wrote to a friend about his health the same month *The Unknown God* was published:

> A few years ago I committed the folly of swimming in Big Tupper after a hot day's work. Had peritonitis at night, but two days' rest restored me. . . . My visits to German springs cured me different years, but last autumn, not having been there, symptoms came on again badly, and threaten the kidneys. I shall try Marienbad (Bohemia) again this summer. My strong constitution is, of course, in my favor; still no one can tell. . . . So you see, I am to battle with disease. God guideth all. You can imagine how devoted and untiring a nurse dear Letitia has been.[6]

Charles, Letitia, and their two youngest children left for Europe shortly after Loring's arrival. The talk was that the elder Brace would resume his duties when he came back in the fall, but it was well understood within the family that he might never return. After Marienbad the Braces went on to Saint Moritz, stopping along the way at the Stelvio Pass so that Brace could show his children "the scene of one of his great walks in the far-away years of his vigorous youth." Nauseated by his illness, Brace went off alone to view the magnificent pass at sunset and to enjoy what his daughter called his "last great pleasure."[7] By the time Brace reached the sanitarium at Saint Moritz his illness had taken such a toll on him that he was confined to his bed, where, through a window, he could look out across the pale green waters of Campfer Lake, toward brilliant snow fields and jagged granite peaks. Far from improving at the sanitarium, he grew steadily weaker, sleeping much of the day and suffering periods of stupor. On August 8 he read an article in a New York newspaper praising the CAS Health

Home on Coney Island and asked his daughter to send the article to Howard Potter. This, apparently, was his last effort on behalf of the charity he had founded and run for nearly thirty-eight years. That night he fell into a coma. He died three days later from Bright's disease, on the evening of Monday, August 11 — the very day Charley Miller was released from prison in Philadelphia.

On August 14, after a quiet ceremony, Charles Loring Brace was laid to rest in the cemetery of a small church beside Lake Campfer, surrounded by those mountains where, on so many occasions, his faith had come closest to being a form of knowledge.

ઝ

The day after Brace's funeral, a lanky, twenty-three-year-old man named Homer Folks arrived in Philadelphia to become the general superintendent of the Pennsylvania Children's Aid Society. The PCAS, founded in 1882, was one of dozens of wholly independent Children's Aid Societies that came into being throughout the United States and Canada during the last decades of the nineteenth century and the first of the twentieth. The PCAS was the largest of Philadelphia's 109 child-caring agencies — but that was not saying much. It operated out of a two-room office, with a tiny staff and a caseload of some 330 children.

Folks, the son of Michigan farmers, had been educated at Harvard, where he had become friends with Charles Birtwell, the head of the Boston Children's Aid Society, and one of the great pioneers of Progressive Era child welfare. By the time Folks took his new job he was well aware of the new wisdom that had been hammered out over the preceding decade at, among other places, the National Conference of Charities and Correction meetings, and he believed that the primary work of the PCAS was not the actual placement of children but the investigation and supervision of the homes into which the children had been placed.

Like Brace before him, Folks was possessed of phenomenal energy and dedication. During his first year at the society, he was almost always on the road visiting placed children and investigating potential foster families. Even as he traveled, he wrote the society's annual reports and publicity literature, as well as position papers that significantly influenced child welfare work during the Progressive Era — that roughly thirty-year period of social and political reform that commenced in the 1890s. He delivered one of these papers, entitled

"Home Care for Delinquent Children," at the 1891 National Conference of Charities and Correction meeting in Indianapolis.

Folks made several controversial points in this paper. First, he declared that, contrary to prevailing opinion, delinquents were not exclusively from the poorer — or as Brace would have said, "dangerous" — classes. What distinguished children convicted of crimes as a group was not their social class but, Folks argued, "a lack of parental oversight due to the loss of one or both parents."[8] Partly on the basis of this conclusion, Folks took a firm stand against the assertions of Hiram Giles and other representatives of the "Asylum-Interest" that such children could and should be cared for only in institutions. On the contrary, given that the source of delinquent children's problems was a lack of parental oversight, the best way to reform them was to place them with carefully chosen and supervised families.

The problem was finding families willing to take such children. Traditionally, juvenile convicts, along with deformed, blind, mentally retarded, or otherwise handicapped children, were considered unplaceable and relegated either to the care of institutions or to placements where incorporation into anything resembling a family was never a real possibility. The New York CAS, for example, commonly sent mildly retarded and deformed but still able-bodied boys to placements in the South where they were little more than substitute slaves. Folks managed to circumvent some families' reluctance to take such children by offering to pay a boarding fee for their care.

The practice of "boarding out" children was first experimented with by the Massachusetts Board of State Charities in 1868 and was deemed such a success that it was sanctioned and to some extent regulated by state law in 1880. Initially, there was no difference between those children boarded out and those placed in what came to be called "free homes." The payment of boarding fees was seen primarily as a way of ensuring that children were not forced to work for their keep and were allowed enough free time to attend school and church and simply to play. Many of the strongest supporters of boarding out during the ensuing decades were anti–child labor advocates.

Although boarding out was clearly in harmony with Brace's emphasis on family care, he condemned the securing of parents by the payment of fees for turning "an act, which is at once one of humanity and prudence, into one purely of business."[9] Brace was not alone in worrying that boarding fees would attract only the most mercenary of foster parents, and it was partly with the goal of preventing boarding families from becoming small businesses that, under the Massachusetts law, they were paid a fee slightly lower than the cost of caring for the child and were forbidden to take in more than two unrelated children.

Folks made an even more compelling argument for the benefits of boarding out in a paper he delivered at a special NCCC meeting held in connection with the 1893 Columbian Exposition in Chicago. Perhaps the greatest weakness of free home placement was that it was never able to meet the needs of what Folks termed "dependent children whose parents are living and have not forfeited their natural rights by unnatural neglect or cruelty."[10] These were children who needed only temporary care because their parents were ill, out of work, or under some other form of duress. Classic orphan train placement in the West did not suit these children well because it made reunification so difficult. But also, even when such children were placed locally, it was hard to find them good homes because many foster parents — arguably the *best* — were reluctant to nurture and love a child they would soon have to give up. Although boarding fees may not have swelled the ranks of these loving parents significantly, there is no question that, for the first time, they gave children needing temporary care a real alternative to orphanages and asylums. And it is partly for this reason that boarding out became so widely employed over the ensuing decades that there is today no other form of family foster care.

There is one other regard in which Folks took a position way ahead of the historical curve in his 1893 paper. For Brace, social work had been primarily a religious enterprise, an attempt to express God's love that improved the soul of everyone involved — charity worker, beneficiary, and, really, the whole of society. But for Folks and much of the generation who came of age during the Progressive Era, social work was first and foremost a matter of public policy. It had to be based on scientific principles and research, thoroughly rational and systematic in its execution, and regulated by equally rational and systematic legislation and oversight bodies. Folks saw scant advantages accruing to needy children merely through being one-half of a mutually beneficial act of charity, especially if that charity was ill organized, inconsistent, or corrupt. Folks also attacked Brace's notion of the importance of bringing the classes together through social work. He did not believe affluent volunteers should play a major role in charity — outside of funding, of course. Social work had to be carried out only by competent and well-trained professionals. In remarks clearly aimed at Brace's anarchistic and idealistic management style, Folks asserted that free home placement as it was practiced by the CAS "is undoubtedly the best plan, provided it is guarded by an ever-vigilant supervision, but is possibly the worst plan of all if not so guarded,"[11] and he declared, "There is no more dangerous enemy to the family plan than he who administers it carelessly."[12]

Folks's public rejection of the labors of affluent volunteers may have had as much to do with his own work situation as his philosophy. The president of the Pennsylvania CAS, Mrs. James C. Biddle, was a pillar of Philadelphia society and a woman with whom Folks had constant disagreements. Shortly after his speech at the Columbian Exposition and his, perhaps, indiscreet remarks about wealthy volunteers, his relations with Mrs. Biddle degenerated to such an extent that he left the CAS to become the general secretary of the State Charities Aid Association (SCAA) in New York City, a position he would hold, despite a brief career in politics, until just before his death in 1947.

The State Charities Aid Association had been founded in 1872 by Louisa Lee Schuyler. Schuyler's mother had been a great friend of Brace's and a prominent CAS contributor. As a young woman, Schuyler had often looked to Brace for guidance. She began her career in charitable work just before the Civil War by helping to organize the Women's Central Relief Association, which was instrumental in the founding of the United States Sanitary Commission headed by Frederick Law Olmsted. Schuyler herself was an important administrator of the Commission throughout the Civil War.

She came up with the idea for the State Charities Aid Association after visiting the Westchester County poorhouse in 1871 and finding it ill staffed, fabulously unsanitary, and barbaric in its treatment of its desperate residents. The association, as she initially conceived of it, was to consist of a number of dedicated, knowledgeable, and influential men and women who could inspect and monitor almshouses, asylums, hospitals, and other public welfare institutions and promote reform generally. Among its founding members were several people associated with the Children's Aid Society, including Charles Loring Brace, Theodore Roosevelt Sr., and Grace Dodge. One of the SCAA's earliest triumphs was the founding of the Bellevue Nurses Training School at Bellevue Hospital — the first nurses' training program in the United States. The association was also an effective lobbying group and was instrumental in the passage of New York's Children's Law of 1875.

As general secretary of the SCAA, Folks was able to put into practice many of the principles regarding the regulation and professionalization of social work that he had outlined at the Columbian Exposition. One of his first initiatives was the founding of the County Agent System, under which each of New York's counties was provided with a paid, ostensibly well-trained agent who worked full-time seeing to the needs of the county's destitute children. The agent's duties included the investigation of troubled families and of foster homes, the placing-out of children, and, when possible, the return of children to their families. It was through this system that Folks also managed to introduce boarding out to New York State.

In 1894, at the New York State Constitutional Convention, he and Louisa Schuyler drafted an amendment that established state supervision of all charitable and correctional institutions, both public and private. It also provided that no wholly or partly private charitable institution could receive payments of state money unless it operated under the rules established by the State Board of Charities. In ensuing years Folks advocated and helped implement state regulations requiring the filing of detailed records for every inmate received at a charitable or correctional institution and establishing a civil service examination to ensure that only competent professionals would be hired as child welfare workers. And in 1898, asserting that there was "fully as much need that the protecting care of the state should be extended to children who are in families as to those who are in institutions," he drafted a piece of legislation entitled "An Act to Prevent Evils and Abuses in Connection with the Placing Out of Children."[13] The law, which required the licensing of all placing-out organizations, was the most dramatic incursion of the state into what Brace had conceived of as the fundamentally private relationship between the agents and beneficiaries of charitable acts.

∽

Progressive Era activists sought to improve child welfare in two ways. One, of which Homer Folks was so prominent an advocate, was to institute regulatory laws and bodies. The other, growing out of the work of Levi Silliman Ives and the Catholic Protectory, was to give families and communities enough support so that children never had to leave home in the first place. This was an important goal of the nation's first juvenile court, founded in Chicago in 1899.

The court was only the latest of a long line of mostly futile efforts to make the criminal justice system more sensitive to the needs of children. The statute establishing the court contained language almost tragically reminiscent of the goals of the early houses of refuge and juvenile asylums: "The care, custody, and discipline of the children brought before the court shall approximate as nearly as possible that which they should receive from their parents, and . . . as far as practicable they shall be treated not as criminals but as children in need of aid, encouragement, and guidance."[14]

Although a proportion of the children who came before the court had committed such serious crimes that incarceration was deemed the only justified punishment, juvenile court judges gave out suspended sentences whenever possible. If a child had no parents, or if those parents were deemed "unworthy," the child was placed in either a free or boarding home and, ideally, adopted. Whenever possible, however, the court tried to keep children with their own families and appointed probation officers to see that the children received every available service to help ensure their permanent reform. Probation officers were considered so essential that they were deemed "the keystone" of the system.[15]

In the early decades of the twentieth century probation officers were not seen as the quasi-police officers that they generally are today, but as something far closer to a modern social worker. Their job, much like that of the early CAS "visitors," was to meet regularly with children and their families and to offer an avuncular form of moral guidance as well as more practical services—references for jobs, for example, or help with school problems, and even payments of money to hard-pressed and "deserving" mothers. The probation officers were, of course, also enforcers who had to make it clear to all parties that if the child did not abide by the conditions of probation, he or she would end up in juvenile prison.

The problem was that there were never enough probation officers to do the job as it was meant to be done. Initially this was because the officers were all volunteers. The founders of the juvenile court system had not asked for appropriations to pay the officers because they had feared that local legislators would balk at the expense, and because they worried that well-paid probation posts would be dispensed not to qualified individuals but as political favors. Eventually probation officers did receive salaries, at first provided exceedingly sparingly by private charities such as the Chicago Women's Club, and eventually by cities and states. But the salaries were never high enough to attract many of the most qualified people to the job, nor to hire enough people for the work to be done as it had been envisioned.

The most comprehensive effort to support poor neighborhoods was conducted by the settlement house movement. The first true settlement house was Toynbee Hall, which was established in the impoverished East End of London in 1884. In many ways, Toynbee Hall was like an early mission, offering education, job training, and other services to adults and children in its surrounding community. Unlike the missions, however, Toynbee Hall's staff did not leave at night. They lived in the house and saw themselves as "settlers" in the slums. And the people they worked with were not the beneficiaries of their charity but their neighbors. For the settlement house residents more than any other single group of reformers who preceded them, the way to solve the problem of poverty was not to punish the poor or preach to them, not to take them from their neighborhoods or raze those neighborhoods to the ground (as was done to Five Points in the 1880s), but to work within the neighborhoods. The settlement house residents felt that, on the basis of careful study, and with dedication and patience, they could take on one issue at a time until, gradually, their neighbors would not be subjected to so many overwhelming pressures and could finally enjoy something like equal opportunity with members of the more fortunate classes.

The first American settlement house was established in New York City in 1886 by Stanton Coit, a young Amherst graduate who had spent several months at Toynbee Hall. Jane Addams also visited Toynbee Hall and returned to her native Chicago in 1888 to found Hull House, the most well-known of all American settlement houses. The movement spread rapidly in the United States. By 1900 there were roughly 100 settlement houses in operation, and ten years later there were 300 more.

When a new settlement house was established, the first service offered the community was usually a kindergarten, because this was seen as the most effective way to establish a relationship with parents and, through them, with the larger neighborhood. Once up and running, in addition to education programs, settlement houses would commonly offer day care for working mothers, a variety of community health services, theaters, and, like Brace's Newsboys' Lodging House, libraries, penny savings banks, gyms, and reading rooms. Settlement house residents were also active lobbyists for any legislation or programs they thought would benefit their poor neighbors. Jane Addams was so dedicated a campaigner for the first juvenile court that it was ultimately established across the street from Hull House.

The great emphasis that these settlements put on personal interaction and on suiting the particular needs of the people in their own neighborhoods was part of what made them so adaptable, so popular, and, in many individual instances, so effective, but it also proved to be their great limitation. There was something deeply sentimental and even quixotic about this notion of ending social injustice by filling the poorest neighborhoods with colonies of well-intentioned, youthful, and energetic scions of the middle and upper classes. Although the best of the houses helped a great many people in moments of need and duress, and some of them, such as Hull House and Lillian Wald's celebrated Henry Street Settlement in New York, became influential bases for social reform, most settlements were too dependent on the vision and energies of one or two charismatic individuals. By the 1920s, having failed to alter substantially the conditions in American slums, settlement houses began to fall out of fashion and, in ever-increasing numbers, close their doors. Jane Addams shared a Nobel Prize in 1931 but, at seventy-one, was in such poor health that she was no longer able to work more than four hours a day. When Edmund Wilson visited Hull House to write a tribute to Addams the following year, he was struck by how wan and obsolete the institution felt in her absence, and he described it as "planted with a proud irrelevance in the midst of those long dark streets."[16]

A few of the settlement houses — including both Hull House and the Henry Street Settlement — survive today, but they are functionally indistinguishable from countless other much more recent community service centers. They are staffed by social workers, psychologists, and other professionals, none of whom actually live at the houses.[17] In the end, the goal of breaking down class divisions by bringing the wealthy into the slums has proven less durable than the spirit of inclusion that inspired it, a spirit that was very much in evidence at the 1909 White House Conference on Dependent Children — attended by Homer Folks, Jane Addams, and Hastings Hart — where modern child welfare was born.

જ઼ૅ

The White House Conference might never have come to pass had it not been for President Theodore Roosevelt's erring memory. After having promised the judgeship at the first juvenile court in the District of Columbia to his good friend James E. West, Roosevelt remembered that he had already offered the position to another political crony. "You've got a draft on me any time you want to call," he told West, "anything you want come in and ask it."[18]

West, an orphan who had grown up in an institution, ultimately called Roosevelt on his promise by asking him to sponsor a conference at the White House on the problems of dependent children. At first Roosevelt was dubious about the value of such an event and said he would agree to sponsor it only if it received the strong support of Homer Folks, who had been his trusted adviser when he was governor of New York. Folks was indeed enthusiastic and expressed his support in a letter to the president, as did Theodore Dreiser, the novelist and editor of the women's magazine *The Delineator,* which published in every issue brief profiles of children who needed to be adopted or placed in a foster family.

The conference, attended by more than 200 of the most prominent figures in American child welfare and social work, was held on January 25 and 26, 1909, a little more than a month before the expiration of Roosevelt's second and final term as president. Homer Folks presided. The concluding report of the conference, which was delivered by Hastings Hart but actually written by Folks, finally codified the wisdom about the proper care of dependent children that had been accumulating at least since the founding of the Children's Aid Society and, in so doing, outlined the goals and values that still dominate child welfare to this very day.

The recommendations began with a resounding affirmation of Brace's most essential insight: "Home life is the highest and finest product of civilization. It is the great molding force of mind and of character. Children should not be deprived of it except for urgent and compelling reasons." But these statements were immediately followed by a forceful indictment of Brace's blanket rejection of poor parents: "Children of parents of worthy character, suffering from temporary misfortune, and children of reasonable efficient and deserving mothers who are without the support of the normal breadwinner, should as a rule be kept with their parents, such aid being given as may be necessary to maintain suitable homes for the rearing of children."[19]

Although the report did recommend family foster care as the

best alternative for normal, noncriminal children who could not stay in their "natural home," its description of how those homes should be found and supervised was also a stark rejection of CAS policy under Brace:

> Such homes should be selected by a most careful process of investigation, carried on by skilled agents though personal investigation and with due regard to the religious faith of the child. After children are placed in homes, adequate visitation, with careful consideration of the physical, mental, moral, and spiritual training and development of each child on the part of the responsible home finding agency, is essential.[20]

In line with the Progressive Era tendency to see government regulation as a corrective to individual corruption and inefficiency, the report also called for state inspection of all public and private child welfare agencies. And finally, it sought to correct the gross inadequacies of virtually all nineteenth-century charities' record-keeping systems by calling for detailed accounts of every child's natural and foster parents' "character and circumstances" based on agents' "personal investigation." The report also recommended that agents visit the children under their care at least annually and, once again, compile detailed records of the children's situations during the entire time that they are under the agency's supervision.

The conference was directly responsible for the development of two important institutions. Established by Congress in 1912, the Children's Bureau, for the first time in history, gathered and disseminated reliable information about the condition of children all across America. The work of the bureau not only called attention to the pressing needs of poor and dependent children but also provided the factual foundation for many programs and laws.

But perhaps the most important and influential products of the conference were the mothers' or widows' pensions, which grew directly out of the recommendation that worthy families suffering temporary economic or other hardships be given such aid "as may be necessary to maintain suitable homes for the rearing of children." The notion of providing home relief to women was not entirely new. From the earliest colonial times destitute soldiers' and fishermen's widows, whose hardship was deemed an act of God and in no way a reflection of character, had been provided with home relief by private charities, usually in the form of food or firewood. What distinguished the mothers' pensions from this traditional form of relief was, first, that they were disbursements of *cash;* second, that they were issued by *government* agencies; and finally, that the moral requirements for eligibility were considerably reconfigured.

The primary goal of the pensions was pragmatic rather than moralistic. They were intended to make it possible for children to stay with their natural families because both foster care and institutionalization were expensive and more likely to produce misfits and criminals who could end up being even greater draws on public coffers. To be eligible for a pension, a woman only had to be deemed a "worthy" mother, but she did not need to be virtuous in more conventional senses of the word. Julian Mack, a Cook County circuit court judge who attended the conference, believed that single mothers should be granted pensions "because if we can stop that mother from giving away her child . . . we are going to save not only the child but the mother too."[21]

Homer Folks came up with the idea of calling these payments "pensions." He wanted to destigmatize them and hoped that they would be seen as money earned by "meritorious services in bearing children and rearing them through infancy."[22] In 1911 Missouri and Illinois became the first states to enact mothers' pension laws, and within two years similar laws had been passed in seventeen other states.

The mothers' pensions were never very substantial, however. Often they were kept below boarding home fees, which were themselves frequently set lower than the average cost of caring for a child. And only 40 percent of the counties legally entitled to issue mothers' pensions ever actually offered them. Also, the municipalities that did offer the pensions often imposed lengthy waiting periods and denied them to selected racial or ethnic groups. Mexican immigrants were denied pensions in Los Angeles, for example, and African Americans were ineligible in Houston, even though they constituted 21 percent of the city's population.[23]

In the end, mothers' pensions are significant not so much for the relief they provided as for the precedent they set. Too scanty to keep many hard-pressed families from breaking up, they were nevertheless the model for a program that, whatever its other drawbacks, enjoyed prodigious success at preserving the ties between mothers and their children: the much maligned "welfare," instituted as Aid to Dependent Children under the Social Security Act of 1935, reconfigured as Aid to Families with Dependent Children (AFDC) in 1962, and eliminated under the so-called Personal Responsibility Act, signed by President Bill Clinton in 1996.

The significance of the 1909 White House Conference on Dependent Children was not by any means confined to the introduction of the Children's Bureau or mothers' pensions. The conference's most important effect by far was the gradual reshaping of the operations and goals of virtually every children's charity and service in the United States — a reshaping that is clearly visible in the development of the Children's Aid Society under the guidance of Loring Brace.

&

Loring Brace had never intended to make a career of child saving. As a result, he lacked the emotional and philosophical loyalties that had made his father so resistant to change. Although the 1909 conference would usher in the most radical restructuring in the CAS's history, Loring began reforming his father's organization almost as soon as he officially took over as secretary. One of his very first actions was to answer the CAS's most vehement and long-standing criticism by decreeing that the society would no longer place any children under twelve who were not Protestants. By the latter half of the 1890s almost all of the orphan train riders came from public or private orphanages in upstate New York, which, like the rest of the country, was largely Protestant. Only a small percentage came from the city itself, and these were usually referred by Protestant agencies. The younger Catholic and Jewish children who needed foster homes and might otherwise have ridden CAS orphan trains were left to the care of the New York Foundling Hospital, the Jewish Home, and other charities of their faiths.

Loring imposed no religious segregation on orphan train riders over twelve, perhaps in part because he believed they were mature enough to make their own decisions regarding religion, but mainly because of the way he decided to answer the criticisms of the "Asylum-Interest." Beginning in 1894 he established a loose partnership with the New York House of Refuge and the New York Juvenile Asylum by agreeing to take their inmates on release, give them two to three months of training at the newly founded Brace Farm School in Westchester County, and then find them placements on farms, mostly in New York State and New England but also in the West and South. Girls were sent to the Goodhue Home on Staten Island, where they were taught manners, deportment, and "domestic arts." In this way,

Loring placated his most bitter local critics (the Asylum-Interest) by performing a service for them and satisfied western opponents, like Lyman P. Alden, by ensuring that older orphan train riders had been trained by professionals. Not all of the farm school graduates, however, had received the first part of their "training" at the refuge or the asylum. Many of them had been residents of the Newsboys' Lodging House or were vagrants referred to the CAS in other ways. But even these had at least learned the basics of milking, livestock care, planting, and picking and had been given time to get over what one CAS document called "the first feeling of intense loneliness which the city boy suffers on going to the country."[24]

The main reason why Loring did not ban older non-Protestants from the orphan trains was that it would have gone so radically against the grain of CAS culture and history. Most of the Newsboys' and Girls' Lodging House residents were Catholic or Jewish, as were the inmates of the asylum and the refuge. Excluding these children would have meant that the orphan trains no longer served New York and would have deprived the lodging houses of what had always been seen as one of their main reasons for being. Also, this age group was not well provided for by any charity, and it would not have been fair to cut them off — at least as long as Loring felt they benefited from the orphan trains.

While, by virtue of their religious diversity, the older boys and girls were a holdover from the early days of the orphan trains, their placements differed from those of the early riders in one important particular: the farmers who took them in were *required* to pay them wages. They were still supposed to send them to school in the winter as well, and to treat them with all the fairness and consideration they owed their own offspring, but the payment of wages made clear that the relationship was not truly familial but primarily a matter of employment. Prior to the opening of the farm school, older orphan train riders had often, of course, been paid wages, but only through their own negotiations with their "employers" and never as a part of official CAS policy. Loring Brace's institution of this policy is characteristic of another aspect of his management of the society.

Loring was an engineer, not a man of the cloth. Under his guidance, CAS literature made only the most cursory references to religion and ceased almost entirely to mention the immortality of the children's souls, their ignorance of the Bible or of Jesus, and even the Christianity of the men and women who wanted to help them. Loring was undoubtedly a man of compassion, with a strong moral sense, but he also had an engineer's deep respect for structural coherence. A large proportion of the changes he made at the CAS were intended to clarify its goals and to make sure that the organization of the society truly reflected and helped to realize those goals.

By establishing a two-tiered system, with the older children essentially being found jobs and the younger ones "foster families" (the new official term as of the mid-1890s), he was eliminating an ambiguity that had dogged the Emigration Plan from its very beginning. He was, of course, also acknowledging the fact that placements of the older children had always been much more like jobs than adoption. Now that the obligations and the benefits of the program were spelled out much more clearly, it was hoped that there would be fewer unmet expectations and thus more happy placements.

Loring also helped clarify CAS placement efforts by establishing separate programs and record-keeping systems for two long-standing categories of orphan train rider that had only intermittently been distinguished from the mass of emigrants: families and single women with children.

The help provided to families hardly changed under Loring's tenure. Essentially, all they were given were job placements and, if necessary, transportation out of town. But in 1901 Loring expanded the society's work with single women substantially by opening a "temporary home for homeless mothers with little children." Many of the women who sought shelter at the home were simply impoverished single mothers, widows, or abandoned wives, but a large percentage of them had fled their husbands as a result of some sort of crisis, most likely battery or abuse. During its first years of operation the women were allowed to remain at the home for only a few days, but in later years they would frequently stay for weeks. The women were given food and clothing, provided with washing and laundering facilities, and helped to solve their larger problems usually in one of three ways. By far the majority of women were found jobs where they would be allowed to keep their children, either locally or in the West. Some of them were helped to move in with family or friends and sometimes provided with transportation. And some, the minority, were helped to reach a reconciliation with their husbands. This remarkably advanced program, ultimately renamed "Emergency Shelter for Women and Children," operated for Loring Brace's entire tenure at the CAS but was discontinued shortly after his retirement in October 1927.

Loring Brace also established a remarkably forward-looking industrial education program for disabled — or, as he referred to them, "crippled and deformed" — children. Every weekday these children would be picked up from and returned to their homes by CAS "wagonettes" — small, horse-drawn omnibuses. Sometimes attendants would have to carry the students up and down several flights of tenement house stairs. At the classes, students would be trained in reading, writing, and basic calculation, as well as some sort of marketable skill that they could practice from their homes to help support their families.

And finally, shortly after the founding of the first juvenile court in 1899, the CAS established its own probation department, which it saw primarily as yet another mechanism for keeping children out of institutions. The probation officer handled the cases of "repentant" boys and girls who had been convicted of "small offenses." He was meant to be a "friend" who would find the children new jobs, or smooth the way for their return to their old employment, and generally guide and advise them until they were "mature enough to recognize responsibilities and able to stand alone."[25] But his friendliness was no doubt compromised in the eyes of many of his charges by the fact that he also had the power to "punish" and "arrest" them.[26] Still, the probation department was yet another example of how the CAS was attempting to help the neighborhoods Brace Sr. had once so scornfully dismissed.

By far the most significant of Loring Brace's reorganization efforts was in part a response to the new oversight and regulation of charitable organization required by new legislation. The official CAS "Record Books," the primary compendium of information about placed children, became considerably more detailed in 1892 — two years into Loring's tenure, and two years before Homer Folks's amendment to the state constitution established state supervision of charities. The books contained more elaborate descriptions of the children's placements and their progress during, and often after, their supervision by the CAS. But the fact that 1892 is also the first year in which the telephone is referred to in the records suggests that the increased detail of the reports may have been due in part to the ease of access offered by this new technology.

The records do not become dramatically different until the years immediately following the passage of New York's new state constitution with its provisions regarding the oversight and regulation of charities. Up through 1894 the "Record Books" had merely been blank, lined ledgers. But beginning in 1895 they contained printed forms that helped standardize the information collected about each child. The forms not only required agents to enter each child's name, age, religion, and similar details about their foster parents but also showed the new emphasis on the importance of visiting the child by requiring the entry of directions to the foster parents' home — information that had never been collected before. Although these records could still be frustratingly incomplete, they were no longer merely jottings intended to jog the memory of readers who were already acquainted with the child.

The most significant change came in 1896 with the institution of the "card files." These were small brown folders — one for each child — that contained a stiff card listing the child's vital statistics and visits from a CAS agent and any other documents related to the child. At first these documents consisted mainly of letters by the children, their foster parents, and sometimes siblings or birth parents. As time passed, however, they became repositories for an ever-expanding number of forms as well as reports and letters from an also rapidly expanding number of experts — teachers, doctors, probation officers, and, finally, social workers and psychiatrists — whom the never satisfied need for supervision and the ever more professionalized and bureaucratized business of child welfare brought into the private lives of the children and their families.

The earliest forms were questionnaires filled out by prospective foster parents that asked not only for basic biographical information but also about their reasons for taking a child. These forms show that, despite the new emphasis on adoption and foster family placement, the society was still perfectly willing to give children to parents who expressed no interest in adoption, or who said their principal reason for having a child around was to have him or her "help with chores." The majority of parents, however, did cite giving the child a home as their main reason for taking him or her in. The questionnaires also reveal that, although the majority of the placements were to couples in their thirties and forties, as many as one-sixth of them were to single women or to very old people — testimony to the fact that, right up until the very end of the Emigration Plan, placing agents often felt that it was better to accept any willing foster parent than to bring a child back to New York.

In a paper delivered sometime in the 1930s, Clara Comstock, one of the most hardworking and beloved of all the placement agents, recounted with clear pride how she used to trick people into becoming foster parents. In one case she asked a couple who had expressed no interest in taking children to baby-sit a child for just one night — ostensibly because the child had no other place to stay. Then, the following morning, while the couple was still under the spell of the child's cuteness and pathetic fate, she rushed in, got them to sign placement forms, then rushed out again before they had time to change their minds.

This first questionnaire was soon followed by others for references, agent preplacement visits, medical and teacher evaluations, and so on. The forms were, of course, a mixed blessing. They were unlikely to reveal anything that an attentive agent would not have picked up by other means, and they forced the agent to spend time doing paperwork that might otherwise have been used attending to the needs of children. But the forms did help clarify the responsibilities of foster parents and agents, as well as the needs of the children. They also signified how seriously the CAS — and by extension, the whole of society — took these responsibilities and needs. And finally, the forms did indeed tend to standardize what had always been a very haphazard process of placement and supervision. At the very least, they required the agent to visit the family and pay some attention to the quality of their relations with the child. The documents show clearly that, from 1896 on, CAS agents visited their charges, on average, nearly one and a half times per year — significantly more frequently than the annual visits that would be recommended by the 1909 conference.

Two other very important documents introduced in 1895 were surrender and permit forms. The surrender forms were legal contracts under which the birth parents gave up all rights to their children, granted the CAS custody, and allowed the children to be placed with foster families. The permit forms granted the society the same rights but were signed by the children themselves, presumably because their parents were dead or otherwise inaccessible. Once again these documents had the advantage of removing ambiguity about the status of the child, and thus easing the adoption process and providing psychological benefit to all parties. They also helped protect the society from the suits by irate parents that had bedeviled it ever since the 1870s.

The increasing "professionalization" of social work during the twentieth century may have cut back on the emotional interchange between worker and child that Brace had so valued, but the ever-denser assemblage of forms, reports, and letters in each card file made for a far more realistic and complete portrayal of children's situations. The card files had begun only as adjuncts to the "Record Books," but by 1916 the files' superior flexibility and capacity had reversed that relationship, and the "Record Books" were discontinued.

Social work's professionalization also substantially diminished the reflexive euphemism of the society's first four decades. Agents still had a tendency to portray placements as successes, but they were far more willing to admit failure and find children more effective forms of treatment.

Finally, these records show how the whole of American society was changing in the twentieth century. Although as early as 1902 Loring Brace could declare that "all over the country there is a great demand for babies,"[27] it was not until the 1920s that this demand translated into a marked increase in the number of adoptions. This trend is something of a puzzle, at least to materialist historians. Why, they ask, should the demand for children to adopt shoot up at the very moment when work prohibitions and an emphasis on education made children more costly and less remunerative than ever before in history? And why were the least remunerative children of all — babies — the ones wanted most? At the end of the nineteenth century mothers still had to pay baby farmers to take their unwanted children, but by 1930 those babies could be sold to desperate adoptive parents on the black market for $1,000 each.[28]

No doubt the exploding demand for young children was partly due to new psychological theories asserting that personality was mostly determined by events in early childhood, and that children adopted after infancy were more likely to be troubled. But the demand was also, certainly, the final fulfillment of the sentimentalization of children that had begun with the Romantics. Once it became forbidden to value children for their economic benefits — for their *capability* — people were no longer so inhibited about yielding to those protective and adoring impulses evoked by a child's *incapability*. And what children were more incapable and adorable than babies? Whatever the source of the demand, it lowered the average age of children placed by the CAS dramatically. By the late 1920s most of the orphan train riders were toddlers and babies, and the society was even picking up newborns at the hospital.

The evolution of social attitudes was also reflected in the name of the department making the placements. Although annual reports continued to refer to it as the Emigration Department well into the twentieth century, as of 1898 it was the Placing-Out Department on the CAS letterhead — a reflection of the growing emphasis on local rather than western placement. By the late 1920s — at which point placements were almost exclusively in the New York area — the division was variously referred to as the Free Home or Home Finding Department — the latter name reflecting the society's experiments with boarding out. By the early 1930s, after the departure of the last orphan train, the division of the CAS making outplacements was renamed the Foster Home Department, the designation it held until the 1960s.

ᴂ

When the first company of orphaned and destitute children left New York for Dowagiac, Michigan, in September 1854, it was hard to see the Children's Aid Society's Emigration Plan as anything other than inspired beneficence. In an era when poor children were commonly judged to be criminals who needed "correction" in brutal, underfunded institutions, the Emigration Plan asserted not merely that destitution was no crime, but that these children were possessed of virtues — strengths, independence, ingenuity, and vitality — that could benefit the whole nation if nurtured in the right environment. At a time when all poor and working-class children had, to one extent or another, to earn their way in the world, the CAS provided orphan train riders with sure jobs. And at a time when children as young as ten traveled hundreds of miles in quest of work, the CAS provided them with free transportation west — to the leading edge of the nation's manifest destiny, where all newcomers had maximum opportunity to build themselves great futures and fortunes.

But then, by a process that was in many ways mysterious — and that Charles Loring Brace was never fully able to apprehend — in a scant few decades almost all of the assumptions that had made the orphan trains seem so admirable lost their validity. Although children were still held to be innocent despite their poverty — at least by people such as those who attended the 1909 White House Conference — they were no longer seen as so capable, strong, or independent. The idea that children, even teenagers, might travel great distances and be left to make their own way in the world came to seem the height of moral and social irresponsibility. Not only could children not be trusted to manage their lives, but the adults who offered to take them in could not be trusted either and had to be subjected to thorough scrutiny and careful supervision. And work, which had once been thought an enriching and thoroughly natural part of childhood, now seemed an impoverishment, depriving children of the superior enrichments of school and play, and depriving adults of work and decent salaries. Even the Great West, which Brace had so often averred had a "nearly inexhaustible demand for labor," had begun to accumulate sizable populations who had built neither great futures nor fortunes and had no money, no jobs, and no hope. And, while Brace's notion that the family was the best place for a child had only gained wider and wider acceptance, that very acceptance had led many people to believe that no child should ever be removed from his or her family except as a last resort. And finally, a growing consensus built that the best way to help poor children was not to send them away but to work with their families, and within their communities, to maximize everybody's opportunity, safety, and happiness.

In 1890, the year of Charles Loring Brace's death, a total of 2,851 children were listed in volume 4 of the "Company Books" — the CAS's official registry of emigrant parties — as having ridden the orphan trains.[29] In 1902, a decade after Loring Brace's influence began to show its first effects at the society, only 712 children emigrated west.[30] The numbers would continue to show a slight but steady decline over the next few years.

The very last party registered in the "Company Books" left New York City on January 22, 1909, just three days before the start of the White House Conference. That final entry is followed by a list of about 130 names of children, most of whom seem to have been placed individually during the following months in the immediate environs of New York City. All the remaining pages in the book are blank.

"Orphan trains" continued to go west for more than twenty years, but they were vastly different affairs than they had been during the program's heyday in the nineteenth century. The parties were considerably smaller. No longer ranging between thirty and one hundred, they were rarely larger than fifteen, and sometimes they contained only two or three children. As the list concluding the final "Company Book" indicates, most of the placements made by the Children's Aid Society during the remaining orphan train years were to homes in New York, New Jersey, and Connecticut. And indeed, even in 1902, when 712 children emigrated west, 726 were placed near New York City (476 of them "at wages"). Although groups of "large boys" — teenagers — were placed until the very end, the average age of the orphan train riders dropped significantly during the final years, and many of the riders were infants. And in part because of being younger, a far larger proportion of orphan train riders were adopted by their new families. In this regard at least, the final orphan trains corresponded far more closely to the ideal that Charles Loring Brace had propounded in the 1850s and '60s.

The orphan train program continued during its final two decades partly out of sentiment — it had been something close to the raison d'être of the CAS for so many years and was still the program with which the society was most readily identified in the public eye — and partly out of institutional inertia. There was a staff of dedicated and respected western placement agents for whom it would be difficult to find other equally satisfying jobs, and then there were the hard-won and expensive placement contracts that had been negotiated with several of the midwestern and western states. In the end, it was the expiration of these contracts that finally brought the orphan train era to a close.

Beginning with Missouri in 1899, the western states began passing laws that either eliminated the placement of poor children from out of state entirely or required placement agencies to put up bonds, usually of $1,000, to ensure that the agency immediately removed — in the words of an Iowa bond from 1907 — "any child having contagious or incurable disease, or having any deformity or being of feeble mind or of vicious character [or] any child . . . which shall become a public charge within the period of five years."[31] Gradually, however, even the states that had allowed bonded placements from the East began to ban them outright. By the time Loring Brace retired in October 1927, after having suffered a mild stroke, there were only five states — Michigan, Kansas, Iowa, Nebraska, and Texas — still allowing the Children's Aid Society to make placements within their borders. But within a mere couple of years these states too had closed their doors to the society. Although it is sometimes said that the program endured into the early 1930s because a few children were spirited out west illegally, one or two at a time, to be placed with or near siblings who had been placed earlier, the last true orphan train carrying children whose placement had not been made in advance left New York City for Sulphur Springs, Texas, on May 31, 1929.

Conclusion: Legacy

Society must act on the highest principles, or its punishment incessantly comes within itself.

— Charles Loring Brace, 1857[1]

THIRTY-THREE of the one hundred biggest contractors doing business with New York City are foster care organizations, among them the Children's Aid Society. But the CAS no longer dominates child welfare as it did during the orphan train era. Beginning shortly after the Second World War, New York's Protestant agencies, whose clientele became increasingly African American, began to lose out in competition for private donations to Catholic and, to some extent, Jewish agencies, whose clientele, merely by virtue of the persisting religious segregation, remained white for longer. Now all of the agencies handle fairly equal portions of black, white, Latino, and Asian children, with black children making up by far the largest category. The three largest child welfare contractors in New York City are Little Flower Children's Services, the Saint Christopher's Home, and the New York Foundling Hospital, which, in 1998, were paid $73 million, $68 million, and $61 million, respectively, from New York City coffers. The Children's Aid Society, the fifteenth largest of the city's sixty child welfare contractors, received only $21 million.[2] It is still, however, one of New York's most highly respected child welfare agencies, and it is one of the seven charities supported by the "Remember the Neediest" campaign run by the *New York Times* during the holiday season.

Significantly, the CAS is now widely praised among child welfare professionals for the care with which it selects, manages, and monitors its foster placements — the very functions for which it was most harshly criticized during Charles Loring Brace's final years. This is not to say that it is perfect. Every child welfare organization, in New York and across the nation, has its share of tragedies, those children whose lives it made more miserable rather than better, and the CAS is no exception.

The bulk of the CAS's work is in foster care. It places some 800 children a year, out of New York's 32,000 total foster care population.[3] Its caseworkers have an average caseload of twenty-two, as opposed to the citywide average of twenty-five. And in the society's "Twelve Months to Permanency Program," which is designed to lessen the amount of time children spend in the limbo of foster care, caseworkers have a load of only fifteen to twenty cases. The ideal caseload recommended by the Child Welfare League is twelve to fifteen, depending on the complexity of the cases.

The CAS also runs Head Start and day-care programs, medical and dental clinics, a summer camp, a teenage pregnancy prevention program, and a "boot camp aftercare" program, which provides the graduates of juvenile boot camps with health care, psychological and career counseling, and — in a revival of the old workshop idea — on-the-job training at a CAS-operated baking business.

One of the society's most ambitious projects is its community schools program. The CAS has turned eight New York public schools into something like the settlement houses. The schools, which are open year-round, fifteen hours a day, and six days a week, not only provide their students with a standard public education but also take advantage of the strong connection that schools automatically have with their surrounding neighborhoods to provide needed social services, such as health care, family programs, before- and after-school care, and a preschool. Another ambitious CAS undertaking has been its Carmel Hill community renewal program. In 1992 the society began providing long-needed repairs and renovations to four run-down, city-owned tenement buildings on a section of 118th Street in Harlem. Once the buildings were in livable condition, the CAS sent in social workers to help the families who had been squatting in the buildings establish legal tenancy and to put them in touch with health care and other family-strengthening social services. Both of these programs position the CAS to take advantage of the city's drive to provide foster care through neighborhood centers and to keep placements local whenever possible. But they also show how far the society has come since the days when Charles Loring Brace thought that the best way to deal with poor children's families and neighborhoods was simply to turn his back on them.

Partly through internal leadership, but mostly because of shifts in social work fashion and new local and federal laws, the CAS no longer places children outside the metropolitan area where it could not adequately monitor them and provide them and their foster and birth families with needed services. The society has also long since ceased to strive to save children by encouraging them to be virtuous or independent. Nowadays the CAS describes its goal as "to ensure the physical and emotional well-being of children and families, and to provide each child with the support and opportunities needed to become a happy, healthy and successful adult."[4] Brace's double-barreled rhetoric is entirely gone. The children are never presented as threats to society but only as innocents in need of help. At the same time, they tend not to be seen as future leaders, or as evolutionarily advanced, but more as victims, dependents, and obligations — a pervasive characterization among contemporary social service organizations dealing with children.

Perhaps the most surprising fact about the way the CAS has evolved is that there is no trace of the most unequivocal of its early successes: the Newsboys' Lodging House. The society does run three group homes, but these are therapeutically oriented and, again, primarily treat their residents as victims in need of help rather than as "independent contractors." The present-day CAS has no program aimed at homeless or street children, and in particular, no program that provides services to teenagers with no strings attached. In this regard as in so many other aspects of its evolution, the CAS is only reflecting broader social attitudes. New York City, like the nation as a whole, has a shocking shortage of services for street children and older teens in general — those who fit into the category of what Brace used to call "large boys," those for whom the orphan trains were a conspicuous failure.

ぷ

Charles Loring Brace's most substantial legacy is the foster care system. Not only were the orphan trains the first step from indenture to modern foster care, but Brace was the first to articulate all of the main arguments still being used to demonstrate the superiority of foster care to institutional care: that children need families; that institutions do not inculcate the attitudes or skills that enable children to thrive in the outside world; and that, in any event, institutions are too expensive.

There are now approximately half a million American children in foster care[5] — a population that, after falling substantially through the mid-twentieth century, reached its all-time highs during the early 1990s. Foster care remains a poor people's institution. Only the tiniest percentage of children who come into the system are middle-class or affluent. The system is also disproportionately black. While African Americans make up 15 percent of the general population, they are 48 percent of the children in foster care. Hispanics are 12 percent of the general population, but 8 percent of foster children. Whites, by contrast, make up only 36 percent of foster children, even though they represent 69 percent of the general population.[6]

The median time that New York foster children spend in the system before being returned permanently to their biological parents or extended family or sent to live with adoptive parents is three years[7] — and this figure includes the large proportion of children who are in and out of the system in only a few days or weeks. Excluding those children, the average amount of time a child spends in the system is four and a half years, a full year and a half longer than allowed by federal guidelines.

Modern foster care is, of course, a decidedly dubious legacy. To call it a "system" is to indulge in the dreamiest of euphemisms. It is little more than an assemblage of afterthoughts and exhausted make-do efforts built on a foundation of contradictory policies and prejudices. It is a system that breeds despair even among its brightest and best, and that turns even the most well-intentioned people into something like the partners of a decaying marriage, who use every opportunity to attack those whom they ought to be helped by and helping, and to whom they are bound by a common destiny.

One of the things that makes modern foster care so difficult to know how to improve is that almost everything said about it is true. It *is* overcrowded, overwhelmed, and often cruel to the very children it is designed to help, and yet it *does* save the lives of thousands of children every year. It *is* pervaded and perverted by class and racial prejudices, and yet it *does* offer vast numbers of poor and minority children their very best chance at decent and satisfying lives. It *is* and always has been unconscionably underfunded, and at the same time it *does* fritter away countless millions of dollars through inefficiency, corruption, and just plain stupidity. It *is* staffed by people who are massively underquali-

fied by both training and inclination for their terribly difficult, demanding, and supremely important work, but there are also many foster care workers with a saint's capacity for hard labor, compassion, and
self-sacrifice.

Foster care can never be painless. It begins, always, with tragedy — the
death, depression, illness, insanity, cruelty, or addiction of parents.
Usually the tragedy is not a discrete event but a series of individually
horrific incidents that occur over a period of years and can build up
such a collective force that they permanently deform a child's character. But even when the tragedy is comparatively minor, and even when
the child is in foster care for only a short period, she is still suffering a
child's most primal nightmare: separation from her mother and father. No child is happy in her new home, at least not in the beginning.
And all children resent their foster parents, at least until they get used
to them, and to the fact that fate has played such a cruel trick on them.
But some children never stop resenting their new mothers and fathers,
even when those parents are decent people doing all they can to make
their foster child happy. And of course, not all foster parents are up to
the terribly difficult job of caring for a traumatized child. Ideally only
the best-qualified men and women should be allowed to become foster parents, but no foster care system anywhere will ever be able to be
so selective: there are just too many children needing care and not
enough people willing to take them.

   To consider foster care is to consider limits. Despite all of our
wishes and best intentions, we simply cannot do everything that we
would like to for a parentless child, or even everything that we should.
We cannot undo the tragedy that brings a child into foster care in the
first place. We cannot guarantee that a drug-addicted mother will respond to therapy, or even go to it, or that a violent father will stop
beating his children. We cannot banish poverty, violence, and social
decay from our inner cities — at least not significantly, and never
soon enough for any particular child. And perhaps most important of
all, we are limited by what we can know. The needs of foster children
are never simple and rarely obvious. Decisions affecting the whole of a
child's future are almost always made on incomplete or confusing evidence, and with only a hazy sense of what their ultimate consequences
might be.

   Most foster care cases begin with an investigation. A report of abuse or neglect is phoned into a local child welfare agency by a child's teacher, doctor, relative, or neighbor. A caseworker, often called a field or protection officer, is sent out to determine whether the report is accurate and, if it is, what should be done with the child. The caseworker's job is easy — in a manner of speaking — if the child is covered with lash marks, cigarette burns, or other obvious signs of abuse. But often the traces even of a brutal beating are hard to distinguish from the ordinary bruises and scars of childhood. And neglect or sexual or psychological abuse often leave no visible traces at all. Caseworkers try to gain insight into parents' and children's true natures by watching how they act, but behavior too can be difficult to evaluate. Some children respond to abuse by becoming subdued or fearful, while others respond in exactly the opposite way, by becoming hyperactive or excessively friendly; moreover, any of these behaviors could be caused simply by the presence of a stranger in the living room. The parents' behavior can be equally hard to evaluate: guilty or innocent, the parent is going to be upset at the intrusion of a government official into private family matters. Guilty or innocent, the parent is going to deny abuse or neglect, with perhaps the most dangerous parents of all — the sociopaths — able to practice the most convincing denials.

Even when caseworkers do uncover textbook evidence of mistreatment, it is often difficult to tell how serious it is. One reason for removing a child from her home is "educational neglect," which is when a child misses school for an extended period of time without being ill or having some other justified reason for absence. But suppose that during an investigation the caseworker finds out that it is the *mother* who is ill, and that she is keeping the child home to nurse her and to help care for a younger sibling. Is this really neglect? What if the mother comes from a village culture where the obligation to help family in trouble is considered more important than the right to education? Is she really neglectful when applying such values in the United States? And would it really be better for a child suffering such "neglect" to be placed in the foster care system?

Although cultural conflicts like this come up all the time in foster care investigations, the cases are rarely so simple. Let us imagine that, as he tries to explain the importance of education in America to this woman, the caseworker notices the smell of alcohol on her breath and, later on, sees an open bottle of whiskey in the kitchen. This is all the evidence he has. None of the other people he has spoken to in his investigation — neighbors, the child's teacher — have said anything about the mother having a drinking problem. But the caseworker thinks that alcohol on the breath at eleven in the morning is evidence enough. What next? Does a drinking problem combined with illness and educational neglect justify removal of the child? Or to put it another way, is it clear that the child would be at greater risk in such a home than in the foster care system?

To answer this question, the caseworker must not only divine secrets that the mother may be keeping from herself (how serious is her drinking?) but also be able to see into the future: Even supposing the mother does not have a true drinking problem now, what will happen if her boyfriend leaves her? Or beats her? Or if she is mugged, raped, or suffers any of the other catastrophes that life so routinely hurls at the very poor? And if she is required to go to Alcoholics Anonymous as a condition of keeping her child, will it help her? Will she go? And what about her medical condition? Suppose the caseworker talks to a doctor (not perhaps the most realistic of suppositions, given the size of most caseloads) and finds out that 60 percent of women with the mother's illness make a full recovery, provided they receive adequate treatment. Is that mother going to be among the 60 percent? Is she going to get the treatment she needs? And how long will recovery take? What will happen to the child in the meantime?

The questions go on and on and on. To make a risk-free decision about what to do with this child — or any child — the caseworker would have to combine the wisdom of Solomon with the omniscience of a deity. All the obscurities of the human heart would have to be transparent to him. The future would have to be an open book. He would have to be able to figure out what life a child might have under each of the possible courses of action (removal, staying with parent, therapy, and so on), and then compare the benefits and drawbacks of each of these possible lives. . . .

Which is to say that there are no risk-free decisions in child welfare. All decisions are based, at least in part, on hunches, educated guesses, superstition, and prejudice. They have to be. And mistakes, inevitably, get made — not just regarding the initial disposition of the child but in every phase of foster care. Even the best trained, most intelligent, diligent, compassionate, and experienced caseworker, with all the best services at her fingertips, can decide to return children to parents who will kill them, or to keep children away from parents whose problems might be easily solved if they were not so distraught at the forced breakup of their family.

Mistakes are an inescapable component of the human condition. And insofar as they are inescapable, insofar as they are a function of the limits of human intelligence and strength, they are not morally culpable, no matter how tragic their consequences. No one can be blamed when their best efforts are not enough. We can only be morally culpable when we truly have a choice, when there is something that we could do to help a child, and we know that we could do it, but we simply don't.

Most of the things that we can and should do to help endangered children are fairly obvious, and have been obvious for a very long time.

At least since Hastings Hart's investigation of the Children's Aid Society's Minnesota placements, we have known how important it is to adequately screen foster parents and to monitor children in their placements. And in fact, we have understood this simple truth for a lot longer, as evidenced by the fact that John Jackson, "the Runaway White Slave Boy," was visited, however ineffectually, by an inspector from the Philadelphia House of Refuge when he was indentured to the Delaware farmer Mr. Mitchell in 1850. There are no longer nearly so many obstacles to screening foster parents and monitoring foster children as there were in the nineteenth century, thanks in part to paved roads, automobiles, telephones, and computers, but also because the trend for the last century has been to place children ever closer to home. Almost all foster children in the larger metropolitan areas are placed within their city's boundaries. If the system of neighborhood-based foster care being proposed in New York, Los Angeles, and elsewhere is actually put into effect, most foster children will be placed within the same community where their biological parents live and the caseworkers who are supposed to look after them have their offices.

The lackadaisical screening and monitoring of the nineteenth century might also be somewhat excused by that era's markedly different attitudes toward children. After all, John Jackson and most of the other older street children who first rode the orphan trains were considered quasi-adults who had already demonstrated their ability to look out for themselves, even if they could still have benefited from contact with a virtuous and loving family. Children nowadays — after the Mary Ellen Wilson case and the successes of the anti–child labor movement — are seen as far more vulnerable, and far more in need of protection, than their counterparts of a century ago. But our universally inefficient and underfunded child welfare system does not remotely begin to provide orphaned, abandoned, or endangered children with the level of protection or sensitive care we know that they need and that we are technically capable of providing.

It is true that, for the most part, dependent children today are far better looked after than those children who were indentured or rode the orphan trains, a substantial portion of whom were never visited even once by representatives of the organizations that placed them. According to a comprehensive 1997 study of the New York City child welfare system, 70 percent of the children under the protection of the Administration for Children's Services (ACS) had at least one face-to-face meeting with a caseworker in a six-month period. The problem is that under state and city regulations, such children and their parents are required to have *two* contacts every *month* with their caseworker. Only 3 percent of the cases studied met this basic standard, and as the original statistic indicates, 30 percent of cases involved no face-to-face contacts between children and their caseworkers for the whole six months.[8] Another sign of the slipshod monitoring of New York's foster children is the fact that the Administration for Children's Services was unable to produce records for 22 percent of the cases randomly selected for the study. There were also huge discrepancies between the information about children in the state's central computer and in the children's files with the ACS. For example, 31 percent of incidents of abuse or neglect reported to the state via its hotline were not even mentioned in the files of the children who were the subjects of those reports.[9] And in 60 percent of the cases the state computers and the local files even disagreed about such basic information as the dates when the ACS first began to investigate the child's situation.[10]

It would be one thing if New York's child welfare system were the worst in the country, but the fact is that it is only average. Although New York State has one of the highest poverty rates in the nation, its child protection services have helped keep its abuse and neglect fatality rates close to the national mean, and it has one of the very highest rates for adoption of children in foster care.[11] There are many reasons why American child welfare agencies tend to do such a terrible job monitoring the children in their care. One of the most obvious is heavy caseloads. The average New York City caseworker is supervising the care of twenty-five children at any one time, which is roughly twice the caseload recommended by the Child Welfare League.[12] But caseloads in the forties and higher are not uncommon in many American cities. When Marcia Robinson Lowry, the executive director of Children's Rights, a child advocacy group, asked a caseworker in Washington, D.C., how often he saw the children in his charge, he laughed bitterly and said, "I'm lucky if I see one of my kids on the evening news!"[13]

Another reason for inadequate monitoring is the quality of the people doing the casework. Child welfare casework — whether it involves the investigation of reports of abuse or the management of children under protection — is terribly demanding intellectually and emotionally. Like the police, caseworkers go in and out of the worst neighborhoods in their cities and routinely place themselves in the middle of dreadful domestic conflicts. Caseworkers are supposed to have police protection when they go to remove a child, but generally they don't get it. Caseworkers also have to be masters of the skills of other professions. Not only must they be shrewd psychologists who have the insight to penetrate deceptions, but they must have the diplomacy to salve furious or frightened parents and children. They must also have a sophisticated understanding of the nature of and treatment for drug addiction, alcoholism, depression, and post-traumatic stress syndrome, since these are conditions that they encounter frequently in their clients. And finally, caseworkers must be able to balance a deep compassion for their clients with a firmness of conviction that will enable them to rip a weeping child away from a pleading mother when that mother is unfit or dangerous.

Common sense would dictate that such professionals be highly trained and paid, but the facts are that frontline caseworkers — those who have the most intimate and influential contact with children and their families — are generally required to have only a bachelor's degree. In New York the median pay for private agency caseworkers is $28,000, with starting salaries in the mid-twenties.[14] These salary levels are particularly shocking when one considers that city garbage truck crew members *start* at $28,000 and have a median salary of $36,000.[15] The Administration for Children's Services has recently raised its starting salary to $28,000, but its pay cap is $50,000.[16] Such

low pay combined with grueling, stressful workloads is a classic for-
mula for burnout; and indeed, the mean annual turnover rate at New
York private agencies is 33 percent, and is nearly 50 percent at a quarter
of the agencies.[17] A foster child told me:

> One time I went through five, six workers in a three-month period.
> They'd just decide they wanted to leave, and I'd end up getting a new
> social worker, a new social worker, a new social worker. They'd leave
> because a lot of them told me they're overworked, underpaid, and on
> high stress. A lot of them told me you have to do this kind of work be-
> cause you love it. You can't do it for the money. They left and they were
> so happy — some went back to school, some went to other agencies. A
> couple I stayed in contact with, and they said, "I'm so relaxed! My
> blood pressure is down!" They got their youth back.[18]

Another effect of the grueling workload and low pay is that child
welfare casework has little social prestige. Most university social work
programs neglect it in favor of clinical psychology, and graduates who
do choose to go into the field are generally looked down upon. Time
and again as I interviewed child welfare and foster care scholars, administrators, and lawyers for this book, I would be asked, always in
tones of mockery, variations of the following: "Have you ever met one
of these caseworkers? Most of them are real troglodytes, believe me!"
Although many intelligent, well-trained, and compassionate men and
women do become frontline caseworkers, there are obviously not
nearly as many of them as there would be if our society granted the
profession respect and remuneration that remotely corresponded to
its difficulty and importance.

Under federal guidelines, children are supposed to be in foster care for
only two years at most after it has been decided that they cannot go
back to their parents and must be adopted. The main reason why
American foster children average four and a half years in the system,
with many children spending five or six years or even longer, is the
inefficiency of the family courts. Like the rest of the child welfare system itself, the family courts are overwhelmed. In many municipalities
there are simply not enough judges, so court calendars get jammed
up; if cases have to be adjourned, months can go by before the next
hearing. And like caseworkers, the lawyers who represent the various

parties in adoption proceedings are overworked and underpaid. In New York City, for example, the average lawyer gets $200 per hour (with corporate lawyers getting $350 to $450 per hour). But lawyers representing private agencies in family court are paid only $85 an hour, and the state-appointed lawyers for birth parents get only $40 for in-court work and a mere $25 for out-of-court work.[19] Again, some of these lawyers are talented and saintly, but not enough, and not nearly as many as there would be if they were paid and respected more in accordance with the other members of their profession.

Another reason for the backlog in family courts is that judges and agencies want to give biological parents time to respond to the therapies and services that might help them solve whatever problem led to the removal of their children. This would seem to be an unavoidable delay, at least as long as we believe that, if at all possible, birth families ought to be kept together. The problem is that very often neither birth parents nor foster parents get the services they need. According to the 1997 study of New York's child welfare system, for example, 76 percent of cases deemed to need family preservation services never got them. Fifty-six percent of birth parents who could have benefited from parenting skills training did not get it. Housing was not provided in 58 percent of the cases for which it was planned. And 43 percent of foster parents did not get needed services such as psychological counseling, medical care, or day care. This study also found that the biggest obstacle to families getting services was not the unwillingness of the recipients to take advantage of the services (169 incidences) but the failure of caseworkers to suggest the services in the first place (197 incidences).[20] As a result, not only are lengthy adjournments sometimes wasted because the biological parents are never given the services the adjournments are ostensibly meant to provide time for, but many family court judges, well aware of how shabbily biological parents are treated by agencies, often issue orders and call for long adjournments simply to force the child welfare agencies to provide parents with the services they should have been getting all along. Essentially what these so-called pro-parent judges are doing is forcing the agencies simply to abide by the law and by accepted social work practices and regulations. This is not wholly an unworthy effort, given the ferocious prejudice against the generally poor, ill-educated, and mightily overburdened birth parents within the child welfare community, but its cost is borne primarily by the children who end up spending unnecessary months and years in the system not knowing whether they are going to go back to their parents or move on to adoption.

Another thing that we can do, and have known we should do for a very long time, is to treat children as individuals. The vast majority of children in foster care have been removed from their families because their mothers have substance abuse problems, but this does not mean that the situations of all of those children are alike. Some alcohol and drug abusers are able to provide their children with considerable love and consistency, even in the midst of their addiction, while others simply forget their children, or come to hate them as nagging rivals to their one and only love. Some addicts truly hit what twelve-step programs call "rock bottom," and then find the strength to rebuild their lives, while others, when they reach a similar crisis in their addiction, only sink into total self-annihilation. The same dichotomy exists in children. Some have the inner strength to thrive despite considerable deprivation and abuse, while others are utterly destroyed by far lesser hardships. Some children have grandparents whom they love, and who can be trusted to give them the care and support they need, while for others the grandparents are the true authors of their misery — since they were the original abusers of the children's abusive parents. For some children it is more important to be placed with siblings than to have unusually compassionate and competent foster parents, while for others the reverse is true. Some children will suffer crippling identity conflicts being raised by families of a different racial or ethnic group, while for others skin color, language, or religion will be insignificant beside the love — or lack thereof — that they find in their new families.

The recognition that children cannot be treated as an identical mass whose problems can be solved by identical treatments was one of the factors leading to the founding of the *Rauhe Haus* in 1832, and that inspired even the largest American orphanages to claim in their publicity circulars that they provided their inmates with a level of attention equivalent to what they would find in families. And of course, it was the recognition that no institution, even those on the "cottage" system, could provide true individual attention that led Charles Loring Brace to institute his Emigration Plan. But as was recognized by Brace's critics and substantiated and elaborated by psychologists and child welfare experts throughout the twentieth century, simply dumping children into families does not, all on its own, constitute individualized treatment. In modern foster care, an effort is supposed to be made not only to ensure the basic competence and decency of the foster families but to make sure that their capacities, interests, and other traits match those of the children placed with them. Unfortunately, 99 percent of foster care placements are made in such a hurry that a true match between child and parent is impossible.

In a typical situation, a caseworker goes into a home and decides to remove a child right away. The child, of course, is distraught, not only on account of the removal but often because of the issues that led to the removal. Nobody wants such a child to have to spend the night in an institution or — as often happens to teenagers, who are particularly hard to place — in the offices of the child welfare agency itself, so placement workers contact potential foster parents immediately, sometimes before the child has even been brought to the agency, and generally without any more knowledge than the child's sex, age, and race. As a result, children with severe psychological or medical needs are often placed with parents who are utterly incapable of handling them. At the same time, parents who might have the strength, training, and desire to handle such children end up being given children with only a normal array of problems and idiosyncrasies. Mismatches on this order are part of the reason that 54 percent of New York foster children undergo the trauma of switching places at least once during their tenure in the system, and 7 percent of children switch placements five times or more.[21]

Given the hurry in which foster children must be placed, matching children to homes can never be perfect, but it can be made worse — sometimes disastrously so — by budget cuts, as New York City's history illustrates. After averaging 21,000 for most of the 1960s, the number of children in foster care in New York began to rise in the early 1970s, peaking at 29,000 in 1975.[22] The city responded by placing a new emphasis on keeping families together rather than removing children. This policy change no doubt seemed progressive and humane during that decidedly liberal era, but it also considerably reduced the amount of money the city spent on foster care boarding fees — a more than welcome side effect given that in 1975 the city was also experiencing the worst financial crisis of its history.

Whatever its true inspiration, the new policy of family preservation encouraged a steady decline in New York's foster care population, which reached a low of 16,230 in 1984.[23] Then came the crack epidemic and the crisis in homelessness, which drove the foster care population to an all-time high of nearly 50,000 in 1991,[24] the beginning of yet another budget crisis. The city responded to the situation by redoubling the emphasis on family preservation. With the best of intentions, but little foresight, Mayor David Dinkins also hired hundreds of new caseworkers in 1990, only to fire most of them in the 1992 budget crunch. During this same period the Child Welfare Administration tried to compensate for its chronic cash shortage by submitting $37 million worth of false casework reports in order to make it look as if the city were substantially in compliance with federal regulations, and thus eligible for incentive payments.[25] With all of this confusion and corruption, the city muddled on, and gradually the crisis lessened. The number of children in foster care began to taper off, and more important, the number of possible placements reached a rough balance with the number of children who needed them.

All of this changed in 1995, the year of the "block grants." The first item of business for the new, decidedly conservative Congress elected in 1994 had been budget cuts, with the bulk of those cuts falling on social service programs. The spoonful of sugar by which this Congress got the states to swallow the bitter pill of reduced funding was the institution of the concept of "block grants." The idea was that while states would be given less money, there would also be fewer restrictions on how they could spend that money. In theory, they could fund their most effective and important programs more generously while cutting supposed "fat" — those programs that were ineffective or insignificant. But in the final analysis, all New York State's "Family and Children's Services Block Grant" really amounted to was a cut of $151 million in the funds available for these services. In response, the city not only made steep child welfare staff cuts but also reduced the boarding fees paid foster parents; the latter cut, in turn, caused a steep decline in the number of families willing to take foster children. This situation only became worse the following year, when a second tier of federal and state budget cuts reduced child welfare funds by an additional $176 million.[26]

The decline in the number of available placements for foster children might never have reached crisis proportions had it not been for the death of six-year-old Elisa Izquierdo. It is hard to imagine a case that could more graphically illustrate the tragic shortcomings of New

York's system for protecting children. Elisa's teachers, doctors, and neighbors had reported their suspicion that she was being abused by her parents to the Child Welfare Administration (CWA) on numerous occasions. A cursory investigation was made into her case, but ultimately, and despite new reports of abuse — some of which simply seem to have gotten lost — Elisa was allowed to remain with parents who, over a period of months, beat her, sexually assaulted her, forced her to drink ammonia and eat her own excrement, and finally bludgeoned her to death in November 1995.[27] When the crime was uncovered, the media were filled with pictures of the big-eyed waif and the shocking testimony of the teachers and doctors who had tried to get help for her. Newspaper editorialists conducted a thoroughly justified excoriation of the CWA for its failure to do its job.

All of this occurred during a decidedly different political environment than had prevailed in New York for the previous decades. The city had a new Republican mayor, Rudolph Giuliani. Newt Gingrich was in Washington, blaming welfare mothers for their own poverty and saying that the best thing for poor children was to take them away from their intractably immoral families and put them into orphanages. In this climate Elisa Izquierdo's death resulted in a radical reversal of child welfare strategy. City caseworkers were encouraged to remove children if there was even the slightest suspicion that they were in danger, and "family preservation" — villainized as "naive," "liberal," and "cruel" — became a decidedly less important goal.

Unfortunately, this policy shift caused a huge surge in the number of children needing foster care just at the point when there were fewer foster parents to take them. Many more children had to spend the night sleeping on pushed-together chairs and on the floor of the newly renamed Administration for Children's Services offices on Laight Street, and residential psychiatric services became crowded with children who didn't particularly need psychological counseling but had no place else to go. The policy shift's most serious consequence, however, was that child welfare agencies rushed a whole new crop of foster parents into service without subjecting them to adequate screening or giving them adequate training. The result was a rise in the number of children abused and killed while in foster care — among them Caprice Reid.

Caprice's story begins in 1983 when Betty Coker, a foster parent affiliated with the Children's Aid Society, adopted a boy and a girl who had been her foster children. Two years later she reversed the adoption and put the children back in foster care. The boy told a city caseworker that Coker had physically and emotionally abused him, but no one ever investigated his complaint. By this time, Coker was no longer working with the CAS.

Eleven years later, in February 1996, a caseworker with Little Flower Children's Services discovered that a group of brothers being cared for by Betty Coker and her daughter, Patricia Coker, had not been washed in weeks, and that the boys' sisters were dressed in stained underpants and shirts smeared with food. Little Flower banned the two women from serving as foster parents with their agency. But only a few months later the Cokers applied to be foster parents with another agency, Louise Wise Services. When this new agency requested evaluations from the Cokers' previous agencies, Little Flower apparently responded with only a tepid rendition of the events that had led them to ban the Cokers from their roster of foster parents. And the Children's Aid Society, not knowing of Betty Coker's adopted son's complaint to a city caseworker, gave her a strong enough recommendation that Louise Wise decided to take the two women on.

On July 22, 1996, three-year-old Caprice Reid and her three brothers were placed with the Cokers. In March 1997 Betty Coker threatened to attack Caprice's biological mother in the Brooklyn Family Court, but this outbreak prompted no investigation of the Cokers' home. The children were left where they were. Nothing at all was done.

Then in June 1997 the Cokers tied Caprice to a chair, refused to feed her for four days, and beat her with a stick until she had bruises all over her body, could not walk, and finally died.[28]

Although the worst of the placement shortage has passed, New York still has many fewer foster care "beds" than it has children to put in them. Michael Wagner, who is in charge of coordinating placements at the Children's Aid Society, said that during any given week he gets an average of fifteen requests for foster care placements from the ACS but has only five openings to offer, and these are generally unsuitable for the calls that come in: mostly for hard-to-place cases, large groups of siblings, sick infants, or suicidal teenagers.[29]

Despite such difficulties, most frontline child welfare workers feel more comfortable with the new child protection directive — epitomized by the slogan "When in doubt, pull 'em out." Rightly or wrongly, caseworkers believe that they have more control when they have removed a child from her parents and placed her in the care of paid employees of the state, and that this control translates into greater safety for the child and, not incidentally, for the caseworkers themselves. But despite this general sympathy with the latest directive, almost every frontline worker I spoke to voiced resentment at the constant shifting of city policies. When debating the pros and cons of child protection versus family preservation, most of these workers share the opinion of Nicholas Scoppetta, whom Mayor Giuliani chose to lead the Administration for Children's Services and enforce his new policy. "[T]his debate is a phony issue and a specious one," Scoppetta said. "It's not whether you err on the side of protecting families or protecting children but whether you accurately assess the needs of the child and the family."[30]

The debate is phony and the policy initiatives promoting either side in the debate are, at best, of limited effectiveness because they do not touch on the most essential element of child welfare work: treating the child as an individual. What matters is not whether the mass of children tend to fare better under a policy of removal or family preservation, but assessing whether any individual child would be better off in a foster home or left with his parents. And then what matters is providing this child and his birth or foster family with the services that will enable *them* — not the mass of children or families — to achieve their best possible outcome. When politicians, in front of TV cameras, proclaim major child welfare policy initiatives, they may earn a few percentage points in popularity polls and a favorable editorial or two, but all they get from frontline child welfare workers, even those who agree with their position, is a dismissive grunt or a cynical shrug of the shoulders. These workers know that almost nothing politicians do makes helping their clients any easier, and that those few improvements that do come along tend to be undone by the next administration, or the next budget crisis. They know that all most changes mean is more pointless forms to fill out.

What these workers need to do the job our society ostensibly wants them to do are lower caseloads, better training, adequate support services (including reliable computerized data banks), and massive cuts in paperwork and inefficient midlevel management. To be fair, Nicholas Scoppetta has made a terrific effort against formidable odds to meet some of these needs. But even with his reductions, New York's caseloads remain at least 50 percent higher than the Child Welfare

League's ideal.[31] The extra training Scoppetta now requires of case-workers (forty-eight as opposed to twenty days in the classroom, and nine months of instructional supervision)[32] is no substitute for a master's degree in social work and still leaves frontline caseworkers largely uninformed about such topics as domestic violence, substance abuse, crisis management, the needs of adolescents, and even the services available to help families in crisis.[33] And while Scoppetta has raised the average pay of caseworkers, it still remains well below that of sanitation workers. Finally, despite much talk about bringing the ACS's computer system into the twentieth century, thus far the city's child welfare records are kept on twenty-six separate systems that cannot talk to one another.

As for providing children and their families with the support services they need to get on their feet (addiction therapy, psychological counseling, and so on), Scoppetta's latest initiative, neighborhood-based foster care, seems a step in the right direction and has considerable sympathy among child welfare professionals. But it is hard to understand how he will be able to disperse the city's relatively centralized foster care and related social services throughout every neighborhood and keep his promise that the initiative will not cost the taxpayer an extra penny. What he is proposing is essentially a massive reduplication of effort. Instead of several big centralized service providers, there will be many smaller ones scattered throughout the city. At the very least this is going to require a considerable rise in real estate expenditures. And likewise, there is going to have to be a substantial escalation of personnel and equipment costs if these scattered centers — and the neighborhood-based foster care initiative itself — are going to be something more than hollow facades.

For more than a century we have known that we should monitor placements well and take care to ensure that foster children — or orphan train riders — are placed in decent homes. For more than a century we have known that every child's needs are different and that, therefore, every child needs a different sort of treatment — and also that every child needs to feel that we care about her for who she is, and not as one of many. At least since the dawn of wage labor we have known that if you need someone to do a difficult and important job, you should pay that person accordingly and only hire the most highly qualified and educated people. We know that we should do all of these things, and we can do them — some of them better now than ever before — but we don't do them. At least, we don't do them anywhere nearly as well as we could.

This is a choice. It is a choice based primarily on money. Yes, money will not solve all of the problems of the child welfare system. It would be simple fantasy to assume that even an ideal system could benefit every child who came into contact with it — or even save the life of every child who was in mortal danger. And certainly there is a lot that can be done to root out inefficiency and corruption in our present system. But to imply that by making a system completely efficient and legitimate — if even that were possible — we would free up enough cash to handle all the current problems of child welfare is no less of a fantasy.

The simple truth is that if we are going to have a child welfare system that does everything we know it can do, and that ostensibly we want it to do, we are going to have to spend more money. There is no way that reducing corruption and inefficiency is going to save more than the cost of the higher salaries necessary to attract a greater number of better-qualified caseworkers, therapists, lawyers, administrators, and other professionals to child welfare work. Nor will it offset the cost of funding family services well enough to do the jobs they are designed for or, finally, the cost of instituting and continually upgrading an integrated computer system that would allow all workers involved with a particular child access to all of the information available and necessary to adequately assess that child's needs and to act on that assessment.

We may believe that the sacredness of children and families is a fundamental American value. We may shake our heads and even shed a tear every time we hear of a child murdered by parents or foster parents whose true danger child welfare agencies failed to assess or act upon. And we may murmur over the newspaper at breakfast, or in front of the television at night, "This is appalling. This shouldn't happen. Something ought to be done." But when it comes time to open up our wallets, we say no. And when we go to the ballot box, we say no.

In these and dozens of other ways we are making a choice. It may be a choice made in ignorance, but ignorance can also be chosen: by a turning of the head, or a refusal to see how a child's misery can be made possible by our action or inaction. It is a choice to save money, but that does not mean it is free of cost.

Child welfare advocates no longer talk about their work as a means of taking the danger out of the "dangerous classes," but the fact remains that the failures of the foster care system end up in prisons in disproportionate numbers. While less than 1 percent of Americans have been in foster care, former foster children make up close to 14 percent of our prison population.[34] Yes, some of those people might have ended up committing crimes anyway, but some of them might have been saved if only they had gotten the help we are more than able to give them.

We all pay the cost of this failure. We pay it in the money we spend to keep an inmate incarcerated — $20,000 a year, which, as has been often pointed out, is close to the annual tuition at Harvard. The total cost of our extraordinarily high incarceration rate — the highest of any industrialized country in the world — is $35 billion a year.[35] We also pay for the failure of our foster care system in the $10 billion we spend annually on police forces,[36] and the additional expenses of security staff, burglar alarms, car alarms, fenced-in communities, crime insurance, and guns. We pay for it in fear, and we pay for it in the suffering we endure when all of our expensive defenses fail to protect us or when they backfire: when our children come across our guns and end up shooting themselves, or their classmates. But the greatest cost of our failure to do what we can do and know we can do is borne by children in the system — not only the Elisa Izquierdos and Caprice Reids, who have died, but also the thousands of children who have endured needless suffering because nobody could be bothered to see what they really needed and help them get it.

Child welfare organizations, even those affiliated with religious groups, also no longer talk about the danger to our eternal souls posed by our failure to give poor children what help we can. But you do not have to be a Christian, Jew, Buddhist, Muslim, or any sort of believer to understand that in our culpability, now and in the past, for the failures of our many mechanisms for helping poor children the moral character of our whole nation suffers, and that our whole nation has a lot to gain by doing what *can be done* and what is *right* to do for the neediest and most defenseless members of our society.

"There's a great work wants doing in this our generation . . ."

Notes

Prologue: Working for Human Happiness

1. George Matsell quoted in *Children and Youth in America: A Documentary History*, 3 vols., edited by Robert H. Bremner et al. (Cambridge, Mass.: Harvard University Press, 1970–74), 1:755.
2. Emma Brace, *The Life of Charles Loring Brace Told Chiefly in His Own Letters* (New York: Charles Scribner's Sons, 1894), 9–10, 71, 291, 69, 283, 284, 483.

Part I: Want

1. Charles Loring Brace, *The Dangerous Classes of New York and Twenty Years' Work Among Them* (New York: Wynkoop & Hallenbeck, 1872; facsimile ed., Silver Spring, Md.: National Association of Social Workers, 1973), 261–63.
2. Harry Morris, "My Life Story," in *Tears on Paper: Orphan Train History*, edited by Patricia J. Young and Frances E. Marks (privately printed, 1990), 228–29.

1. The Good Father

1. Paul Boyer, *Urban Masses and Moral Order in America: 1820–1920* (Cambridge, Mass.: Harvard University Press, 1978), 13–14.
2. Harriet Beecher Stowe, quoted in Joan D. Hedrick, *Harriet Beecher Stowe: A Life* (New York: Oxford University Press, 1994), 17.
3. Harriet Beecher Stowe, quoted in Brace, *The Life of Charles Loring Brace*, 3.
4. Harriet Beecher Stowe, *Oldtown Folks* (Boston: Houghton Mifflin, 1911), 2:38–39.
5. Catharine Beecher, quoted in Hedrick, *Harriet Beecher Stowe*, 26.
6. Ibid., 27.
7. Ibid., 24, 25.
8. Quoted in Kristine Elisabeth Nelson, "The Best Asylum: Charles Loring Brace and Foster Family Care" (Ph.D. diss., University of California at Berkeley, 1980), 15.
9. Ibid., 15–16.
10. Quoted in ibid., 19.
11. Geraldine Youcha, *Minding the Children: Child Care in America from Colonial Times to the Present* (New York: Charles Scribner's Sons, 1995), 22.
12. Nelson, "The Best Asylum," 48.

13. Quoted in ibid., 52.

14. Ibid., 68.

15. Mrs. Louisa Gurney Hoare, *Hints for the Improvement of Early Education and Nursery Discipline* (Dover: Samuel C. Stevens, 1826), 5–6.

16. Lydia Maria Child, *The Mother's Book* (Boston: Carter and Hendee, 1832), title page.

17. Lydia H. Sigourney, *Letters to Mothers* (New York: Harper & Brothers, 1842), 45.

18. Lydia Maria Child, *Letters from New York* (New York: C. S. Francis and Co., 1843), 196.

19. Child, *The Mother's Book,* 63.

20. Catharine Beecher quoted in Nelson, "The Best Asylum," 85, 86.

21. Child, *The Mother's Book,* 135.

22. Brace, *The Life of Charles Loring Brace,* 62–63.

23. Ibid., 34.

24. Ibid., 4.

25. Ibid., 75.

26. Ibid., 10–11.

27. Ibid., 7–8.

28. Horace Bushnell, "Unconscious Influence," *The American Pulpit* (Worcester, Mass.) 2, no. 10: 232–33.

29. Ibid., 230.

30. Ibid., 236.

31. Ibid., 240.

32. Ibid.

33. Brace, *The Life of Charles Loring Brace,* 4.

34. Ibid., 12.

35. Ibid., 16–17.

36. Ibid., 26.

37. Ibid., 62.

38. Ibid., 9–10.

39. Charles Caper McLaughlin, ed., *The Papers of Frederick Law Olmsted,* vol. 1, *1822–1852* (Baltimore: Johns Hopkins University Press, 1977).

40. Brace, *The Life of Charles Loring Brace,* 107–8.

41. Frederick Law Olmsted quoted in Thomas Bender, *Toward an Urban Vision: Ideas and Institutions in Nineteenth-Century America* (Baltimore: Johns Hopkins University Press, 1991), 159; originally from Broadus Mitchell, *Frederick Law Olmsted: A Critic of the Old South* (Baltimore: Johns Hopkins University Press, 1924), 39.

42. Frederick Law Olmsted quoted in Elizabeth Stevenson, *Park Maker: A Life of Frederick Law Olmsted* (New York: Macmillan, 1977), 27.

43. Brace, *The Life of Charles Loring Brace,* 61–62.

44. McLaughlin, *The Papers of Frederick Law Olmsted,* 1:313–15.

45. Brace, *The Life of Charles Loring Brace,* 38–39.

46. Ibid., 44–46.

2. Flood of Humanity

1. Kenneth T. Jackson, ed., *The Encyclopedia of New York City* (New Haven: Yale University Press, 1995), 923.

2. Quoted in Stevenson, *Park Maker*, 14.

3. Charles Dickens, *American Notes* (New York: Penguin, 1985), 128.

4. Ibid., 138.

5. Michael B. Katz, *In the Shadow of the Poorhouse: A Social History of Welfare in America* (New York: Basic Books, 1986), 4.

6. Jackson, *The Encyclopedia of New York City*, 359.

7. Ted C. Hinckley, *Alaskan John G. Brady: Missionary, Businessman, Judge, and Governor, 1878–1918* (Columbus: Ohio State University Press, 1982), 3.

8. Katz, *In the Shadow of the Poorhouse*, 8.

9. Claudia Goldin's study cited in Viviana A. Zelizer, *Pricing the Priceless Child: The Changing Social Value of Children* (New York: Basic Books, 1985), 58.

10. Edward K. Spann, *The New Metropolis: New York City, 1840–1857* (New York: Columbia University Press, 1981), 262.

11. George Matsell quoted in Bremner et al., *Children and Youth in America*, 1:755; see also Christine Stansell, *City of Women: Sex and Class in New York, 1789–1860* (New York: Alfred A. Knopf, 1986), 195.

12. Miriam Z. Langsam, *Children West: A History of the Placing-Out System of the New York Children's Aid Society, 1853–1890* (Madison: State Historical Society for the Department of History, University of Wisconsin, 1964), vii.

13. Brace, *The Life of Charles Loring Brace*, 58–59.

14. Ibid., 61.

15. Ibid., 63.

16. Ibid., 64.

17. Ibid., 62–63.

18. Jackson, *The Encyclopedia of New York City*, 1007.

19. Ibid., 219.

20. Brace, *The Life of Charles Loring Brace*, 73–74.

21. Ibid., 16.

22. Ibid., 70.

23. Ibid., 79–80.

24. Ibid., 79.

25. Child, *Letters from New York*, 210.

26. Ibid., 201, 206.

27. Ibid., 204.

28. Brace, *The Life of Charles Loring Brace*, 76.

29. Ibid., 77–78.

30. Ibid., 88.

31. Ibid., 82–83.

32. Ibid., 146.

33. Ibid., 90.

34. Charles Loring Brace, *Home-Life in Germany* (New York: Charles Scribner, 1853), 265.

35. Ibid., v.

36. Brace, *The Life of Charles Loring Brace*, 114.

37. Boyer, *Urban Masses*, 95.

38. Child, *Letters from New York*, 209.

39. Brace, *Home-Life in Germany*, 91.

40. Ibid., 96.
41. Brace, *The Life of Charles Loring Brace*, 98–100.
42. Ibid., 102.
43. Ibid., 103.
44. Ibid., 128.
45. Charles Loring Brace, *Hungary in 1851; With an Experience of the Austrian Police* (New York: Charles Scribner, 1852), 274.
46. Ibid., 278.
47. All the details and quotes pertaining to Brace's interrogation are from *Hungary in 1851*, 279–91.
48. Ibid., 300–301.
49. Ibid., 302.
50. Ibid., 326–27.
51. Quoted in Brace, *The Life of Charles Loring Brace*, 145.

Part II: Doing

1. William Colopy Desmond, *Sketches and Incidents in the Office of the Children's Aid Society*, handwritten journal (CAS archives), 177.
2. Children's Aid Society, *Record Book 6*, 442.

3. City Missionary

1. Brace, *The Life of Charles Loring Brace*, 148.
2. For the sake of comparison, Brace's six-dollar weekly salary for part-time teaching at the Rutgers Institute brought him approximately three hundred dollars annually.
3. Brace, *The Life of Charles Loring Brace*, 153–54.
4. Ibid., 178.
5. Ibid., 181.
6. Ibid., 182.
7. Ibid., 180.
8. Ibid., 179.
9. The location of both the Old Brewery and the original mission is now occupied by the New York County Court House, not so much by coincidence as design. After nearly a century of trying to reform Five Points, the city finally gave up in the 1880s and simply razed the entire neighborhood, replacing it with parks and outsized marble edifices dedicated to the law and civic bureaucracy.
10. Brace, *The Dangerous Classes*, 77–78.
11. Brace, *The Life of Charles Loring Brace*, 180.
12. Brace, *The Dangerous Classes*, 158.
13. Ibid., 145–46.
14. Ibid., 78.
15. John Earl Williams, *First Annual Report of the Executive Committee of the Children's Mission to the Children of the Destitute* (Boston: Benjamin H. Greene, 1850), 1.

16. The statistics and the *Evening Post* report come from Spann, *The New Metropolis,* 253.
17. Ibid., 255.
18. Williams, *First Annual Report,* 6.
19. Brace, *The Dangerous Classes,* 98–99.
20. Ibid., 302.
21. All quotes in this section from Brace, *The Dangerous Classes,* 80–81.
22. Charles Loring Brace, *Short Sermons to News Boys.* The cover and title pages are missing, but the book seems to have been published in the mid-1860s. From the collection of the Children's Aid Society.

4. Draining the City, Saving the Children

1. Brace, *The Life of Charles Loring Brace,* 160.
2. Charles Loring Brace, first publicity circular of the Children's Aid Society, New York (publisher unknown, March 1853).
3. Brace, *The Dangerous Classes,* 82.
4. Ibid., 96.
5. Ibid., 76–77.
6. Charles Dickens, *Martin Chuzzlewit* (New York: Penguin, 1968), 317–18.
7. All information regarding a typical newsboy's day is from John Morrow, *A Voice Among the Newsboys* (New York: privately published, 1860), 127–33.
8. Brace, *The Dangerous Classes,* 109.
9. Charles Loring Brace, *Eleventh Annual Report of the Children's Aid Society* (New York: Wynkoop & Hallenbeck, 1864), 12.
10. Brace, *The Dangerous Classes,* 100.
11. Ibid., 102.
12. See chapter 6.
13. Brace, *The Dangerous Classes,* 102–3.
14. Ibid., 105.
15. Ibid., 109.
16. Ibid., 106.

5. Journey to Dowagiac

1. Langsam, *Children West,* 17.
2. Brace, *The Dangerous Classes,* 410.
3. Bruce Bellingham, "'Little Wanderers': A Socio-historical Study of the Nineteenth-Century Origins of Child Fostering and Adoption Reform, Based on Early Records of the New York Children's Aid Society" (Ph.D. diss., University of Pennsylvania, 1984), 313–14.
4. Ibid., 302.
5. Ibid., 185–86.
6. Ibid., 182.
7. Ibid., 186.
8. Charles Loring Brace, "Daily Journal."

9. Brace, *The Dangerous Classes,* 225.

10. Brace, "Daily Journal" (emphasis in the original).

11. Brace, *First Annual Report,* 19.

12. Langsam, *Children West,* 27.

13. Brace, *The Dangerous Classes,* 227–28.

14. Ibid., 334–35.

15. LeRoy Ashby, *Endangered Children: Dependency, Neglect, and Abuse in American History* (New York: Twayne Publishers, 1997), 24.

16. Brace, *The Dangerous Classes,* 407–8; William W. Sanger, M.D., *The History of Prostitution: Its Extent, Causes, and Effect Throughout the World* (New York: Harper & Bros., 1858), 481.

17. Langsam, *Children West,* 35.

18. Marilyn Irvin Holt, *The Orphan Trains: Placing Out in America* (Lincoln: University of Nebraska Press, 1992), 48.

19. All the quotes are from E. P. Smith's journal, which was published in Charles Loring Brace, *Third Annual Report of the Children's Aid Society* (New York: M. B. Wynkoop, 1856), 54–60.

20. Emphasis in the original.

21. Most likely the girls were German, speakers of *deutsch,* and therefore called "Dutch" by nineteenth-century Americans.

22. Emphasis in the original.

23. Emphasis in the original.

24. Children's Aid Society, "Company Books," vol. 1, 1.

25. Brace, *The Life of Charles Loring Brace,* 192–93.

6. A Voice Among the Newsboys

1. Brace, *The Life of Charles Loring Brace,* 197–98.

2. Ibid., 195.

3. Ibid., 204.

4. Ibid., 211.

5. Ibid., 220.

6. Except where otherwise noted, all information concerning Johnny Morrow and his family comes from Morrow, *A Voice Among the Newsboys.*

7. Anna Hope, "The Boy Who Confessed His Sin," *The Independent* (late 1854 or 1855); reprinted in *Newsboy,* edited by Jack Bales (Horatio Alger Society newsletter, Jacksonville, Ill.), 16, no. 1 (August 1977): 21–22.

8. Emphasis in the original.

9. Emphasis in the original.

10. Emphasis in the original.

11. Actually there were eight. Johnny seems to have forgotten to count himself.

12. Emphasis in the original.

13. Children's Aid Society, record book, vol. 4, 76.

14. Charles Loring Brace, "A News Boy's Funeral," *The Independent,* June 6, 1861; reprinted in Charles Loring Brace, *Ninth Annual Report of the Children's Aid Society* (New York: Wynkoop & Hallenbeck, 1862), 34–37.

15. Charles Loring Brace, "The Little Theologue," reprinted in Bales, *Newsboy.*
16. Brace, "A News Boy's Funeral."
17. The third anniversary of the founding of the CAS, or the second anniversary of the founding of the Newsboys' Lodging House, the first in February and the second in March.
18. Probably Washington Square.
19. William Colopy Desmond, "Incidents and Sketches Among the Newsboys" (handwritten journal in CAS archives), pt. 4, 123–24.
20. Ibid., pt. 3, 59.
21. "Cars" generally refers to streetcars but can also refer to railroad cars.
22. His stepmother.
23. William Colopy Desmond, "Incidents and Sketches," 81–83.
24. Langsam, *Children West,* 27.
25. Emphasis added.
26. Brace, "A News Boy's Funeral."
27. Hope, "The Boy Who Confessed His Sin."
28. Brace, "A News Boy's Funeral."
29. Ibid.

7. Happy Circle

1. Charles Loring Brace, *Sixth Annual Report of the Children's Aid Society* (New York: Wynkoop, Hallenbeck & Thomas, 1859), 9.
2. Bellingham, "Little Wanderers,'" 52.
3. Ibid., 335.
4. Henry W. Thurston, *The Dependent Child* (1930; reprint, New York: Arno Press, 1974), 132–33.
5. Based on figures in Children's Rights/Marisol Joint Case Review Team, *Marisol v. Giuliani Case Record Review: Services to Children in Foster Care and Their Families* (December 1997), 119.
6. Children's Aid Society, "Record Book," vol. 3, 296.
7. Ibid., vol. 6, 442.
8. Bellingham, "Little Wanderers,'" 237.
9. Brace, first CAS publicity circular.
10. Jackson, *The Encyclopedia of New York City,* 298, 1007; Spann, *The New Metropolis,* 253.
11. Charles Loring Brace, *Fourth Annual Report of the Children's Aid Society* (New York: Wynkoop, Hallenbeck & Thomas, 1857), 6.
12. Nelson, "The Best Asylum," 222.
13. Quoted in ibid., 223.
14. Langsam, *Children West,* 27; Nelson, "The Best Asylum," 212.
15. Bremner et al., *Children and Youth in America,* 1:673.
16. Nelson, "The Best Asylum," 224 (emphasis in the original).
17. Ibid., 225.
18. Bremner et al., *Children and Youth in America,* 1:744–45.
19. Nelson, "The Best Asylum," 224.

20. Bremner et al., *Children and Youth in America,* 1:743–44.

21. Brace, *The Dangerous Classes,* 235.

22. Ibid., 238–40 (emphasis in the original).

23. Charles Loring Brace, *The Best Method of Disposing of Our Pauper and Vagrant Children* (New York: Wynkoop, Hallenbeck & Thomas, 1859), 14.

24. Nelson, "The Best Asylum," 214.

25. Brace, *The Dangerous Classes,* 238.

26. Brace, *The Life of Charles Loring Brace,* 239–40.

27. Ibid., 232, 245.

28. Ibid., 234.

29. Ibid., 237.

30. Ibid., 242.

31. Ibid., 248.

32. Ibid., 249.

33. Ibid., 244 (emphasis in the original).

34. Ibid., 245.

35. Ibid., 246.

36. Ibid., 265.

37. Ibid., 255.

38. Charles Loring Brace, *A Statement to the Public of a Portion of the Work of the Children's Aid Society* (publisher unknown [probably Wynkoop & Hallenbeck], 1863), 1, 2.

39. Jackson, *The Encyclopedia of New York City,* 191–92.

40. *The Irish World* (New York), May 9, 1874, 1.

41. Nelson, "The Best Asylum," 350.

42. Brace, *The Dangerous Classes,* 199.

43. Levi Silliman Ives, *New York Catholic Protectory, First Annual Report, 1864,* quoted in Bremner et al., *Children and Youth in America,* 1:748.

44. Quoted in Bremner et al., *Children and Youth in America,* 1:748.

45. Ives discontinued the protectory's outplacement program after experimenting with it for a year, but it was reinstated after his death.

46. Ashby, *Endangered Children,* 50.

47. Annette R. Fry, *The Orphan Trains* (New York: Macmillan, 1994), 37.

48. Brace, *The Dangerous Classes,* 408.

49. Young and Marks, *Tears on Paper,* 257–59, 345–46; Fry, *The Orphan Trains,* 89–92.

50. Fry, *The Orphan Trains,* 44.

51. Author interview, Springdale, Ark., October 3, 1997.

52. Holt, *The Orphan Trains,* 137.

53. Brace, *The Dangerous Classes,* 435–37.

54. Ibid., 439; Langsam, *Children West,* 17.

8. Almost a Miracle

1. Brace, *The Dangerous Classes,* 261.

2. Ibid., 262.

3. CAS, *Fiftieth Annual Report,* vii.

4. Quoted in Hinckley, *Alaskan John G. Brady.*

5. Ibid., 355, 370.

6. Brace, *The Dangerous Classes,* 262.

7. Fry, *The Orphan Trains,* 64.

8. Children's Aid Society, "Record Book," vol. 7, 36.

9. Ibid., 36.

10. Hinckley, *Alaskan John G. Brady,* 14.

11. Ibid., 14.

12. Ibid., 11.

13. Ibid., 15.

14. Brace, *The Dangerous Classes,* 263.

15. Hinckley, *Alaskan John G. Brady,* 29–30.

16. Ibid., 35.

17. Ibid., 37.

18. Ibid., 60.

19. Ibid., 67.

20. Ibid., 240.

21. N. Scott Mommaday, "The American West and the Burden of Belief," in *The West: An Illustrated History* by Geoffrey C. Ward (Boston: Little, Brown, 1996), 381.

22. Hinckley, *Alaskan John G. Brady,* 119–20.

23. Ibid., 120.

24. Ibid., 165.

25. Ibid., 172.

26. Ibid., 192.

27. Ibid., 195.

28. Ibid., 276.

29. Children's Aid Society, "Record Book," vol. 7, 35.

30. *The National Cyclopedia of American Biography* (New York: James T. White & Co., 1898), 1:320.

31. Robert Sobel and John Raimo, eds., *Biographical Directory of Governors of the United States, 1789–1978* (Westport, Conn.: Meckler Books, 1978), 3:1171–72.

32. Ibid.

33. Hinckley, *Alaskan John G. Brady,* 211.

34. Ibid., 212.

35. Ibid., 224.

36. Ibid., 278, 282–83.

37. Ibid., 184.

38. Ibid., 362.

39. Charles Loring Brace, 2nd, *The Children's Aid Society of New York in Its Seventieth Year* (publisher unknown, 1923), 10.

40. Children's Aid Society, *Sixty-fifth Annual Report* (New York, 1917), 12–13.

41. Ibid., 13. The *Sixty-fifth Annual Report* actually lists 113,503 Emigration Plan placements. But because this list includes some adults and many children who were entered as new cases two or three times, a conservative estimate seems more realistic.

42. Brace, *Best Method,* 16; Brace, *The Dangerous Classes; The Children's Aid Society of New York: Its Emigration or Placing-Out System and Its Results* (New York, 1910), 11.

Part III: Redoing

1. Brace, *First Annual Report,* 27–29.

9. Invisible Children

1. Brace, *The Life of Charles Loring Brace,* 257.
2. Charles L. Brace, *The Races of the Old World: A Manual of Ethnology* (New York: Charles Scribner, 1863), 494–95.
3. Ibid., 462–63.
4. Ibid., 467.
5. Ibid., 441.
6. Bellingham, "'The Little Wanderers,'" 246.
7. Brace, *Sixth Annual Report,* 37.
8. Charles Loring Brace, letter to Colonel J. Howland, April 2, 1863, CAS Archive.
9. Brace, *Fourth Annual Report,* 57.
10. Charles Loring Brace, *Second Annual Report of the Children's Aid Society* (New York: M. B. Wynkoop, 1855), 27.
11. Brace, *The Dangerous Classes,* 214.
12. Charles Loring Brace, *Sixteenth Annual Report of the Children's Aid Society,* New York: Wynkoop & Hallenbeck, 1869, 33.
13. Charles Loring Brace, *Fifteenth Annual Report of the Children's Aid Society* (New York: Wynkoop & Hallenbeck, 1868), 46.
14. Brace 2nd, *The Children's Aid Society of New York,* 10.
15. Brace, *The Life of Charles Loring Brace,* 364–65. In this same letter, Brace mentioned that, twenty-nine years after her death, he still missed his sister Emma so deeply that he could not bear to read her letters and thought of her constantly.
16. Holt, *The Orphan Trains,* 64.
17. Thurston, *The Dependent Child,* 133.
18. Brace, *The Dangerous Classes,* 106, 303.
19. Ibid., 115.
20. Brace, first CAS publicity circular, 2.
21. Charles Loring Brace, *Thirteenth Annual Report of the Children's Aid Society* (New York: Wynkoop & Hallenbeck, 1866), 13.
22. Charles Loring Brace, *Twenty-fifth Annual Report of the Children's Aid Society* (New York: Wynkoop & Hallenbeck, 1879), 20–21.
23. Brace, *Thirteenth Annual Report,* 13–14.
24. Brace, *Eleventh Annual Report,* 12.
25. Brace, *The Dangerous Classes,* 115.
26. Ibid., 115.
27. Brace, *Thirteenth Annual Report,* 13.
28. Charles Loring Brace, *Twelfth Annual Report of the Children's Aid Society* (New York: Wynkoop & Hallenbeck, 1865), 16.
29. Brace, *The Dangerous Classes,* 115.
30. Stansell, *City of Women,* 181; Timothy J. Gilfoyle, *City of Eros: New York City, Prostitution, and the Commercialization of Sex* (New York: Norton, 1992), 69.

31. Sanger, *The History of Prostitution,* 455.

32. Ibid., 481.

33. Ibid., 488.

34. Brace, *Twelfth Annual Report,* 14.

35. Ibid., 14.

36. Brace, *Twenty-fifth Annual Report,* 21.

37. Brace, *Eleventh Annual Report,* 12.

38. Ibid., 15.

39. Brace, *Twenty-fifth Annual Report,* 24.

40. Bellingham, "Little Wanderers,'" 329.

41. Sanger, *The History of Prostitution.* 178.

42. Marguerite Thomson, interview with the author, Springdale, Ark., October 2, 1997.

43. Alice Bullis Ayler, interview with the author, Springdale, Ark., October 3, 1997.

44. Brace, *The Dangerous Classes,* 116.

45. Mary Warner Blanchard, *Oscar Wilde's America: Counterculture in the Gilded Age* (New Haven: Yale University Press, 1998), 13.

46. Ibid., 15, 17.

47. Carl Bode, "Introduction" to *Ragged Dick and Struggling Upward* by Horatio Alger (New York: Penguin, 1986), xvii.

48. Ibid., xiv (emphasis in the original).

10. Neglect of the Poor

1. Brace, *The Life of Charles Loring Brace,* 267.

2. Ibid., 215.

3. Ibid., 279.

4. Ibid., 283–84.

5. Quoted in Ashby, *Endangered Children,* 64.

6. Langsam, *Children West,* 27.

7. Brace, *The Life of Charles Loring Brace,* 330.

8. *New York Times,* February 8 and 15, 1871; *New York Tribune* and *New York Evening Post,* February 15, 1871.

9. Langsam, *Children West,* 22.

10. Brace, *The Life of Charles Loring Brace,* 335–36.

11. Ibid., 338.

12. Brace, quoted in Nelson, "The Best Asylum," 214.

13. Langsam, *Children West,* 56.

14. Ibid., 56–57.

15. *History of Johnson County, Iowa* (Iowa City: n.p., 1883), 423.

16. Holt, *The Orphan Trains,* 100–101.

17. Langsam, *Children West,* 57.

18. Ibid., 57–58.

19. Nelson, "The Best Asylum," 233.

20. *New York Times,* April 10, 1874, quoted in Bremner et al., *Children and Youth in America,* 2:186.

21. *New York Times*, April 22, 1874, quoted in Bremner et al., *Children and Youth in America*, 2:189.
22. Ashby, *Endangered Children*, 62.
23. Zelizer, *Pricing the Priceless Child*, 176.
24. Bremner et al., *Children and Youth in America*, 2:291–92.
25. Nelson, "The Best Asylum," 236–37; Langsam, *Children West*, 58–59.
26. Nelson, "The Best Asylum," 236.
27. Quoted in Langsam, *Children West*, 60.
28. Brace, *The Life of Charles Loring Brace*, 362.
29. Ibid., 403.
30. Quoted in Bremner et al., *Children and Youth in America*, 2:307.
31. All quotes from Hastings H. Hart study ibid., 2:305–9.
32. Charles Loring Brace, *Thirty-second Annual Report of the Children's Aid Society* (New York: Wynkoop & Hallenbeck, 1885).
33. Quoted in Holt, *The Orphan Trains*, 58–59.
34. From Harry Morris, "My Life Story by Harry Morris (Shorty)," collected in Young and Marks, *Tears on Paper*, 205–12.
35. Quoted in Holt, *The Orphan Trains*, 149.
36. Nelson, "The Best Asylum," 244.

11. The Trials of Charley Miller

1. Except where otherwise noted, all information in this chapter comes from the transcript of Charley Miller's trial, December 8–11, 1890, in Cheyenne, Wyoming, and reports in the *Cheyenne Daily Leader*, September 23, 1890, to April 23, 1892.
2. Children's Aid Society, "Record Book," vol. 27, 90.
3. Amos Barber's correspondence provided by the Wyoming State Archives, Department of Commerce.
4. T. A. Larson, *History of Wyoming* (Lincoln: University of Nebraska Press, 1965), 230.

12. The Death and Life of Charles Loring Brace

1. Brace, *The Life of Charles Loring Brace*, 279–80.
2. Ibid., 430.
3. Ibid., 449–50.
4. Ibid., 462.
5. Ibid., 463–64.
6. Ibid., 470.
7. Ibid., 478.
8. Walter I. Trattner, *Homer Folks: Pioneer in Social Welfare* (New York: Columbia University Press, 1968), 24.
9. Quoted in Zelizer, *Pricing the Priceless Child*, 186.
10. Bremner et al., *Children and Youth in America*, 2:324.
11. Ibid.
12. Quoted in Trattner, *Homer Folks*, 27.

13. Ibid., 48.
14. Quoted in Walter I. Trattner, *From Poor Law to Welfare State* (New York: Free Press, 1989), 118.
15. Ibid., 120.
16. Quoted in Michael Shapiro, *Solomon's Sword* (New York: Times Books, 1999), 153.
17. The original Hull House building is now a museum, and the social work of the institution is carried out by the Hull House Association, an affiliation of social service agencies. Only the director of the Henry Street Settlement is required to live at the settlement house itself.
18. Trattner, *Homer Folks*, 104.
19. Quoted in Bremner et al., *Children and Youth in America*, 2:365.
20. Ibid., 2:366–67.
21. Katz, *In the Shadow of the Poorhouse*, 126–27.
22. Trattner, *Homer Folks*, 115.
23. Ashby, *Endangered Children*, 96–97.
24. Children's Aid Society, "Argument upon Senator Brown's Bill Entitled an Act to Regulate the Placing-Out of Children," 1897, 5 (CAS Archives).
25. CAS, *Fiftieth Annual Report*, 21.
26. Ibid., 24.
27. Ibid., 25.
28. Zelizer, *Pricing the Priceless Child*, 14.
29. Langsam, *Children West*, 27.
30. CAS, *Fiftieth Annual Report*, 15.
31. CAS Archives

Conclusion: Legacy

1. Brace, *Fourth Annual Report*.
2. Center for New York City Law, New York University, *City Law* 4, no. 5 (September–October 1998): 97, 98–104.
3. Ann McCabe, CAS director of foster care and adoption services, interview with the author, New York City, October 26, 1998; and Administration for Children's Services (ACS) Public Affairs Office.
4. Children's Aid Society, *1998 Annual Report*, inside front cover statement.
5. Michael R. Petit, et al., *Child Abuse and Neglect: A Look at the States, 1999 CWLA Stat Book* (Washington, D.C.: CWLA Press, 1999), 72.
6. Ibid., 95.
7. Rachel L. Swarns, "Three Years After a Girl's Murder, Five Siblings Lack Stable Homes," *New York Times*, August 4, 1998.
8. "*Marisol v. Giuliani*, Case Record Review: Services to Families with Open Indicated Cases," prepared by Marisol Joint Case Review Team, September 5, 1997, 6.
9. Ibid., 23.
10. Ibid., 3.
11. Petit et al., *Child Abuse and Neglect*, 225, 53, 136–37.
12. "Under Attack, Foster Agencies Link Lapses to Budget Cuts," *New York Times*, February 26, 1998.

13. Marcia Robinson Lowry, interview with the author, New York City, October 6, 1998.

14. Special Child Welfare Advisory Panel (SCWAP) (New York City), *Advisory Report on Front Line and Supervisory Practice,* March 9, 2000, 55.

15. New York City Department of Sanitation Press Office, October 6, 2000.

16. ACS web page (career opportunities), July 27, 1999.

17. SCWAP, *Advisory Report,* 56.

18. Name withheld for privacy, interview with the author, New York City, January 22, 1999.

19. SCWAP, *Advisory Report,* 46.

20. *Marisol v. Giuliani,* 2:47, 48; 3:51.

21. Ibid., 3:5.

22. New York State Social Services Department, "1983 Annual Report, Statistical Supplement."

23. ACS public affairs office.

24. A portion of that rise, perhaps as much as 25 percent, may have been due to the decision in 1988 to begin counting children placed with family members as part of the foster care population.

25. Nina Bernstein, "City and State Pay $49 Million to Settle Foster Care Fraud Lawsuit," *New York Times,* November 11, 1998.

26. Bob Herbert, "An Unending Tragedy," *New York Times,* February 26, 1998.

27. Swarns, "Three Years After a Girl's Murder, Five Siblings Lack Stable Homes"; Dale Russakoff, "The Protector," *The New Yorker,* April 21, 1997, 61.

28. Rachel L. Swarns, "Foster Agencies Called Lax, and Faulted in a Girl's Death," *New York Times,* January 21, 1999.

29. Michael Wagner, interview with the author, New York City, November 18, 1998.

30. Russakoff, "The Protector," 62.

31. SCWAP, *Advisory Report,* 12.

32. ACS Press Office, September 18, 2000.

33. SCWAP, *Advisory Report,* 12.

34. Carolyn Harlow, U.S. Bureau of Justice Statistics (USBOJS) Office of Justice Programs.

35. Jim Stephan, USBOJS Office of Justice Programs.

36. Sue Lindgren, USBOJS Office of Justice Programs.

Bibliography

Children's Aid Society Archives

Brace, Charles Loring. 1853. "Daily Journal." Typed manuscript.
Brace, Charles Loring. N.d. (cover and title page missing). *Short Sermons to News Boys.*
Company Books. 1854–1909. Vols. 1–4. Handwritten register.
Desmond, William Colopy. 1857–59. *Sketches and Incidents in the Office of the Children's Aid Society.* Handwritten journal.
Macy, John, and C. C. Tracy. 1855–57. *Incidents and Sketches Among the Newsboys.* Handwritten journal.
Record Books. 1854–1916. Vols. 2–57. Handwritten registers and journals.

Books and Pamphlets

Ashby, LeRoy. 1997. *Endangered Children: Dependency, Neglect, and Abuse in American History.* New York: Twayne Publishers.
Ashton, T. S. 1969. *The Industrial Revolution, 1760–1830.* London: Oxford University Press.
Bellingham, Bruce. 1984. "'Little Wanderers': A Socio-historical Study of the Nineteenth-Century Origins of Child Fostering and Adoption Reform, Based on Early Records of the New York Children's Aid Society." Ph.D. diss., University of Pennsylvania.
Bender, Thomas. 1987. *New York Intellect.* Baltimore: Johns Hopkins University Press.
———. 1975. *Toward an Urban Vision.* Baltimore: Johns Hopkins University Press.
Blanchard, Mary Warner. 1998. *Oscar Wilde's America: Counterculture in the Gilded Age.* New Haven, Conn.: Yale University Press.
Bode, Carl. 1986. "Introduction" to *Ragged Dick and Struggling Upward* by Horatio Alger. New York: Penguin.
Boyer, Paul. 1978. *Urban Masses and Moral Order in America: 1820–1920.* Cambridge, Mass.: Harvard University Press.
Brace, Charles Loring. 1868. *Address on Industrial Schools Delivered to the Teachers of the Schools, November 13th, 1868.* New York: Wynkoop & Hallenbeck.
———. 1859. *The Best Method of Disposing of Our Pauper and Vagrant Children.* New York: Wynkoop, Hallenbeck & Thomas.

————. 1853 (March). "Children's Aid Society." Publicity circular. N.p.

————. 1973. *The Dangerous Classes of New York and Twenty Years' Work Among Them.* Facsimile ed., Silver Spring, Md.: National Association of Social Workers. (Originally published 1872, New York: Wynkoop & Hallenbeck).

————. 1864. *Eleventh Annual Report of the Children's Aid Society.* New York: Wynkoop & Hallenbeck.

————. 1868. *Fifteenth Annual Report of the Children's Aid Society.* New York: Wynkoop & Hallenbeck.

————. 1854. *First Annual Report of the Children's Aid Society.* New York: C. W. Benedict.

————. 1885. *Forty-second Annual Report of the Children's Aid Society.* New York: Wynkoop & Hallenbeck.

————. 1853. *Home-Life in Germany.* New York: Charles Scribner.

————. 1852. *Hungary in 1851; With an Experience of the Austrian Police.* New York: Charles Scribner.

————. 1863. *The Races of the Old World: A Manual of Ethnology.* New York: Charles Scribner.

————. 1855. *Second Annual Report of the Children's Aid Society.* New York: M. B. Wynkoop.

————. 1869. *Sixteenth Annual Report of the Children's Aid Society.* New York: Wynkoop & Hallenbeck.

————. 1859. *Sixth Annual Report of the Children's Aid Society.* New York: Wynkoop, Hallenbeck & Thomas.

————. 1863. *A Statement to the Public of a Portion of the Work of the Children's Aid Society.* N.p.

————. 1856. *Third Annual Report of the Children's Aid Society.* New York: M. B. Wynkoop.

————. 1866. *Thirteenth Annual Report of the Children's Aid Society.* New York: Wynkoop & Hallenbeck.

————. 1865. *Twelfth Annual Report of the Children's Aid Society.* New York: Wynkoop & Hallenbeck.

————. 1879. *Twenty-fifth Annual Report of the Children's Aid Society.* New York: Wynkoop & Hallenbeck.

Brace, 2nd, Charles Loring. 1923. *The Children's Aid Society of New York in Its Seventieth Year.* New York: Children's Aid Society.

————. 1903. *Fiftieth Annual Report of the Children's Aid Society for Year Ending October 1, 1902.* New York: Wynkoop, Hallenbeck, Crawford.

Brace, Emma. 1894. *The Life of Charles Loring Brace Told Chiefly in His Own Letters.* New York: Charles Scribner's Sons.

Bremer, Francis J. 1995. *The Puritan Experiment: New England Society from Bradford to Edwards.* Hanover, N.H.: University Press of New England.

Bremner, Robert H., et al., eds. 1970–74. *Children and Youth in America: A Documentary History.* Vols. 1–3. Cambridge, Mass.: Harvard University Press.

Bushnell, Horace. 1847. *Discourse on Christian Nurture.* Boston: Massachusetts Sabbath School Society.

————. 1985. *Sermons.* New York: Paulist Press.

Child, Lydia Maria. 1843. *Letters from New York*. New York: C. S. Francis and Co.

————. 1832. *The Mother's Book*. Boston: Carter and Hendee.

Children's Mission. 1856. *Light Dawning: Fruits of the Children's Mission*. Boston: John Wilson & Son.

Children's Rights/Marisol Joint Case Review Team. 1997 (December). *Marisol v. Giuliani Case Record Review: Services to Children in Foster Care and Their Families*. Vols. 1–3.

Cook, Jeanne F. 1994. "Experiences of Orphan Train Riders: Implications for Child Welfare Policy." Ph.D. diss., University of South Carolina.

Delbanco, Andrew. 1995. *The Death of Satan: How Americans Have Lost the Sense of Evil*. New York: Farrar, Straus and Giroux.

Dickens, Charles. 1985. *American Notes for General Circulation*. New York: Penguin. (Originally published in 1842)

————. 1984. *Martin Chuzzlewit*. New York: Penguin. (Originally published in 1843–44)

Dykstra, Robert R. 1968. *The Cattle Towns*. New York: Alfred A. Knopf.

Ellington, George. 1869. *Women of New York; or, The Underworld of the Great City*. New York: New York Book Co.

Executive Committee of the Children's Mission to the Children of the Destitute. 1850. *First Annual Report of the Executive Committee of the Children's Mission to the Children of the Destitute*. Boston: Benjamin H. Greene.

Fry, Annette R. 1994. *The Orphan Trains*. New York: Macmillan.

Gilfoyle, Timothy J. 1992. *City of Eros: New York City, Prostitution, and the Commercialization of Sex*. New York: Norton.

Governors of the Alms House. 1856. *Seventh Annual Report of the Governors of the Alms House, New York, for the Year 1855*. New York: Hall, Clayton & Co.

Hedrick, Joan D. 1994. *Harriet Beecher Stowe: A Life*. New York: Oxford University Press.

Hinckley, Ted C. 1982. *Alaskan John G. Brady: Missionary, Businessman, Judge, and Governor, 1878–1918*. Columbus: Ohio State University Press.

Hoare, Mrs. Louisa Gurney. 1826. *Hints for the Improvement of Early Education and Nursery Discipline*. Dover: Samuel C. Stevens.

Holloran, Peter C. 1989. *Boston's Wayward Children: Social Services for Homeless Children, 1830–1930*. Rutherford, N.J.: Fairleigh Dickinson University Press.

Holt, Marilyn Irvin. 1992. *The Orphan Trains: Placing Out in America*. Lincoln: University of Nebraska Press.

Jackson, Kenneth T., ed. 1995. *The Encyclopedia of New York City*. New Haven, Conn.: Yale University Press.

Johnson, Mary Ellen, ed. *Orphan Train Riders: Their Own Stories*. Vols. 1–4. Baltimore: Gateway Press, 1992–97.

Katz, Michael B. 1986. *In the Shadow of the Poorhouse: A Social History of Welfare in America*. New York: Basic Books.

Kett, Joseph F. 1971. "Adolescence and Youth in Nineteenth-Century America." In *The Family in History: Interdisciplinary Essays*, edited by Theodore K. Rabb and Robert I. Rothberg, pp. 95–110. New York: Harper Torchbooks.

Knitzer, Jane, Mary Lee Allen, and Brenda McGowan. 1978. *Children Without Homes:*

An Examination of Public Responsibility to Children in Out-of-Home Care. Washington, D.C.: Children's Defense Fund.

Langsam, Miriam Z. 1964. *Children West: A History of the Placing-Out System of the New York Children's Aid Society, 1853–1890.* Madison: State Historical Society for the Department of History, University of Wisconsin.

Larson, T. A. 1965. *History of Wyoming.* Lincoln: University of Nebraska Press.

McCabe, James D. 1970. *Lights and Shadows of New York Life; or, Sights and Sensations of the Great City.* New York: Farrar, Straus and Giroux.

Morrow, John. 1860. *A Voice Among the Newsboys.* New York: privately published.

Nelson, Kristine Elisabeth. 1980. "The Best Asylum: Charles Loring Brace and Foster Family Care." Ph.D. diss., University of California at Berkeley.

Olmsted, Frederick Law. 1977. *The Papers of Frederick Law Olmsted (1822–1852).* Vol. 1. Edited by Charles Caper McLaughlin. Baltimore: Johns Hopkins University Press.

Optic, Oliver. 1876. *Going West; or, The Perils of a Poor Boy.* Boston: Lee and Shepard.

Pollock, Linda A. 1983. *Forgotten Children: Parent-Child Relations from 1500 to 1900.* Cambridge: Cambridge University Press.

Reynolds, David S. 1995. *Walt Whitman's America.* New York: Vintage.

Sanger, M.D., William W. 1851. *The History of Prostitution: Its Extent, Causes, and Effect Throughout the World.* New York: Harper & Bros.

Shapiro, Michael. 1999. *Solomon's Sword.* New York: Times Books.

Sigourney, Lydia H. 1842. *Letters to Mothers.* New York: Harper & Bros.

Smith Rosenberg, Carroll. 1971. *The Rise of the American City, 1812–1870.* Ithaca, N.Y.: Cornell University Press.

Sobel, Robert, and John Raimo, eds. 1978. *The Biographical Directory of the Governors of the United States, 1789–1978.* Vol. 4. Westport, Conn.: Meckler Books.

Spann, Edward K. 1981. *The New Metropolis: New York City, 1840–1857.* New York: Columbia University Press.

Special Child Welfare Advisory Panel (NYC). 2000 (March 9). *Advisory Report on Front Line and Supervisory Practice.*

Stansell, Christine. 1986. *City of Women: Sex and Class in New York, 1789–1860.* New York: Alfred A. Knopf.

Stevenson, Elizabeth. 1977. *Park Maker: A Life of Frederick Law Olmsted.* New York: Macmillan.

Stowe, Harriet Beecher. 1911. *Oldtown Folks.* Boston: Houghton Mifflin.

Thurston, Henry W. 1974. *The Dependent Child.* New York: Arno Press.

Trattner, Walter I. 1989. *From Poor Law to Welfare State: A History of Social Welfare in America.* New York: Free Press.

———. 1968. *Homer Folks: Pioneer in Social Welfare.* New York: Columbia University Press.

Vogt, Martha Nelson, and Christina Vogt. 1979. *Searching for Home: Three Families from the Orphan Trains.* Privately published.

Youcha, Geraldine. 1995. *Minding the Children: Child Care in America from Colonial Times to the Present.* New York: Scribner.

Young, Patricia J., and Frances E. Marks, eds. 1990. *Tears on Paper: Orphan Train History.* Privately published.

Zelizer, Viviana A. 1985. *Pricing the Priceless Child: The Changing Social Value of Children.* New York: Basic Books.

Articles

Bernstein, Nina. 1999 (June 22). "Pattern Cited in Missed Signs of Child Abuse." *New York Times.*

———. 2000 (September 13). "Family Needs Far Exceed the Official Poverty Line." *New York Times.*

Brace, Charles Loring. 1977 (August). "The Little Theologue." *The Independent* (date unavailable). Reproduced in *Newsboy* (Horatio Alger Society newsletter, Jacksonville, Ill.) 16, no. 1, 22–23.

Bushnell, Horace. 1848. "Unconscious Influence." *The American Pulpit* (Worcester, Mass.) 2, no. 10.

City Law. 1998 (September-October). "Sewage Disposal and Foster Care Lead in the Top 100 for Fiscal Year 1998." *City Law* 4, no. 5, 97–104.

Dykstra, Robert. 1996 (Winter). "Field Notes: Overdosing on Dodge City." *Western Historical Quarterly,* 505–14.

Gopnik, Adam. 1997 (March 31). "Olmsted's Trip." *The New Yorker,* 96–104.

Herbert, Bob. 1998 (February 26). "An Unending Tragedy." *New York Times.*

Hoaglund, Kenneth G. 1982 (Spring). "'The Least of These': Visions of the Mid-Nineteenth-Century City Missions Movement in New York." *Imprint* 7, no. 1, 26–32.

Hope, Anna. 1977 (August). "The Boy Who Confessed His Sin." *The Independent* (late 1854 or 1855). Reproduced in *Newsboy* (Horatio Alger Society newsletter, Jacksonville, Ill., edited by Jack Bales) 16, no. 1, 21–22.

Kilborn, Peter T. 1997 (April 21). "Priority on Safety Is Keeping More Children in Foster Care." *New York Times.*

Pear, Robert. 1997 (May 1). "House Passes Bill to Encourage Adoption of Abused Children." *New York Times.*

Russakoff, Dale. 1997 (April 21). "The Protector." *The New Yorker,* 50–71.

Swarns, Rachel L. 1999 (January 21). "Foster Agencies Called Lax, and Faulted in a Girl's Death." *New York Times.*

Index